Jacob Mayer

German for Americans

Jacob Mayer

German for Americans

ISBN/EAN: 9783337322205

Printed in Europe, USA, Canada, Australia, Japan

Cover: Foto ©ninafisch / pixelio.de

More available books at **www.hansebooks.com**

German for Americans.

A PRACTICAL GUIDE FOR SELF-INSTRUCTION

AND

FOR COLLEGES AND SCHOOLS.

CONTAINING

PRONUNCIATION; GRAMMAR; Sentences with special reference to Grammar; Table of CLASSIFICATION of IRREGULAR VERBS; Exercises; DIALOGUES; PHRASEOLOGY alphabetically arranged; List of WORDS SIMILAR IN SOUND; VOCABULARY with Nouns classified according to Gender; German and English PROVERBS; Rules to determine the GENDER OF NOUNS, etc., etc.

BY

DR. JACOB MAYER.

SECOND EDITION.

PHILADELPHIA:
I. KOHLER, No. 911 ARCH STREET.
1889.

PREFACE.

A book, especially an elementary book, ought to speak for itself, and thus a preface to this "Practical Guide" would seem to be superfluous, if the author did not think it his duty to advance some hints concerning some of its contents, and the arrangement and use thereof. There is naturally nothing new in this book; grammatical rules do not change, and their application cannot but be in accordance with the language in speaking and writing. Self-evidently the German language offers no exception to this rule; but it has peculiarities and features which make its acquisition somewhat difficult to the English-speaking American who is desirous of conversing in it at home and abroad. There is, for instance, the pronunciation, the gender, the syntax, the idiomatic expression, the classification of nouns and verbs, and many another particular inherent in the genius of the language, which appear to rise, each and all of them, as obstacles difficult for the student to overcome. In this book, however, they are treated and arranged in such a manner as to render the study of German comparatively easy; the reader will notice this by merely superficially glancing over the pages of the book, and the student will find it verified by the rapid progress he is sure to make in his studies. And as for the teacher, he will find various remarks and suggestions quite familiar to him, inasmuch as they surely have occurred to him, in full or in part, in his public profession and private contemplation, without having been touched upon in any other elementary book. Thus he will be pleased with the pronunciation added to each word, and warranting correctness in reading; the grammatical rules, though simple in form and comparatively few in number, still completely covering the whole ground; the various tables and lists, to be used for reference as well as for information; the collection of phrases and dialogues, arranged with due regard to the peculiarities of the language and the needs of the student at home and abroad; the vocabulary with nouns classified according to gender; the English and German proverbs in their mutual adaptation; and finally the practical rules and indications to determine the gender of the nouns, explained and exemplified in the vocabulary (containing about five thousand words) by the "classification of the nouns according to gender," the three genders on the same page and in alphabetical connection and succession.

The author hopes in this way to meet the wishes and expectations of both the teachers and students, and therefore recommends his "German for Americans" to the favor of the American friends of the German tongue.

Philadelphia, May, 1889.

INDEX.

	PAGE
GERMAN ALPHABET, and KEY to the pronunciation of German words	5
Reading Exercises	7
Declension of Nouns and the Article	9
The Adjective (Eigenschaftswort)	13
Numerals (Zahlwörter)	16
Pronouns (Fürwörter)	17
The Verb (Zeitwort)	20
Table of Classification of Irregular Verbs	25
Irregular Verbs	26
The Preposition (Verhältnißwort)	34
The Adverb (Umstandswort)	35
The Conjunction (Bindewort)	37
The Interjections (Empfindungswörter)	37
Exercises	38
Syntactical Remarks	57

PRACTICAL PART—Praktischer Theil:

General Terms and Phrases (gewöhnliche Ausdrücke und Redensarten)	58
Addresses, Salutations (Anreden, Begrüßungen)	61
Answers and Counter-Salutations (Antworten und Gegengrüße)	62
Receiving a Visitor (Beim Empfangen eines Besuches)	63
Asking. Requesting (Bitten, Fragen)	64
Complying, Acceding (Einwilligen)	65
Refusing with Regrets (Verweigern mit Bedauern)	66
Affirming (Bejahen)	67
Denying (Verneinen)	68
Admiring, Wondering (Bewundern, wundern)	69
News (Neuigkeiten)	70
Queries and Answers (Fragen und Antworten)	72
Possibility and Probability (Die Möglichkeit und Wahrscheinlichkeit)	75
Surprise (Ueberraschung)	76
Consultation (Berathung)	77
Eating and Drinking (Essen und Trinken)	78

	PAGE
Addresses, Titles (Anreden, Titulaturen)	85
Going and Coming (Gehen und Kommen)	87
Speaking (Sprechen)	89
Days, Dates, Months (Tage, Daten, Monate)	91
Joys, Sorrows (Freuden, Leiden)	94
SENTENCES with special reference to Grammar (Sätze mit besonderer Rücksicht auf die Grammatik)	95

DIALOGUES—Gespräche:

Of the State of Health (Vom Befinden)	104
Rising (Vom Aufstehen)	105
Going to Bed (Vom Schlafengehen)	106
Dressing (Vom Ankleiden)	106
Breakfast (Vom Frühstück)	107
Dinner (Vom Mittagessen)	108
The Time (Von der Zeit)	109
The Weather (Vom Wetter)	110
Age (Vom Alter)	111
Writing (Vom Schreiben)	111
Sea Voyage (Seereise)	111, 112
On the Railroad (Auf der Eisenbahn)	113
In a Hotel (In einem Gasthofe)	114
Renting Rooms (Zimmer miethen)	115
With a Physician (Mit einem Arzte)	116
With a Tailor (Mit einem Schneider)	117
In a Shoe Store (In einem Schuhladen)	118
PHRASEOLOGY alphabetically arranged (Phraseologie alphabetisch geordnet)	119
WORDS SIMILAR IN SOUND (Aehnlich lautende Wörter)	133
VOCABULARY with the nouns classified according to Gender	148

GERMAN AND ENGLISH PROVERBS:

I. German	199
II. English	207
RULES TO DETERMINE THE GENDER OF NOUNS	216

GERMAN WRITING ALPHABET.

a b c d e f g h i j k l m n o p q

r s t u v w x y z

A B C D E F G H I J

K L M N O P Q R S St

T U V W X Y Z

ä ö ü ai au äu ei eu

ch ck ph ss sch sp st th tz

Aß, Lenz, Chor, Dach, ~~~, Forst, Grund, Haus, Inn, Joch, Kind, Lenz, Mond, Nacht, Ort, Pfuhl, Quell, Rast, Sand, Ur~~, Tisch, Uhr, Volk, Wald, Zeit.

———

Die Sprache ist die Scheide der That; wir nehmen das unsichtbare Schwert und meinen unblutige Dinge.

Die schöne deutsche Sprache hat für das Tiefste und Höchste ihre vollkommen entsprechenden Worte.

Suchet, so werdet ihr finden!

INTRODUCTION.

THE ALPHABET OF THE GERMAN LANGUAGE.

𝔄 a (A a) 𝔅 b (B b) ℭ c (C c) 𝔇 d (D d) 𝔈 e (E e) 𝔉 f (F f) 𝔊 g (G g)
𝔥 h (H h) 𝔍 i (I i) 𝔍 j (J j) 𝔎 k (K k) 𝔏 l (L l) 𝔐 m (M m) 𝔑 n (N n)
𝔒 o (O o) 𝔓 p (P p) 𝔔 q (Q q) 𝔑 r (R r) 𝔖 ſ ß (S s ss sz or ss)
𝔗 t (T t) 𝔘 u (U u) 𝔙 v (V v) 𝔚 w (W w) 𝔛 x (X x) 𝔜 y (Y y) 𝔷 z (Z z).

The pronunciation (sound) of these letters is as follows:—a like *a* in *father*; e like *a* in *fate*; i like *ee* in *meet*; u like *oo* in *boot*; j (yott) like *y* in *year*; g like *g* in *gold*; b, d, g, p, t, as if sounded with the *a* in *fate*, hence ba, da, etc.; c the same but sharp: tsa; f, l, m, n, o, ſ, as in English; h like *h* in *harvest*; k with the same vowel sound, as in *ka-hin*; q like *coo* in *cool*; r like *er* in *error*; v like *f* (fow); w like the English *v* with the vowel sound of *a* in *fate* (va); x = *iks*; y (as vowel = *ee*, and as consonant = *j*) has the original Greek designation of *Ypsilon*; and z like *ts* in *hearts* is called tsett.

Now read the German alphabet according to the German pronunciation. 𝔄 (father), 𝔅 (fate), ℭ (tsa), 𝔇, 𝔈, 𝔉, 𝔊, 𝔥, 𝔍, 𝔎, 𝔏, 𝔐, 𝔑, 𝔒, 𝔓, 𝔔, 𝔑, 𝔖, 𝔗, 𝔘, 𝔙, 𝔚, 𝔛, 𝔜, 𝔷. Accordingly the

KEY

to the pronunciation of German words, in conformity with the above, is in this book as follows:—

I. VOWELS.

𝔄, a, 𝔄a (long):   ä = fäther;   𝔄, a (short): ȧ = ȧsk;   gar, gär; bann, dȧn.
𝔈, e   "   ā = fāte;   short: ą; short: e = kettle; ber, där; er-ben, ar'-ben.
𝔍, i   "   ee = meet;   short: i = in;   bir, deer; bin, bin.
𝔒, o   "   ō = ōld;   short: o = not; ver, för; voll, foll.
𝔘, u   "   oo = pool;   short: ụ = bụll; gut, goot; zum, tsum.
𝔄i, ai   "   I = mīne;   𝔑ain, rīn; always long.
𝔈i, ei   "   the same I;   𝔙eil, bīl; always long.
𝔄̈, 𝔄e, ä   "   ai = chair;   short: ą = met; 𝔅är, bair; hȧt-te, hạt'-te.

𝔄u, au, always like *ou* in *out*, somewhat subdued: auf, ouf.
𝔄̈u, äu, and 𝔈u, eu, like *oi* in *oil*: 𝔏äufe, loi'-fe; 𝔈ule, oi'-le; beugen, boi'-gen.

NOTE.—The accent (′) following the syllable, as in hạt'-te, loi'-fe, oi'-le, boi'-gen (see above), indicates that the accent falls on that syllable.

(5)

𝔍𝔥, i𝔥, ie, like *ee* in *bee*, *see* = i𝔥m, wir, die; cem, veer, dee.

𝔒, ö can be pronounced by giving the lips a round form and in this position utter a sound like e, when the proper sound of ö will be produced. It is similar to the English *i* in *girl*, *sir*, *whirl*, and *u* in *hurt*, and will be marked, when long, ï, and short ĭ in this book = 𝔒fen, böſe; ï'-fen, bĭ'-ze.

ü, ŭ requires the same position of the lips and the attempt to pronounce *ee* long or *i* short (*in*). The former is marked ü, and the latter ŭ = über, dünn; ü'-ber, dŭn.

II. CONSONANTS.

𝔅 differs only at the end of a syllable from the English *b*, being then pronounced like *p* (𝔚eib = vīp).

ℭ (tsä), before *e*, *i*, *y* = *ts*; before *a*, *o*, *u* = *k*; met with only in words of foreign origin (central = tsen-träl'; 𝔎onvent = kon'-vent').

ℭ𝔥, c𝔥. (1) At the beginning of a word (*a*) of French derivation like *sh* (ℭ𝔥arade = shä-rä'-da), and (*b*) from other languages and before a consonant like *k* (ℭ𝔥amäleon = kä-mai'-la-on'; ℭ𝔥ronik = krö'-nik). (2) In the middle or at the end of a word: after ä, ö, ü, e, i, y, ei, eu and äu, harder than the German *j*, and softer than the German *g*, with a strong leaning toward the former; and after *a*, *o*, *u*, *au* like the Scotch *ch* in *Loch* (Lomond). We mark the former 𝔥 (𝔗öc𝔥terc𝔥en = tĭ𝔥'-ter-𝔥en'), and the latter *ch* (𝔅uc𝔥 = booch); c𝔥 before ſ like *k* (𝔄c𝔥ſel = äk'-sel; 𝔒c𝔥s = oks).

The ck (only in the middle and at the end of a word) stands for *kk* (𝔑ock = rokk; backen = bäk'-ken); never preceded by a consonant.

𝔇 the same as in English, but hard at the end of a syllable or word (𝔥und = hunt).

𝔊 like *g* in *good*; but in some parts of Germany like 𝔥 and *ch* at the end of a word or syllable (gütig = gü'-ti𝔥; ℒug und 𝔗rug = looch unt trooch). Preceded by the letter *n* it has the same value as *ng* in *thing* = 𝔇ing.

𝔥, 𝔥 is only aspirated at the beginning of a syllable, as in English (𝔥ut, hoot); at the end of a grammatical syllable (ge𝔥-en = gäh'-en) it should not be aspirated at all, but where, in writing, the syllables are so divided as to carry the 𝔥 to the next syllable, it becomes a feeble aspirate (ge-𝔥en, gä'-hen). Still we read gäh'-en. Preceded by a vowel and followed by a consonant, it has no sound at all, but merely serves to indicate that the vowel is long. [See above: 𝔍𝔥, i𝔥, ie.]

𝔎, k is always sounded, both after n (𝔅ank = bänk) and before n (𝔎nall = knäl).

𝔑, n always plain *N*, *n*; but when followed by *g* it sounds like *ng* in *song*, and never like *ng* in *finger*.

𝔔, q (koo) has but one sound, viz., *k* or *c* hard. It never occurs by itself, but is always followed by u, which two letters are then pronounced like kw (𝔔uelle = kväl'-le; quer = kvär). In foreign words the foreign pronunciation is retained.

𝔑, r has always a sharp sound like the rough, rolled, dental, initial *R*, *r* in English (𝔑aritäten = rä'-ree-tai'-ten; 𝔉riedric𝔥 = free'-dri𝔥).

𝔖, ſ, ſſ, ß, s. Mark: 𝔖, ſ (used only at the beginning of a syllable), is soft like the English *z* (𝔖and = zänt; ſehr = zār); ſ after a consonant has also a soft sound (ℒinſe = lin'-ze; 𝔄mſel = äm'-zel), except after b, c𝔥, and p (𝔈rbſe =

ạrp'-se ; Achſe = ạk'-se ; Stöpſel, see below), but the end syllable ſal always reads zäl ; ſſ is invariably sharp (eſſen = ạs'-sen), and more so is ß (ſʒ) in one sound (daß = dảss), which always occurs at the end of a syllable. So does s (das = dảs ; dasſelbe = dảs-zạl'-be) with the simple hard sound of the ſ.

Sp, ſp sounds almost like *shp* at the beginning of a syllable (Spiel = shpeel) ; but in the middle or near the end of a word or syllable it resumes its original character (Weſpe = vạs'-pe). The same rule applies to

St, ſt (Stadt = shtảt ; Liſt = list ; Stöpſel = shtĭp'-sel).

Sch, ſch = *sh*. For instance : Schaf = shảf ; raſch = rảsh.

T, t and Th, th are pronounced *t* (That = tät). In the naturalized words with the termination tion, the *t* sounds like *ts* (Nation = nảt'-sec-ōn' ; Portion = port'-sec-ōn'). The new orthography drops the h after t in nearly all words with th.

V, v occurs only in few German words, where it is pronounced like *f* (Vater = fä'-ter ; viel = feel), but it assumes the original sound of *v* (w) in originally foreign words (Vaſe = vả'-ze ; Evangelium = ả'-vản-gả'-li-ụm') ; if they, however, terminate in v, the sound of *f* is preferred (Motiv = mo-teef' ; brav = brảf ; Nerv = nerf).

W is like the English *v* (will = vill ; war = vảr).

Pf, pf = *pf* (Pfenning = pfen'-ning ; Kopf = kopf).

Ph, ph = *ph* (Phantom = fản-tōm' ; Philoſophie = fee'-lō-zo-fee').

Instead of double *z* (ʒʒ) ß, preceded by a vowel, is used (Troß = trots) ; the simple z interchanges with C in naturalized foreign words (Zentner = Cent'-ner).

READING EXERCISES.

I. CONSIDERING THE VOWELS.

A, a ; ả.—Aar, Bab, Char, Da, Fahl, Gar, Haar, Jahr, Kahn, Lahn, Mal, Naht, Paar, Qual, Rath, Saat, Staar, Ba'(ter), Wahl, Zahn.

A, a ; ạ.—Alt, Ball, Damm, Fall, Gaſt, Haft, Jack'(e), Karl, Land, Mann, Narr, Pfaff'(e), Quart, Rand, Sack, Stadt, Wald, Zack'(en).

E, e ; ả.—Bee'r(e), Der, Er, Fehl, Geb'(en), Heer, Jeb'(er), Kehl'(e), Lehm, Meer, Pferd, Quer, Reh, See, Theer, Wehr, Zehn.

E, e ; e, ạ.—Bett, Des, Elf, Fell, Gelb, Herr, Jetzt, Kerl, Letzt, Menſch, Netz, Peſt, Quell'(e), Reſt, Selbſt, Sped, Stell'(e), Schred, Ten'n(e), Ver-, Weſt, Kerres, Zelt.

J, i ; ee.—Bier, Dir, Flie'g(e), Gier, Igel, Ihm, Knie, Lieb, Mir, Nie, Phi'l(o), Sie, Thier, Vier, Wien, Ziel.

J, i ; i.—Bin, Did, Flink, Glitſch, Hin, Irr, Kinn, Lip'p(e), Quit, Riff, Sitz, Spin'n(e), Strich, Schimpf, Tritt, Wind, Zip'f(el).

O, o ; ō.—Brob (Brot), Chrom, Dom, Froh, Goth'(a), Hob, Joſt, Kohl, Lohn, Mond, Noth, O'(fen), Pol, Quot'(e), Roh, Soph'(a), Spohr, Stoß, Schon, Ton, Thor, Vor, Wohl, Zon'(e).

O, o ; o.—Bonn, Con'(to), Dorf, Forſt, Gott, Holz, Klotz, Loch, Mord, Noch, Poſt, Quoll, Roſt, Son'n(e), Spott, Strold, Schroff, Toll, Voll, Won'n(e), Vorf, Zorn.

U, u; oo.—Bu′b(e), Chur, Du, Fuh′r(e), Gut, Hut, Ju′b(el), Klug, Lu′p(e), Muth, Nu, Pfuhl, Ruhm, Such′(e), Spuhl, Stuhl, Schur, Schnur, Thun, Zu′b(er).

U, u; u.—Bunt, Dumm, Frucht, Gunst, Huld, Kurz, Luchs, Mund, Nuß, Pfund, Rumpf, Sucht, Spuck, Stun′b(e), Schuld, Trupp, Ulk, Wur′z(el), Zunft.

Ai, ai; I.—Aich′(en), Bai, Faisch, Gaiß, Hai, Kai′(ser), Laib, Mais, Rain, (Sayn).

Ei, ei; I.—Beil, Dein, Ei, Fleiß, Geist, Heil, Klein, Leim, Mein, Neid, Pfeil, Rhein, Seil, Spei′(er), Stein, Scheit, Theil, Veil′(chen), Weib, Zeit.

Ä, ä; ai.—Ähr′(e), Bär, Dä′n(e), Fäh′r(e), Hä′(ring), Krä′m(er), Lä′b(en), Mäb′(chen), Nächst, Pär′(chen), Räb′(er), Säg′(e), Spät, Stä′b(e), Schä′(len), Thä′t(ig), Bä′(ter), Wäh′r(en), Zäh′l(en).

Ä, ä; (e), a.—Äl′t(er), Blät′t(er), Däch′(er), Fläch′(e), Glät′t(e), Härt′(e), Käl′t(e), Län′b(er), Män′n(er), När′r(in), Pfäl′z(er), Säß′(e), Späß′(e), Stäl′l(e), Schränk′(e), Täp′p(isch), Wäl′b(er).

Au, au; ou.—Au, Baum, Dauer, Frau, Glaube, Haus, Jau′(che), Kraut, Lauch, Maut, Pfau, Rauch, Saul, Staub, Schlauch, Tau, Zaum.

Äu, äu; Eu. eu; oi.—Äu′ße-re′, Äu′geln, Räu′me; Säu′le; Euch, Eugen′, Eu′ter; Beu′le, Scheu.

Ih, ih, ie; ee.—Bier, Dieb, Gier, Hieb, Ihm, Knie, Lieb, Nie, Schier, Zier.

Ö, ö [lang]; ī [long].—Öf(en), Bö′s(e), Chö′r(e), Fröh′(lich), Hört, Kö′nig, Löb′(lich), Möh′r(e), Nöth′(ig), Röh′r(e), Schön, Tö′n(e).

Ö, ö [kurz]; ī [short].—Dör′f(er), Göt′t(er), Hör′n(er).

Ü, ü [lang]; ü [long].—Brü′h(e), Früh, Gü′t(e), Hü′(gel), Jü′(ten), Kü′(bel), Kühn, Mü′(be), Pfühl, Rü′(be), Spühl, Thür, Wühl, Zü′(rich).

Ü, ü [kurz]; ī [short].—Bün′b(el), Drück′(en), Flüg′(ge), Grütz′(e), Hüt′t(e), Zür′(gen), Kürz′(lich), Müß′(e), Nütz′(lich), Pfütz′(e), Rüst′(ig), Sün′(be), Stück′(e), Schür′z(e), Thür′m(e).

II. CONSIDERING THE CONSONANTS.

B, b.—Blech; Dieb, Leib, Weib, Gieb, Hieb, Lieb, Ob, Aub, Üb, Trüb.

C, ch, ck.—Cen-sur′, Ce′-res, Ci-ca′-be, Ci′-ce-ro; Can-can, Ca-non; Con-vent, Cur, Cu′-pi-do′; Cy′-pern, Cy′-rus; Chal-bä′-er, Christ, Chauf-see′; Richt(ig), Häß′-lich; Buch′-sta-be, Pracht, Noch, Rauch; Decke, Beck, Sack.

D, b.—Dau′-men, Dünn; Haub, Laub, Mund.

G, g.—Gut, Gott, Grab, Gold, Ge-nug′, Ge-räu′-mig.

H, h.—Hab, Hut, Haus; Deh′-nen, Fleh′-en, Ge-h′-eu; Rauh, Roh, Rüh′-rig.

K, k.—Kalb, Kloß, Krank, Kork; Rück′-kehr, Krück′-en-kopf.

N, n.—Nen′-nen, Neu′-ling, Ni′-be-lung′-en, Neu′-e-rung′-en.

Q, q.—Quab′-be, Qual, Quack′-sal′-ber, Qua-brat′, Qua-ran-tai′-ne.

R, r.—Roth, Ru′-the, Raub, Räu′-ber; Krä′-mer, Her-uu′-ter.

S, s, ss, ß, s.—Salz, Sach(e), Sim′-son, Sohn; Biu′-sen, Gäu′-se, Trüb′-sal, Ge-schreib′-sel, An′-häng-sel, El′-se, Hop′-sa, Hir′-se; Asse, Fäs′-ser, Ruf′-sen, Tas′-sen; Lachs, Füch′-se; Gruß, Schuß, Faß, Fleiß, Fluß; Loos, Moos, Reis, das-selb(e), ba-selbst′.

Sp, sp.—Spaß, Spund, Spruch, Sprosse; Espe, Raspel, Ge-lisp′-el, Mispel, Ge-spenst′, Hospi-tal′.

St, ſt.—Stall, Straße, Stand, Strauch; Oſtern, Luſtig, Koſt'-bar; Bruſt, Durſt, Laſt, Dreiſt.

Sch, ſch.—Schatz, Schrei, Schlaf; Flaſche, Wäſche; Raſch, Ge-klatſch'.

T, t.—Tand, Ton, Thon, Tha'-ler, Thür, Thor; Aktion', Lektion', Operation'.

V, v.—Va'-ter, Vet'-ter, Ge-vat'-ter, Vieh, Viel, Vogel, Volk; Fre'-vel, Brav, Guſtav, Na-iv'.

Pf, pf.—Pfahl, Pfund; Hopfen, Karpfen; Napf, Strumpf.

Ph, ph.—Phalanr, Phan-taſt', Pha'-ſe, Phleg'-ma, Phi'-lipp, Phos'-phor, Phra'-ſe, Phy'-ſik.

3, z.—Zentner, Zit-ro'-ne, De-zem'-ber, Pro-zent', Re-zept' [see rule on Z]; Zelle, Ziffer, Zirkel; Bron'-ze, Po-li-zei'; Dif'-fe-renz', Diſtanz', No-tiz'.

DECLENSION OF NOUNS AND THE ARTICLE.

There are three genders, viz., masculine, feminine, neuter (männlich, män'-lih—weiblich, vīp'-lih—ſächlich, zah'-lih), and three kinds of declension, viz., the strong, the feeble, the mixed declension (die ſtarke, die ſchwache, die gemiſchte Deklination, dee shtär'-ke, dee shväch'-e, dee ge-mish'-te dąk'-li-näts'-yōn). The noun, both in *singular* (Einzahl, In'-tsäl) and in *plural* (Mehrzahl, mär'-tsäl), appears in a sentence in either of the four different forms—called *Cases* (Fälle)—

Nominativ (*first case*, answering the question "who"—wer?—or "which"—was?)

Genitiv (*second case*, " " " "of whom"—weſſen?—or "of which"—weſſen?)

Dativ (*third case*, " " " "to whom"—wem?—or "to which"—wem?)

Akkuſativ (*fourth case*, " " " "whom"—wen?—or "which"—was?)

STRONG DECLENSION.

SINGULAR.

Masculine.	*Feminine.*	*Neuter.*
1. Der Hund, the dog.	Die Hand, the hand.	Das Land, the land.
2. Des Hund-es, of the —.	Der Hand, of the —.	Des Land-es, of the —.
3. Dem Hund-e, to the —.	Der Hand, to the —.	Dem Land-e, to the —.
4. Den Hund, the —.	Die Hand, the —.	Das Land, the —.

PLURAL.

1. Die Hund-e, the dogs.	Die Händ-e, the hands.	Die Länder, the lands.
2. Der Hund-e, of the —.	Der Händ-e, of the —.	Der Länder, of the —.
3. Den Hund-en, to the —.	Den Händ-en, to the —.	Den Ländern, to the —.
4. Die Hund-e, the —.	Die Händ-e, the —.	Die Länder, the —.

Such being the declined forms of the definite article (des beſtimmten Artikels, das be-shtim'-ten är-tik'-kels), and the forms of the strong declension of the nouns in gender, number and cases, the following table will point out the changes as distinct marks of the declined articles and nouns, viz.:

SINGULAR.

Masculine.	Feminine.	Neuter.
1. De-r ——.	D-ie ——.	D-as ——.
2. De-s ——es.	D-er ——.	D-es ——es.
3. De-m ——e.	D-er ——.	D-em ——e.
4. De-n ——.	D-ie ——.	D-as ——.

PLURAL.

1. D-ie ——e.	D-ie Hä——e.	D-ie Lä——er.
2. D-er ——e.	D-er —ä——e.	D-er —ä——er.
3. D-en ——en.	D-en —ä——en.	D-en —ä——ern.
4. D-ie ——e.	D-ie —ä——e.	D-ie —ä——er.

The indefinite article „ein" (m.), „eine" (f.), „ein" (n.), has the same termination as the definite article, viz., (m.) ein, eines, einem, einen; (f.) eine, einer, einer, eine; (n.) ein, eines, einem, ein; and so the substantive. There is no plural, of course.

MONOSYLLABIC MASCULINE NOUNS OF THE STRONG DECLENSION.

1. WITH THE VOWEL u LONG, PL. ü=oo, PL. ü.

Bug, bow, bough; Fuß, foot; Fluch, curse; Flug, flight; Gruß, salute, greeting; Huf, hoof; Hut, hat; Krug, pitcher; Muth, courage; Pfuhl, pool; Ruf, call, fame; Schwur, oath; Stuhl, chair; Spuk, ghost, spectre; Zug, draught, train. The same with prefixes: Ab'-zug, deduction; Ein'-zug, entry; Vor'-zug, preference; Aus'-zug, extraction.

2. WITH THE VOWEL u SHORT, PL. ü=ü, PL. ĭ.

Bruch, rupture; Bund, covenant; Busch, bush; Duft, scent; Dunst, mist; Durst, thirst (no pl.); Fluß, river; Grund, ground; Guß, gush, font; Muff, muff; with prefix: Ge-nuß', enjoyment; Ge-ruch', smell; Puff, puff, thump; Puz, finery; Rumpf, trunk, rump; Sprung, leap, jump; Sumpf, swamp; Sturz, fall; Spund, bung; Schlund, gullet, gulf, abyss; Strumpf, stocking; Trumpf, trump; Wurf, cast, throw. With prefixes: Ab'-wurf, offal; Aus'-wurf, refuse, outcast, expectoration; Ein'-wurf, objection; Ent-wurf', sketch; Vor'-wurf, reproach.

3. WITH THE VOWEL o LONG, PL. ö=PL. ĭ LONG.

Chor, choir; Floh, flea; Hof, court, yard; Schooß, lap; Schlot (no modification of the vowel in pl.), chimney, flue; Schrot (the same), small shot; Strom, stream; Tod (no pl.), death; Ton, sound; Thon (no pl.), clay; Thron (no modific.), throne.

4. WITH THE VOWEL o SHORT, PL. ö=PL. ĭ SHORT.

Block, block; Bock, buck; Frosch, frog; Koch, cook; Korb, basket; Kloz, log, trunk; Kopf, head; Knopf, button; Kropf, crop, craw; Probst, provost; Pflock, plug; Rock, coat; Sporn, spur; Stock, cane, stick; Stoff (no modific.), stuff, matter; Topf, pot; Tropf, dunce; Zoll, custom, duty; Zopf, pigtail; Zorn, anger.

5. WITH THE VOWEL a LONG, PL. ä=ā, PL. ai.

Aal (no modific.), eel; Aar (the same), eagle; Aas (pl. Ä-fer), carrion; Bart, beard; Draht, wire; Gram, grief; Pfahl, pale; Saal, saloon; Stab, staff; Tag (no modific.), day; Dieb'-stahl, theft.

6. WITH THE VOWEL a SHORT, PL. ä=ä, PL. a.

Ball, ball; Band, volume; Brand, conflagration; Damm, dam; Dampf, vapor; Drang, pressure; Empfang', reception; Fall, fall, case; Fang, catch; Frack, dress-coat; Gang, walk, gait; with prefixes: Ab'-gang, exit; Aufgang, ascent; Ausgang, egress; Durchgang, passage; Eingang, entrance; Ue'-bergang, transition; Umgang, rotation; Un'-tergang, going down, ruin; Vorgang, occurrence; Haß (no pl.), hatred; Kamm, comb; Klang, sound; Knall, clap, crack; Krampf, cramp; Kranz, wreath; Mann (pl. Männer), man; Markt, market; Platz, place; Rand (pl. Rän'-der), edge; Rang, rank; Sack, sack; Satz, leap, dregs, sentence; with prefixes: Ab'-satz, stop, sale, heel; Ansatz, deposit; Aufsatz, head-dress, essay; Aussatz, (no pl.), leprosy; Beisatz, apposition; Einsatz, deposit; Ge'-gensatz, contrast; Nachsatz, conclusion; Umsatz, sale, exchange; Vorsatz, purpose; Zusatz, addition, appendix, codicil; Schatz, treasure; Schwall, billow, throng; Schwamm, sponge; Schwanz, tail; Spaß, jest, fun; Stall, stable; Stamm, stem, stock; Stand, position, stand; Strand, strand; Strang, rope; Tanz, dance; Wald (pl. Wälder), forest; Wall, rampart; Zank (no pl.), quarrel; Zwang (no pl.), compulsion.

7. WITH THE VOWEL i (ie) LONG=ee, PL. THE SAME.

Brief, letter; Dieb, thief; Dienst, service; Hieb, hit, stroke; Kiel, quill, keel; Kies, gravel; Pie'-ke, spade; Quiek, squeak; Ried, reed; Sieg, victory; Spieß, spear; Stieg, path; Stiel, handle, stalk; Stier, bull; Stil, style.

8. WITH THE VOWEL i SHORT=i, PL. THE SAME.

Blick, glance; Filz, felt; Fisch, fish; Hirsch, stag; Hirt, shepherd; Pilz, mushroom; Quirl, twirling stick; Ring, ring; Riß, rent, cleft; Ritt, ride; Schild, shield; Schilf, bulrush; Schirm, shelter; Sitz, seat; Stift, tag, tack; Tisch, table; Wind, wind; Wink, hint; Wirth, host; Witz, wit; Zins, rent, interest; Zisch, whiz, hiss; Zitz, chintz, teat.

9. WITH THE VOWEL e LONG=ā, PL. THE SAME.

Herd, hearth; Klee (no pl.), clover; Krebs, crab; Weg, way; Werth, value.

10. WITH THE VOWEL e SHORT=a (elder).

Berg, mountain; Helm, helmet; Kelch, goblet; Kerl, fellow; Kern, kernel; Klecks, blot; Knecht, servant; Lenz, spring; Netz, net; Pelz, fur; Pfenn, peg, pin; Text, text; West, west.

11. WITH THE DOUBLE VOWEL au, PL. äu=ou, PL. oi, ALWAYS LONG.

Bau, building; Baum, tree; Bauch, belly; Bausch, pad; Brauch, usage; with the prefix Ge-, custom, and with the prefix Ver-, consumption, consume; Gaul, horse; Gaum(en) (no modific.), palate; Hauch, breath; Kauf, purchase, the same with the prefix Ein-, and "sale" with the prefix Ver-, and Aus'-ver-kauf', selling out; Knauf, knob; Kauz (prop. owl), but applied to men of odd habits; Kraut (pl. Kräuter), herb; Lauf, course; Laut (no modific.), sound; Pfau (no modific.), peacock; Raum, space; Rausch, inebriation; Saum, hem; Schaum, foam; Schlauch, leather bag or bottle; Schmaus, feast, banquet; Strauch, shrub; Strauß, nosegay; (Thau, dew; Tausch, barter, no pl.); Traum, dream; Zaum, bridle; Zaun, fence.

12. WITH OTHER DOUBLE VOWELS: ai=I, eu=oi.

Hai, shark; Hain, grove; Kai, quay; Mai, May; Mais, Indian corn; Maisch, mash of distillers and brewers; Rain, green strip of land as boundary; Deut, penny; Kreuz, cross.

All these monosyllabic masculine nouns of the *strong declension* have es in the Genitive singular, and en in the Dative plural; and they terminate in a consonant with the exception of the two naturalized foreign words, Kai and Mai.

There are 23 monosyllabic feminine nouns of the strong declension, viz.: Brust, breast; Frucht, fruit; Gruft, tomb, vault, sepulchre; Kluft, cleft; Kunst, art; Luft, air; Lust, joy, pleasure, lust; Nuß, nut.—Bank, bench; Gans, goose; Hand, hand; Kraft, force; Macht, power; Magd, maid-servant; Nacht, night; Naht, seam; Stadt, town, city.—Braut, bride; Faust, fist; Haut, skin; Laus, louse; Maus, mouse; Sau, sow.

There are 24 monosyllabic neuter nouns of the strong declension, viz.: Aas (Äser), carrion; Band, ribbon; Blatt, leaf; Dach, roof; Fach, case, pannel, shelf; Faß, barrel; Kalb, calf; Lamm, lamb; Land, land; Rad, wheel.—Blut (oo, no pl.), blood; Buch (oo), book; Tuch (oo), cloth; Gut (oo), estate, manor, commodity; Obst, fruit; Lied, song; Brett, board, plank; Feld, field; Geld, money; Mensch, low woman; Nest, nest; Haus, house; Kleid, dress; Maul, mouth (of an animal).

DISTINCTIVE MARKS OF THE STRONG DECLENSION.

SINGULAR.		PLURAL.	
1. —		e, er	Mostly with modification of vowels: a, ä; o, ö, etc.
2. es, s (ens)	Feminine nouns remain unchanged.	e, er	
3. e (may be omitted)		en, ern, en	
4. like the first.		e, er	

DISTINCTIVE MARKS OF THE WEAK DECLENSION.

SINGULAR.	PLURAL.	
1. —	en, n	No modification of vowels.
2. en, n	en, n	
3. en, n	en, n	
4. en, n	en, n	

The mixed declension has in the *singular* the marks of the *strong* declension, and in *plural* the mark of the *weak* declension; no feminine nouns belong to it.

Example of the declension of a noun of more than one syllable with indefinite article. Strong declension:

SINGULAR.

1. Ein Vater (In fü'-ter), father.   Eine Stadt (Ine shtàt), city.
2. Eines Vaters.   Einer Stadt.
3. Einem Vater.   Einer Stadt.
4. Einen Vater.   Eine Stadt.

   1. Ein Beispiel (In bī'-shpeel), example.
   2. Eines Beispieles (or is).
   3. Einem Beispiele.
   4. Ein Beispiel.

Decline: der Wald, forest; der Bach, brook; der Fisch, fish; die Frucht, fruit; der Mantel, mantel; das Schreibbuch, copybook; der Ritter, knight.

Examples of the weak declension:

SINGULAR.	PLURAL.
1. Der Mensch (dār mansh), man.	Die Menschen.
2. Des Menschen.	Der Menschen.
3. Dem Menschen.	Den Menschen.
4. Den Menschen.	Die Menschen.

SINGULAR.	PLURAL.
1. Der Bote (där bō'-te), messenger.	Die Boten.
2. Des Boten.	Der Boten.
3. Dem Boten.	Den Boten.
4. Den Boten.	Die Boten.
1. Die Feder (dee fä'-der), pen.	Die Federn.
2. Der Feder.	Der Federn.
3. Der Feder.	Den Federn.
4. Die Feder.	Die Federn.

Decline: der Fürst (first), prince; der Bär (bair), bear; der Preuße (proi'-sse), Prussian; die Frau (frou), woman; die Rose (rō'-ze), rose.

Examples of the mixed declension:

SINGULAR.	PLURAL.
1. Der Strahl (där shträl), beam, ray.	Die Strahlen.
2. Des Strahles.	Der Strahlen.
3. Dem Strahle.	Den Strahlen.
4. Den Strahl.	Die Strahlen.
1. Das Herz (dás harts), heart.	Die Herzen.
2. Des Herzens.	Der Herzen.
3. Dem Herzen.	Den Herzen.
4. Das Herz.	Die Herzen.

Proper nouns remain unchanged except in the second case, where they receive an s, as for instance: Karls, Berthas, Schillers ꝛc. Proper nouns of males ending in s, ß, sch, x, z, and of females in e, have the Genitive termination ens, and in conversational language the third and fourth cases in en; for instance: Heinz (hints), Heinzens, Heinzen; Max (máx), Maxens, Maxen; Auguste (ougus'-te), Augustens, Augusten.

THE ADJECTIVE (Eigenschaftswort—I'-gen-sháfts-vort').

It indicates the quality, condition, or character of a noun; for instance: der fleißige Schüler (där flī'-ssi-ge' shü'-ler), the *diligent* pupil; der Schüler ist fleißig, the pupil is diligent. Du bleibst bescheiden, thou remainest modest.

Before the noun it is attributive, as: der gute Mann (där goo'-te mán), the good man; preceded by a verb it is predicative, as: aller Anfang ist schwer (ál'-ler án'-fáng ist shvär), every beginning is difficult.

If an adjective needs for its completion a certain object, it puts this object either in the second, or in the third, or in the fourth case; for instance: ein guter Dolmetscher ist mehrerer Sprachen mächtig (īn goo'-ter dol'-mat'-sher ist mä'-re-rer' shprä'-chen mah'-tig), a good interpreter is master of various languages. Here the adjective „mächtig" (potent, able) is completed by the object „mehrere Sprachen" (various languages), which, however, must be put in the Genitive case, viz.: mehrerer Sprachen, in obedience to „mächtig", which governs the Genitive. Another instance (Dative): leichter Sinn ist den Kindern eigen, (līh'-ter zin ist dän kin'-dern ī'-gen), a light mind is peculiar (incomplete adjective, admitting the question "to whom?" Answer:) to children. A third instance (Accusative): dieses Brod ist einen Tag alt (dee'-zes brōt ist ī'-nen tāg ált), this loaf of bread is one day old. It is old (alt); how old? Followed by the Accusative „einen Tag" (one day).

The following adjectives govern the GENITIVE:—

Anſichtig (ån'-zih'-tig), have a sight of.
Bar (bår), destitute, bare, devoid.
Bedürftig (be-dirf'-tig), needy.
Befliſſen (be-flis'-sen), studious.
Begierig (be-gee'-rig), desirous.
Benöthigt (be-nī'-tigt), in need of.
Beraubt (be-roupt'), bereaved.
Bewußt (be-vyst'), conscious.
Eingedenk (in'-ge-dank'), in memory of, remembring.
Fähig (fai'-ih or ig), able, capable.
Froh (frō), glad.
Gewahr (ge-vär'), aware, sensible (of).
Gewärtig (ge-var'-tig), expectant.
Gewiß (ge-vis'), sure, certain.
Gewohnt (ge-vönt'), accustomed.
Habhaft (häp'-häft), having.
Inne (in'-ne), with werben (var'-den), to perceive.
Kundig (kun'-dig), acquainted with, skilled, expert.
Ledig (lā'-dig), rid.
Leer (lār), empty, void.
Los (lōs), free, untied.
Mächtig (mäh'-tig), master of.
Müde (mü'-de), tired (of).
Quitt (kvit), quits.
Satt (zåt), satiated; filled.
Schuldig (shul'-dig), guilty (of).
Sicher (zih'-her), sure, safe.
Theilhaftig (til'-hàf'-tig), participant.
Ueberdrüſſig (ü'-ber-drīs'-sig), weary, tired of.
Verdächtig (fer-dah'-tig), suspected.
Verlustig (fer-lus'tig), forfeit.
Voll (foll), full.
Werth (värt), deserving, worthy.
Würdig (vīr'-dig), worthy.

The DATIVE is governed by adjectives signifying something *favorable* or *unfavorable*, *useful* or *hurtful*, *kind* or *unkind*, a *vicinity* or a *distance;* as:

Angenehm (àn'-ge-nām), pleasant.
Angst (mir ist ångst), uneasy (I am).
Bange (mir ist bång'-e), afraid (I am).
Bequem (be-kvām'), convenient.
Dienlich (deen'-lih), serviceable.
Feind (fīnt), inimical.
Folgsam (folg'-zàm), obedient.
Freundlich (froint'-lih), friendly.
Gehorsam (ge-hör'zàm), obedient.
Geneigt (ge-nīgt'), favorable.
Gewogen (ge-vō'-gen), kind, well disposed.
Gnädig (gnai'-dig), gracious.
Gram (gräm), grudging.
Günstig (gīns'-tih), favorable.
Gut (goot), good.
Heilsam (hīl'-zàm), salutary.
Hinderlich (hin'-der-lih'), troublesome.
Hold (holt), kind, affectionate.
Lieb (leep), sweet.
Nützlich (nīts'-lih), useful.
Passend (pås'-sent), suitable, appropriate.
Schädlich (shait'-lih), injurious.
Schmerzlich (shmarts'-lih), painful.
Schwer (shvär), heavy, difficult.
Süß (züss), sweet.
Theuer (toi'-er), dear.
Treu (troi), faithful.
Uebel (ü'-bel), evil.
Verhaßt (fer-håst'), hated.
Vortheilhaft (för'-tīl-häft'), profitable.
Weh (vā), ill.
Werth (värt), worth, in the sense of dear.
Wichtig (vih'-tig), important.
Willkommen (vill-kom'-men), welcome.
Zuträglich (tsoo'-träg'-lih), useful, profitable.
Zuwider (tsoo-vee'-der), repugnant.

The ACCUSATIVE is governed by adjectives expressing a *measure, weigh*, *age*, etc., as for instance:

Hoch (hōch), high.
Lang (lång), long.
Breit (brīt), broad.
Tief (teef), deep.
Groß (grōss), great, large.
Schwer (shvär), heavy (with designation of weight).
Alt (ålt), old (with designation of age).
Werth (värt), worth (with the value indicated), etc.

We say: einen (Accus.) Fuß hoch (ī'-nen foos hōch), one foot high; eine (Accus.) Meile lang (ī'-ne mī'-le lång), a mile long; keinen Cent werth (kī'-nen tsånt värt), not worth a cent, etc.

COMPARISON OF ADJECTIVES.

The degrees of comparison can be formed—

(1) In a *regular* way by adding er to the Positive to make the Comparative, and eſt (ſt) to make the Superlative.. Modifications of vowels are frequent. Example: Fein (fīn), fine; fein-er (fī'-ner), finer; fein-ſt (fīnst), finest. Kurz (kŭrts), short; fürz-er (kĭr'-tser), shorter; fürz-eſt (kĭr'-tsest), shortest. Hoch (hōch), high; höh-er (hīh'-er), higher; höchſt (hihst), highest. (In Old German the Comparative was höcher (hī'-her), which change of h or ch in a more delicate aspirate h took place in various words).

(2) In an *irregular* way, when Comparative and Superlative are formed from a word different from the Positive, as: gut (goot), good; beſſer (bes'-ser), better; beſt (best), best. Viel (feel), much; mehr (mār), more; meiſt (mīst), most. In this form the Superlative is used as adverb; in conjunction with the preposition an (än), at, to, on, and the articles, syllables of declension are added, as; am feinſt-en (äm fīn'-sten), the finest; der, die, das höch-ſte (hīh'-ste), highest; mein beſt-er (mīn best'-er), my best (one).

DECLENSION OF ADJECTIVES.

The adjective always precedes the noun, and ends in the nominative case in e when preceded by the definite article, or by a numeral or pronoun with the termination of the gender, as: manch-es (numeral), many a. unnütze (adjective), useless, Wert (nonn), word: män'-hes un-nüt'-se vort; dieſ-er (pronoun), this, hoh-e (adj.), high, Berg (n.), mountain: dee'-zer hōh'-e barg; der (article) rauſchend-e (adj.), rushing, Bach (n.), brook: dār rou'-shen-de' bäch. But it assumes the termination of the gender if not preceded by any such word, which has the termination; as: froh-er Muth (frō'-er moot), cheerful courage; gut-e Laune (goo'-te lou'-ne), good humour; reines Silber (rī'-nes zil'-ber), pure silver; ein (īn), mein (mīn), ihr (eer), un-ſer (ŭn'-zer), eu-er (oi'-er), fein (kīn), wahr-er (vä'-rer), Freund (froint), mas.: a, my, her, our, your, no true friend. Ein-e (ī'-ne), mein-e (mī'-ne), etc., wah-re (vä'-re), Freun-din (froin'-din), fem.; a, my, etc., true female friend. Ein, mein, etc., trau-ri-ges (trou'-ri-ges'), Schickſal (shik'-zäl'), n.; a, my, etc., sad fate.

The adjective has a *strong* and a *weak* declension; in the former it is not preceded by an article, etc., and terminates in all four cases like the article; in the latter it is preceded by the article, and receives in all cases (except in the nominative of all three genders, and the accusative of the neuter in the singular) n or en, the latter especially in the plural.

EXAMPLES OF THE STRONG DECLENSION.

SINGULAR.	PLURAL.
1. Kalt-er Wind (kält'-ter vint), cold wind.	Kalt-e Wind-e.
2. Kalt-en Wind-es, of — —.	Kalt-er Wind-e.
3. Kalt-em Wind-e, to — —.	Kalt-en Wind-en.
4. Kalt-en Wind, cold —.	Kalt-e Wind-e.
1. Warm-e Luft (vär'-me luft), warm air.	Warm-e Lüft-e.
2. Warm-er Luft, of — —.	Warm-er Lüft-e.
3. Warm-er Luft, to — —.	Warm-en Lüft-en.
4. Warm-e Luft, warm —.	Warm-e Lüft-e.
1. Edle-s Metall (äd'-les me-täll'), precious metal.	Edl-e Metall-e.
2. Edl-en Metall-es, of — —.	Edl-er Metall-e.
3. Edl-em Metall-e, to — —.	Edl-en Metall-en.
4. Edle-s Metall, precious —.	Edl-e Metall-e.

NOTE.—It will be observed that from euphonic reasons the genitive masculine and neuter ends in en, instead of es.

EXAMPLES OF THE WEAK DECLENSION.

SINGULAR.

1. Der gut-e Sohn (dār goo'-te zōn), the good son.
2. Des gut-en Sohn-es, of ———.
3. Dem gut-en Sohn-e, to ———.
4. Den gut-en Sohn, the ——.

1. Die lieb-e Tochter (dee lee'-be toch'-ter), the dear daughter.
2. Der lieb-en Tochter, of ———.
3. Der lieb-en Tochter, to ———.
4. Die lieb-e Tochter, the ——.

1. Das froh-e Kind (dās fröh'-e kint), the glad child.
2. Des froh-en Kindes, of ———.
3. Dem froh-en Kind-e, to ———.
4. Das froh-e Kind, the ——.

PLURAL.

Die gut-en Söhn-e.
Der gut-en Söhn-e.
Den gut-en Söhn-en.
Die gut-en Söhn-e.

Die lieb-en Töchter.
Der lieb-en Töchter.
Den lieb-en Töchtern.
Die lieb-en Töchter.

Die froh-en Kinder.
Der froh-en Kinder.
Den froh-en Kindern.
Die froh-en Kinder.

NUMERALS (Zahlwörter—tsül'-vĭr'-ter).

I. CARDINAL NUMBERS (Grundzahlen—grunt'-tsü'-len).

1, eins (īns).
2, zwei (tsvī).
3, drei (drī).
4, vier (feer).
5, fünf (fĭnf).
6, sechs (zaks).
7, sieben (zee'-ben).
8, acht (acht).
9, neun (noin).
10, zehn (tsān).
11, elf (alf).
12, zwölf (tsvĭlf).
13, dreizehn (drī'-tsān).
14, vierzehn (feer'-tsān).
15, fünfzehn (fĭnf'-tsān).
16, sechzehn (zah'-tsān).
17, siebenzehn (zee'-ben-tsān).
18, achtzehn (acht'-tsān).
19, neunzehn (noin'-tsān).
20, zwanzig (tsvan'-tsih).
21, einundzwanzig (īn'-unt-tsvan'-tsih).
22, zweiundzwanzig (tsvī'-unt-tsvan'-tsih).
30, dreißig (drī'-ssih, or ssig).
31, einunddreißig (īn'-unt-drī'-ssih).
40, vierzig (feer'-tsih).
41, einundvierzig (īn'-unt-feer'-tsih).
42, zweiundvierzig (tsvī'-unt-feer'-tsih).
49, neunundvierzig (noin'-unt-feer'-tsih).
50, fünfzig (fĭnf'-tsih).
51, einundfünfzig (īn'-unt-fĭnf'-tsih).
60, sechzig (zah'-tsih).
66, sechsundsechzig (zeks'-unt-zah'-tsih).
70, siebenzig (zee'-ben-tsih).
78, achtundsiebenzig (acht'-unt-zee'-ben-tsih).
80, achtzig (acht'-tsih).
90, neunzig (noin'-tsih).
100, hundert (hun'-dert).
1000, tausend (tou'-zent).

II. ORDINAL NUMBERS (Ordnungszahlen—ord'-nungs-tsä'-len).

The ordinal numbers are formed by adding t to the cardinals from *two* to *nineteen*, and ſt from *twenty* upward. For instance: neunt (noint), ninth; zwanzigſt (tsvan'-tsihst), twentieth. They are, however, never used in this form, but always with te or ſte, *like adjectives*, before a noun or in the sense of a noun, and preceded by the article, as: der zweite Mann (dār tsvī'-te man), the second man; der dreißigſte August (dār drī'-ssih-ste ou-gust'), the thirtieth of August. In this (adjective) form they are also declined like adjectives in both declensions.

First and *last* are in German „erſt" (ārst), from Old German „er" (ār). *early*, and „letzt" (latst), from O. G. „lat" (lāt), *late*. Der erſte Mai (ārst'-e mī), the first of May; letztes Mal (mūl), last time.

The ordinal number, like the adjective, is not affected by the article denoting the gender.

The adverbial *ly* of second*ly*, etc., is rendered n⸗, as: zweitens (tsvī'-tens), etc. „Dritte" (drit'-te), *third*, is irregular, and „achte" (äch'-te), *eighth*, (not acht-te), is correct.—In the compound numbers from 20 upward the English ordinals are cardinals in German, viz.: twenty-*fifth* = fünfundzwanzigste.

1. Der (die, das) erste (dār, dee, dås ęrs'-te), the first.
2. „ zweite (tsvī'-te), the second.
3. „ dritte (drit'-te), the third.
4. „ vierte (feer'-te), the fourth.
5. „ fünfte (fĭnf'-te), the fifth.
6. „ sechste (ząks'-te), the sixth.
7. „ siebente (zee'-ben-te), the seventh.
8. „ achte (äch'-te), the eighth.
9. „ neunte (noin'-te), the ninth.
10. „ zehnte (tsān'-te), the tenth.
11. „ elfte (ạlf'-te), the eleventh.
12. „ zwölfte (tsvĭlf'-te), the twelfth.
13. „ dreizehnte (drī'-tsān'-te), the thirteenth.
20. „ zwanzigste (tsvän'-tsig-ste'), the twentieth.
21. „ einundzwanzigste (īn'-ụnt-tsvän'-tsig-ste'), the twenty-first.
22. „ zweiundzwanzigste (tsvī'-ụnt-tsvän'-tsig-ste'), the twenty-second.
30. „ dreißigste (drī'-ssih [or ig]-ste'), the thirtieth.
31. „ einunddreißigste (īn'-ụnt-drī'-ssig-ste'), the thirty-first.
40. „ vierzigste (feer'-tsig-ste'), the fortieth.
43. „ dreiundvierzigste (drī'-ụnt-feer'-tsig-ste'), the forty-third.
50. „ fünfzigste (fĭnf'-tsih-ste'), the fiftieth.
54. „ vierundfünfzigste (feer'-ụnt-fĭnf'-tsig-ste'), the fifty-fourth.
60. „ sechzigste (zạh'-tsig-ste'), the sixtieth.
70. „ siebenzigste (zee'-ben-tsig-ste'), the seventieth.
80. „ achtzigste (ächt'-tsig-ste'), the eightieth.
90. „ neunzigste (noin'-tsig-ste'), the ninetieth.
100. „ hundertste (hụn'-dert-ste'), the hundredth.
1000. „ tausendste (tou'-zent-ste'), the thousandth.
10,000. „ zehntausendste (tsān'-tou'-zent'-ste'), the ten-thousandth.

The German „fach" (fäch), added to a cardinal number, answers the English "fold;" as: zwiefach (instead of zweifach)—tsvee'-fäch—*twofold*, etc. "Single" is rendered einfach (īn'-fäch).

"Times," indicating repetition, is rendered „mal" (mäl): *four times* is viermal (feer'-mäl), etc.; *once*, einmal (īn'-mäl); *twice*, zweimal (tsvī'-mäl), etc.

Fractional numbers are: ½, ein Halb (īn hålp); ⅓, ein Drittel (īn drit'-tel); ¾, drei Viertel (drī feer'-tel), etc.

PRONOUNS (Fürwörter—für'-vĭr'-ter).

I. PERSONAL—Persönlich[e]—per zjụ'-li-ḥ[e'].

Ich (iḥ), I; du (doo), thou; er (ār), he; sie (zee), she; es (ạs), it; wir (veer), we; ihr (eer), you, ye; sie (zee), they.

Genitive.—Meiner (mī'-ner); deiner (dī'-ner); seiner (zī'-ner); ihrer (ee'-rer); seiner; unser (ụn'-zer); euer (oi'-er); ihrer (ee'-rer).

Dative.—Mir (meer); dir (deer); ihm (eem); ihr (eer); ihm; uns (ụns); euch (oiḥ); ihnen (ee'-nen).

Accusative.—Mich (miḥ); dich (diḥ); ihn (een); sie; es; uns; euch; sie.

In addressing one or more persons of good standing, „Sie" (zee) is used instead of „Ihr" (eer), you.

„Du" (doo), thou, is used among relatives and friends. Parents never address a child of theirs with „Sie" (zee), you, nor will children address their parent thus, except perhaps among the very higher classes and in presence of strangers.

II. POSSESSIVE—Besitzanzeigend[e]—be-zits'-ån-tzī'-gend[e']

are in place of a Genitive, in answer to the question „wessen?" (vas'-sen), "of whom?" and always closely in connection with a noun, hence of an *adjective* character. Referring to persons they are also a kind of *personal* pronouns with three persons and the three distinctions of gender of the third person singular. They are as follows: mein (mīn), my; dein, thy; sein (*m.*), his; ihr (eer), her; sein (*n.*), its; unser, our; euer, your; ihr, their.

Pronouns of a *substantive* character are treated as nouns. They read as follows: der, (die, das) Meinige (mī'-ni-ge'), mine; Deinige, thine; Seinige, his; Ihrige, hers; Unsrige (unz'-ri-ge'), ours; Eurige, yours; Ihrige, theirs. They have a small initial, when the person or thing they refer to, is mentioned previously. For instance: nicht (niht) dein Buch (booch), sondern (zon'-dern) das meinige, *not thy book, but mine.*

The nominative *masculine*, and the nominative and accusative *neuter* have the termination of the strong declension (-er, -es), if no article is used, as: dein Vater (fä'-ter) ist gut (goot), und meiner (instead of der meinige) ist es auch (ouch), *thy father is good, and mine is it also.* Nimm sein Geld und meines, take (thou) his money and mine.

Declension of *adjective* character (strong), of *substantive* character (weak):

SINGULAR.
1. Mein Arm (årm), my arm.
2. Mein-es Arm-es, of — —.
3. Mein-em Arm-e, to — —.
4. Mein-en Arm, my —.

PLURAL.
Meine Arme (år'-me), my arms.
Meine-r Arme, of — —.
Meine-n Arme-n, to — —.
(like nominative).

1. Meine Lippe (lip'-pe), my lip.
2. Meine-r Lippe, of — —.
3. Meine-r Lippe, to — —.
4. (like nominative.)

Meine Lippen (lip'-pen), my lips.
Meine-r Lippen, of — —.
Meine-n Lippen, to — —.
(like nominative).

1. Mein Auge (ou'-ge), my eye.
2. Mein-es Auge-s, of — —.
3. Mein-em Auge, to — —.
4. (like nominative.)

Meine Augen (ou'-gen), my eyes.
(like the preceding).

The reflexive "self" and "selves," joined to the third person of the personal pronouns of all three genders in the third and fourth cases of either the singular or plural number, is rendered in German simply by „sich" (zih); as: er gab (gåp) es sich (selbst), *he gave it to himself;* sie sagte (zåg'-te) es sich (selbst), *she said it to herself;* das Kind (kint) wusch (vush) sich, *the child washed itself;* sie verbargen (fer-bår'-gen) sich, *they hid themselves,* etc.

III. DEMONSTRATIVE—Hinweisend[e]—hin'-vī'-zen-d[e'].

Fundamentally: dies- and jen-, whence dieser (dee'-zer), diese, dieses, *this,* or *this one;* and jener (yä'-ner), jene, jenes, *that* or *that one;* and the plural number diese, *these,* and jene, *those.* They have, as is obvious, the termination of the respective article, and suffer the article to be used in their place; thus we say (emphatically): der Mann, instead of dieser or jener Mann. They are also declined as the article, and so is the article itself, when used in their place in an adjective character; but in a substantive character the genitive singular des, der, des is changed into dessen (das'-sen), deren (dā'-ren), dessen; and the genitive plural der into deren or derer, and the dative plural den into denen (dā'-nen). Here is the full declension of it:

SINGULAR, Einzahl.			PLURAL, Mehrzahl.
1. der	die	das	die
2. dessen	deren	dessen	deren (derer)
3. dem	der	dem	denen
4. den	die	das	die

NOTE.—Deren refers to a preceding noun, derer contains the noun, as: Keine (kī'-ne) Könige (kī'-ni-ge') mehr (mār), wir hatten (hät'-ten) deren genug (ge-noog'), no more kings, we had *of them* enough. Das ist das Ende derer, die Gott leugnen (loig'-nen), such is the end *of those* that deny God.

„jen" with an additional „ig" (jenig) assumes the adjective and substantive character of the pronoun, and becomes by prefixing the article (derjenig) emphatically demonstrative. In this form the article claims its customary declension, and the pronominal addition is declined either as an adjective, or as a noun of the second declension, thus:

SINGULAR (that —— or *he, she* who)   PLURAL (those —— or *they* who)

1. derjenige	diejenige	dasjenige	diejenigen
(dār'-yā'-ni-ge')			
2. desjenigen	derjenigen	desjenigen	derjenigen
3. demjenigen	derjenigen	demjenigen	denjenigen
4. denjenigen	diejenige	dasjenige	diejenigen

The same is the case with „selb" (zalp), *same*, when thus added to the article, viz.: derselbe, dieselbe, dasselbe, dieselben.

IV. RELATIVE—Beziehend[e]—be-tseeh'-en-d[e']

are: welcher (val'-her), welche, welches, pl. welche; or wer (vār), (*m.*), or der, die, das (as pronouns), or finally was, with reference to things, all answering the English *who*, or *which*, or *that*, and being declined as above.

V. INTERROGATIVE—Fragend[e]—frā'-gen-d[e']

are: wer? *who;* was? *what;* welch-er, -e, -es? *which, which one;* was für —— (für)? *what* ——; was für ein? eine? ein? Declension like the article when used as demonstrative pronoun, and in was für ein, eine, ein, the indefinite article only.

VI. INDEFINITE—Unbestimmt[e]—un'-be-shtim'-t[e']

representing persons, are: man (mán), *one*, meaning *a person;* jemand (yā'-mánt), *somebody;* niemand (nee'-mánt), *nobody;* jedermann (yā'-der-mán'), *everybody;* einer (ī'-ner), *one;* keiner, *none;* wenige (vā'-ni-ge'), *few;* viele (fee'-le), *many;* manche (mán'-he), *many a, some;* jed-er (yā'-der), -e, -es, *every, each;* jeglich-er (yāg'-li-her'), -e, -es, *every, each.*

The following refer to things: etwas (at'-vás), *something;* nichts (nihts), *nothing;* vieles (fee'-les), *much;* manches (mán'-hes), *many a thing;* etliches (at'-li-hes'), *something;* alles (ál'-les), *everything;* the latter four used in a substantive sense.

Declension.—Man, etwas, nichts cannot be declined at all; the others, which originally are *indefinite numerals*, and have the *termination of the definite article*, are declined *strong*, as:

    1. einer   2. eines   3. einem   4. einen
    1. wenige   2. weniger 3. wenigen 4. wenige, etc.

Jemand is declined as follows: 1. jemand; 2. jemand-es (yä'-man-des'); 3. jemand-em (jemand); 4. jemand-en. The same, niemand. Jedermann has only a genitive: jedermann's (yä'-der-mans').

THE VERB (das Zeitwort—dás tsĭt'-vort).

This class of words, designating activity and passivity, with (and without) reference to the various divisions of *time* (whence it is called „Zeitwort", *the word of the time* or *times*), is the very life of the language, and claims, therefore, the greatest attention, especially in German.

It has never less than two syllables (except the auxiliary verb „sein", *to be*, and „thun"—toon—originally thu-en), viz.: the fundamental monosyllabic word or sound (as tanz—tänts—), and the verbal termination „en" (hence: tanzen—tän'-tsen—*to dance*).

In all moods and tenses of conjugation the n (and also mostly the e and n) of this terminal syllable is dropped by all three persons in the singular and the second person in plural, but retained by the first and third persons of the plural number. The first person singular invariably drops the n without admitting any other sound in its place; as: loben (lō'-ben), lobe (lō'-be), *praise*. The second person singular, also dropping the n (and sometimes en), is distinguished by the termination st: lobest (lō'-best), *praisest*. The third person drops, besides the en, also the s of the st, retaining the t, and thus reads lobt (lōbt). *praises*. Also the second person is often rendered in the same way without the e after the fundamental syllable, viz.: lobst, instead of lobest. The second person plural ends in et (or t), like the third person singular (lobet or lobt), while the first and third persons plural always end in en (loben).

The auxiliary verb „sein", *to be*, being irregular, has features entirely distinct from the forms indicated above, and requires, therefore, a special study.

Conjugation—Konjugation (con'-yoo'-gäts-yōn')—of the auxiliary verb—des Hilfszeitworts (hilfs'-tsĭt'-vorts') „sein", *to be*,—and of the regular verb—und des regelmäßigen (rā'-gel-mai'-ssi-gen') Zeitwortes (tsĭt'-vor'-tes) „loben", *to praise*.

Indicative mood, Indikativ (in'-di-kä-teef')—*present tense,* gegenwärtige Zeit (gä'-gen-var'-ti-ge' tsĭt).

Ich bin	ih bin	I am	Ich lobe	lō'-be	praise
Du bist	doo bist	thou art	Du lobest	lō'-best	praisest
Er, sie, es ist	är, zee, as ist	he, she, it is	Er, sie, es lobt	lōbt	praises
Wir sind	veer zint	we are	Wir loben	lō'-ben	praise
Ihr seid	eer zīt	you are	Ihr lobet	lō'-bet	praise
Sie sind	zee zint	they are	Sie loben	lō'-ben	praise

The auxiliary verb „haben" (hä'-ben), *to have*, drops the syllable „ben" in the second and third person singular, indicative mood, present tense, admitting st and t respectively in its place.

There is a third auxiliary verb in German, viz.: „werden" (var'-den). *to be, to become, to get*, which changes the e of the first syllable into i, drops the syllable „den" and takes the usual st in the second and d in the third person singular.

Konjugation der Hilfszeitwörter (-vīr'-ter) „haben" und „werden" im (in dem) Indikativ der Gegenwart (-vårt).

Ich habe	Wir haben	Ich werde	Wir werden
Du hast	Ihr habet	Du wirst (virst)	Ihr werdet
Er hat	Sie haben	Er wird (virt)	Sie werden

Participle past—Partizipium or Mittelwort (mit'-tel-vort') der Vergangenheit (fer-gàng'-en-hīt')—of „haben" is gehabt (ge-hápt'), of „sein" gewesen (ge-vā'-sen) and geworden (ge-vor'-den) or worden, and of „werden" geworden.

„Haben" in the sense of *possessing* is followed by a noun or adjective in the accusative; as: ich habe Geld (galt), *I have money;* du hast genug (ge-noog'), *thou hast enough.* „Werden" in the sense of *becoming, getting, growing*, is followed by an adjective or a noun in the nominative case; as: ich werde alt (ált), *I am getting old;* er wird ein Mann (màn), *he becomes a man;* sie wird eine schöne (shī'-ne) Jungfrau (yung'-frou), *she is going to be* (becoming) *a beautiful young lady.* „Haben" indicates and forms, in connection with another verb, the past; „werden", in connection with a verb, constitutes the future. Example: der Herr (hàr) hat (hàt) gegeben (ge-gā'-ben), *the Lord has given;* ich werde leben (lā'-ben), *I shall live;* du wirst kommen (kom'-men), *thou will come.* „Werden" can be the auxiliary of „haben", as: ich werde haben, *I shall have,* but „haben" is never the auxiliary of „werden"; thus we do not say: ich habe gewesen (ge-vā'-zen), *I have been,* but: ich bin gewesen, *I am been.*

FURTHER CONJUGATION OF THE AUXILIARY VERBS.

Ich hatte (hát'-te), had;	hätte (hạt'-te)	Ich war (vär); wäre (vā'-re),	was
Du hattest (hát'-test), hadst "		Du warst (vàrst),	wast
Er hatte (hát'-te), had "		Er war (vàr),	was
Wir hatten (hát'-ten), had "		Wir waren (vä'-ren),	were
Ihr hattet (hát'-tet) " "		Ihr waret (vä-ret),	"
Sie hatten (hát'-ten) " "		Sie waren (vä'-ren),	"

Ich habe gehabt (ge-hápt), have had		Ich bin gewesen (ge-vā'-zen), have been	
Du hast gehabt " hast had		Du bist gewesen " hast been	
etc.		etc.	

Ich hatte gehabt,	had had	Ich war gewesen,	had been
Du hattest gehabt,	hadst had	Du warst gewesen,	hadst been
etc.		etc.	

Ich werde haben,	shall have	Ich werde sein,	shall be
Du wirst haben,	wilt have	Du wirst sein,	wilt be
etc.		etc.	

Ich werde gehabt haben,	shall have had	Ich werde gewesen sein,	shall have been
Du wirst gehabt haben,	wilt have had	Du wirst gewesen sein,	wilt have been
etc.		etc.	

Ich würde (vīr'-de) haben, I should have
Du würdest haben, thou wouldst have
Er würde haben, he would have
Wir würden haben, we should have
Ihr würdet haben, you would have
Sie würden haben, they would have

Ich würde sein, I should be
Du würdest sein, thou wouldst be
Er würde sein, he would be
Wir würden sein, we should be
Ihr würdet sein, you would be
Sie würden sein, they would be

Ich würde gehabt haben, I should have had
etc.   etc.

Ich würde gewesen sein, I should have been
etc.   etc.

Habe! Habet! Haben Sie! Have!
Laßt (làst) uns haben! Let us have!

Sei! Seid! Seien (zī'-en) Sie! Be!
Laßt uns sein! Let us be!

Besides these *perfect* auxiliary verbs, there are other *defective* ones, viz.: dürfen (dür'-fen), *to be permitted, may;* können (kin'-nen), *to be able, can;* lassen (lås'-sen), *to let, to suffer to;* mögen (mĭ'-gen), *to like, wish, may;* müssen (müs'-sen), *to have to, to be to, must;* sollen (zol'-len), *to be obliged to, to be said to;* wollen (vol'-len), *to will, to be willing.*

CHANGES IN THE CONJUGATION OF THESE VERBS.
(Indicative mood, present tense.)

Singular.—First and third person: darf (därf); kann (kån); mag (måg); muß (mŭs); soll (zol); will (vil). Second person adds st, but to muß it adds t, mußt.

Plural.—First and third persons have the original verb (infinitive), and the second person has t for the ending en, as: können, ihr könnt. Lassen has the a modified in ä in the second person singular: lässest, and the second person plural is both lasset and lasst, or laßt.

REGULAR AND IRREGULAR VERBS.
(Regelmäßige und unregelmäßige Zeitwörter.)

The verbs with e, i, ei in the first of the two radical syllables are either *regular* or *irregular*, whereas those with a, o, u, au, eu, and their modifications in the same place are, with rare exceptions, *regular*. The regular verbs retain the vowel of the first syllable unchanged in all conjugations, and have their participle past ending in et or t. For instance: loben, lobte, gelobt (ge-löpt'); beten (bā'-ten), *to pray*, betete (bā'-te-te'), gebetet (ge-bā'-tet).

All verbs, regular and irregular, have „ge" prefixed to form the participle past, except those with the prefixes be, ent, er, ver (fer) and miß; as: ge-lobt, from loben; ge-erbt (ge-arpt'), from erben (ar'-ben), *inherited* (a legacy); but be-erbt (a person), not ge-be-erbt, and so ent-erbt (ent-arpt'), *disinherited*, er-erbt (a competence), ver-erbt (fer-arpt'), *transmitted, left as inheritance.*

The participle past of the irregular verbs ends in en, as: lesen (lā'-zen), *to read;* participle past: gelesen (ge-lā'-zen), *read;* schreiben (shrī'-ben), *to write;* geschrieben (ge-shree'-ben), *written,* etc.

All verbs derived from nouns are regular, as: kleiden (klī'-den), *to dress;* from the noun Kleid (klīt), *dress;* Imperfect: kleidete (klī'-de-te'); participle past: gekleidet (ge-klī'-det).

Regular are furthermore intransitive irregular verbs when (1) either used transitively, or (2) turned into a transitive verb, as : (1) erschrecken (er-shrak'-ken), *to be frightened;* Imperfect: erschrak (-shråk'); participle past: erschrocken (er-shrok'-ken); Transitive: erschrecken, *to frighten;* Imperfect: erschreckte (er-shrak'te); participle past: erschreckt. (2) fallen (fäl'-len), *to fall;* fiel (feel), gefallen (ge-fäl'-len); but fällen (fal'-len), *to fell;* fällte (fal'-te), gefällt (ge-falt'), *felled.*

The irregular verbs change the radical vowel in the Imperfect and participle past, as follows:

I. i or e in a (ä, å) and u (oo, ŭ),
        also o (ō, o), as: singen (zing'-en), *to sing;* sang (zång), gesungen (ge-zŭng'-en) ;—stehlen (shtā'-len), *to steal;* stahl (shtäl), gestohlen (ge-shtō'-len).

II. „ „ „ „ „ e (ā), as: bitten (bit'-ten), *to ask for;* bat (båt), gebeten (ge-bā'-ten);—geben (gā'-ben), gab (gåp), gegeben (ge-gā'-ben).

III. ie in o (ö) and o (o), as: fliegen (flee'-gen), *fly;* flog (flōg), geflogen (ge-flō'-gen);—sieden (zee'-den), *boil;* sott (zot), gesotten (ge-zot'-ten).

IV. ei in i (i) and ie (ee), as: leiden (lī'-den), *suffer;* litt (lit), gelitten (ge-lit'-ten);—bleiben (blī'ben), *remain;* blieb (bleep), geblieben (ge-blee'-ben).

V. a in ie (ee) and a (à), as: halten (hàl'-ten), *keep;* hielt (heelt), gehalten (ge-hàl'-ten).

VI. a in u (oo) and e (ü), as: graben (grü'-ben), *dig;* grub (groop), gegraben (ge-grü'-ben).

CONJUGATION OF REGULAR VERBS.

Konjugation regelmäßiger (rä'-gel-mä'-ssi-ger') Zeitwörter.

Lieben (lee'-ben), to love.
Liebend (lee'-bent), loving; participle present.
Geliebt (ge-leept'), loved; participle past.

ACTIVE FORM.	PASSIVE FORM.
(Thätige Form—tä'-ti-ge' forrm.)	(Leidende Form—lī'-den-de' forrm.)

1. *Present tense,* Gegenwart (gä'-gen-vàrt').

Ich liebe (lee'-be), I love
Du lieb-est (lee'-best), or lieb-st (leepst), thou lovest
Er (sie, es) lieb-t (leept), he (she, it) loves
Wir lieben (veer), we love
Ihr liebt (eer), you love
Sie lieben (zee), they love

Ich werde geliebt, I am loved, etc.

[See conjugation of the auxiliary verb „sein".]

2. *Imperfect,* jüngste Vergangenheit (yìng'ste fer-gàng'-en-hīt').

Ich lieb-te (leep'-te), I loved
Du lieb-test (leep'-test), thou lovedst
Er lieb-te (leep'-te). he loved
Wir lieb-ten (leep'-ten), we loved
Ihr lieb-tet (leep'-tet), you loved
Sie lieb-ten (leep'-ten), they loved

Ich wurde (war) geliebt, I was loved, etc.

3. *Perfect,* Vergangenheit.

Ich habe geliebt, I have loved
Du hast geliebt, thou hast loved
Er hat geliebt, he has loved
Wir haben geliebt, we have loved
Ihr habt geliebt, you have loved
Sie haben geliebt, they have loved

Ich bin geliebt worden, I have been loved, etc.

4. *Pluperfect,* längste Vergangenheit (làng'-ste ——).

Ich hatte geliebt, I had loved
Du hattest geliebt, thou hadst loved
Er hatte geliebt, he had loved
Wir hatten geliebt, we had loved
Ihr hattet geliebt, you had loved
Sie hatten geliebt, they had loved

Ich war geliebt worden, I had been loved, etc.

| ACTIVE FORM. | PASSIVE FORM. |

5. First future, erste Zukunft (ärs'-te tsoo'-kunft).

| Ich werde lieben, I shall love
Du wirst lieben, thou wilt love, etc. | Ich werde geliebt werden, I shall be loved, etc. |

6. Second future, zweite Zukunft (tsvī'-te ——).

| Ich werde geliebt haben, I shall have loved
Du wirst geliebt haben, thou shalt have loved, etc. | Ich werde geliebt worden sein, I shall have been loved, etc. |

7. First conditional future, erste bedingte Zukunft (—— be-ding'-te ——).

| Ich würde lieben, I should love
Du würdest lieben, thou wouldst love, etc. | Ich würde geliebt werden, I should be loved, etc. |

8. Second conditional future, zweite bedingte Zukunft.

| Ich würde geliebt haben, I should have loved
Du würdest geliebt haben, thou wouldst have loved, etc. | Ich würde geliebt worden sein, I should have been loved, etc. |

THE INTERROGATIVE (fragende, frä'-gen-de') FORM

simply places the pronoun behind the verb, as: Liebe ich? *Do I love?* etc. And with the negative: Lieben Sie nicht (niht)? *Do you not love?* etc. Answer in the negative: Ich liebe nicht, I do not love, etc.

The Monosyllabic Prepositions an (an), auf, aus, bei (bī), durch (durh), mit, nach (näch), um (um), vor (för), zu (tsoo), and the adverbs ab (äp) and ein (īn), prefixed to a verb and thus making it a compound verb, are separated from the same in the present and imperfect tenses, and placed after the verb, even at the end of the sentence in which the verb prevails; as: anbieten (än'-bee'-ten), *to offer* = ich biete Ihnen meine Dienste an, *I offer you my services.*

The Imperative drops the terminal n in the singular, and substitutes t in the plural; as: fragen (frä'-gen), *to ask;* singular: frage; plural: fraget; but seib (zīt), be (you), instead of seit, which means: *since.* [See also the list of irregular verbs below.]

Table of the Classification of Irregular Verbs.

No. of Class.	Infinitive.	Past Perf.	Past Partic.	Infinitive.	Past Perfect.	Past Participle.
I.	e	a	e	Sehen, to see	sah	gesehen
II.	e i	a	o	Helfen, to help Sinnen, to reflect	half sann	geholfen gesonnen
III.	i	a	u	Trinken, to drink	trank	getrunken
IV.	a	ie	a	Fallen, to fall	fiel	gefallen
V.	ei	ie i	ie i	Schreiben, to write Beißen, to bite	schrieb biß	geschrieben gebissen
VI.	ä, au e, i, ie ö, ü	o	o	Schießen, to shoot	schoß	geschossen
VII.	a	u	a	Schlagen, to beat	schlug	geschlagen
VIII.	a, e, i, o ö, u, ü	a, o, u	a, o, u *See corresponding number in following list.*	Brennen, to burn; bringen, to bring; denken, to think; dürfen, to be permitted; haben, to have; kennen, to know; können, to be able, can; mögen, to be allowed, may; müssen, to be obliged, must; nennen, to name; rennen, to run; senden, to send; sollen, to be obliged, shall; thun, to do; wenden, to turn; wissen, to know; wollen, to be willing, will.		

IRREGULAR VERBS.—Un(un)regelmäßige Zeitwörter.

The figures indicate the class to which the verbs belong. [See Table of Classification on preceding page.]
The asterisk (*) marks the verbs which are also conjugated regularly, when they have an active or a transitive sense.
The persons and tenses not indicated here, are regular, or are formed from the persons and tenses given.

PRESENT INFINITIVE.	PAST.	PAST PARTICIPLE.	PRES. INDICATIVE.	IMPERATIVE.
7 Backen (bäk'-ken), to bake	buk (book)	gebacken	du bäckst (bäkst)	
2 Bedingen (be-ding'-en), to stipulate	bedang (-däng)	bedungen (-dung/–)		
Bedürfen, see dürfen				
2 Befehlen (be-fā'-len), to command	befahl (-fäl)	befohlen (-fō'-len)	er befiehlt (-feelt')	befiehl (-feel')
5 Befleißen (be-flī'-ssen), sich, zih, to apply (one's self)	befliß (-flis)	beflissen		
2 Beginnen (be-gin'-nen), to begin	begann (-gän)	begonnen (-gon'–)		
5 Beißen (bī'-ssen), to bite	biß (biss)	gebissen (-biss–)		
2 Bergen (bär'-gen), to hide	barg (bärg)	geborgen (-bor'–)	du birgst (birgst)	birg (birg)
2 Bersten (bär'-sten), to burst	barst (bärst)	geborsten (-bōr'–)	er birst (birst)	birst (birst)
Besinnen, see sinnen				
Besitzen, see sitzen				
8 Betrügen (be-trü'-gen), to cheat	betrog (-trōg)	betrüge (-trü'-ge)	betrogen (-trō'-gen)	
6 Bewegen* (be-vā'-gen), to induce	bewog (-vōg)	bewogen (-vō'–)		
6 Biegen (bee'-gen), to bend	bog (bōg)	gebogen (-bō'–)		
6 Bieten (bee'-ten), to offer	bot (bōt)	geboten (-bō'–)		
2 Binden (bin'-den), to bind	band (bant)	gebunden (-bun'–)		
1 Bitten (bit'-ten), to request	bat (bät)	gebeten (-bā'–)		
4 Blasen (blä'-zen), to blow	blies (blees)	geblasen (-blä'–)	du bläsest (blai'–) er bläs't (blais't)	
5 Bleiben (blī'-ben), to remain	blieb (bleep)	geblieben (-blee'–)		
5 Bleichen (blī'-hen), to fade	blich (blih)	geblichen (-blih'–)		
2 Braten (brä'-ten), to roast	briet (breet)	gebraten (-brä'–)	du brätst (braitst) er brät (brait)	
2 Brechen (brah'-en), to break	brach (bräch)	gebrochen (-broch'–)	er bricht (briht)	brich (brih)
8 Brennen (bren'-nen), to burn	brannte (brän'–)	gebrannt (-bränt')		
8 Bringen (bring'-en), to bring	brachte (bräch'–)	gebracht (-brächt')		

³Denken (daŋk′-ken), to think	dachte (däсht′-)		
³Dingen (ding′-en), to hire	bung (dung)		
⁶Dreschen (dresh′-shen), to thrash	drosch (drosh)		
³Dringen (dring′-en), to urge	drang (drång)		
⁸Dürfen (dür′-fen), to be allowed	burfte (durf′-)		er darf (därf)
Einschlafen, see schlafen		gehacht (-dächt′-)	
Empfangen, see fangen		gebungen (-dung-)	ich binge (ding′-e) {bringe (ding′-e)
Empfehlen, see befehlen		gedroschen (-drosh-)	bu brischeft (drish′-) {brisch (drish)
Empfinden, see finden		gebrungen (-drung′-)	
		geburft (-durft′-)	
²Entrinnen (ent-rin′-nen), to escape	see gewinnen		
Entsprechen, see sprechen			
Erbleichen, see bleichen			
Erfrieren, see frieren			
Erführen, see führen			
⁶Erlöschen (er-lish′-shen), to extinguish	erlosch (-losh′)	erloschen (-losh′-)	bu erlischeft (-lish′-)
Erlaufen, see laufen			
⁶Erschallen (er-shäl′-len), to resound	erschott (-shol′)	erschollen (-shol′-)	
Erscheinen, see scheinen			
²Erschrecken* (er-shrak′-ken), to be frightened	erschraf (-shräk′-)	erschrocken (-shrok′-)	er erschrickt (-shrik′-)	erschrick (-shrik′)
Ertrinken, see trinken			
Erwägen, see wägen			
¹Essen (ns′-sen), to eat	aß (iss)	gegessen (-gns′-)	du ißeft (iss′-)	iß (iss)
⁷Fahren (fä′-ren), to drive	fuhr (foor)	gefahren (-fä′-)	er fährt (fairt)	
⁴Fallen (fäl′-len), to fall	fiel (feel)	gefallen (-fäl′-)	bu fällft (fälst)	
⁴Fangen (fäng′-en), to catch	fing (fing)	gefangen (-fäng′-)	er fängt (fängt)	
⁶Fechten (fäh′-ten), to fight, fence	{focht (focht) {fechtete(fäh′-te-te′-)	gefochten (-fäh′-)	bu fichtft (fihtst)	fich (fiht)
	fand (fänt)		bu fechteft (fäh′-test)	
³Finden (fin′-den), to find	flocht (flocht)	gefunden (-fun′-)		
⁶Flechten (flah′-ten), to braid	flog (flôg)	geflochten (-floch-)		
⁶Fliegen (flee′-gen), to fly	floh (flō)	geflogen (-flō′-)		
⁶Fliehen (fleeh′-en), to flee	floß (floss)	geflohen (-flōh′-)		
⁶Fließen (flee′-ssen), to flow		geflossen (-flos′-)		
¹⁷Fressen, to devour, see essen				
⁶Frieren (free′-ren), to freeze	fror (frōr)	gefroren (-frō′-)	er flieht (liht)	flieht
⁶Gähren (gai′-ren), to ferment	gohr (gōr), (also reg.)	gegohren (-gō′-)		

PRESENT INFINITIVE.	PAST.	PAST PARTICIPLE.	PRES. INDICATIVE.	IMPERATIVE.
²Gebären (ge-bai'-ren), to bear	gebar (ge-bär')	geboren (–bō'–)	fie gebärt (–bairt')	
¹Geben (gā'-ben), to give	gab (gäp)	gegeben (–gāp'–)	bu giebſt (geepst)	gieb (geep)
Gebieten, see bieten				
⁵Gedeihen (ge-dīh'-en), to prosper	gebieh (–deeh')	gediehen (–teeh'–)		
Gefallen, see fallen				
⁴Gehen (gāh'-en), to go	ging (ging)	gegangen (–gäng'–)		
³Gelingen (ge-ling'-en), to succeed	gelang (–läng')	gelungen (–lung'–)		
²Gelten (gel'-ten), to be worth	galt (gält)	gegolten (–gol'–)	bu giltſt (giltst)	
¹Genießen (ge-nee'-ssen), to enjoy	genoß (–nūs')	genoſſen (–nos'–)		
Gerathen, see rathen				
¹Geſchehen (ge-shaih'-en), to happen	geſchah (–shäh')	geſchehen	es geſchieht (–sheet')	
²Gewinnen (ge-vin'-nen), to win	gewann (–vän')	gewonnen (–von'–)		
⁶Gießen (gee'-ssen), to pour	goß (goss)	gegoſſen (–gos'–)		
⁵Gleichen (glīl'-hen), to resemble	glich (glih)	geglichen (–glih'–)		
⁵Gleiten (glīt'-en), to glide	glitt (glit)	geglitten (–glit'–)		
⁶Glimmen (glim'-men), to glimmer	glomm (glom)	geglommen (–glom'–)		
⁷Graben (grā'-ben), to dig	grub (groop)	gegraben	gräbſt (graipst)	
⁵Greifen (grī'-fen), to grasp	griff (grif)	gegriffen (–grif'–)		
⁸Haben (hā'-ben), to have	hatte (hät'-te)	gehabt (–häpt')	er hat (hät)	
⁴Halten (häl'-ten), to hold	hielt (heelt)	gehalten	bu hältſt (hältst)	
⁴Hangen (häng'-en), to hang, (intrans.)	hing (hing)	gehangen		
Hauen (how'-en), to hew, lash	hieb (heep)	gehauen		
⁶Heben (hā'-ben), to lift	hob (hōp)	gehoben (–hō'–)		
⁴Heißen (hī'-ssen), to call, bid	hieß (hees)	geheißen		
²Helfen (hel'-fen), to help, aid, assist	half (hälf)	geholfen (–hol'–)	er hilft (hilft)	hilf
Kennen (kan'-nen), to know	kannte (kän'–)	gekannt		
⁸Klimmen (klim'-men), to climb	klomm (klom)	geklommen		
³Klingen (kling'-en), to sound	klang (kläng)	geklungen (–klung'–)		
⁵Kneifen (knī'-fen), to pinch	see greifen			
²Kommen (kom'-men), to come	kam (käm)	gekommen	{ kömmſt (komst) / kömmſt (kimst)	
⁸Können (kin'-nen), to be able	konnte (kon'–)	gekonnt	er kann (kän)	

Infinitive	Preterite	Past Participle	Present	Imperative
5 Kreischen (krī'-shen), to screech	kreischte (krīsh'-te)	gekrischen (-krish'-)		
6 Kriechen (kree'-hen), to creep	kroch (kroch)	gekrochen		
7 Küren (kü'-ren), to choose, (also reg.)	kor (kōr)	gekoren		
7 Laden (lā'-den), to load	lud (loot)	geladen	lädst (laidst)	
" to invite	regular			
4 Lassen (lās'-sen), to let	ließ (lees)	gelassen	lässest (las'-sest)	laß (lās)
4 Laufen (low'-fen), to run	lief (leef)	gelaufen	läufst, läuft (loist)	
5 Leiden (lī'-den), to suffer	litt (lit)	gelitten		
5 Leihen (līh'-en), to lend, to borrow	lieh (leeh)	geliehen		
1 Lesen (lā'-zen), to read	las (lās)	gelesen	liesest (lee'-zest) / liest (leez't)	lies (lees)
1 Liegen (lee'-gen), to lie	lag (lāg)	gelegen (-lā'-)		
1 Lügen (lü'-gen), to lie (tell a falsehood)	log (lōg)	gelogen (-lō'-)		
7 Mahlen (mā'-len), to grind	regular	gemahlen		
5 Meiden (mī'-den), to shun, avoid	mied (meet)	gemieden (-mee'-)		
6 Melken (mal'-ken), to milk	molk	gemolken (-mol'-)		
19 Messen (mās'-sen), to measure	maß (mās)	gemessen	missest (mis'-sest) / mißt (mist)	miß (mis)
19 Mißfallen (mis-fāl'-len), to displease	see fallen			
3 Mißlingen (mis-ling'-en), to fail	see gelingen			
8 Mögen (mō'-gen), to be allowed	mochte (moch'-te)	gemocht	magst (mägst)	
8 Müssen (müs'-sen), to be obliged	mußte (mus'-te)	gemußt	du mußt	
2 Nehmen (nā'-men), to take	nahm (nām)	genommen (-nom'-)	nimmt (nimt)	nimm (nim)
3 Nennen (nan'-nen), to name	nannte (nan'-te)	genannt		
5 Pfeifen (pfī'-fen), to whistle	see greifen			
6 Pflegen (pflā'-gen), to attend to, to nurse; to cultivate; to be wont, to be in habit of, to use	pflog (pflōg). (but the regular form is preferable)	gepflogen (-pflō'-)		
5 Preisen (prī'-zen), to praise	pries (prees)	gepriesen (-pree'-)		
6 Quellen (kval'-len), to spring forth	quoll (kvoll)	gequollen (-kvol'-)	quillt (kvilt)	
4 Rathen (rā'-ten), to advise	rieth (reet)	gerathen		
5 Reiben (rī'-ben), to rub	see bleiben			
5 Reißen (rī'-ssen), to tear	see pfeifen			
5 Reiten (rī'-ten), to ride	see reißen			
3 Rennen (ran'-nen), to run, to race	rannte (rän'-)	gerannt		

PRESENT INFINITIVE.	PAST.	PAST PARTICIPLE.	PRES. INDICATIVE.	IMPERATIVE.
⁶Riechen (ree′-hen), to smell	roch (roch)	gerochen		
³Ringen (ring′-en), to wrestle	see fingen			
²Rinnen (rin′-nen), to run, flow	rann (rän)	geronnen (–ron′–)		
⁴Rufen (roo′-fen), to call	rief (reef)	gerufen (–roo′–)		
Salzen (zal′-tsen), to salt	regular	gesalzen		
⁶Saufen (zow-fen), to drink excessively	soff (zoff)	gesoffen		
⁶Saugen (zow′-gen), to suck	sog (zōg)	gesogen (–zō′–)		
⁷Schaffen (shaf′-fen), to create	schuf (shoof)	geschaffen (–shaf′–)		
²Schaffen, to work, provide	regular			
⁵Scheiden (shī′-den), to separate	see meiden			
⁵Scheinen (shī′-nen), to shine	see meiden			
²Schelten (shel′-ten), to scold	schalt (shält)	gescholten (–shol′–)	schiltst (shiltst) schiltst (sheerst)	schilt (shilt) (also regular)
²Scheren (shai′-ren), to shear	schor (shōr)	geschoren (–shō′–)		
⁶Schieben (shee′-ben), to shove	schob (shōp)	geschoben (–shō′–)		
⁶Schiessen (shee′-ssen), to shoot	schoss (shoss)	geschossen (–shoss′–)		
³Schinden (shin′-den), to flay	schund (shund)	geschunden (–shun′–)		
⁷Schlafen (shlä′-fen), to sleep	schlief (shleef)	geschlafen	er schläft (shlaift) schläfst (shlaigst)	
²Schlagen (shlä′-gen), to beat	schlug (shloog)	geschlagen		
⁵Schleichen (shlī′-hen), to sneak	schlich (shlih)	geschlichen (–shlih′–)		
⁶Schleifen (shlī′-fen), to grind	see preceding			
⁵Schleissen (shlī′-ssen), to slit	see preceding			
⁶Schliessen (shlee′-ssen), to shut	see schiessen	geschlissen (–shliss′–)		
³Schlingen (shling′-en), to twist, twine, wind	see flingen			
⁵Schmeissen (shmī′-ssen), to fling	see schleissen			
⁶Schmelzen (shmal′-tsen), to melt	see fiechten			
⁵Schneiden (shnī′-den), to cut	see reiten			
⁶Schrauben (shrow′-ben), to screw	schrob (shrōp)	geschroben (–shrō′–)	(also regular)	
⁵Schreiben (shrī′-ben), to write	see bleiben			
⁵Schreien (shrī′-en), to cry	see preceding			
⁵Schreiten (shrī′-ten), to stride	see reiten			
⁶Schroten (shrō′-ten), to bruise, to grind		gefchroten		
⁶Schwären (shvai′-ren), to fester	schwor (shvōr)	geschworen (–shvō′–)		

⁵Schweigen (shvī'-gen), to be silent	schwieg (shveeg)	geschwiegen (–shvee'–)	schwillst (shvilst)
Schwellen (shval'-len), to swell	schwoll (shvoll)	geschwollen (–shvol'–)	
²Schwimmen (shvim'-men), to swim	schwamm (shvām)	geschwommen (–shvom'–)	
³Schwinden (shvin'-den), to vanish	schwand (shvānd)	geschwunden (–shvun'–)	
³Schwingen (shving'-en), to swing	see *preceding*		
¹Schwören (shvï'-ren), to swear	schwur (shvoor)	geschworen (–shvō'–)	
¹Sehen (zäh'-en), to see	sah (zäh)	gesehen (–zäh'–)	sei, seist (see conjugation)
¹Sein (zīn), to be	war (vär)	gewesen (–vä'–zen)	bin, bist, ist, sind, seid
¹¹Senden (zan'-den), to send	{ sandte (zänd'–) sendete (zan'-de-te')	gesandt (–zänt') gesendet (–zan'–)	(*also regular*)
⁴Sieden (zee'-den), to boil	sott (zot)	gesotten (–zot'-ten)	
³Singen (zing'-en), to sing	see klingen		
³Sinken (zing'-ken), to sink	sank (zank)	gesunken (–zunk'–)	
²Sinnen (zin'-nen), to muse	sann (zän)	gesonnen (–zon'–)	
¹Sitzen (zit'-sen), to sit	saß (zäs)	gesessen (–zes'–)	{ 3d person singular, soll (zoll)
⁸Sollen (zol'-len), to be obliged, shall	see schreien		
⁵Speien (shpī'-en), to spit	see sinnen		
²Spinnen (shpin'-nen), to spin			
⁵Spleißen (shplī'-ssen), to split	spließ (shpleess)	gesplissen (–shpliss'–)	
²Sprechen (shprah'-hen), to speak	see brechen		
⁵Sprießen (shpree'-ssen), to sprout	proß (shpross)	gesprossen (–shpross'–)	
³Springen (shpring'-en), to spring	see singen		
²Stechen (stah'-hen), to sting	see brechen		
⁷Stehen (shtäh'-en), to stand	stand (shtänd)	gestanden (–shtän'–)	stiehlst (shteelst)
²Stehlen (shtäh'-len), to steal	stahl (shtähl)	gestohlen (–shtō'–)	stiehl (shteel)
⁵Steigen (shtī'-gen), to mount, rise	see schweigen		stirbst (shtirpt)
²Sterben (shtar'-ben), to die	starb (shtärp)	gestorben (–shtor'–)	stirb (shtirp)
⁶Stieben (shtee'-ben), to disperse	stob (shtōp)	gestoben (–shtō'–)	
⁴Stoßen (shtō'-ssen), to push	stieß (shtees)	gestoßen (–shtō'–)	{ stößest (shtï'-seest) stößt (shtïsst)
⁵Streichen (shtrī'-hen), to stroke	see schleichen		
⁵Streiten (shtrī'-ten), to quarrel	see reiten		
¹Thun (toon), to do	that (tāt)	gethan (–tän')	{ thue (too'-e), thust (toost), thut (toot) } thue (too'-e)

PRESENT INFINITIVE.	PAST.	PAST PARTICIPLE.	PRES. INDICATIVE.	IMPERATIVE.
⁷Tragen (trä'-gen), to carry, bear, wear	trug (troog)	getragen (-trȧ'-)	trägſt (traigst) trifft (trift)	
²Treffen (traf'-fen), to hit	traf (traf)	getroffen (-trof'-)	trifft (trift)	triff (trif)
⁵Treiben (trī'-ben), to drive	see ſchreiben			
¹Treten (trā'-ten), to tread	trat (trāt)	getreten (-trā'-)	trittſt (trŭtst)	tritt (trit)
⁶Triefen (tree'-fen), to drip, trickle	see gießen			
³Trinken (tring'-ken), to drink	see ſinken			
⁶Trügen (trü'-gen), to deceive	see lügen			
²Verbergen (fer-bar'-gen), to hide	see bergen			
⁵Verbieten (fer-bee'-ten), to prohibit	see bieten			
⁵Verbleiben (fer-blī'-ben), to remain	see bleiben			
⁵Verbleichen (fer-blī'-ḣen), to grow pale	see bleichen			
²Verderben (fer-dar'-ben), to perish	see ſterben			
⁶Verdrießen (fer-dree'-ssen), to vex	see ſprießen			
¹Vergeſſen (fer-gas'-sen), to forget	see meſſen			
⁵Vergleichen (fer-glī'-ḣen), to compare	see gleichen			
⁴Verlaſſen (fer-läs'-sen), to forsake	see laſſen			
⁶Verlieren (fer-lee'-ren), to lose	verlor (-lōr')	verloren (-lō'-)		
⁶Verlöſchen (fer-lësh'-shen)to extinguish	verloſch (-losh)	verloſchen (-losh'-shen)		
⁸Verſchwinden (fer-shvin'-den), to disappear	see ſchwinden			
⁶Verwirren (fer-vir'-ren), to confuse		verworren (fer-vor'-ren)		
⁵Verzeihen (fer-tsīh'-en), to pardon				
⁷Wachſen (väk'-sen), to grow	wuchs (vuks)	gewachſen (-vä'-)	wächſ't (vakst)	
⁶Wägen (vai'-gen), to weigh	wog (vōg)	gewogen (-vō'-)		
⁷Waſchen (väsh'-shen), to wash	wuſch (vṳsh)	gewaſchen (-väsh'-)	{ wäſcheſt (våsht'-) wäſcht (vāsht) *also regular* }	
⁶Weben (vā'-ben), to weave	wob (vōp)	gewoben (-vō'-)		
⁵Weichen (vī'-ḣen), to give way, to yield	see gleichen			
⁵Weiſen (vī'-zen), to show	see preiſen			
⁸Wenden (van'-den), to turn	see ſenden			
²Werben (var'-ben), to recruit, enlist	warb (varp)			
²Werden (var'-den), to become	*see conjugation*	geworden (-vor'-)	ſie wirbt (virpt)	wirb (virp)
²Werfen (var'-fen), to throw	see helfen			

EXPLANATORY REMARKS.

(See Table of the Classification of Irregular Verbs.)

I. The first class changes the radical vowel e into a in the past perfect, and resumes it in the past participle. Example: geben (gā'-ben), to give; past perfect, gab (gäp); past participle, gegeben (ge-gā'-ben). To this class must be added bitten (bit'-ten), to beg, entreat, which, on account of the vowel i, seems to belong to either the second or third class; but in order to be distinguished from bieten (bee'-ten), to offer, and beten (bā'-ten), to pray, worship, and from the past participle form of the second and third classes, it claims its place among the first class of irregular verbs, viz.: bitten, bat (bät), gebeten (ge-bā'-ten).

II. The second class changes the radical vowel e or i into a in the past perfect, and in the past participle into o. Example: nehmen (nā'-men), to take, nahm, genommen; gewinnen (ge-vin'-nen), to win, gewann, gewonnen. To these must be added gebären (ge-bai'-ren), to bear, produce, with ä instead of e or i in the root; hence gebar (ge-bär'), geboren (ge-bō'-ren).

III. The third class changes the radical vowel i into a in the past perfect, and in the past participle into u. Example: singen (sing'-en), to sing, sang, gesungen; except dingen (ding'-en), to hire, and schinden (shin'-den), to flay, the past perfect of which is: dung (dung) and schund (shunt).

IV. The fourth class changes the radical vowel a into ie in the past perfect, and resumes it in the past participle. Example: rathen (rä'-ten), to guess, advise, rieth (reet), gerathen (ge-rä'-ten). The following with a different radical vowel belong to the same class, viz.: laufen (lou'-fen), to run, lief (leef), gelaufen (ge-lou'-fen); heißen (hī'-ssen), to order, hieß (hees), geheißen (ge-hī'-ssen); rufen (roo'-fen), to call, rief (reef), gerufen (ge-roo'-fen); stoßen (shtō'-ssen), to push, stieß (shtees), gestoßen (ge-shtō'-ssen).

V. The fifth class changes the radical vowel ei into ie in the past perfect, and into i in the past participle or before a double consonant. Example: schreiben (shrī'-ben), to write, schrieb (shreep), geschrieben (ge-shree'-ben); schneiden (shnī'-den), to cut, schnitt (shnitt), geschnitten (ge-shnit'-ten); gehen (gäh'-en), to go, belongs by its past perfect ging (ging) to the same, and by its past participle gegangen (ge-gäng'-en) to the preceding class.

⁶Wiegen (vee'-gen), to weigh	see mögen		
⁸Winden (vin'-den), to wind	see binden		
⁶Wissen (vis'-sen), to know	wußte (vus'-te)	gewußt (-vust-)	{ weißt (vist), weiß (viss), will, willst, will }
⁵Wollen (vol'-len), to will	regular	regular	
⁵Zeihen (tsih'-en), to accuse of	see bleiben		
⁶Ziehen (tseeh'-en), to draw	zog (tsōg)	gezogen (-tsō'-)	
³Zwingen (tsving'-en), to compel	zwang (tsvang)	gezwungen (-tsvųn'-)	

Note.—The derivative and compound verbs, of inseparable or separable particles, are conjugated like their primitives. Ex.: entwerfen (ent-var'-fen), to project, and vorwerfen (fōr'-var'-fen), to reproach, like werfen, to throw; ausgehen (ous'-gäh'-en), to go out, like gehen, to go; vorschreiben (fōr'-shrī'-ben), to prescribe, like schreiben, to write, etc.

VI. The sixth class changes the radical vowels ä, au, e, i, ie, ö, ü into o in the past perfect and past participle. Example: gähren (gai'-ren), to ferment, gohr (gōr), gegohren (ge-gō'-ren); saugen (zou'-gen), to suck, sog (zōg), gesogen (ge-zō'-gen); saufen (zou'-fen), to drink to excess, soff (zoff), gesoffen (ge-zof'-fen); heben (hä'-ben), to lift, hob (hōp), gehoben (ge-hō'-ben); verwirren (fer-vir'-ren), to embroil, confuse, verworr (fer-vorr'), verworren (fer-vor'-ren); bieten (bee'-ten), to offer, bot (bōt), geboten (ge-bō'-ten); schwören (shvȳ'-ren), to swear, schwor (shvōr), geschworen (ge-shvō'-ren); betrügen (be-trü'-gen), to cheat, deceive, betrog (be-trōg), betrogen (be-trō'-gen).

VII. The seventh class changes the radical vowel a into u in the past perfect, and resumes it in the past participle. Example: graben (grä'-ben), to dig, grub (groop), gegraben (ge-grä'-ben ; stehen (stäh'-en), to stand, formerly stund (shtunt), now stand (shtänt), gestanden (ge-shtän'-den).

VIII. The eighth class comprises seventeen verbs with seven radical vowels, viz.: a, e, i, o, ö, u, ü, changed into a, o, u in the past perfect and past participle. Example: brennen (brän'-nen), to burn, brannte (brän'-te), gebrannt (ge-bränt'), burnt; können (kin'-nen), to be able, konnte (kon'-te), was able, could, gekonnt (ge-kont'), was (or have been) able; müssen (mis'-sen), to be obliged, must, mußte (mus'-te), was obliged, gemußt (ge-must'), was obliged.

THE PREPOSITION (Verhältnißwort—fer-halt'-niss-vort')

indicates the *position* or *relation* in which a verb, used in a sentence, stands to the object connected with it in the same sentence; as: der Baum (boum), *tree*, steht (shtät), *stands* [verb], in, *in* [preposition], dem Garten (gär'-ten), *garden*.

It answers the interrogative wo (vō)? *where?*; wohin (vo-hin')? *whither?*; von wann (fon vän)? *from when?*; woher (vō-hār')? *from what place?*; bis wann (biss vän)? *till when?* For instance: Wohin gehst Du? (—— gäst doo), *whither art thou going?* Answer: In mein Zimmer (—— —— tsim'-mer), *into my room.*

It is followed by either the genitive, dative, or accusative.

Prepositions with the Genitive, characterized in English by "of" following them, are:

    anstatt or statt (än-shtät'), *instead of;*
    außerhalb (ou'-sser-hälp'), *without, outside of;*
    innerhalb (in'-ner-hälp'), *within, inside of;*
    diesseit[s] (dees'-zīt[s], *on this side of;*
    jenseit[s] (yän'-zīt[s], *on the other side of;*
    entlang (ent-läng') or längs (längs), *along, on the side of;*
    halben (häl'-ben) or halber (häl'-ber), *on account of;*
    kraft (kräft) or vermöge (fer-mȳ' ge), *by virtue of;*
    laut (lout), *according to, in pursuance of;*
    mittels-st (mit'-tels-st) or vermittelst (fer-mit'-telst), *by means of;*
    ob (ōp), *on account of;*
    oberhalb (ō'-ber-hälp'), *above, on the top of;*
    unterhalb (un'-ter-hälp), *below, under the foot of;*
    troß (trots), *in spite of;*
    ungeachtet (un'-ge-äch'-tet), *notwithstanding, in spite of;*
    um —— willen (um —— vil'-len), *for the sake of;*
    unfern (un-färn) or unweit (un-vīt), *not far off or from;*
    während (vai'-rent), *during, in the time of;*
    wegen (vä'-gen), *on account of;*
    zufolge (tsoo-fol'-ge), *in pursuance of.*

Entlang (but not längs), ungeachtet, wegen and zufolge precede or follow, halben or halber always follows, and um —— willen encloses the object. For instance: wegen des Vaters, or des Vaters wegen; des Friedens halber (—— free'-dens ——), on account of peace; um seines Sohnes willen (—— zī'-nes zō'-nes ——), for the sake of his son.

Entlang, preceded by the object, governs the accusative; längs, trotz and zufolge are also used with the dative.

Mark: It is correct to say meinet- (mī'-net), deinet-, seinet-, ihret-, unsert-, euret-halben, -wegen or -willen—not meiner-, deiner-, etc.)

The Dative require:

aus (ous), *out, out of, from;*
außer (ous'-ser), *except, besides;*
bei (bī), *with, near, by;*
binnen (bin'-nen), *within;*
entgegen (ent-gā'-gen), *toward, against;*
gegenüber (gā'-gen-ü'-ber), *opposite;*
gemäß (ge-mais'), *in conformity with;*
mit (mit), *with;*

nach (näch), *after, to;*
nächst (naihst), *next to;*
nebst (näpst), *together with;*
samt (zämt), *together with;*
seit (zīt), *since;*
von (fon), *of, from, by;*
zu (tsoo), *to;*
zuwider (tsoo-vee'-der), *against.*

Place entgegen, gegenüber, gemäß, zuwider after the object.

The Accusative is governed by:

durch (durh), *through, by;*
für (fīr), *for;*
gegen (gā'-gen), *toward, against;*

ohne (ō'-ne) or sonder (zon'-der), *with-*
um (um), *about, around;* [*out;*
wider (vee'-der), *against.*

The following prepositions govern the Dative when the verb indicates a rest, and the Accusative, when a motion in a certain direction is expressed by the verb. The former answers the question wo? *where?* and the latter wohin? (vo-hin') *whither?*

an (än), *on, at, to;*
auf (ouf), *on, upon;*
hinter (hin'-ter), *behind;*
in, *in, into;*
neben (nā'-ben), *near, by the side of, besides, close by;*

über (ü'-ber), *over, above;*
unter (un'-ter), *under, among, below, beneath, amid, betwixt;*
vor (fōr), *before;*
zwischen (tsvish'-shen), *between, betwixt, among[st].*

Examples: Das Bild (bilt), *picture,* hängt (hängt), *hangs*—*where?*—an der [dative] Wand (vänt), *wall.* Hänge (hang'-e), *hang* [imperat. trans.] das Bild-wohin?—an die [accusative] Wand.

THE ADVERB (Umstandswort—um'-shtänts-vort')

qualifies a verb, an adjective, or other adverb. In the first of these qualifications it has its comparisons like an adjective, of which the following are irregular:

bald (bält), *soon;*
eher (äh'-er), *sooner;*
am ehesten (äh'-e-sten'), *soonest.*

gern (garn), *willingly;*
lieber (lee'-ber), *more willingly;*
am liebsten (leep'-sten), *most willingly.*

The other adverbs designate—

(A) The place where something exists or is done.

allenthalben (äl'-lent-häl'-ben), *everywhere;*
da (dä), *here, there;*

dort (dorrt), *there;*
draußen (drou'-ssen), *without, out of doors, abroad;*

drinnen (drin'-nen), *within;*
daheim (dā-hīm), *at home;*
fort (forrt), *away, on, forth;*
heim (hīm), *home;*
herab (her-áp'), *down, down here;*
herauf (her-ouf'). *up, up here;*
hernieder (her-nee'-der), *down;*
hinab (hin-áp'), *down;*
hinan (hin-án'), *up, up to;*
hinauf (hin-ouf'), *up, up to;*
hinten (hin'-ten), *behind;*
links (links), *on or to the left;*

nirgends (nir'-gents), *nowhere;*
oben (ō'-ben), *above;*
rechts (rahts), *on or to the right;*
stromab (shtröm-áp'), *down the river, or with the current;*
stromauf (shtröm-ouf'), *up or against the stream or current;*
überall (ü'-ber-áll'), *everywhere;*
unten (un'-ten), *below;*
vorn (forrn), *in front;*
vorwärts (fōr'-vąrts), *forward, on;*
weiter (vī'-ter), *farther, further.*

(B) The time when or how often a thing is done.

bald (bált), *soon;*
beständig (be-shtan'-dig), *constantly;*
bisher (biss-hār'), *hitherto, till now;*
dann (dann), *then;*
darauf (dár-ouf'), *thereupon, on it;*
eben (ā'-ben), *just, exactly;*
ehemals (ā'-he-mäls'), *formerly;*
einst (īnst), *once;*
endlich (ant'-lih), *at last, finally;*
ewig (ā'-vig), *eternally, forever;*
früh (frü), *early;*
gegenwärtig (gā'-gen-vąr'-tih), *present, at present, now;*
gestern (gas'-tern), *yesterday;*
heute (hoi'-te), *to-day;*
immer (im'-mer), *always, ever;*
jährlich (yār'-lih), *yearly, annually;*
jetzt (yatst), *at present, now;*
jüngst (yīngst), *lately;*
lange (láng'-e), *long time;*
monatlich (mō'-nät-lih'), *monthly;*

morgen (morr'-gen), *to-morrow;*
nachher (nāch-hūr'), *afterward;*
nächstens (naih'-stens), *soon;*
neulich (noi'-lih), *lately;*
nie (nee), *never;*
noch (noch), *yet;*
nun (noon), *now;*
oft (offt), *often;*
seitdem (zīt-dām'), *since, since then;*
seither (zīt-hār'), *since, since that time;*
spät (shpait), *late;*
später (shpai'-ter), *later, later on;*
stets (shtāts), *continually;*
stündlich (shtīnt'-lih), *hourly;*
täglich (taig'-lih), *daily;*
vorher (fōr-hār'), *before, previously;*
wöchentlich (vīh'-hent-lih'), *weekly;*
zeitlebens (tsīt'-lā'-bens), *all my, his, etc., life;*
zuletzt (tsoo-latst'), *at last, lastly.*

(C) The manner in which a thing is done.

allerdings (ál'-ler-dings'), *undoubtedly, sure enough, indeed;*
also (ál'-zō), *thus, so, then, therefore;*
anders (án'-ders), *otherwise, differently, in another way;*
außerordentlich (ou'-sser-or'-dent-lih'), *extraordinary;*
doch (doch), *yet, nevertheless, pray;*
durchaus (durh-ous'), *throughout, thoroughly, absolutely;*
durchaus nicht (―― niht), *not at all, by no means, not in the least;*
ebenso (ā'-ben-zō'), *likewise;*
etwa (at'-vā'), *perhaps, by chance, anywhere;*
freilich (frī'-lih), *of course, certainly, indeed, to be sure;*
gar (gār), *quite, entirely, very, even;*
gewiß (ge-viss'), *certainly;*

höchst (hīhst), *at best, at most;*
ja (yā), *yes, aye, yea;*
jedenfalls (yā'-den-fálls'), *at all events, in any case;*
keineswegs (kī'-nes-vāgs'), *by no means;*
nicht (niht), *not;*
recht (rąht), *right;*
sehr (zār), *very, exceedingly;*
sicherlich (zih'-her-lih'), *surely;*
so (zō), *so;*
unbedingt (un'-be-dingt'), *unconditionally;*
überaus (ü'-her-ous'), *exceedingly;*
vermuthlich (fer-moot'-lih), *presumably;*
vielleicht (feel-līht'), *perhaps;*
wahrhaftig (vār-háf'-tih), *truly, verily;*
wahrscheinlich (vār-shīn'-lih), *probably;*
wirklich (virk'-lih), *really.*

THE CONJUNCTION (Bindewort—bin'-de-vort')

connects sentences or words with one another, and is either *co-ordinate*, beiordnend (bī'-ord'-nent), or *subordinate*, unterordnend (un'-ter-ord'-nent).

Die beiordnenden Bindewörter sind:

aber (ä'-ber), *but;*
allein (al-līn'), *but;*
also (äl'-zō), *consequently;*
auch (ouch), *also;*
bald—bald (bält), *at one time—at another;*
daher (dä-hār'), darum (dür-um'), *therefore;*
denn (dan), *for, than;*
dennoch (dan'-noch), *nevertheless;*
dessenungeachtet (das'-sen-un'-ge-ácht'-tet), *nevertheless;*
deshalb (das'-hälp), deswegen (das-vā'-gen), *therefore;*
doch (doch), *yet, still;*

entweder—oder (ent-vā'-der—ō'-der), *either—or;*
desto (das'-tō), preceded in the first part of the sentence by je (yā), *the—the;*
indessen (in-das'-sen), *however;*
jedoch (ye-doch'), *yet, however, nevertheless;*
mithin (mit-hin'), *consequently;*
nämlich (naim'-lih), *namely, to wit;*
oder (ō'-der), *or;*
sonach (zo-näch'), *therefore;*
sondern (zon'-dern), *but;*
sowohl—als (zo-vōl'-äls), *as well—as;*
und (unt), *and;* [nor.
weder—noch (vā'-der—noch), *neither—*

Die unterordnenden Bindewörter sind:

als (äls), *as, when, than;*
als ob (äls op), *as if;*
auf daß (ouf däs), damit (dä-mit'), *in order that;*
bis (bis), *until;*
da (dä), *as, since;*
daß (däss), *that;*
ehe (äh'-e), *before;*
falls (fäls), *in case;*
indem (in-dām'), *as, while, whereas;*
je, see desto;
nachdem (nach-dām'), *after;*
ob (op), *whether, if;*
obgleich (op-glīh'), obschon (-shōn'), obwohl (-vōl'), *although;*

seit (zīt), seitdem (-dām'), *since;*
sobald als (zo-bält' äls), *as soon as;*
so oft als (zo oft äls), *as often as;*
um zu (um tsoo), followed by Infin., *in order to;*
während (vai'-rent), *while;*
wann (vän), *when;*
weil (vīl), *because;*
wenn (van), *if, when;*
wenn nicht (van niht), *unless;*
weshalb (ves-hälp'), weswegen (ves-vā'-gen), *wherefore;*
wo (vō), *where;*
wofern (vo-fārn'.), *if, provided;*
zwar (tsvär), *indeed, certainly, it is true.*

THE INTERJECTIONS (Empfindungswörter—emp-fin'-dungs-vīr'-ter)

are words thrown (interjected) into a sentence, to express (1) JOY, as: ha (hä); heißa (hī'-säh); juchhei (yuch-hī'); ei (ī); ah (üh); hurrah (hur-räh'), etc.— (2) PAIN, as: ach (ach); weh (vä), *woe;* o weh; au; leider (lī'-der), *alas,* etc.— (3) FEAR, as: uh (oo); huh (hoo), etc.—(4) DISGUST, as: pfui (pfui), *fi;* fi (fee), etc.—(5) WONDER, as: hah (häh); ach (ach); ih (eeh); o, etc.—(6) A CONFIRMATION, as: ja (yä), *yes;* nein (nīn), *no;* fürwahr (fīr-vär'), *truly, indeed;* wahrlich (vär'-lih), *verily;* wahrhaftig (vär-häf'-tih), *truly, indeed.*—(7) A WILL, as: heda (hā'-dä); pst! holla (hol'-lah); fort (forrt), *away!* marsch (märsh), *march;* wohlan (vōl-än'), *well, come on!*

EXERCISES.

1.

Der, den, die, das, the.
Vater (fä'-ter), father.
Mutter (mut'-ter), mother.
Bruder (broo'-der), brother.
Schwester (shvas'-ter), sister.
und (unt), and.
ein (in), eine (ī'-ne), a, an.
klein, —er, —e, —es (klīn), little, small.
Knabe (knä'-be), boy.
Mädchen (mait'-hen), girl.

mein, —en, —e (mīn), my.
Kind (kint), child.
dein, —en, —e (dīn), thy.
gut, —er, —e, —es (goot), good.
sein, —en, —e (zīn), his.
ihr, —en, —e (eer), her.
jung, —er, —e, —es (yung), young.
ist (ist), is.
auch (ouch), also.
noch (noch), still, yet.

Der Vater, die Mutter, der Bruder und die Schwester. Der gute Vater,
The father, the mother, the brother and the sister. The good father,

die gute Mutter, der gute Bruder und die gute Schwester. Ein kleines Kind,
the good mother, the good brother and the good sister. A little child,

ein guter Knabe und ein gutes Mädchen. Mein Bruder und meine Schwester,
a good boy and a good girl. My brother and my sister,

mein kleiner Bruder und meine kleine Schwester. Mein Bruder ist gut und
my little brother and my little sister. My brother is good and

meine Schwester ist auch gut. Der gute kleine Knabe und das gute kleine
my sister is also good. The good little boy and the good little

Mädchen. Dein Bruder ist klein und deine Schwester ist auch klein. Seine kleine
girl. Thy brother is small and thy sister is also small. His little

Schwester ist ein gutes Mädchen und sein kleiner Bruder ist ein guter Knabe.
sister is a good girl and his little brother is a good boy.

Mein Bruder ist noch jung, meine Schwester ist auch jung.
My brother is still young, my sister is also young.

2.

Ich habe (ih hä'-be), I have.
du hast (doo hást), thou hast.
er (är), sie (zee), es (ess) hat (hát), he, she, it has.
unser (un'-zer), unsre (un'-zre), unsren (un'-zren), unsern (un'-zarn), our.
euer (oi'-er), eure (oi'-re), euern (oi'-ern), your.

Feder (fä'-der) [f.], pen, feather.
Buch (booch) [n.], book.
gross (grōss), great, big, large.
Haus (houss) [n.], house.
Garten (gär'-ten) [m.], garden.
dieser (dee'-zer), diesen (dee'-zen), diese (dee'-ze), this.
Pferd (pfärt) [n.], horse.

(38)

sehr (zūr), very.
wir haben (veer hä'-ben), we have.
Ihr habt, Sie haben (eer häpt), you have.
sie haben (zee hä'-ben), they have.

aber (ä'-her), but.
gesehen (ge-zäh'-en), seen.
Sohn (zōn), son.
Tochter (toch'-ter), daughter.

Ich habe eine gute Feder und ein großes Buch. Du hast auch ein Buch.
I have a good pen and a large book. Thou hast also a book.
Ich habe einen guten Bruder und du hast eine gute Schwester. Meine Schwester
I have a good brother and thou hast a good sister. My sister
hat eine kleine Feder. Hat er euer Buch gesehen? Sie hat Euren Bruder gesehen.
has a little pen. Has he your book seen? She has your brother seen.
Unser Haus ist groß, aber unser Garten ist klein. Dieser kleine Knabe ist mein
Our house is large, but our garden is small. This little boy is my
Sohn und dieses kleine Mädchen ist meine Tochter. Unsre Schwester ist noch jung.
son and this little girl is my daughter. Our sister is still young.
Habt Ihr einen Garten? Wir haben einen großen Garten und ein großes Haus.
Have you a garden? We have a large garden and a large house.
Euer Pferd ist gut, aber unser Pferd ist auch gut. Habt Ihr meinen Sohn gesehen?
Your horse is good, but our horse is also good. Have you my son seen?
Ich habe euren Sohn und eure Tochter gesehen. Er ist groß und sie ist noch
I have your son and your daughter seen. He is tall and she is yet
klein. Wir haben ein Pferd, aber es ist noch sehr jung. Meine kleine Schwester
little. We have a horse, but it is yet very young. My little sister
hat ein großes Buch. Habt Ihr (haben Sie) auch ein Buch? Habt Ihr (haben
has a large book. Have you also a book? Have you
Sie) den großen Garten gesehen?
the large garden seen?

3.

Welcher (val'-her), —e, —es, who, which.
welchen, whom, which.
gekauft (ge-koust'), bought.
Hut (hoot) [m.], hat.
Uhr (oor) [f.], watch.
Federmesser (fä'-der-mas'-ser) [n.], pen-[knife.
Freund (froint) [m.], friend.

gefunden (ge-fun'-den), found.
verloren (fer-lō'-ren), lost.
für (fīr), for.
wo (vō), where.
reich (rih), rich.
Oheim (ō'-hīm), Onkel (ong'-kel), uncle.
nicht (niht), not.

Wir haben einen Vater, welcher gut ist. Wir haben eine Mutter, welche gut
We have a father, who good is. We have a mother, who good
ist. Ich habe ein Buch, welches sehr gut ist. Meine Schwester hat eine Feder,
is. I have a book, which very good is. My sister has a pen,
welche sehr klein ist. Das Buch, welches Sie gekauft haben, ist gut, aber es ist
which very small is. The book, which you bought have, is good, but it is

klein. Unser Vater hat ein Pferd, welches noch jung ist. Ich habe einen Freund,
small. Our father has a horse, which yet young is. I have a friend,
welcher sehr reich ist, aber er ist noch jung. Das Haus, welches Ihr habt, ist
who very rich is, but he is still young. The house, which you have, is
klein, aber euer Garten ist groß. Unser Oheim hat das Buch, welches Sie gesehen
small, but your garden is large. Our uncle has the book, which you seen
haben. Das Pferd, welches wir gekauft haben, ist noch jung. Ich habe einen kleinen
have. The horse, which we bought have, is yet young. I have a little
Hut; dein Hut ist groß. Mein Bruder hat eine Uhr. Haben Sie auch eine
hat; thy (your) hat is big. My brother has a watch. Have you also a
Uhr? Meine Uhr ist klein, aber sie ist sehr gut. Der kleine Knabe, welchen ihr
watch? My watch is small, but it is very good. The little boy, whom you
gesehen habt, ist mein Bruder. Das kleine Mädchen, welches ihr gesehen habt,
seen have, is my brother. The little girl, whom you seen have,
ist meine Schwester. Ich habe ein Federmesser verloren. Habt Ihr mein Federmesser
is my sister. I have a penknife lost. Have you my penknife
gefunden? Wir haben das Pferd gesehen, welches euer Vater gekauft hat.
found? We have the horse seen, which your father bought has.
Wo habt ihr dieses Federmesser gefunden? Mein Vater hat für meinen Bruder
Where have you this penknife found? My father has for my brother
eine Uhr gekauft. Diese Feder ist für meine Schwester.
a watch bought. This pen is for my sister.

4.

Von (fon), of; [*genitive case.*]
von, aus (ous), from.
nützlich (nüts'-lih), useful.
König (kĭ'-nig) [*m.*], king.
Königin (kĭ'-ni-gin'), queen.
Näherin (naih'-e-rin), seamstress.

Brief (breef) [*m.*], letter.
wo (vö), where.
Nachbar (nách'-bär) [*m.*], neighbor.
Nachbarin (nách-bä-rin'), female neigh-
Hund (hunt) [*m.*], dog. [bor.
erhalten (er-hál'-ten), received.

Der Freund meines Bruders ist noch jung. Das Buch meiner Schwester
The friend of my brother is still young. The book of my sister
ist sehr nützlich. Das Haus meines Onkels ist sehr klein, aber sein Garten ist
is very useful. The house of my uncle is very small, but his garden is
groß. Habt Ihr den Brief meiner Schwester erhalten? Die Näherin hat von
large. Have you the letter of my sister received? The seamstress has from
Ihrer Schwester einen Brief erhalten. Ich habe den Hund meines Nachbars
your sister a letter received. I have the dog of my neighbor
gesehen. Unsere Nachbarin hat die Königin gesehen. Dieser kleine Knabe hat
seen. Our (lady) neighbor has the queen seen. This little boy has

das Federmesser seiner Schwester verloren. Ich habe das Buch gesehen, welches
the penknife of his sister lost. I have the book seen, which
mein Bruder von unserm Onkel erhalten hat. Wo ist der Hund unseres Nach-
my brother from our uncle received has. Where is the dog of our neigh-
bars? Meine Freundin hat das Pferd des Königs gesehen. Dieses nützliche
bor? My (fem.) friend has the horse of the king seen. This useful
Buch hat der Sohn meines Nachbars von seinem Onkel erhalten; aber das Buch
book has the son of my neighbor from his uncle received; but the book
seines Vaters hat er verloren. Wo haben Sie die Schwester der Königin
of his father has he lost. Where have you the sister of the queen
gesehen? Ich habe die Schwester der Näherin gesehen, welche für diesen kleinen
seen? I have the sister of the seamstress seen, who for this little
Knaben ein sehr nützliches Buch gekauft hat. Die Tochter unsers Nachbars ist
boy a very useful book bought has. The daughter of our neighbor is
klein, aber sein Sohn ist groß. Habt Ihr die Feder meiner Schwester gefunden?
small, but his son is tall. Have you the pen of my sister found?
Meine Nachbarin hat eine Feder erhalten, welche sehr gut ist. Die Königin hat
My (fem.) neighbor has a pen received, which very good is. The queen has
von dem König ein Pferd erhalten, welches sehr gut und noch sehr jung ist.
from the king a horse received, which very good and still very young is.

5.

An (àn) [*followed by accus.*], zu (tsoo),
  to; [*dative, when not translated.*]
an meinen Vater, or
meinem Vater, to my father.
an meine Mutter, or
meiner Mutter, to my mother.
geschickt (ge-shikt'), sent.

gegeben (ge-gā'-ben), given.
geliehen (ge-leeh'-en), lent.
verkauft (fer-kouft'), sold.
geschrieben (ge-shree'-ben), written.
Vetter (fet'-ter) [*m.*], Base (bä'-ze) [*f.*],
  cousin.
Geld (galt) [*n.*], money.

Ich habe mein Federmesser meinem Vetter gegeben. Mein Bruder hat einen
I have my penknife to my cousin given. My brother has a
Brief an seinen Onkel geschrieben. Meine Schwester hat ein Buch an ihre Base
letter to his uncle written. My sister has a book to her cousin
geschickt. Mein Vater hat diesem Kinde ein Federmesser gegeben. Wo habt Ihr
sent. My father has to this child a penknife given. Where have you
das Geld, welches ich eurer Schwester geliehen habe? Habt Ihr Eurem Vetter
the money, which I to your sister lent have? Have you to your cousin
das Buch geschickt? Ich habe Eurem Onkel das Federmesser geliehen, welches ich
the book sent? I have to your uncle the penknife lent, which I
von meinem Onkel erhalten habe. Mein Onkel hat sein Pferd seinem Nachbar
from my uncle received have. My uncle has his horse to his neighbor

verkauft. Habt Ihr euren Garten an euren Onkel verkauft? Haben Sie Ihrem
  sold. Have you your garden to your uncle sold? Have you to your

Nachbarn einen Brief geschrieben? Ich habe meinem Bruder dein Buch geliehen.
neighbor   a   letter written? I have to my brother thy book   lent.

Unsere Nachbarin hat die Feder erhalten, welche Sie von meinem Bruder
Our (fem.) neighbor has the pen received, which you from my   brother

gekauft haben.
bought have.

6.

Oft (oft), often.
Gärtner (gart'-ner) [m.], gardener.
Magd (mügt), maid-servant.
krank (kránk), sick.
spricht (shpriht), speaks.
immer (im'-mer), always.
Thür (tür) [f.], door.

offen (of'-fen), open.
ich denke an (ih deng'-ke an), I think of.
Geschenk (ge-shank') [n.], present.
Kaufmann (kouf'-mán) [m.], merchant.
Mann (mán), man.
Papier (pá-peer') [n.], paper.
treu (troi), faithful.

Die Tochter der Nachbarin ist noch jung. Der Sohn des Nach-
The daughter of the (fem.) neighbor is still young. The son of the neigh-

bars ist krank. Habt Ihr das Pferd des Kaufmannes gesehen? Wo ist das
bor is sick. Have you the horse of the merchant   seen? Where is the

Messer der Magd? Ich denke an den Gärtner, welcher immer von dem guten
knife of the maid-servant? I think of the gardener, who always of the good

Kinde spricht. Die Thür eures Hauses ist offen. Die Näherin hat von der
child speaks. The door of your house is open. The seamstress has from the

Königin ein Geschenk erhalten. Unsere Magd ist des Gärtners Schwester. Der
queen a present received. Our maid-servant is the gardener's sister. The

Sohn des Kaufmannes ist sehr krank. Die Magd der Nachbarin ist sehr
son of the merchant is very sick. The maid-servant of the neighbor is very

treu. Wo habt Ihr dieses Papier gekauft? Wir haben von dem Sohne des
faithful. Where have you this paper bought? We have from the son of the

Kaufmannes einen Brief erhalten. Er hat das Geld von dem Onkel dieses jungen
merchant   a   letter received. He has the money from the uncle of this young

Mannes erhalten. Mein Freund spricht immer von der Tochter unserer Freundin.
man received. My friend speaks always of the daughter of our (f.) friend.

Ich denke oft an deine Schwester. Dieser Brief ist von dem Vetter des Gärtners.
I think often of thy sister. The letter is from the cousin of the gardener.

Ich habe der Tochter des Nachbars ein Geschenk gegeben. Dieser Mann hat sein
I have to the daughter of the neighbor a present given. This man has his

Pferd an den Bruder des Kaufmannes verkauft. Habt Ihr an den Vetter eures
horse to the brother of the merchant sold. Have you to the cousin of your

Freundes geschrieben? Ich habe an den Freund unserer Base ein Geschenk geschickt.
friend written? I have to the friend of our (f.) cousin a present sent.

7.

Bücher (bü'-her), books.
Federn (fä'-dern), pens.
Geschenke (ge-shäng'-ke), presents.
zufrieden (tsoo-free'-den), satisfied.
kurz (kurts), short.
Tag (täg) [*m.*], day.
lang (läng), long.
schon (shön), already.
sind (zint), are.

Nacht (nächt) [*f.*], night.
Blume (bloo'-me) [*f.*], flower.
schön (shïn), beautiful.
Stuhl (shtool) [*m.*], chair.
glücklich (glïk'-lih), happy, lucky, fortunate.
angekommen (än'-ge-kom'-men), arrived.
Mädchen (mait'-hen) [*pl.*], girls.
diese (dce'-ze) [*pl.*], these.

Die Bücher meines Bruders sind nützlich. Die Federn meiner Schwester sind
The books of my brother are useful. The pens of my sister are
gut. Die Kinder des Nachbars sind krank. Die Geschenke meines Oheims sind
good. The children of the neighbor are sick. The presents of my uncle are
schön. Die kleinen Mädchen sind schon zufrieden. Ich habe meine schönen
beautiful. The little girls are already satisfied. I have my beautiful
Blumen der Tochter meines Freundes gegeben. Die Freunde unseres Vetters
flowers to the daughter of my friend given. The friends of our cousin
sind angekommen. Lange Tage, kurze Nächte. Ich bin glücklich, und meine Schwester
are arrived. Long days, short nights. I am happy, and my sister
ist zufrieden. Ich habe diesen Stuhl an den Gärtner verkauft. Meine Base
is satisfied. I have this chair to the gardener sold. My (fem.) cousin
hat ein Geschenk von Blumen erhalten, sie ist sehr glücklich. Diese Mädchen sprechen
has a present of flowers received, she is very happy. These girls speak
immer von den großen Gärten des Kaufmannes. Die Söhne und Töchter des
always of the large gardens of the merchant. The sons and daughters of the
Nachbars haben schöne Bücher und gute Federn. Der junge Gärtner des
neighbor have beautiful books and good pens. The young gardener of the
Nachbars ist angekommen, er hat dem Sohne des Nachbars ein schönes Federmesser gegeben. Er spricht immer von glücklichen Tagen, schönen Blumen und guten
neighbor is arrived, he has to the son of the neighbor a beautiful penknife given. He speaks always of happy days, beautiful flowers and good
Mädchen. Ich habe meinem Onkel das Papier geschickt, welches Ihr gekauft habt.
girls. I have to my uncle the paper sent, which you bought have.
Mein Bruder spricht immer von unserer Base, und mein Vetter denkt immer
My brother speaks always of our (f.) cousin, and my cousin thinks always
an seine Schwester. Habt Ihr meine Blumen schon gesehen? Ich habe das Geld für
of his sister. Have you my flowers already seen? I have the money for
diese Blumen erhalten und ich bin zufrieden. Diese Tage sind schön. Diese Thür
these flowers received and I am satisfied. These days are beautiful. This door

ift offen. Diefer Stuhl ift groß. Diefer Mann ift treu. Ich denke an die Geschenke,
is open. This chair is large. This man is faithful. I think of the presents,
welche angekommen find.
which arrived are.

8.

Reicher (rī'-her), richer.
größer (grī'-sser), larger, greater.
treuer (troi'-er), more faithful.
schöner (shī'-ner), more beautiful.
besser (bas'-ser), better.
als (àls), than.
der größte (— grīss'-te), am größten (àm ——), the greatest.
der reichste, am reichsten (— rīh'-ste, —-sten), the richest.
der treueste (troi'-e-ste'), am treuesten, the most faithful.
der beste (bas'-te), am besten, best.
der, die, das meinige (mī'-ni-ge'), den meinigen [accus. m. sing.], die meinigen [pl.], mine.
der, die, das deinige (dī'-ni-ge'), den deinigen (accus. m. sing.], die deinigen [pl.], thine.
der, die, das seinige (zī'-ni-ge'), den seinigen [accus. m. sing.], die seinigen [pl.], his.
der, die, das ihrige (eeh'-ri-ge'), den ihrigen [accus. m. sing.], die ihrigen [pl.], hers.
der, die, das unsrige (un'-zri-ge'), den unsrigen [accus. m. sing.], die unsrigen [pl.], ours.
der, die, das eurige (oi'-ri-ge'), Ihrige (eeh'-ri-ge'), den eurigen, Ihrigen [accus. m. sing.], die eurigen [pl.], yours.
der, die, das ihrige [pl.], den ihrigen [accus. m. sing.], die ihrigen [pl.], theirs.
ihr, ihre, ihren [pl.], their.
jener (yä'-ner), jene, jenes, jenem; der-, die-, dasjenige (-yä'-ni-ge'), denjenigen [accus. m. sing.], that.
jene, diejenigen [pl.], those.
Land (lànt) [n.],
Gegend (gä'-gent) [f.], } country.
Stadt (shtàt) [f.], town, city.
Männer (man'-ner),
Menschen (man'-shen), } men.
Welt (valt) [f.], world.
Sonne (zon' ne) [f.], sun.
Mond (mònt) [m.], moon.
hell (hall), clear.
angenehm (àn'-ge-näm), agreeable.
ich liebe (lee'-be),
habe gern (— gàrn), } I like.
Katze (kàt'-se) [f.], cat.
fleißig (flī'-ssig), diligent.

Er ift reicher, als ich. Die Sonne ift größer, als der Mond. Der Tag ift
He is richer, than I. The sun is larger, than the moon. The day is
heller, als die Nacht. Meine Schwester ift fleißiger, als mein Bruder.
clearer, than the night. My sister is more diligent, than my brother.
Diese Gegend ift schöner als diejenige, welche wir gesehen haben. Unsere Katze
This country is more beautiful than that, which we seen have. Our cat
ift besser, als die eurige. London ift die größte Stadt der Welt. Die Tage
is better, than yours. London is the largest city of the world. The days
find kürzer, als die Nächte. Ein Hund ift treuer, als eine Katze. Das
are shorter, than the nights. A dog is more faithful, than a cat. The
Land ift angenehmer, als die Stadt. Meine Feder ift besser, als die deinige,
country is more agreeable, than the city. My pen is better, than thine,
aber diejenige, welche dein Bruder gekauft hat, ift noch besser. Unser Hund ift
but that, which thy brother bought has, is still better. Our dog is

treuer, als der eurige, aber eure Bücher sind nützlicher, als die unsrigen.
more faithful, than yours, but your books are more useful, than ours.
Diese Blume ist schön, die Blume meiner Schwester ist schöner, und
This flower is beautiful, the flower of my sister is more beautiful, and
diejenige deiner Mutter ist die schönste. Diese Knaben sind fleißiger,
that of thy mother is the most beautiful. These boys are more diligent,
als jene. Unser Nachbar ist der reichste Mann der Stadt. Mein Hund ist
than those. Our neighbor is the richest man of the city. My dog is
treu, der eurige ist treuer, aber derjenige unsers Nachbars ist der
faithful, yours is more faithful, but that of our neighbor is the most
treueste. Der Kaufmann, welcher jenes große Haus gekauft hat, ist einer der
faithful. The merchant, who that large house bought has, is one of the
reichsten Männer der Stadt. Ich habe mein Buch verloren und dasjenige meines
richest men of the town. I have my book lost and that of my
Vetters. Ich habe fleißige und treue Menschen gern. Die Sonne ist die treue
cousin. I like diligent and faithful men. The sun is the faithful
Uhr der Welt. Katzen sind oft nützlicher, als Hunde.
watch of the world. Cats are often more useful, than dogs.

9.

Es giebt (— geept), es ist, da ist (dä —), there is.
es giebt, es sind, da sind, there are.
viel (feel), much.
viele (fee'-le) [pl.], many.
mehr (mär), more.
wenig (vā'-nig), little.
wenige (vā'-ni-ge'), few.
so viel als (zō feel äls), as much as.
so viele als, as many as.
wie viel? (vee feel), how much?
wie viele, how many?
weniger (vā'-ni-ger'), less.
zu viel, too much.
zu viele, too many.
zu groß, too large.
zu klein, too small.
arm (ärm), poor.

Frau (frou), woman.
Frauen (frou'-en), women.
geben Sie mir (gā'-ben — —), gebet mir, give me.
getrunken (ge-trung'-ken), drunk.
gegessen (ge-gas'-sen), eaten.
genug (ge-nug'), enough.
Wasser (vás'-ser) [n.], water.
Brot (brōt) [n.], bread.
Butter (but'-ter) [f.], butter.
hier (heer), here.
Baum (boum) [m.], tree.
Zimmer (tsim'-mer) [n.], room.
so (zō), so.
hungrig (hung'-rig, -rih), hungry.
etwas (at'-vás), something.
Bier [n.], beer.

Der reiche Mann hat viel Geld. Mein Freund hat mehr Geld, als ich.
The rich man has much money. My friend has more money, than I.
Habt Ihr viel Brod? Gebt mir ein wenig Butter. Dies ist Brot genug.
Have you much bread? Give me a little butter. This is bread enough.
Da ist ein wenig Bier. Es giebt viele große Bäume in diesem Garten.
There is a little beer. There are many large trees in this garden.

Es giebt viele schöne Häuser in dieser Stadt. Diese Frau hat viele
There are many beautiful houses in this town. This woman has many
Kinder. Ich habe weniger Geld, als Sie, aber ich bin glücklicher, als Sie,
children. I have less money, than you, but I am happier, than you.
Mein Bruder hat mehr Bücher, als Sie. Ich habe zu viel Brot und Butter
My brother has more books, than you. I have too much bread and butter
gegessen, und Sie haben zu viel Wasser getrunken. Wie viele Bäume giebt es
eaten, and you have too much water drunk. How many trees are there
in Eurem Garten? In unserm Garten sind so viele Bäume, als in dem
in your garden? In our garden there are as many trees, as in
eurigen. In diesem Zimmer (da) sind zu wenige Stühle. Diese arme Frau ist
yours. In this room there are too few chairs. This poor woman is
hungrig, gebt ihr ein wenig Brot. Wie viele Kinder habt Ihr? Wir haben
hungry, give her a little bread. How many children have you? We have
weniger Kinder, als unser Nachbar. Dieser Mann hat zu viele Blumen in
less children, than our neighbor. This man has too many flowers in
seinem Garten. Gebt diesem armen Manne etwas Brod, er ist so hungrig.
his garden. Give this poor man some bread, he is so hungry.

10.

Leinwand (lĭn′-vànt) [*f.*], linen.
Tasse (täs′-se) [*f.*], cup.
Stück (shtĭk) [*n.*], piece.
Glas (gläs) [*n.*], glass.
Flasche (fläsh′-she) [*f.*], bottle.
Pfund (pfunt) [*n.*], pound.
Elle (ăl′-le) [*f.*], ell, yard.
Paar (pär) [*n.*], pair, couple.
Dutzend (dŭt′-tsent) [*n.*], dozen.
Korb (korp) [*m.*], basket.
halb (hälp), half.
Thee (tā) [*m.*], tea.
Kaffee (käf′-fā) [*m.*], coffee.
Handschuh (hänt′-shoo) [*m.*], glove.

Taschentuch (täsh′-shen-tooch′) [*n.*], handkerchief.
Strumpf (shtrumpf) [*m.*], stocking.
Schuh (shoo) [*m.*], shoe.
Stiefel (shtee′-fel) [*m.*], boot.
Hemd (hąmpt) [*n.*], shirt.
Halsbinde (häls′-bĭn′-de) [*f.*], cravat.
Bleistift (blī′-shtĭft′) [*m.*], lead-pencil.
Tinte (tĭn′-te) [*f.*], ink.
Koffer (kof′-fer) [*m.*], trunk.
Zucker (tsŭk′-ker) [*m.*], sugar.
drei (drī), three.
zehn (tsān), ten.

✗ Meine Mutter hat meinem Vetter drei Paar Handschuhe, drei Paar
My mother has to my cousin three pair of gloves, three pair of
Strümpfe und ein Dutzend Hemden geschickt. In diesem Koffer (da) sind drei
stockings and a dozen shirts sent. In this trunk there are three
Dutzend Paar Stiefel und ein halbes Dutzend Halsbinden. Ich habe von meinem
dozen pair of boots and half a dozen of cravats. I have from my
Onkel einen Hut und eine Uhr, ein Federmesser, zehn Federn und ein Dutzend
uncle a hat and a watch, a penknife, ten pens and a dozen

Bleistifte erhalten. Mein Bruder hat ein Paar Schuhe und ein Paar
lead-pencils received. My brother has a pair of shoes and a pair of
Stiefel gekauft. Mein Onkel hat meiner Schwester zehn Dutzend Ellen Lein-
boots bought. My uncle has to my sister ten dozen yards of linen
wand und ein Dutzend Taschentücher geschickt. Wir haben der Näherin Ihrer
and a dozen handkerchiefs sent. We have to the seamstress of your
Freundin zehn Pfund Zucker geschickt. Meine Nachbarin hat diesem kleinen
(f.) friend ten pounds of sugar sent. My (f.) neighbor has to this little
Knaben eine Tasse Kaffee und Brot und Butter gegeben. Ich habe ein Glas
boy a cup of coffee and bread and butter given. I have a glass of
Wasser getrunken. Jenes schöne Mädchen hat meinem Bruder einen Korb
water drunk. That beautiful girl has to my brother a basket
gegeben, und er hat ihr ein Paar Strümpfe geschickt. Diese Tasse Thee ist für
given, and he has to her a pair of stockings sent. This cup of tea is for
Sie, und dieses Pfund Zucker ist für Ihren Bruder. Ich habe von meinem
you, and this pound of sugar is for your brother. I have from my
Vater einen Bleistift und ein wenig Dinte erhalten.
father a lead-pencil and a little ink received.

11.

[See Cardinal Numbers, page 16.]

Thaler (tä'-ler) [m.], dollar.
Jahr (yähr) [n.], year.
Monat (mö'-nät) [m.], month.
Woche (voch'-e) [f.], week.
Stunde (shtun'-de) [f.], hour.
Minute (mi-noo'-te) [f.], minute.
heute (hoi'-te), to-day.
spät (shpait), late.
früh (frü), early.
nicht (niht), not. [night.
vierzehn Tage (feer'-tsān tä'-ge), a fort-
ein Vierteljahr (īn feer'-tel-yähr), three months.
Ehefrau (ā'-he-frou'), wife. [months.
ein halbes Jahr (— häl'-bes yähr), six

eine Viertelstunde (—feer'-tel-shtun'-de), a quarter of an hour.
eine halbe Stunde, half an hour.
Wie viel Uhr ist es? What o'clock is it?
es ist ein Uhr, it is one o'clock.
es ist halb drei Uhr, it is half past two o'clock.
es ist ein Viertel auf vier, it is a quarter past three.
Um wie viel Uhr? At what o'clock?
es wird (virt) gleich (glīh) schla(ä'-)gen, it is going to strike.
es hat soe(ä'-)ben geschla(ä'-)gen, it has struck just now.
Fenster (fan'-ster) [n.], window.

In diesem Zimmer sind zwei Tische und sechs Stühle. Ich habe von meinem
In this room there are two tables and six chairs. I have from my
Onkel ein Federmesser und zehn Federn, einen Hut und eine Uhr, drei Taschen-
uncle a penknife and ten pens, a hat and a watch, three pocket-
tücher und einen halben Dollar erhalten; und mein Bruder hat zehn Dollars
handkerchiefs and a half dollar received; and my brother has ten dollars

erhalten. In dem Garten unsers Nachbars giebt es zwanzig große Bäume. In
received. In the garden of our neighbor there are twenty large trees. In

diesem Zimmer (da) sind zwei Fenster und drei Thüren. Wie viel haben Sie
this room there are two windows and three doors. How much have you

für Ihren Hut gegeben? Ich habe drei Dollars für meinen Hut und vier Dollars für
for your hat given? I have three dollars for my hat and four dollars for

meine Weste gegeben. Wir haben heute fünf Briefe erhalten. Meine Schwester
my waistcoat given. We have to-day five letters received. My sister

hat ein halbes Dutzend Taschentücher und drei Paar Handschuhe erhalten.
has a half dozen pocket-handkerchiefs and three pair of gloves received.

Mein Vater hat fünf Dollars an die Frau des Gärtners geschickt. Wie alt sind Sie?
My father has five dollars to the wife of the gardener sent. How old are you?

Ich bin neunzehn Jahre alt. Wie alt ist Ihr Bruder? Mein Bruder ist zwanzig
I am nineteen years old. How old is your brother? My brother is twenty

Jahre alt und meine Schwester achtzehn. Mein Vetter ist noch nicht zwölf Jahre alt.
years old and my sister eighteen. My cousin is yet not twelve years old.

Es ist noch nicht vierzehn Tage, daß ich hier bin. Es ist ein halbes Jahr, daß mein
It is yet not two weeks, that I here am. It is a half year, that my

Bruder in Berlin ist. Ein Tag hat vierundzwanzig Stunden, eine Stunde hat sechzig
brother in Berlin is. A day has twenty-four hours, an hour has sixty

Minuten. Eine Woche hat sieben Tage, vier Wochen sind noch nicht ein Monat, ein
minutes. A week has seven days, four weeks are yet not a month, a

Monat hat dreißig Tage. Ein Jahr hat dreihundert fünf und sechzig Tage, oder
month has thirty days. A year has three hundred five and sixty days, or

zwölf Monate, oder zwei und fünfzig Wochen. Dieses ist das Jahr achtzehn hundert
twelve months, or two and fifty weeks. This is the year eighteen hundred

sieben und achtzig. Ist die Welt noch nicht älter als sechs tausend Jahre? Sehr
seven and eighty. Is the world yet not older than six thousand years? Very

viel älter. Wie viel Uhr ist es? Es ist ein Uhr, zwei Uhr, ein Viertel bis
much older. What o'clock is it? It is one o'clock, two o'clock, a quarter of

drei, halb fünf Uhr. Wie viel Uhr ist es nach Ihrer Uhr? Es ist drei Uhr,
three, half past four. What o'clock is it by your watch? It is three o'clock,

ein Viertel nach vier, drei Viertel auf sechs Uhr. Es ist noch nicht sechs Uhr. Es
a quarter past four, a quarter of six o'clock. It is yet not six o'clock. It

hat sieben Uhr geschlagen. Es wird gleich acht Uhr schlagen. Um wie viel
has seven o'clock struck. It is going to eight o'clock strike. At what

Uhr habt Ihr den Brief erhalten? Um halb zwölf Uhr.
o'clock have you the letter received? At half past eleven o'clock.

12.

[See Conjugation of Auxiliary Verbs, page 20.]

Güte (gü'-te), kindness.
liebt, hat gern, likes.
arbeiten (ar'-bī-ten), to work.
traurig (trou'-rig, –riḣ), sad.
unglücklich (un–), unhappy.
Eltern (ạl'-tern), parents.

faul (foul), lazy.
gemacht (ge-măcht'), made.
Aufgabe (ouf'-gä'-be) [*f.*], exercise.
vernünftig (fer-nïnf'-tig, –tiḣ), reasonable.
Obst (ōpst) [*n.*], fruit (of trees).

Ich habe viele Bücher, ich bin glücklich. Du bist nicht zufrieden. Du hast
I have many books, I am happy. Thou art not satisfied. Thou hast
nicht Güte genug für deine Freunde. Mein Bruder ist glücklich, er hat viele
not kindness enough for thy friends. My brother is happy, he has many
Freunde. Meine Schwester ist fleißig, sie arbeitet gern. Wir sind nicht traurig,
friends. My sister is diligent, she likes to work. We are not sad,
wir haben unsere Bücher nicht verloren. Ihr seid nicht unglücklich, Ihr habt Eure
we have our books not lost. You are not unhappy, you have your
Eltern nicht verloren. Meine Brüder sind nicht faul, sie haben ihre Aufgaben
parents not lost. My brothers are not lazy, they have their exercises
gemacht. Diejenigen, welche zufrieden sind, sind glücklich. Ihr habt wenig Geld,
made. Those, who satisfied are, are happy. You have little money,
aber Ihr seid immer fleißig. Sie sind noch jung, aber Sie sind vernünftiger,
but you are always diligent. You are yet young, but you are more reasonable,
als Ihr Vetter. Sind Sie immer glücklich? Haben Sie viele Freunde? Ist er
than your cousin. Are you always happy? Have you many friends? Is he
zufrieden? Hat er Geld genug? Diese Kinder sind krank, sie haben zu
satisfied? Has he money enough? These children are sick, they have too
viel Obst gegessen.
much fruit eaten.

13.

[See Conjugation of Auxiliary Verbs, page 21.]

Tugendhaft (too'-gent-häft'), virtuous.
man (män), one (you, they).
ehemals (ā'-he-mäls'), formerly.
Tante (tän'-te), aunt.
Neffe (näf'-fe), nephew.
Nichte (niḣ'-te), niece.

Großvater (grōs'-fä'-ter), grandfather.
Großmutter (–mut'-ter), grandmother.
jetzt (yatst), at present.
Zahl (tsäl) [*f.*], number.
bescheiden (be-shī'-den), modest.
thätig (tai'-tig), active.

Ich war ehemals sehr glücklich. Ich hatte viele Bücher und Freunde. Mein
I was formerly very happy. I had many books and friends. My
Großvater war immer dein Freund, er hatte auch viele Güte für
grandfather was always thy (your) friend, he had also much kindness for

deine   Schwester.   Meine Nichte war   immer bescheiden und thätig.   Man liebt die
thy (your) sister.   My   niece was always modest and active.   One likes the
Menschen, welche tugendhaft sind.   Dein Neffe hatte sein Geld verloren, er war sehr
men,   who virtuous are.   Thy nephew had his money lost, he was very
unglücklich;   jetzt   ist er zufrieden.   Unsere Großmutter war oft in dem Garten
unhappy; at present is he satisfied.   Our grandmother was often in the garden
unsres Oheims.   Sie hatte eine große   Zahl   Blumen in ihrem Hause. Dieser
of our uncle.   She had   a   great number of flowers in her house.   This
fleißige Knabe war ehemals sehr krank; man liebt ihn, er ist bescheiden und
diligent boy was formerly very sick; one likes him, he is modest and
tugendhaft.   Ihr waret ehemals reich und   hattet viele Freunde;   jetzt sind
virtuous.   You were formerly rich and (you) had many friends; at present are
wir reich und haben Eure Freunde.   Ich habe eine fleißige und eine faule Nichte, eine
we rich and have your friends.   I have a diligent and a lazy niece, a
tugendhafte und bescheidene   Base, einen reichen und einen armen Vetter, und einen
virtuous and modest (f.) cousin, a rich and a poor cousin, and a
sehr thätigen Neffen.   Wo waren   deine   Schwestern?   In dem Hause unserer
very active nephew.   Where were thy (your) sisters?   In the house of our
   Nachbarin, welche die beste Frau von der Welt ist.
   (f.) neighbor, who the best woman of the world is.

14.

[See Conjugation of Auxiliary Verbs, page 21.]

Geschäft (ge-shaft') [n.], business.
Frühstück (frü'-shtĭk') [n.], breakfast.
Mittagessen (mit'-täg-as'-sen) [n.], dinner.
zusammen (tsoo-zäm'-men), together.
gestern (gas'-tern), yesterday.
kochen (koch'-chen), to cook, boil.

will (vill), wird (virt), will.
Dame (dä'-me), lady.
meine Damen (mī'-ne dä'-men)! ladies.
Herr (har'), gentleman.
Vergnügen (ter-gnü'-gen) [n.], pleasure.
bereiten (be-rī'-ten), to prepare.
kann (kän), can.

Haben Sie meinen Bleistift gehabt?   Ich bin in Ihrem Zimmer gewesen, aber
Have you my lead-pencil had?   I have in your room been, but
mein Bruder hat Ihren Bleistift gehabt.   Wo ist Ihre Frau? Meine Frau ist
my brother has your lead-pencil had.   Where is your wife? My wife is
noch nicht angekommen; sie war gestern   noch in dem Hause ihrer Tante in New
yet not   arrived; she was yesterday still in the house of her aunt in New
York. Wer wird mein Frühstück bereiten?   Wer kann ein gutes Mittagessen kochen?
York. Who will my breakfast prepare?   Who can a good dinner   cook?
Diese Dame kann kochen und dieser Herr kann arbeiten.   Wo sind Sie gewesen,
This lady can cook and this gentleman can work.   Where have you been,

meine Damen? Wir hatten wenig Geschäfte und waren zusammen in dem Garten
  ladies?   We had little business and were together in the garden
einer guten Freundin. Wir waren gestern sehr glücklich, wir hatten viel Vergnügen.
of a good (f.) friend. We were yesterday very happy, we had much pleasure.
Man kann nicht immer Vergnügen haben, aber man ist glücklich, wenn man immer
One can not always pleasure have, but one is happy, when one always
zufrieden und tugendhaft gewesen ist. Gestern waren wir in jener Stadt, heute sind
satisfied and virtuous been is. Yesterday were we in that town, to-day are
wir hier; gestern haben wir ein gutes Mittagessen gehabt, heute haben wir ein sehr
we here; yesterday have we a good dinner had, to-day have we a very
gutes Frühstück.
good breakfast.

15.

[See Conjugation of Auxiliary Verbs, page 21.]

morgen (morr'-gen), to-morrow.
Birne (birr'-ne) [*f.*], pear.
einige (i'-ni-ge'), a few.
schön (shjn), fine.
Abendessen (ü'-bent-as'-sen) [*n.*], supper.
Gesellschaft (ge-zall'-shaft) [*f.*], company, society.
daß (dáss), that.
Wetter (vat'-ter) [*n.*], weather.
mit, bei (bi), with.
Theater (tā-ā'-ter) [*n.*], theater.
müde (mü'-de), tired, fatigued. [dress.
Vortrag (fŏr'-trāg') [*m.*], lecture, ad-
Abend (ü'-bent) [*m.*], evening.

Das Wetter ist heute schön, aber gestern war es noch schöner. Morgen
The weather is to-day fine, but yesterday was it still finer. To-morrow
wird es acht Tage, daß ich im Theater gewesen bin. Heute Abend werden
will it (be) eight days, that I in the theater have been. This evening shall
wir Bier und Obst haben, die Gesellschaft wird sehr groß und das Abendessen
we beer and fruit have, the company will very large and the supper (will)
gut sein. Der Vortrag dieses Herrn war sehr gut, aber der meines Onkels
good be. The address of this gentleman was very good, but that of my uncle
wird noch viel besser sein. Diese Dame wird diesen Abend bei mir sein. Ich werde
will still much better be. This lady will this evening with me be. I shall
genug Papier, Federn und Tinte haben. Birnen sind gutes Obst, ich esse sie gern.
enough paper, pens and ink have. Pears are (a) good fruit, I like them.
Werden Sie morgen Abend im Theater sein? Werden wir viel Vergnügen
Will you to-morrow evening in the theater be? Shall we much pleasure
haben? Ich werde zu müde sein. Mit diesem Dollar wirst du zwölf Dollars
have? I shall too tired be. With this dollar wilt thou twelve dollars
erhalten haben. Dies wird zu viel für dich gewesen sein. Ich werde morgen
received have. This will too much for thee have been. I shall to-morrow

vier Wochen hier gewesen sein und mehr Vergnügen gehabt haben, als Diejenigen,
four weeks here have been and more pleasure have had, than those,
welche nicht hier gewesen sind. Meine Vetter würden nicht so traurig gewesen sein,
who not here have been. My cousins would not so sad have been,
wenn sie Briefe von ihrem Vater erhalten hätten. Er hatte meinen Hut gehabt,
if they letters from their father received had. He had my hat had,
aber er hatte nicht meine Handschuhe gehabt.
but he had not my gloves had.

16.

[*See Conjugation of Auxiliary Verbs, page 21.*]

gesagt (ge-zägt'), said.
alle (ál'-le), all.
rauchen (rou'-chen), to smoke.
Tabak (tä'-bák) [*m.*], tobacco.
Zigarre (tsi-gär'-re) [*f.*], cigar.

geraucht (ge-roucht'), smoked.
gethan (ge-tän'), done.
Zigarette (tsi'-gä-rat'-te) [*f.*], cigarette.
nichts (nihts), nothing.
schädlich (shait'-lih), injurious, hurtful.

Ich würde glücklich sein, wenn ich Bücher und Freunde hätte. Ich würde mehr
I should happy be, if I books and friends had. I should more
Vergnügen haben, wenn mein Vetter hier wäre. Ich habe es dir schon oft
pleasure have, if my cousin here were. I have it to thee already often
gesagt, daß es sehr schädlich ist, Zigaretten zu rauchen. Ich würde reicher sein,
said, that it very injurious is, cigarettes to smoke. I should richer be,
wenn ich nicht so viel geraucht hätte. Nicht alle Menschen würden zufrieden und
if I not so much smoked had. Not all men would satisfied and
glücklich sein, wenn sie Millionen hätten. Ich werde dies morgen früh gethan
happy be, if they millions had. I shall this to-morrow morning done
haben. Was hast du mit meinem Hunde gethan? Wenn ich Ihren Hund gesehen
have. What hast thou with my dog done? If I your dog seen
hätte, würde ich nichts damit gethan haben. Ich denke oft an Das, was Sie
had, should I nothing with it done have. I think often of that, which you
würden gesagt haben, wenn Sie alle diese Blumen gesehen hätten. Wenn Sie fünfzig
would said have, if you all these flowers seen had. If you fifty
Briefe geschrieben haben, werden Sie müde sein. Ich würde nicht mit mir zufrieden
letters written have, will you tired be. I should not with myself satisfied
sein, wenn ich nicht fleißig gearbeitet hätte. Die Mädchen würden nicht so schön
be, if I not diligently worked had. The girls would not so handsome
sein, wenn sie nicht so bescheiden und tugendhaft wären. Ich würde nichts gesagt
be, if they not so modest and virtuous were. I should nothing said
haben, wenn Sie die Uhr nicht verloren hätten, die ich Ihnen geliehen hatte.
have, if you the watch not lost had, which I to you lent had,

17.

[*See Conjugation of Regular Verbs, pp. 23 and 24, and List of Irreg. Verbs, p. 26 sq.*]

kommen (kom'-men) [*irr.*], to come.
liebenswürdig (lee'-bens-vïr'-dig), amiable.
sprechen (shprah'-hen) [*irr.*], to speak.
glauben (glou'-ben) [*r.*], to believe.
zu Mittag essen (tsoo mit'-täg äs'-sen) [*irr.*], to dine.
antworten (änt'-vor'-ten) [*r.*], to answer.
Licht (liht) [*n.*], light.

warum (vär-um'), why? what for?
hoffen (hof'-fen) [*r.*], to hope.
gehorchen (ge-horr'-hen) [*r.*], to obey.
vortrefflich (for-traff'-lih), excellent, -ly.
rein (rīn), clean, pure, purely.
reinigen (rī'-ni-gen) [*r.*], to clean, purify.
thun (toon) [*irr.*], to do.
erwarten (er-vär'-ten) [*r.*], to expect.

Ich liebe meine Brüder und Schwestern. Du liebst Deine Freunde und er liebt
I love my brothers and sisters. Thou lovest thy friends and he loves

sie auch. Deine Schwester liebt unsere Großmutter und glaubt, daß sie auch von
them also. Thy sister loves our grandmother and believes, that she also by

ihr geliebt wird. Wir erwarten, daß Ihr auf den Brief antwortet, welchen wir Euch
her loved is. We expect, that you the letter answer, which we to you

geschrieben haben. Ich kam in das Haus meines Onkels und aß mit ihm zu Mittag.
written have. I came into the house of my uncle and dined with him.

Sie haben das Zimmer vortrefflich gereinigt; ich hoffe, daß Sie jetzt so liebenswürdig
You have the room excellently cleaned; I hope, that you now so amiable

sein werden, Ihre Freunde darin zu erwarten. Gott sprach: Es werde Licht! und es
will be, your friends in it to expect. God spoke: It be light! and it

wurde Licht. Gute Kinder gehorchen ihrem Vater und ihrer Mutter. Ich bin
was light. Good children obey to their father and to their mother. I am

mit Dir, spricht Dein Gott. Er glaubte glücklich zu sein, wenn seine schöne
with thee, speaks thy God. He believed happy to be, if his beautiful

Base käme. Sie bereitete Thee und Kaffee für ihn und erwartete ihn
(f.) cousin came. She prepared tea and coffee for him and expected him

gestern Abend in dem Hause ihrer Tante. Aber er kam nicht; ich glaube, er
yesterday evening in the house of her aunt. But he came not; I believe, he

hatte zu viel zu thun. Warum kamst Du nicht, mein Freund? Warum antwortetest
had too much to do. Why camest thou not, my friend? Why answeredst

Du nicht auf den Brief, den meine Mutter die Güte hatte, Dir zu schreiben?
thou not on the letter, which my mother the kindness had, to thee to write?

Frühstückt Ihr heute nicht mit meinem Bruder? Wir frühstücken heute mit Deinem
Breakfast you to-day not with my brother? We breakfast to-day with thy

Bruder und essen morgen mit Ihrem Onkel zu Mittag; wir hoffen, ein gutes
brother and dine to-morrow with your uncle (at noon); we hope, a good

Mittagessen zu haben.
dinner to have.

18.

[See Conjugation of Verbs, page 23.]

tadeln (tä'-deln), to blame.
neu (noi), new.
schreiben (shri'-ben), to write.
letzt (latst),
vergangen (fer gäng'-en), } last
Kleid (klīt) [*n.*], dress.
Kleider (kli'-der), dresses.
weil (vīl), because.
gerufen (ge-roo'-fen), called.
bezahlen (be-tsä'-len), to pay.
versprechen (fer-shprǎh'-hen), to promise.
schicken (shik'-ken), to send.
Mantel (män'-tel) [*m.*], mantle.
Monat (mō'-nät), month.
Schleier (shlī'-er) [*m.*], veil.
nachher (näch-hār'), afterward

Ehemals liebte ich diesen jungen Mann, weil er bescheiden und fleißig war;
Formerly loved I this young man, because he modest and diligent was;

wir arbeiteten oft zusammen und schickten Geld an seinen Vater, der sehr arm ist.
we worked often together and sent money to his father, who very poor is.

Jetzt aber ist er faul und immer hungrig, und kann essen und trinken den ganzen
At present but is he lazy and always hungry, and can eat and drink the whole

Tag, und sein Vater ist ärmer als je. Ich sagte ihm gestern: Arbeite und sei
day, and his father is poorer than ever. I said to him yesterday: Work and be

ein guter Sohn; er aber antwortete nichts. Meine Mutter erwartete ihre Base,
a good son; he but answered nothing. My mother expected her (f.) cousin,

welche vergangene Woche in Boston war; aber sie kam nicht. Dieser Herr
who last week in Boston was; but she came not. This gentleman

tadelte seinen Gärtner, weil er nicht genug gearbeitet hatte; der Gärtner versprach
blamed his gardener, because he not enough worked had; the gardener promised

ihm nachher, morgen mehr zu arbeiten, als heute. Ich habe Ihren Brief
to him afterward, to-morrow more to work, than to-day. I have your letter

beantwortet, aber Sie nicht den meinigen. Warum kamen Sie gestern nicht in unser
answered, but you not mine. Why came you yesterday not in our

Haus? Wir erwarteten Sie den ganzen Abend. Ich habe das Paar Handschuhe
house? We expected you the whole evening. I have the pair of gloves

noch nicht bezahlt, welches ich vergangenen Monat gekauft habe. Mein Bruder war
yet not paid, which I last month bought have. My brother was

hier und sagte, Sie hätten ihm ein Buch versprochen; warum schicken Sie es ihm
here and said, you had to him a book promised; why send you it to him

nicht? Haben Sie schon gefrühstückt? Gefrühstückt haben wir schon, aber noch
not? Have you already breakfasted? Breakfasted have we already, but yet

nicht zu Mittag gegessen. Haben Sie meine neuen Kleider gesehen? Den Schleier, den
not dined. Have you my new dresses seen? The veil, the

Hut, die Schuhe und Stiefel? Wo haben Sie sie gekauft?
hat, the shoes and boots? Where have you them bought?

19.

[See Conjugation of Verbs, page 23.]

Mittag (mit'-täg) [m.], noon, mid-day.
Vormittag (för'-m-) [m.], forenoon.
Nachmittag (näch'-m-) [m.], afternoon.
diesen Abend (dee'-zen ä'-bent), to-night.
nicht länger (niht lang'-er), no longer.
Geschäft (ge-shaft') [n.], business.
müßig (mü'-ssig), idle.
vergebens (fer-gü'-bens), in vain.

Ich werde diesen Abend noch mit dem Herrn sprechen, der diesen Nachmittag
I shall to-night yet with the gentleman speak, who this afternoon
mit Ihrem Onkel angekommen ist. Sie werden nicht länger müßig sein und auch nicht
with your uncle arrived is. You will no longer idle be and also no
länger an mich denken, wenn Sie in London im Geschäfte sind. Vergebens habe
longer of me think, if you in London in (the) business are. In vain have
ich den Mann gerufen, der diesen Vormittag bei Ihnen gewesen war und Ihren Damen
I the man called, who this forenoon with you been had and to your ladies
die schönen Blumen verkaufte, welche ihm der Gärtner gegeben hatte. Ihr
the beautiful flowers sold, which to him the gardener given had. Your
Vater tadelt Sie; warum? Weil Sie öfter an Ihr Vergnügen als an Ihre
father blames you; why? Because you more often of your pleasure than of your
Arbeit denken. Ihren Bruder lobt er, weil er immer fleißig ist. Sie tadeln
work think. Your brother praises he, because he always diligent is. You blame
mich, und ich habe nichts gethan; wie Sie sagen, weil Sie nichts gethan haben,
me, and I have nothing done; as you say, because you nothing done have,
tadle ich Sie, Sie sind immer müßig.
blame I you, you are always idle.

20.

[See Conjugation of Verbs, page 23.]

Warten (vàrr'-ten), to wait.
spielen (shpee'-len), to play.
kaufen (kou'-fen), to buy.
ehrlich (är'-lih), honest.
Politik (po'-li-tik') [f.], politics.
Politiker (po-lee'-ti-kar') [m.], politician.
schlau (shlou), keen, cunning, sharp, sly.
gerade (ge-rä'-de), straight.

Ich würde ein wenig länger warten, wenn ich könnte; aber ich kann nicht, ich muß
I should a little longer wait, if I could; but I can not, I must
einen neuen Hut kaufen. Er würde nicht so reich sein, wenn er nicht ein schlauer
a new hat buy. He would not so rich be, if he not a cunning
Politiker wäre. Du würdest nicht so glücklich sein, wenn Du nicht so viele Freunde
politician were. Thou wouldst not so happy be, if thou not so many friends
hättest. Er würde ihn nicht loben, wenn er nicht ehrlich wäre und seine Arbeit nicht
hadst. He would him not praise, if he not honest were and his work not

gut gemacht   hätte. Wir würden mit Ihnen   zu Mittag essen, wenn wir
well made (or done) had. We should with you dine (or take dinner), if we
hungrig wären. Dieser Mann würde nicht mit Ihnen getrunken haben, wenn er nicht
hungry were. This man would not with you drunk have, if he not
ein Politiker wäre. Sie würden nicht so traurig sein, wenn Sie Ihr Geld nicht
a politician were. You would not so sad be, if you your money not
verloren hätten. Sie würden gewartet haben, wenn sie keine Geschäfte gehabt hätten.
lost had. They would waited have, if they no business had had.
Ich würde ihn geliebt haben, wenn er mich nicht beleidigt hätte. Wir würden mit
I should him loved have, if he me not offended had. We should with
unserm Vetter gefrühstückt haben, wenn er uns eingeladen hätte. Diese jungen Damen
our cousin breakfasted have, if he us invited had. These young ladies
würden das Vergnügen nicht so sehr lieben, wenn sie nicht so viele Freunde hätten.
would pleasure not so much love, if they not so many friends had.

21.

Mir (meer), mich (mih), to me, me.
dir (deer), dich (dih), to thee, thee.
ihm (eem), ihn (een), to him, him.
ihr (eer), sie (zee), to her, her.
es, sie, ihn (of things), it.
uns (uns), us.
Ihnen (ee'-nen), Euch (oih), Sie (zee),
   to you, you.
ihnen, sie, to them, them.
gedacht (ge-dácht'), thought.
gesprochen (ge-shproch'-en), spoken.

gegen (gä'-gen), toward.
gegen, wider (vee'-der), against.
vor (för), before.
nach (näch), after.
undankbar (un'-dánk-bär'), ungrateful.
gehen Sie (güh'-en zee), gebe (gäh'-e),
   go [*imperative to second person*].
Schneider (shni'-der), tailor.
gebracht (ge-brächt'), brought.
verweigert (fer-vi'-gert), refused.

Komm mit mir, gehe nicht mit ihm. Ihr kamt vor mir an,* sie
Come with me, go not with him. You arrived before me,* she
kam nach ihm an. Wollen Sie mit mir zu Mittag essen? Euer Bruder hat
arrived after him. Will you with me dine? Your brother has
uns ein nützliches Buch gegeben. Diese Uhr ist für Sie. Dein Bruder ist immer
us a useful book given. This watch is for you. Thy brother is always
gegen uns. Ihr Vetter ist bei uns gewesen. Diese Flasche ist für ihn und jener
against us. Your cousin has with us been. This bottle is for him and that
Korb ist für sie. Ich liebe ihn so sehr wie sie. Ihr seid undankbar gegen ihn
basket is for her. I love him as much as her. You *have* ungrateful toward him
gewesen. Ich habe Sie gestern gesehen.   Haben Sie
been. I have you yesterday seen (better: I saw you yesterday). Have you

---

* See lesson 7. Infinitive: ankommen (án'-kom'-men), to arrive. Compare List of Irregular Verbs, page 28: kommen, to come; and see rule on *Compound Verbs*, page 24.

ihnen genug gegeben? Wir haben Ihre Brüder nicht gesehen, aber wir haben an
them enough given? We have your brothers not seen, but we have (to)
sie geschrieben. Der Schneider hat dir vorigen Monat einen neuen Rock geschickt, und
them written. The tailor has thee last month a new coat sent, and
du hast ihn heute noch nicht bezahlt. Sie haben ihm mehr gegeben als mir, und ihr
thou hast it to-day yet not paid. You have him more given than me, and her
mehr als ihm. Sie haben mich um mein Federmesser gebeten? hier ist es. Wenn
more than him. You have me for my penknife asked? here is it. If
Sie mich um eine gute Zigarre gebeten hätten, würde ich sie sicherlich nicht verweigert
you me for a good cigar asked had, should I it surely not refused
haben, Sie können mir es glauben.
have, you may me it believe.

REMARKS ON THE DUE ARRANGEMENT OF WORDS IN SENTENCES IN THEIR
NECESSARY RELATIONS, ACCORDING TO THE ESTABLISHED
USAGE IN THE GERMAN LANGUAGE.

Simple sentences are as in English: Der Mensch ist sterblich (shtarp'-lih), man is mortal. Mein Freund übertreibt (ü'-ber-tript') meine Tugenden (too'-gen-den'), my friend exaggerates my virtues. If this sentence is preceded by an *adjective clause*, the subject follows the predicate, viz.: Treu (troi) in seiner Liebe zu mir— faithful in his love to me—übertreibt [pred.] mein Freund [subj.], etc. The predicate generally following the subject, the verb, constituting the predicate, allows the very object and all words forming a clause, to come between itself and the subject, so that it (the verb) appears at the end of the sentence, in which it is the predicate, *if the sentence assumes a conditional, a dependent form.* For instance: Da (since) mein Freund [subj.] meine Tugenden [obj.] übertreibt [pred.], etc. Or as in the last sentence above: „Sie hatten gebeten"; Sie hatten (mich) gebeten; Sie hatten (mich um eine gute Zigarre) gebeten. The subjunctive form with the conditional „wenn", or the sentence beginning with another conjunction, as for instance: da, als, nachdem, etc., places the *auxiliary* verb—in this instance hätten— at the very end of the sentence, to wit: „Wenn Sie gebeten [verb. trans.] hätten [auxil.];" wenn Sie (mich) gebeten hätten; wenn Sie (mich um eine gute Zigarre) gebeten hätten; and in the second part of the sentence, instead of: ich würde —— haben, or more fully: ich würde (verweigert) haben; or finally: ich würde (nicht verweigert) haben—we make the predicate „verweigert" in its subjunctive mode (würde ——) to precede the subject „ich," and we say: (so) würde [subj.] ich sie (sicherlich) nicht verweigert [verb trans.] haben [auxil.].

PRACTICAL PART.
Praktischer Theil
(präk'-ti-sher' tïl).

GENERAL TERMS AND PHRASES.
Gewöhnliche Ausdrücke und Redensarten.
(ge-vĭn'-li-ḫe')   (ous'-drĭk'-ke)   (rā'-dens-är'-ten)

I beg you.	Ich bitte Sie.	iḫ bit'-te zee.
May I ask you?	Darf ich Sie bitten?	därf iḫ zee bit'-ten.
Pray!	Bitte!	bit'-te.
Do!	Doch! O doch!	doch! ō doch.
Give me —	Geben Sie [gieb] mir —	gā'-ben zee [geep] meer—
— some bread.	— Brod, n.	— brōt.
— some butter.	— Butter, f.	— bụt'-ter.
— some meat.	— Fleisch, n.	— flīsh.
— some cheese.	— Käse, m.	— kai'-ze.
— some ham.	— Schinken, m.	— shing'-ken.
— some tea.	— Thee, m.	— tā.
— some coffee.	— Kaffee, m.	— káf'-fe.
Bring me —	Bringen Sie [bring] mir—	bring'-en zee [bring] meer
— some chocolate.	— Schokolade, f.	— shok'-kō-lä'-de.
Give me a glass of wine.	Geben Sie [gieb] mir ein Glas Wein.	gā'-ben zee [geep] meer īn gläs vīn.
Lend me —	Leihen Sie [leihe] mir —	lī'-en zee [lī'-e] meer—
— some money.	— Geld; — etwas Geld.	— galt; at'-väs galt.
Sir.	Herr! Mein Herr!	harr! nīn harr.
Madam.	Madame! Geehrte Frau!	mä-dü'-me! ge-ür'-te frou.
Miss.	Fräulein!	froi'-līn.
Do me the pleasure.	Erweisen Sie mir das Vergnügen.	er-vī'-zen zee meer dás fergnü'-gen.
I thank you.	Ich danke Ihnen [Dir].	iḫ dang'-ke ee'-nen [deer].
You are very kind.	Sie sind sehr gütig.	zee zint zär gü'-tig.
You are very polite.	Sie sind sehr höflich.	zee zint zär hḭf'-liḫ.
Much obliged.	Sehr verbunden.	zür fer-bụn'-den.
I am ready.	Ich bin bereit, fertig.	iḫ bin be-rīt', fạr'-tig.
It is true.	Es ist wahr.	es ist vär.
Is it true?	Ist es wahr?	ist es vär?
It is so.	Es ist so; so ist's.	es ist zō.
Yes; certainly.	Ja; gewiß.	yü; ge-viss'.
No; surely not.	Nein; sicherlich nicht.	nīn; ziḫ'-er-liḫ' niḫt.
You are right.	Sie haben Recht.	zee hä'-ben rạht.
You are mistaken.	Sie irren sich.	zee ir'-ren ziḫ.
By no means.	Keineswegs.	kī'-nes-vägs.
Of course.	Natürlicherweise.	nä-tür'-li-ḫer'-vī-ze.

Just so; indeed.	Gerade so; wirklich.	ge-rii'-de zō; virk'-lih.
I believe so.	Ich glaube, ja.	ih glou'-be, yü.
I believe not.	Ich glaube, nein.	ih glou'-be, nīn.
Is it possible?	Ist es möglich?	ist es mǐg'-lih?
Upon my honor!	Auf Ehre!	ouf ä'-re!
Believe me.	Glaube[n Sie] mir.	glou'-be[n zee] meer.
It is possible.	Es ist möglich.	es ist mǐg'-lih.
As true as —	So wahr als —	zō vär äls —
Very likely.	Wahrscheinlich.	vär-shīn'-lih.
I will.	Ja, ich will.	yü, ih vill.
No, I will not.	Nein, ich will nicht.	nīn, ih vill niht.
May be that —	Es mag sein, daß —	es mäg zīn, däs —
Probably.	Wahrscheinlich.	vär-shīn'-lih.
Possibly.	Möglich.	mǐg'-lih.
That'll do.	Das reicht hin, ist genug.	däs rīht hin, ist ge-nug'.
I guess.	Ich vermuthe, glaube.	ih fer-moo'-te, glou'-be.
Naturally so.	Ganz natürlich.	gänts ná-tür'-lih.
Never mind.	Es macht nichts aus.	es mächt nihts ous.
No matter.	Es kommt nicht darauf an.	es komt niht därouf' än.
That is understood.	Das versteht sich, ist verstanden.	däs fer-shtät' zih, ist fer-shtán'-den.

Where do you come from?	Woher kommen Sie?	vo-hār' kom'-men zee?
I come from —	Ich komme von —	ih kom'-me fon —
I am going to —	Ich gehe nach —	ih gäh'-e näch —
Go upward, up stairs.	Gehe[n Sie] hinauf.	gäh'-e[n zee] hin-ouf'.
Go down, down stairs.	Gehe[n Sie] hinunter.	gäh'-e[n zee] hin-un'-ter.
Go in; step in; enter.	Gehe[n Sie] hinein; treten Sie ein.	gäh'-e[n zee] hin-īn'; trä'-ten zee īn.
Come here.	Komme[n Sie] hierher.	kom'-me[n zee] heer-hār'.
Stay; wait; one moment.	Warte[n Sie]; einen Augenblick.	vår'-te[n zee]; ī'-nen ou'-gen-blick'.
You go too fast.	Sie gehen zu rasch.	zee gäh'-en tsoo räsh.
Why? What for?	Warum? Wofür?	vär-um'? vō-für'?
How so?	Wie so?	vee zō?
Because; for the reason that —	Weil; aus dem Grunde, —	vīl; ous däm grun'-de, —
Open the door.	Oeffne[n Sie] die Thür.	ǐff'-ne[n zee] dee tür.
The door is open, closed.	Die Thür ist offen, ist zu.	dee tür ist of'-fen, ist tsoo.
Open the window.	Oeffne[n Sie] das Fenster.	ǐff'-ne[n zee] däs fǎn'-ster.
Shut the window.	Mache[n Sie] das Fenster zu.	mäch'-che[n zee] däs fǎn'-ster tsoo.
Fix the curtain.	Mache[n Sie] den Vorhang zurecht.	mäch'-che[n zee] dän för'-häng tsoo-räht'.
Let the blinds down.	Lasse[n Sie] die Jalousien herunter.	läs'-se[n zee] dee jäl'-loo-zeen' her-un'-ter.
Lock the door, if you please.	Verschließe[n Sie] die Thür gefälligst.	fer-shlee'-sse[n zee] dee tür ge-fäll-'ligst.

Speak loud.	Sprich [sprechen Sie] laut.	shprih [shpräh'-hen zee] lout.
You speak too low.	Sie sprechen [Du sprichst] zu leise.	zee 'shpräh'-hen [doo shprihst] tsoo lī'-se.

Your voice is hardly audible.	Ihre [Deine] Stimme ist kaum hörbar.	ee'-re [dī'-ne] shtim'-me ist koum hṛ'-bär.
Do not cry out.	Schreie[n Sie] nicht.	shrī'-e[n zee] niht.
Do not whisper.	Flüstre[ern Sie] nicht.	flīs'-tre[ern zee] niht.
I cannot understand him.	Ich kann ihn nicht verstehen.	ih kån een niht fer-shtäh'-en
He stammers.	Er stottert.	är shtot'-tert.
She speaks through the nose.	Sie näselt.	zee nai'-zelt.
Do you speak German?	Sprechen Sie Deutsch?	shprah'-hen zee doitsch?
A little; very little.	Ein wenig; sehr wenig.	īn vä'-nig; zūr vä'-nig.
I know but little.	Ich kann nur wenig.	ih kån nur vä'-nig.
This is unknown to me.	Das ist mir unbekannt.	dås ist meer un'-be-kånt'.
What have you done?	Was haben Sie [hast Du] gethan'?	vås hä'-ben zee [håst doo] ge-tün'?
Why do you not answer?	Warum antworten Sie [-test Du] nicht?	vür-um' ånt-vor'-ten zee [-test doo] niht?
Let me speak.	Lassen Sie [lass'] mich sprechen.	lås'-sen zee [lås] mih shprah'-hen.
Help me; lend me a hand.	Helfen Sie [hilf] mir; steh [en Sie] mir bei.	hål'-fen zee [hilf] meer; shtäh'[en zee] meer bī.
Make haste; hurry up.	Beeile Dich; mache[n Sie] rasch.	be-ī'-le dih; måch'-che[n zee] råsh.

Call again.	Sprechen Sie wieder vor.	shprah'-hen zee vee'-der för.
Come soon back again.	Komme[n Sie] bald wieder.	kom'-me[n zee] bålt vee'-der.
Make your stay short.	Halten Sie sich nicht lange auf.	hål'-ten zee zih niht läng'-e ouf.
Will you go with me?	Wollen Sie [willst Du] mit mir gehen?	vol'-len zee [vilst doo] mit meer gäh'-en?
Whither shall we go?	Wohin sollen wir gehen?	vo-hin' zol'-len veer gäh'-en?
I am tired.	Ich bin müde.	ih bin mü'-de.
You need not run.	Sie brauchen nicht zu laufen.	zee brou'-chen niht tsoo lou'-fen.
Move on; onward.	Weiter; vorwärts.	vī'-ter; för'-varts.
If you would only be willing.	Wenn Sie nur wollten.	van zee nur vol'-ten.
What can I do?	Was kann ich thun?	vås kån ih toon?
It is not my fault.	Es ist nicht meine Schuld.	es ist niht mī'-ne shult.
What do you take me for?	Wofür halten Sie mich?	vo-für' hål'-ten zee mih?
I feel quite comfortable.	Ich fühle mich ganz behaglich.	ih fü'-le mih gånts be-hüg'-lih.
It does not suit me.	Es passt mir nicht.	es påst meer niht.
His every day's talk.	Sein alltägliches Geschwätz.	zīn ål-taig'-li-hes ge-shvats.
He is everybody's friend.	Er ist Jedermann's Freund.	är ist yä'-der-mån's froint.
She minds nobody.	Sie achtet auf Niemanden.	zee åch'-tet ouf nee'-mån'-den.
Was anybody here?	War Jemand hier?	vür yä'-månt heer?
Somebody inquired for you.	Jemand hat nach Dir gefragt.	yä'-månt håt nåch deer ge-frügt'.

ADDRESSES. SALUTATIONS.
Anreden. Begrüßungen.
(ȧn'-rā'-den) (be-grü'-ssṳng-en)

Good morning; good evening.	Guten Morgen; guten Abend.	goo'-ten mor'-gen; goo'-ten ü'-bent.
I wish you a good day.	Ich wünsche Ihnen einen guten Tag.	iḫ vïn'-she ee'-nen ī'-nen goo'-ten tüg.
Good afternoon, sir.	Guten Nachmittag.	goo'-ten näch'-mit-tüg'.
I am glad to see you.	Ich freue mich, Sie zu sehen.	iḫ froi'-e miḫ, zee tsoo zäh'-en.
How are you to-day?	Wie befinden Sie sich heute?	vee be-fin'-den zee ziḫ hoi'-te?
I hope to see you well.	Ich hoffe, Sie recht wohl zu sehen.	iḫ hof'-fe, zee raḫt völ tsoo zäh'-en.
How do you do?	Wie geht es Ihnen?	vee güt es ee'-nen?
How is your health?	Wie ist Ihr Befinden?	vee ist eer be-fin'-den?
You look very well, indeed.	Sie sehen wirklich sehr gut aus.	zee zäh'-en virk'-liḫ zär goot ous.
How is your father; mother?	Wie geht's Ihrem Vater? Ihrer Mutter?	vee güt's ee'-rem fü'-ter? ee'-rer mṳt'-ter?
I hope the children are well.	Ich hoffe, daß die Kinder alle wohl sind.	iḫ hof'-fe, däs dee kin'-der äl'-le völ zint.
I have not seen you for many days.	Ich habe Sie seit lange nicht gesehen.	iḫ hä'-be zee zīt läng'-e niḫt ge-zäh'-en.
I very often thought of you.	Ich habe oft an Sie gedacht.	iḫ hä'-be oft än zee ge-dächt'.
I intended to call on you.	Ich beabsichtigte, Sie zu besuchen.	iḫ be-äp'-ziḫ'-tiḫ-te, zee tsoo be-zoo'-chen.
I only came to see you.	Ich kam nur, Sie zu besuchen.	iḫ käm nṳr, zee tsoo be-soo'-chen.
Do I disturb you?	Störe ich vielleicht?	shtī'-re iḫ feel-liḫt?
You are fortunately at home.	Sie sind glücklicherweise zu Hause.	zee zint glik'-lee'-ḫer-vī'-ze tsoo hou'-ze.
I am not going to stay long.	Ich will nicht lange bleiben.	iḫ vil niḫt läng'-e blī'-ben.
I must go now.	Ich muß jetzt gehen.	iḫ mṳs yatst gäh'-en.
I cannot stay any longer.	Ich kann nicht länger verweilen.	iḫ kän niḫt läng'-er fer-vī'-len.
Very glad to have seen you.	Sehr froh, Sie gesehen zu haben.	zär frō, zee ge-zäh'-en tsoo hä'-ben.
No, no, don't trouble yourself.	Nein, nein, bemühen Sie sich nicht.	nīn, nīn, be müh'-en zee ziḫ niḫt.
Give my regards to your lady, to your father, mother, brother, sister.	Meine achtungsvollen Grüße an Ihre Frau, an Ihren Vater, Ihre Frau Mutter, Ihren Bruder, Ihre Schwester.	mī'-ne äch'-tṳngs-fol'-len grü'-sse än ee'-re frou, än ee'-ren fü'-ter, ee'-re frou mṳt'-ter, ee'-ren broo'-der, ee'-re shvas'-ter.
Please remember me to—	Empfehlen Sie mich —	emp-fä'-len zee miḫ —
We shall meet again.	Auf Wiedersehen.	ouf vee'-der-zäh'-en.
Good-bye; adieu; farewell.	Leben Sie wohl; Adieu.	lä'-ben zee völ; ȧd-yī'.

ANSWERS AND COUNTER-SALUTATIONS.
Antworten und Gegengrüße.
(ánt'-vor'-ten)   (gā'-gen-grü'-sse)

Good morning, — evening, sir.	Guten Morgen, — Abend.	goo'-ten mor'-gen, — ä'-bent.
I wish you the same.	Ich wünsche Ihnen dasselbe.	ih vin'-she ee'-nen däs-zal'-be.
The same to you.	Desgleichen.	des-glī'-hen.
So am I, indeed.	Ja wohl, ich bin's.	yä vōl, ih bin's.
Quite well, thank you.	Ganz wohl, danke Ihnen.	gánts vōl, dáng'-ke ee'-nen.
Thank you, I am; and you?	Danke, ich bin's; und Sie?	dáng'-ke, ih bin's; unt zee?
As usual, thank you.	Wie gewöhnlich, danke Ihnen.	vee ge-vīn'-lih, dáng'-ke ee'-nen.
I cannot complain.	Ich kann nicht klagen.	ih kán niht klä'-gen.
You, too, look excellent.	Sie sehen auch vortrefflich aus.	zee zäh'-en ouch for-trąf'-lih ous.
How is your family?	Was macht Ihre Familie?	vás mácht ee'-re fá-mee'-li-ye'?
You are quite a stranger.	Sie halten sich so fremd.	zee hál'-ten zih zō frámt.
Business before pleasure.	Erst das Geschäft, dann das Vergnügen.	ąrst dás ge-shąft', dąn dás fer-gnü'-gen.
You are very kind.	Sie sind sehr gütig.	zee zint zär gü'-tig.
You may expect me tomorrow.	Sie dürfen mich morgen erwarten.	zee dir'-fen mih mor'-gen er-vár'-ten.
You are heartily welcome.	Sie sind herzlich willkommen.	zee zint hárts'-lih vil-kom'-men.
It is a treat to see you.	Es thut Einem wohl, Sie zu sehen.	es toot ī'-nem vōl, zee tsoo zäh'-en.
I should be sorry to have missed you.	Es würde mir leid sein, Sie verfehlt zu haben.	es vir'-de meer līt zīn, zee fer-fält' tsoo hü'-ben.
Be not in a hurry.	Eilen Sie nicht!	ī'-len zee niht!
A very short visit.	Ein sehr kurzer Besuch.	īn zär kur'-tser be-zooch'.
I am very sorry, indeed.	Das thut mir sehr leid.	dás toot meer zär līt.
I am very much obliged to you.	Ich bin Ihnen sehr verbunden.	ih bin ee'-nen zär fer-bun'-den.
No trouble at all.	Durchaus keine Mühe.	durh-ous' kī'-ne müh'-e.
Don't forget to remember me to —	Vergessen Sie nicht, mich — zu empfehlen.	fer-gąs'-sen zee niht, mih — tsoo emp-fā'-len.
I will pay my respects to —	Ich möchte — meine Achtung bezeigen.	ih mih'-te — mī'-ne ách'-tung be-tsī'-gen.
I thank you for your kind call.	Ich danke Ihnen für Ihren freundlichen Besuch.	ih dáng'-ke ee'-nen fīr ee'-ren froint'-li-hen be-zooch'.
I will not forget —	Ich werde nicht vergessen,	ih vär'-de niht fer-gąs'-sen
Please God.	So Gott will!	zō gott vill!
Good day.	Gehaben Sie sich wohl!	ge-hü'-ben zee zih vōl!

RECEIVING A VISITOR.
Beim Empfangen eines Besuches.
(bīm)   (emp-fáng′-en)   (ī′-nes)   (be-zoo′-ches)

Is it you, indeed?	Bist Du es wirklich?	bist doo es virk′-lih?
What a pleasant surprise!	Welch' angenehme Ueberraschung!	velh' án′-ge-nä′-me ü′-ber-rash′-shung.
So unexpected and welcome.	So unerwartet und so willkommen.	zō un′-er-vár′-tet unt zō vil-kom′-men.
Let me take your overcoat.	Lass' mich Deinen Ueberrock nehmen.	lás mih dī′-nen ü′-ber-rock′ nä′-men.
Let me have your hat and cane.	Lass' mich Deinen Hut und Stock haben.	lás mih dī′-nen hoot unt shtock hä′-ben.
Sit down; be seated.	Setze Dich.	zat′-se dih.
Make yourself at home.	Thue als wärest Du zu Hause.	too′-e áls vai′-rest doo tsoo hou′-ze.
It is an age since I saw you last.	Ich habe Dich in einer Ewigkeit nicht gesehen.	ih hä′-be dih in ī′-ner ā′-vig-kīt′ niht ge-zäh′-en.
You look remarkably well.	Du siehst merkwürdig gut aus.	doo zeest mark′-vür′-dig goot ous.
How are they all at home?	Wie befinden sich die Deinigen alle?	vee be-fin′-den zih dee dī′-ni-gen áľ-le?
I wish they were with you here.	Ich wünsche, sie wären hier bei Dir.	ih vīn′-she, zee vai′-ren heer bī deer.
Would not my wife enjoy it!	Wie würde meine Frau sich freuen!	vee vīr′-de mī′-ne frou zih froi′-en!
Will she not be surprised!	Wird sie nicht erstaunt sein?	virt zee niht er-shtount′ zīn?
The children are in school.	Die Kinder sind in der Schule.	dee kin′-der zint in dar shoo′-le.
O yes, they will recognize you.	Gewiss werden sie Dich erkennen.	ge-viss′ var′-den zee dih er-kan′-nen.
Now tell me some news.	Jetzt erzähle mir etwas Neues.	yatst er-tsai′-le meer at′-vás noi′-es.
News of yourself and family.	Neues von Dir und Deiner Familie.	noi′-es fon deer unt dī′-ner fá-mee′-li-ye′.
I hope, you'll stay a week.	Ich hoffe, Du wirst eine Woche hier bleiben.	ih hof′-fe, doo virst ī′-ne voch′-e heer blī′-ben.
There is plenty of room and food.	Wir haben Raum und Essen genug.	veer hä′-ben roum unt as′-sen ge-noog′.
Yes, you will have to stay.	Ja, Du musst hier bleiben.	yü, doo must heer blī′-ben.
Listen, the children are coming.	Horch, die Kinder kommen.	horh, dee kin′-der kom′-men.
My wife will be here directly.	Meine Frau wird sogleich hier sein.	mī′-ne frou virt zo-glīh′ heer zīn.
Excuse yourself? Why?	Dich entschuldigen? Wofür?	dih ent-shul′-di-gen′? vo-für′?
We treat you as our best friend.	Wir behandeln Dich als unsern besten Freund.	veer be-hán′-deln dih áls un′-zern bas′-ten froint.
Some refreshment, of course.	Etwas Erfrischung natürlich.	at′-vás er-frish′-shung nä-tür′-lih.

I'll send for your valise.	Ich will Deine Reisetasche holen lassen.	ih vill dī'-ne rī'-ze-tåsh'-she hō'-len lås'-sen.
That's right; write home.	Das ist recht: schreibe nach Hause.	dås ist raht: shrī'-be nåch hou'-ze.
Remember me kindly to them.	Bestelle ihnen meine freundlichsten Grüße.	be-shtål'-le ee'-nen mī'-ne froint'-lih-sten' grü'-sse.

ASKING. REQUESTING.
Bitten. Fragen.
(bit'-ten) (frä'-gen)

I come to speak to you.	Ich komme, um mit Ihnen zu sprechen.	ih kom'-me, um mit ee'-nen tsoo shprah'-hen.
I have a favor to ask of you.	Ich muß Sie um eine Gefälligkeit bitten.	ih mus zee um ī'-ne ge-fål-lig-kīt' bit'-ten.
Will you grant me a favor?	Wollen Sie mir eine Gefälligkeit erweisen?	vol'-len zee meer ī'-ne ge-fål'-lig-kīt' er-vī'-zen?
May I request it of you?	Darf ich Sie darum bitten?	dårf ih zee dår-um bit'-ten?
Allow me to explain —	Gestatten Sie mir, zu erklären —	ge-shtåt'-ten zee meer, tsoo er-klai'-ren —
Please listen to me.	Hören Sie mich gefälligst an.	hȳ'-ren zee mih ge-fål'-ligst ån.
May I trouble you?	Darf ich Sie belästigen?	dårf ih zee be-lås'-ti-gen'?
I beg your pardon, if —	Ich bitte um Vergebung, wenn —	ih bit'-te um fer-gā'-bung, van —
I am sorry if I trouble you.	Es thut mir leid, wenn ich Sie störe.	es toot meer līt, van ih zee shtȳ're.
I wish you would help me.	Ich wünsche, Sie möchten mir helfen.	ih vin'-she, zee möh'-ten meer hal'-fen.
You will oblige me infinitely.	Du wirst mich unendlich verbinden.	doo virst mih un-ånt'-lih fer-bin'-den.
When may I call on you?	Wann darf ich zu Ihnen kommen?	vån dårf ih tsoo ee'-nen kom'-men?
Excuse me: Does Mr. S. live here?	Entschuldigen Sie: Wohnt Herr S. hier?	ent-shul'-di gen' zee: vōnt harr S. heer?
Would you really be so kind?	Würden Sie wirklich so gütig sein?	vïr'-den zee virk'-lih zō gü'-tig zīn?
It is hard, but I must tell you.	Es kommt mir hart an: aber ich muß Ihnen sagen, —	es komt meer hårt ån: ü-ber ih mus ee'-nen zü'-gen, —
May I have the paper?	Kann ich das Blatt haben?	kån ih dås blåt hä'-ben?
I want it only for a minute.	Ich wünsche es nur auf eine Minute.	ih vïn'-she es nur ouf ī'-ne mi-noo'-te.
May I ask you for a loan of 100 dollars?	Darf ich Sie um ein Darleben von 100 Dollars bitten?	dårf ih zee um īn där-läh'-en fon 100 dol-lärs' bit'-ten?
Please take along this box.	Nehmen Sie diese Schachtel gefälligst mit.	nä'-men zee dee'-ze shåch'-tel ge-fål-ligst mit.
Will you kindly inquire —?	Wollen Sie gütigst nachfragen —?	vol'-len zee gü'-tigst nåch'-frä'-gen —?
It would be a great service to me.	Es würde mir von großem Nutzen sein.	es vïr'-de meer fon grō'-ssem nut'-sen zīn.
Do, I beg of you.	Bitte, seien Sie so gut.	bit'-te, zī'-en zee zō goot,

I will thank you for all details.	Ich werde Ihnen für alle Einzelheiten dankbar sein.	ih var'-de ee'-nen fir äl'-le In'-tsel-hi'-ten dank'-bär zin.
Will you kindly show me the way to —?	Wollen Sie mir gütigst den Weg nach — zeigen?	vol'-len zee meer gü'-tigst dän väg nach — tsi'-gen?
I appeal to your generosity.	Ich wende mich an Ihre Großmuth.	ih van'-de mih än ee'-re grōs'-moot.
For Heaven's sake, leave me not!	Um des Himmels willen, verlaß' mich nicht!	um des him'-mals vil'-len, fer-läs mih niht!
I am in a fix.	Ich bin in großer Verlegenheit.	ih bin in grö'-sser fer-lä'-gen-hīt'.
Help me, do, help me!	Bitte, bitte, helfen Sie mir!	bit'-te, bit'-te, hạl'-fen zee meer!

COMPLYING. ACCEDING.

Einwilligen.

(In-vil'-li-gen')

Willingly.	Gern.	garn.
Presently.	Sogleich.	zo-glīh'.
Undoubtedly.	Ohne Zweifel.	ō'-ne tsvi'-fel.
Assuredly; certainly.	Sicherlich.	zih'-er-lih'.
Why not?	Warum nicht?	vär-um' niht?
With all my heart.	Mit ganzem Herzen.	mit gän'-tsem hạr'-tsen.
With pleasure.	Mit Vergnügen.	mit fer-gnü'-gen.
I am at your disposal.	Ich stehe Ihnen zur Verfügung.	ih shtäh'-e ee'-nen tsur fer-fü'-gung.
Just as you desire.	Ganz wie Sie wünschen.	gänts vee zee vin'-shen.
I cannot refuse you anything.	Ich kann Ihnen nichts abschlagen.	ih kän ee'-nen nihts äp'-shlä'-gen.
I will do it with pleasure.	Ich will es mit Vergnügen thun.	ih vill es mit fer-gnü'-gen toon.
Most cordially.	Herzlich gern.	harts'-lih garn.
I agree with you.	Ich bin Ihrer Ansicht.	ih bin ee'-rer än'-ziht.
I have no objection.	Ich habe nichts dagegen.	ih hä'-be nihts dä-gā'-gen.
I am not opposed to it.	Ich bin nicht dagegen (dawider).	ih bin niht dä-gā' gen (dä-vee'-der).
I agree to it; I will.	Ich gehe es ein; ich will wohl.	ih gäh'-e es īn; ih vill vōl.
Well, I consent.	Nun, ich bin's zufrieden.	nụn, ih bin's tsoo-free'-den.
You need but command.	Sie haben nur zu befehlen.	zee hä'-ben nụr tsoo be-fä'-len.
I am at your command.	Ich stehe Ihnen zu Befehl.	ih shtäh' e ee'-nen tsoo be-fäl'.
Dispose of me.	Verfüge[n Sie] über mich.	fer-fü'-ge[n zee] ü'-ber mih.
You may count (depend, rely) on me.	Sie dürfen auf mich rechnen (sich auf mich verlassen).	zee dir'-fen ouf mih rạh'-nen (zih ouf mih fer-läs'-sen).
It pleases me to be of any service to you.	Es macht mir Vergnügen, Ihnen nützlich sein zu können.	es mächt meer fer-gnü'-gen, ee'-nen nits'-lih zin tsoo kin'-nen.
You shall have it.	Du sollst es haben.	doo zolst es hä'-ben.

5

I will do it for you with great pleasure.	Ich will es mit dem größten Vergnügen für Sie thun.	ih vill es mit däm grīs'-ten fer-gnü'-gen fir zee toon.
I shall be most happy to do it.	Ich werde mich glücklich schätzen, es thun zu können.	ih vŭr'-de mih glĭk'-lih shät'-sen, es toon tsoo kin'-nen.

REFUSING WITH REGRETS.
Verweigern mit Bedauern.
(fer-vī'-gern)   (be-dou'-ern)

I cannot.	Ich kann nicht.	ih kån niht.
It is impossible.	Es ist unmöglich.	es ist un·mȫg'-lih.
I cannot consent to it.	Ich kann es nicht zugeben.	ih kån es niht tsoo'-gā-ben.
I am very sorry, but I cannot do it.	Es thut mir sehr leid, allein ich kann es nicht thun.	es toot meer zār līt, ål-līn' ih kån es niht toon.
I assure you, it is not my fault.	Ich versichere Sie, es ist nicht meine Schuld.	ih fer-zih'-re zee, es ist niht mī'-ne shult.
I must refuse.	Ich muß es abschlagen.	ih mus es åp'-shlä'-gen.
I regret that I cannot render you this service.	Ich bedaure, daß ich Ihnen den Dienst nicht erweisen kann.	ih be-dou'-re, dås ih ee'-nen dän deenst niht er-vī'-zen kån.
At another time.	Auf ein anderes Mal.	ouf īn ån'-de-res' mäl.
Indeed I am extremely sorry not to be able to oblige you (to render you this service) (to comply with your request).	Wirklich, es thut mir außerordentlich leid, Ihnen nicht gefällig sein (diesen Dienst nicht leisten) (Ihrem Ersuchen nicht willfahren) zu können.	virk'-lih, es toot meer ou·sser-or'-dent-lih' līt, ee'-nen niht ge·fäl'-lig zīn (dee'-sen deenst niht lī'-sten) (ee'-rem er-zoo'-chen niht vil·fä'-ren) tsoo kin'-nen.
Excuse me; I beg your pardon.	Entschuldigen Sie mich; verzeihen Sie.	ent-shul'-di-gen' zee mih; fer-tsī'-en zee.
I beg you to spare me in these matters.	Bitte, mich mit dergleichen zu verschonen.	bit'-te, mih mit der-glī'-hen tsoo fer-shō'-nen.
I would rather be excused.	Ich bitte, mich zu entschuldigen (bedanke mich ganz gehorsamst).	ih bit'-te, mih tsoo ent-shul'-di-gen' (be-dång'-ke mih gånts ge-hōr'-zämst).
I reserve it for another time.	Ich behalte es mir für ein anderes Mal vor.	ih be·hål'-te es meer fīr īn án'-de·res' mäl fōr.
The moment is (the circumstances are) not favorable.	Der Augenblick ist (die Umstände sind) nicht günstig.	där ou'-gen·blik' ist (dee um'-shtän'·de zint) niht gins'-tig.
It is not my fault.	Es ist nicht meine Schuld.	es ist niht mī'-ne shult.
I cannot help it.	Ich kann nicht dafür.	ih kån niht då·fūr'.
I have not the money.	Ich habe das Geld nicht.	ih hü'-be dås galt niht.
It is not in my power.	Es ist nicht in meiner Macht.	es ist niht in mī'-ner mächt.
I am exceedingly sorry.	Es thut mir außerordentlich leid.	es toot meer ou'·sser·or'·dent-lih līt.
I am embarrassed myself.	Ich bin selbst in Verlegenheit.	ih bin zulpst in fer-lā'·gen·hīt'.

AFFIRMING.

Bejahen.
(be-yü′-hen)

English	German	Pronunciation
Certainly.	Gewiß.	ge-vis′.
That is true.	Das ist wahr.	dás ist vär.
It is the truth.	Es ist die Wahrheit.	es ist dee vär′-hīt.
You may believe me.	Sie können es mir glauben.	zee kīn′-nen es meer glou′-ben.
I am not joking.	Ich scherze nicht.	iḥ shar′-tse niḥt.
I saw it with my own eyes.	Ich habe es mit meinen eignen Augen gesehen.	iḥ hä′-be es mit mī′-nen Ig′-nen ou′-gen ge-zäh′-en.
I give you my word for it.	Ich gebe Ihnen mein Wort darauf.	iḥ gā′-be ee′-nen mīn vort där-ouf′.
I will answer for it.	Ich stehe Ihnen dafür.	iḥ shtäh′-e ee′-nen dá-für′.
Upon my honor.	Auf meine Ehre.	ouf mī′-ne ā′-re.
I am serious.	Ich bin im Ernst.	iḥ bin im arnst.
I'll tell you what.	Ich will Ihnen etwas sagen.	iḥ vill ee′-nen at′-vás zä′-gen.
I assure you that —	Ich versichere Sie, daß —	iḥ fer-ziḥ′-he-re′ zee, dás —
I promise you that —	Ich verspreche Ihnen, daß —	iḥ fer-shpraḥ′-he ee′-nen, dás —
I can assure you.	Ich kann Sie versichern.	iḥ kán zee fer-ziḥ′-hern.
This is what I can assure you.	Das kann ich Ihnen versichern.	dás kán iḥ ee′-nen fer-ziḥ′-hern.
Rely upon what I tell you.	Rechnen Sie auf das, was ich Ihnen sage.	raḥ′-nen zee ouf dás, vás iḥ ee′-nen zä′-ge.
Depend upon it.	Verlassen Sie sich darauf.	fer-lás′-sen zee ziḥ där-ouf′.
You may rest assured.	Sie können versichert sein.	zee kīn′-nen fer-ziḥ′-ḥert zīn.
Believe me.	Glaube[n Sie] mir.	glou′-be[n zee] meer.
'tis a fact.	Es ist eine Thatsache.	es ist ī′-ne tät′-zách′-e.
Without any doubt.	Ohne allen Zweifel.	ō′-ne ál′-len tsvī′-fel.
There's no doubt.	Da ist nicht zu zweifeln.	dä ist niḥt tsoo tsvī′-feln.
Can any man doubt it.	Kann man daran zweifeln?	kán mán där-án′ tsvī′-feln?
Undoubtedly.	Unzweifelhaft.	un′-tsvī′-fel-háft′.
I have it not from hearsay.	Ich habe es nicht von Hörensagen.	iḥ hä′-be es niḥt fon hȳ′-ren-zä′-gen.
I saw it in his own handwriting.	Ich habe es in seiner eignen Handschrift gesehen.	iḥ hä′-be es in zī′-ner Ig′-nen hánd′-shrift ge-zäh′-en.
I'll swear that —	Ich will schwören, daß —	iḥ vill shvȳ′-ren, dás —
I take an oath on it.	Ich schwöre einen Eid darauf.	iḥ shvȳ′-re ī′-nen It där-ouf′.
I say it is so; I say yes.	Ich sage ja.	iḥ zä′-ge yü.
I maintain that —	Ich behaupte, daß —	iḥ be-houp′-te, dás —
I suppose [it is] so.	Ich vermuthe es [ist so].	iḥ fer-moo′-te es [ist zō].
I fancy so.	Ich kann es mir einbilden.	iḥ kán es meer īn′-bil′-den.
I think so too.	Ich glaube [denke] es auch.	iḥ glou′-be [dang′-ke] es ouch.
You may easily imagine that —	Sie können leicht denken, daß —	zee kīn′-nen līḥt dang′-ken, dás —

English	German	Pronunciation
You must know it.	Sie müssen es wissen.	zee mĭs'-sen es vĭs'-sen.
I have a notion that —	Ich habe eine Idee, daß —	ih hāb'-be ī'-ne i-dā', dås
I am inclined to think —	Ich bin geneigt, zu glauben —	ih bin ge-nīgt', tsoo glou'-ben —
It is certain that —	Es ist gewiß, daß —	es ist ge-vis', dås —
Yes, it is true.	Ja, es ist wahr.	yä, es ist vär.
It is but too true.	Es ist nur zu wahr.	es ist nur tsoo vär.
I should not say so, if—	Ich würde es nicht sagen, wenn —	ih vïr'-de es niht zä'-gen, van —
I don't doubt it.	Ich zweifle nicht daran.	ih tsvī'-fle niht där-än'.
I protest that —	Ich versichere Ihnen, daß —	ih fer-zih'-he-re' ee' nen, dås —
It sounds incredible; still —	Es klingt unglaublich; jedoch —	es klinkt un-gloup'-lih; yedoch' —
My word of an honest man.	Mein Wort als ein ehrlicher Mann.	mīn vort åls īn är'-li'-her mån.
Honestly.	Wahrhaftig.	vär'-häf'-tig.
It is but plain truth what I say.	Es ist die reine Wahrheit, was ich sage.	es ist dee rī'-ne vär'-hīt', vås ih zä'-ge.
This gentleman is witness.	Dieser Herr ist Zeuge.	dee'-zer harr ist tsoi'-ge.
He certainly will tell the truth.	Er wird gewiß die Wahrheit sagen.	är virt ge-vis' dee vär'-hīt' zä' gen.
As sure as I live.	So wahr ich lebe.	zō vär ih lā'-be.
He was present himself.	Er war selbst zugegen.	är vär zalpst tsoo-gā' gen.
Unquestionably.	Unstreitig.	un-shtrī'-tig.
No exaggeration.	Keine Uebertreibung.	kī'-ne ü'-ber-trī'-bung.
Just as I tell you.	Gerade wie ich Ihnen sage.	ge-rä'-de vee ih ee'-nen zä'-ge.
Yes, indeed.	Ja, in der That.	yä, in där tät.

DENYING.

Verneinen.

(fer-nī'-nen)

English	German	Pronunciation
Not at all.	Gar nicht; durchaus nicht.	gär niht; durh-ous' niht.
By no means.	Keineswegs; ganz und gar nicht.	kī'-nes vägs'; gånts unt gär niht.
It is false.	Das ist falsch.	dås ist fålsh.
There is no such thing.	Es ist nichts daran.	es ist nihts där-än'.
It is a falsehood.	Es ist eine Lüge.	es ist ī'-ne lü'-ge.
It cannot be.	Es kann nicht sein.	es kån niht zīn.
It is impossible.	Es ist unmöglich.	es ist un-mǖg'-lih.
I doubt it.	Ich bezweifle es.	ih be-tsvī'-fle es.
It is incomprehensible.	Es ist unbegreiflich.	es ist un'-be-grīf'-lih.
You are mistaken.	Sie irren sich.	zee ir'-ren zih.
There is not a word of truth in it.	Es ist kein wahres Wort daran.	es ist kīn vä'-res vort där-än'.
You have been imposed on.	Man hat Ihnen etwas weiß gemacht.	mån håt ee'-nen åt'-vås vīs ge-måcht'.
I don't think so.	Ich glaube es nicht.	ih glou'-be es niht.
Unheard of.	Unerhört.	un'-er-hĭrt'.
That can't be true.	Das kann nicht wahr sein.	dås kån niht vär zīn.

Do you think so?	Glauben Sie?	glou′-ben zee?
Who would believe it?	Wer sollte das glauben?	vär zoll′-te dås glou′-ben?
Most willingly I would, but I can't.	Sehr gern, aber ich kann nicht.	zär gɐrn, ü′-ber iḥ kån niḥt.
The whole thing is fictitious.	Die ganze Sache ist erdichtet.	dee gån′-tse zåch′-e ist erdiḥ′-tet.
I will certainly not do it.	Ich will es bestimmt nicht thun.	iḥ vill es be-shtimt′ niḥt toon.
I don't believe it.	Ich glaube es nicht.	iḥ glou′-be es niḥt.
It's too good to be true.	Es ist zu gut, um wahr zu sein.	es ist tsoo goot, um vär tsoo zīn.
No, you cannot go along.	Nein, Du kannst nicht mitgehen.	nīn, doo kånst niḥt mit′-gäh′-en.
I positively refuse.	Ich verweigere es ganz bestimmt.	iḥ fer-vī′-ge-rɐ′ es gånts be-shtimt′.
Certainly not.	Sicherlich nicht.	ziḥ′-er-liḥ′ niḥt.
Respectfully declined.	Achtungsvoll abgewiesen.	åch′-tungs-foll′ åp′-ge-vee′-zen.
"No peace to the wicked."	„Kein Friede für die Bösewichte."	kīn free′-de fir dee bī′-ze-viḥ′-te.
I never saw him before.	Ich habe ihn nie vorher gesehen.	iḥ hä′-be een nee for-här′ ge-zäh′-en.

ADMIRING, WONDERING.

Bewundern, wundern.

(be-vun′-dern)

That is very fine, excellent.	Das ist sehr schön, vortrefflich.	dås ist zär shīn, for-traff′-liḥ.
It is wonderful, astonishing.	Es ist wunderbar, zum Erstaunen.	es ist vun′-der-bär′, tsum er-shtou′-nen.
That astonishes me.	Das wundert mich.	dås vun′-dert miḥ.
That surprises me.	Das überrascht mich.	dås ü′-ber-råsht′ miḥ.
I am much surprised at it.	Das wundert mich sehr.	dås vun′-dert miḥ zär.
It is startling at first.	Es macht erst stutzig.	es måcht ärst shtut′-sig.
Who would have thought it?	Wer hätte das denken sollen?	vär hat′-te dås dang′-ken zol′-len?
I was stupefied.	Ich war ganz verdutzt.	iḥ vär gånts fer-dutst′.
You cannot form any idea of it.	Sie können sich keinen Begriff davon machen.	zee kīn′-nen ziḥ kī′-nen be-griff′ dä-fon′ måch′-en.
I wonder that I did not notice it before.	Es wundert mich, daß ich es nicht früher beobachtet habe.	es vun′-dert miḥ, dås iḥ es niḥt früh′-er be-öb′-åch′-tet hä′-be.
How charming is this sight!	Wie reizend ist dieser Anblick!	vee rī′-tsent ist dee′-zer ån′-blik′!
What magnificence! [—brilliancy!]	Welche Pracht! [—r Glanz!]	val′-ḥe prächt! [—r glånts!]
I cannot express my astonishment.	Ich kann mein Erstaunen nicht ausdrücken.	iḥ kån mīn er-shtou′-nen niḥt ous′-drik′-ken.
It is more than a nine days wonder.	Das ist nicht von vorübergehender Wichtigkeit.	dås ist niḥt fon for-ü′-ber-gäh′-en-der′ viḥ′-tig-kīt′.
Can I trust my eyes?	Kann [darf] ich meinen Augen trauen?	kån [dårf] iḥ mī′-nen ou′-gen trou′-en?

It surprises me.	Es überrascht mich.	es ü'-ber-rásht' mih.
It astonishes me.	Es setzt mich in Erstaunen.	es zątst mih in er-shtou'-nen.
How grand a storm at sea!	Wie großartig ist ein Sturm zur See!	vee grōs'-ár'-tig ist ĭn shtųrm tsur zā!
I think it must be awful.	Ich denke, es muß schauerlich sein.	ih dąng'-ke, es mųs shou'-er-lih' zin.
I don't know whether I am dreaming, sleeping or awake.	Ich weiß nicht, ob ich träume, schlafe oder wache.	ih vĭs niht, op ih troi'-me, shlii'-fe ō'-der vách'-e.
It is simply amazing.	Es ist einfach erstaunlich.	es ist ĭn'-fách er-shtoun'-lih.
"How wonderful are thy works, O Lord!"	„Wie wunderbar sind Deine Werke, o Herr!"	vee vųn'-der-bär' zint dī'-ne vạr'-ke, ō hąrr!
There he stood spellbound.	Er stand da festgebannt.	ạr shtánt dü fạst'-ge-bánt'.
The grandeur is indescribable.	Die Großartigkeit ist unbeschreiblich.	dee grōs'-ár'-tig-kīt' ist ųn'-be-shrīp'-lih.
Absorbed in that immensity I see —	In das Unermeßliche versunken, sehe ich —	in dás ųn'-er-mąs'-li-he' fer-zųng'-ken, zäh'-e ih —
I see the sun rise—I worship.	Ich sehe die Sonne aufgehen—ich bete an.	ih zūh'-e dee zon'-ne ouf'-gāh'-en—ih bā'-te án.

NEWS.

Neuigkeiten.

(noi'-ig-kī'-ten)

What news is there?	Was giebt's Neues?	vás gipt's noi'-es?
Any news?	Etwas Neues?	ạt'-vás noi'-es?
What is the talk down town?	Was sagt man drunten in der Stadt.	vás zügt mán drųn'-ten in dar shtát?
Is there anything new?	Giebt es etwas Neues?	gipt es ąt'-vás noi'-es?
Is there any news to-day?	Giebt es heute Neuigkeiten?	gipt es hoi'-te noi'-ig-kī'-ten?
Have you heard of anything?	Haben Sie etwas gehört?	hii'-ben zee ąt'-vás ge-hịrt'?
Do you know anything new?	Weißt du etwas Neues?	vĭst doo ąt'-vás noi'-es?
What is the best news?	Was sagt man Gutes?	vás zügt mán goo'-tes?
What is the news in your quarter?	Was giebt's Neues in Ihrem Stadttheil.	vás gipt's noi'-es in ee'-rem shtát'-tīl'?
Have you anything to tell us?	Haben Sie uns etwas zu sagen?	hii'-ben zee ųns ąt'-vás tsoo zii'-gen?
Hav'nt you heard of anything?	Haben Sie nichts gehört?	hii'-ben zee nihts ge-hịrt'?
There is no news.	Es giebt nichts Neues.	es gipt nihts noi'-es.
I know no news.	Ich weiß nichts Neues.	ih vĭs nihts noi'-es.
I have not heard of anything.	Ich habe nichts gehört.	ih hii'-be nihts ge-hịrt'.
What do the papers say?	Was sagen die Zeitungen?	vás zü'-gen dee tsī'-tųng'-en?
There's good [bad] news.	Gute [schlechte] Neuigkeiten.	goo'-te [shląh'-te] noi'-ig-kī'-ten.

English	German	Pronunciation
Whence have you got this news?	Woher haben Sie diese Nachricht?	vo-hār' hā'-ben zee dee'-ze näch'-riht'?
How do you know it?	Wieso wissen Sie das?	vee'-zō' vis'-sen zee dás?
This news has not been confirmed.	Diese Nachricht hat sich nicht bestätigt.	dee'-ze näch'-riht' hát zih niht be-shtai'-tigt.
I've not heard speak of it.	Ich habe nicht davon sprechen hören.	ih hā'-be niht dä-fon' shprah'-en hȳ'-ren.
Did you hear from your brother?	Haben Sie von Ihrem Bruder gehört?	hā'-ben zee fon ee'-rem broo'-der ge-hirt'?
No, not for the last two months.	Nein, nicht seit zwei Monaten.	nīn, niht zīt tsvī mō'-nä'-ten.
I expect a letter from him every day.	Ich erwarte jeden Tag einen Brief von ihm.	ih er-vär'-te yā'-den tāg ī'-nen breef fon eem.
Did you read the papers?	Haben Sie die Zeitungen gelesen?	hā'-ben zee dee tsī'-tung-en ge-lā'-zen?
I've read no papers to-day.	Ich habe heute keine Zeitung gelesen.	ih hā'-be hoi'-te kī'-ne tsī'-tung ge-lā'-zen.
Did you read that in any paper?	Haben Sie das in irgend einer Zeitung gelesen?	hā'-ben zee dás in ir'-gent ī'-ner tsī'-tung ge-lā'-zen?
It's mentioned only in a private letter.	Es ist nur in einem Privatschreiben erwähnt worden.	es ist nur in ī'-nem pri-vät'-shrī'-ben er-vaint' vor'-den.
Do they know who received the letter?	Weiß man, wer diesen Brief empfangen hat?	vīs mán, vār dee'-zen breef emp-fāng'-en hát?
Yes, they say it is Mr.—	Ja, man sagt, es sei Herr—	yü, mán zägt, es zī hárr—
They doubt this news very much.	Man bezweifelt diese Nachricht sehr.	mán be-tsvī'-felt dee'-se näch'-riht' zār.
This news wants confirmation.	Diese Neuigkeit bedarf noch der Bestätigung.	dee'-ze noi'-ig-kīt' be-därf' noch dar be-shtai'-ti-gung'.
From whom have you had this news?	Von wem haben Sie diese Neuigkeit?	fon vām hā'-ben zee dee'-ze noi'-ig-kīt'?
How do you know that?	Wie wissen Sie das?	vee vis'-sen zee dás?
I've had this news from good authority.	Ich habe diese Neuigkeit aus guter Quelle.	ih hā'-be dee'-ze noi'-ig-kīt' ous goo'-ter qval'-le.
I've had it from the first hand.	Ich habe sie aus erster Hand.	ih hā'-be zee ous ārs'-ter hánt.
I give you my authority.	Ich nenne Ihnen meinen Gewährsmann.	ih nan'-ne ee'-nen mī'-nen ge-vairs'-mán'.
That report has proved false.	Es war ein falsches Gerücht.	es vär in fál' shes ge-riht'.
This news is no longer talked of.	Man spricht nicht mehr von dieser Neuigkeit.	mán shpriht niht mār fon dee'-zer noi'-ig-kīt'.
Do they still speak of war?	Spricht man immer noch von Krieg?	shpriht mán im'-mer noch fon kreeg?
Do they think, we shall have peace?	Glaubt man, daß wir Frieden haben werden?	gloupt mán, dás veer free'-den hā'-ben vār'-den?
It is not likely.	Es ist nicht wahrscheinlich.	es ist niht vär-shīn'-lih.
What news can you tell us?	Was können Sie uns Neues erzählen?	vás kin'-nen zee uns noi'-es er-tsai'-len?
I heard that—	Ich habe gehört, daß—	ih hā'-be ge-hirt, dás—
The news are very bad.	Das sind sehr schlechte Neuigkeiten.	dás zint zār shlah'-te noi'-ig-kī-ten.

QUERIES AND ANSWERS.
Fragen und Antworten.
(frä'-gen)   (ànt'-vor'-ten)

English	German	Pronunciation
Have you anything to tell me?	Haben Sie mir etwas zu sagen?	hä'-ben zee meer ät'-vàs tsoo zä'-gen?
I have a word to tell you.	Ich habe Ihnen ein Wort zu sagen.	iḣ hä'-be ee'-nen ïn vort tsoo zä'-gen.
Will you listen to me?	Wollen Sie mich anhören?	vol'-len zee miḣ àn'-hÿ'-ren?
Listen to me.	Hören Sie mich an.	hÿ'-ren zee miḣ àn.
Do you wish to speak to me?	Wünschen Sie mit mir zu sprechen?	vïn'-shen zee mit meer tsoo shpräḣ'-en?
Yes, I should like to speak to you.	Ja, ich wünsche es.	yä, iḣ vïn'-she es.
What is it?	Was ist's?	vàs ist's?
What is your pleasure?	Was wünschen Sie?	vàs vïn'-shen zee?
Would you see the man?	Möchten Sie den Mann sehen?	miḣ'-ten zee dän màn zäh'-en?
How does he look?	Wie sieht er aus?	vee zeet ạr ous?
Quite decent.	Ganz anständig.	gànts àn'-shtạn'-dig.
What do [did] you say?	Was sag[t]en Sie?	vàs zäg'[t]en zee?
I say [said] nothing.	Ich sag[t]e nichts.	iḣ zäg'[t]e niḣts.
Do you understand me?	Verstehen Sie mich?	fer shtäh'-en zee miḣ?
I did not understand you.	Ich habe Sie nicht verstanden.	iḣ hä'-be zee niḣt fershtän'-den.
Why do you not answer?	Warum antworten Sie nicht?	vär-um' ànt'-vor'-ten zee niḣt?
Is an answer needed?	Bedarf es einer Antwort?	be därf' es ï'-ner ànt'-vort?
Did you not tell me that —	Sagten Sie mir nicht, daß —	zäg'-ten zee meer niḣt, dàs —
Are you in earnest.	Sind Sie im Ernst?	zint zee im ạrnst?
Why shouldn't I?	Warum sollte ich nicht?	vär um' zoll'-te iḣ niḣt?
Whom do you take me for?	Für wen halten Sie mich?	fïr vän häl'-ten zee miḣ?
Are you not Mr. —?	Sind Sie nicht Herr —?	zint zee niḣt hạrr —?
I was always of opinion —	Ich war immer der Meinung, —	iḣ vär im'-mer dạr mï'-nụng, —
I have been told so.	Man hat es mir gesagt.	màn hät es meer ge-zägt'.
What do you mean?	Was meinen Sie?	vàs mï'-nen zee?
Precisely what I say.	Gerade was ich sage.	ge-rä'-de vàs iḣ zä'-ge.
How do you call that?	Wie nennen Sie das?	vee nạn'-nen zee dàs?
It is called —	Es heißt; wird genannt; man nennt es —	es hïst; virt ge-nànt'; màn nạnt es —
May I ask you?	Darf ich Sie fragen?	därf iḣ zee frä'-gen?
Why not? What do you want?	Warum nicht? Was wollen Sie?	vär-um' niḣt? vàs vol'-len zee?
Do you know Mr. —?	Kennen Sie Herrn —?	kạn'-nen zee hạrrn —?
I know him by sight.	Ich kenne ihn von Ansehen.	iḣ kạn'-ne een fon àn'-zäh'-en.
Do you know that —	Wissen Sie, daß —	vis'-sen zee, dàs —
I did not know that —	Ich wußte nicht, daß —	iḣ vụs'-te niḣt, dàs —
I know nothing of it.	Ich weiß nichts davon.	iḣ vïs niḣts dä-fon'.

Will you please come here?	Wollen Sie gefälligst herkommen?	vol'-len zee ge-fal'-ligst här'-kom'-men?
What do you want me for?	Was wollen Sie von mir?	vás vol'-len zee fon meer?
I have to speak to you.	Ich habe mit Ihnen zu sprechen.	ih hä'-be mit ee'-nen tsoo shprah'-en.
Hear! Listen!	Hört!	hĭrt!
I want to speak to you.	Ich muß Dich sprechen.	ih mus dih shprah'-en.
What is it? What is your pleasure?	Was ist's? Was steht zu Diensten?	vás ist's? vás shtät tsoo deen'-sten?
I do not speak to you.	Ich spreche nicht zu Ihnen [Euch, Dir].	ih shprah'-e niht tsoo ee'-nen [oih, deer].
What do you say? What is it you say?	Was sagen Sie?	vás zä'-gen zee?
Did you say anything?	Sagten Sie etwas?	zägt'-ten zee ät'-vás?
I missed hearing it.	Ich habe es überhört.	ih hä'-be es ü'-ber-hĭrt.
What did you say?	Was sagten Sie?	vás zäg'-ten zee?
I said nothing.	Ich sagte nichts.	ih zäg'-te nihts.
Do you hear[?] what I say?	Hören Sie[?] was ich sage?	hĭ'-ren zee[?] vás ih zä'-ge?
Do you understand me?	Verstehen Sie mich?	fer-shtäh'-en zee mih?
I did not hear [understand] you.	Ich hörte [verstand] Sie nicht.	ih hĭr'-te [fer-shtänt'] zee niht.
Listen to me.	Höre mir zu.	hĭ'-re meer tsoo.
You do not listen to me.	Du hörst mir nicht zu.	doo hĭrst meer niht tsoo.
Do you understand what I say?	Verstehst Du, was ich sage?	fer-shtäst doo, vás ih zä'-ge?
Will you be so kind as to repeat?	Wollen Sie gefälligst wiederholen?	vol'-len zee ge-fal'-ligst vee'-der-hö'-len?
I understand you well.	Ich verstehe Sie wohl.	ih fer-shtäh'-e zee völ.
You speak plainly [distinctly].	Sie sprechen deutlich.	zee shprah'-en doit'-lih.
Why don't you answer me?	Warum antworten Sie mir nicht?	vär-um' ánt'-vor'-ten zee meer niht?
Do not speak so loud.	Sprich nicht so laut.	shprih niht zö lout.
Do not make so much noise.	Mach' nicht so viel Lärm.	mách' niht zö feel lärm.
Did you not tell me that —	Haben Sie mir nicht gesagt, daß —	hä'-ben zee meer niht ge-zägt', dás —.
Who told you so?	Wer hat Ihnen das gesagt?	vär hát ee'-nen dás ge-zägt'?
I do not like to speak about it.	Ich spreche nicht gern darüber.	ih shprah'-e niht gärn dä-rü'-ber.
Somebody told me so.	Jemand hat es mir gesagt.	yä'-mánt hát es meer ge-zägt'.
I heard it.	Ich hörte es.	ih hĭr'-te es.
How do you call that in German?	Wie heißen Sie das auf Deutsch?	vee hĭ'-ssen zee dás ouf doitsh?
It is called —	Es heißt —	es hĭst —
May I ask you?	Darf ich [man] Sie fragen?	dárf ih [mán] zee frä'-gen?
I don't know a word of it.	Ich weiß kein Wort davon.	ih vis kin vort dä-fon'.
Ridiculous.	Lächerlich.	lah'-her-lih'.
Why is it ridiculous?	Warum ist es lächerlich?	vär-um' ist es lah'-her-lih'?
Because Dutch is not German.	Weil holländisch nicht deutsch ist.	vil hol'-län'-dish' niht doitsh ist.
Don't I speak German?	Spreche ich nicht deutsch?	shprah'-e ih niht doitsh?

Of course you do.	Versteht sich.	fer-shtät' zih.
Well, why then is it ridiculous?	Nun, warum ist es denn lächerlich?	nun, vär-um' ist es dan läh'-her-lih'?
Because you call it Dutch.	Weil Sie es „holländisch" nennen.	vīl zee es hol'-län'-dish' nan'-nen.
Do not the German Americans call it so?	Nennen die Deutsch-Amerikaner es nicht so?	nan'-nen dee doitsh'-ä-mä'-ri-kä'-ner es niht zō?
Not that I know of.	Nicht, daß ich wüßte.	niht, dás ih vīs'-te.
Did you never hear it?	Haben Sie es nie gehört?	hä'-ben zee es nee ge-hịrt'?
Not from the lips of educated people.	Nicht von den Lippen [im Munde] Gebildeter.	niht fon dän lip'-pen [im mun'-de] ge-bil'-de-ter'.
I never heard of it.	Ich habe nie davon gehört.	ih hä'-be nee dä-fon' ge-hirt'.
Who is this man?	Wer ist dieser Mann?	vär ist dee'-zer män?
I do not know him.	Ich kenne ihn nicht.	ih kán'-ne een niht.
Does he not look ill?	Sieht er nicht krank aus?	zeet är niht kránk ous?
What may be the matter with him?	Was mag ihm fehlen? [mit ihm los sein?]	väs mäg eem fä'-len? [mit eem lōs zīn?]
God knows.	Gott mag's wissen.	gott mäg's vis'-sen.
You will accompany me, will you not?	Nicht wahr? Sie wollen mich begleiten.	niht vär? zee vol'-len mih be-glī'-ten.
What are you thinking of?	Was fällt Ihnen ein?	väs fält ee'-nen īn?
Business before pleasure.	Erst das Geschäft, dann das Vergnügen.	ärst das ge-shaft, dan das fer-gnü'-gen.
Isn't it so?	Nicht wahr?	niht vär?
You have been there before, have you not?	Nicht wahr? Sie sind schon dort gewesen.	niht vär? zee zint shōn dort ge-vä'-zen.
I have.	Ja wohl.	yä vōl.
I met you last year, did I not?	Nicht wahr? Ich habe Sie voriges Jahr getroffen.	niht vär? ih hä'-be zee fō'-ri-ges' yär ge-trof'-fen.
I think so; yes, you did.	Ich glaube wohl; ja, ganz recht.	ih glou'-be vōl; yä, gánts raht.
You know him, do you not?	Nicht wahr? Sie kennen ihn.	niht vär? zee ken'-nen een.
I do not.	O nein.	ō nīn.
The boy plays well, does he not?	Nicht wahr? Der Knabe spielt gut.	niht vär? där knä'-be shpeelt goot.
Indeed, he does.	Ja wahrhaftig; wirklich; in der That.	yä vär'-häf'-tig; virk'-lih; in där tät.
You did that for me; isn't it so?	Nicht wahr? Sie thaten das für mich.	niht vär? zee tä'-ten dás fīr mih.
Altogether for you, Madam.	Ganz und gar für Sie, Madam.	gánts unt gär fīr zee, mä-däm'.
You do not go with him, do you?	Nicht wahr? Sie gehen nicht mit ihm.	niht vär? zee gūh'-en niht mit eem.
No, Miss!	Nein, mein Fräulein.	nīn, mīn froi'-līn.
You advanced him the money, did you not?	Nicht wahr? Sie streckten ihm das Geld vor.	niht vär? zee shtrak'-ten eem dás galt för.
I did, Sir!	Ja wohl [mein Herr]!	yä vōl [mīn harr]!
You will write to-day, will you not?	Nicht wahr? Sie werden heute schreiben.	niht vär? zee vär'-den hoi'-te shrī'-ben?
No, Sir, to-morrow.	Nein, morgen.	nīn, mor'-gen.
Can she understand me, Madam?	Kann sie mich verstehen, Madam?	kán zee mih fer-shtäh'-en, mä-däm'?
She can, Sir.	O ja; ganz gut.	ō yä; gánts goot.

English	German	Pronunciation
May I come in?	Darf ich hinein kommen?	därf ih hin-īn' kom'-men?
You are welcome, my boy.	Du bist willkommen, mein Junge.	doo bist vil-kom'-men, mīn yung'-e.
You will stay here over night, will you not?	Nicht wahr? Sie wollen hier übernachten.	niht vär? zee vol'-len heer ü'-ber-nách'-ten.
I will.	Ja; ja wohl.	yä; yä vūl.
Suppose we explore this place before supper?	Was halten Sie davon, wenn wir vor dem Abendessen uns diesen Ort erst ansehen?	väs häl'-ten zee dä-fou', van veer för däm ü'-bent-as'-sen uns dee'-zen ort ärst an'-zäh'-en?
I am with you.	Ich bin dabei.	ih bin dä-bī'.
This is a snug little place, don't you think so?	Nicht wahr? Es ist ein niedliches Oertchen.	niht vär? es ist īn neet'-li-hes' īrt'-hen.
Yes, it is.	Ei ja!	I yä!
Shall we now return?	Sollen wir jetzt umkehren?	zol'-len veer yätst um'-kā'-ren?
Just as you please.	Wie Sie wollen.	vee zee vol'-len.
Yes, let us do so.	Ich denke, ja.	ih dạng'-ke, yä.
We enjoyed the walk, didn't we?	Nicht wahr? Wir haben einen schönen Spaziergang gemacht.	niht vär? veer hä'-ben ī'-nen shī'-nen shpä-tseer'-gäng ge-mächt'.
I think so.	Ich glaube.	ih glou'-be.
Yes, we did; at least I did.	Ja wohl; ich kann es mindestens von mir sagen.	yä vōl; ih kän es vā'-nig-stąns' fon meer zä'-gen.

POSSIBILITY AND PROBABILITY.
Die Möglichkeit und Wahrscheinlichkeit.
(mīg'-lih-kīt')   (vär-shīn'-lih-kīt')

English	German	Pronunciation
That's possible.	Das ist möglich.	däs ist mīg'-lih.
It is possible, but not practicable.	Es ist möglich, aber nicht thunlich.	es ist mīg'-lih, ü'-ber niht toon'-lih.
It is probable [improbable].	Es ist wahrscheinlich [unwahrscheinlich].	es ist vär'-shīn'-lih [un'-vär'-shīn'-lih].
It is likely enough.	Es ist wahrscheinlich genug.	es ist vär'-shīn'-lih ge-noog'.
Impossible; unlikely; not likely.	Unmöglich; unwahrscheinlich.	un-mīg'-lih; un'-vär-shīn'-lih.
It is more than probable.	Es ist mehr als wahrscheinlich.	es ist mär äls vär-shīn'-lih.
May be; perhaps.	Kann sein; möglich; vielleicht.	kän zīn; mīg'-lih; feel-līht'.
We may possibly reach Berlin to-day.	Wir können Berlin möglicherweise heute erreichen.	veer kīn'-nen bạr-leen' mīg'-li-her-vī'-ze hoi'-te er-rī'-hen.
There is nothing impossible in it.	Es ist nichts Unmögliches dabei.	es ist nihts un'-mīg'-li-hes' dä-bī'.
Nothing surprising.	Nichts Erstaunliches.	nihts er-shtoun'-li-hes'.
Not at all surprising.	Ganz und gar nicht [keineswegs] erstaunlich.	gänts unt gär niht [kī'-nes-vūgs'] er-shtoun'-lih.
I shouldn't wonder.	Es sollte mich nicht wundern.	es zoll'-te mih niht vun'-dern.
It might be so.	Es könnte wohl sein.	es kīn'-te vōl zīn.

English	German	Pronunciation
It may be so.	Es kann wohl sein.	es kán völ zīn.
There is the bare possibility that —	Es ist eben möglich, daß —	es ist ä'-ben mig'-lih, dás
I do not wonder at it.	Ich wund're mich nicht darüber.	ih vun'-dra mih niht där-ü'-ber.
I should not wonder at it.	Ich würde mich nicht darüber wundern.	ih vir'-de mih niht där-ü-ber vun'-dern.
I should not be surprised.	Ich würde nicht erstaunen.	ih vir'-de niht er-shtou'-nen.
Of course.	Natürlich; versteht sich.	nä-tür'-lih; fer-shtāt' zih.
No wonder.	Das ist ganz einfach.	dás ist gánts īn'-fách.
That's understood.	Das versteht sich.	dás fer-shtāt zih.
It is a matter of course.	Es ist ganz natürlich.	es ist gánts nä-tür'-lih.
That's natural.	Das ist natürlich.	dás ist ná-tür'-lih.
Self-evident.	Selbstverständlich; augenscheinlich.	zalpst'-fer-shtant'-lih; ou'-gen shīn'-lih.

SURPRISE.

Ueberraschung.

(ü'-ber-rásh'-shung)

English	German	Pronunciation
What!	Wie!	vee!
Indeed! Really?	Wirklich! [?]	virk'-lih! [?]
You don't say so.	Ist das so? Wahrhaftig!	ist dás zō? vär'-häf'-tig!
Is it so?	Ist es so?	ist es zō?
Is it possible?	Ist es möglich?	ist es mig'-lih?
How is that possible?	Wie ist das möglich?	vee ist dás mig'-lih?
Who would ever have expected that —	Wer würde je erwartet haben, daß	vär vir'-de yā er-vär'-tet hä'-ben, dás —
I am quite dumbfounded!	Ich bin ganz verblüfft!	ih bin gánts fer-blifft'!
Did you ever hear of such a thing?	Haben Sie je so etwas gehört?	hä'-ben zee yā zō at'-vás ge-hīrt'?
I cannot believe it.	Ich kann es nicht glauben.	ih kán es niht glou'-ben.
Such a striking resemblance!	Solch' eine täuschende Aehnlichkeit!	zolh' ī'-ne toi'-shen-de āin'-lih-kīt'!
He is out of his wits.	Er ist ganz außer sich.	är ist gánts ou'-sser zih.
I cannot think how —	Ich kann nicht begreifen, wie —	ih kán niht be-grī'-fen, vee —
I never dreamt of meeting you here.	Es hätte mir nicht geträumt, Sie hier zu treffen.	es hat'-te meer niht ge-troimt', zee heer tsoo traf'-fen.
I cannot realize it yet.	Es will mir noch nicht in den Kopf.	es vill meer noch niht in dän kopf.
You astonish me.	Sie setzen mich in Erstaunen.	zee zat'-sen mih in er-shtou'-nen.
I am thunderstruck.	Ich bin wie vom Donner gerührt.	ih bin vee fom don'-ner ge-rürt'.
So sudden!	So plötzlich!	zō plits'-lih!
He is astounded.	Er ist wie vom Himmel gefallen.	är ist vee fom him'-mel ge-fäl'-len.
Quite unexpected!	Ganz unerwartet!	gánts un'-er-vär'-tet!
Rather strange.	Eigentlich auffallend.	ī'-gent-lih ouf'-fäl-lent.

A strange sort of business!	Eine befremdende Geschichte!	I'-ne be-frąm'-den-de' ge-shih'-te!
Are you in earnest?	Ist es Ihnen ernst?	ist es ee'-nen ąrnst?
And you expect me to believe it?	Und Sie erwarten, daß ich das glaube?	ųnt zee er-vár'-ten, dás ih dás glou'-be?
Is it really you, or your ghost?	Sind Sie es wirklich, oder ist's Ihr Geist?	ziut zee es virk'-lih, ō'-der ist's eer gīst?
Am I not dreaming?	Träume ich nicht?	troi'-me ih niht?
Have you lost your wits?	Bist Du verrückt geworden?	bist doo fer-rïkt' ge-vor'-den?
Don't my eyes deceive me?	Täuschen mich meine Augen nicht?	toi'-shen mih mī'-ne ou'-gen niht?
And you kept it a secret all the while?	Und Sie haben es die ganze Zeit geheim gehalten?	ųnt zee hä'-ben es dee gąn'-tse tsīt ge-hīm' ge-hál'-ten?
You here in G., and I did not know it!	Du hier in G., und ich wußte es nicht!	doo heer in G., ųnt ih vųs'-te es niht!
It took him by surprise.	Es hat ihn überrascht.	es hát een ü'-ber-rásht'.
What a happy meeting!	Welch' ein glückliches Wiedersehen!	vąlh' īn glïk'-li-hes' vee'-der-zäh'-en!

CONSULTATION.

Berathung.

(be-rä'-tųng)

You have admonished me.	Sie haben mich gewarnt.	zee hä'-ben mih ge-várnt'.
Now advise me.	Jetzt rathen Sie mir.	yątst rä'-ten zee meer.
What course is to be taken?	Was soll man anfangen?	vás zoll mán án'-fáng'-en?
What shall we do?	Was wollen wir machen?	vás vol'-len veer mách'-en?
What's to be done?	Was soll man thun?	vás zoll mán toon?
What remains for us to do now?	Was bleibt uns nun zu thun übrig?	vás blīpt ųus noon tsoo toon üb'-rig?
Let us see.	Wir wollen sehen.	veer vol'-len zäh'-en.
We must resolve upon something.	Wir müssen uns zu etwas entschließen.	veer mïs'-sen ųns tsoo ąt'-vás ent-shlee' ssen.
We must decide upon something.	Wir müssen uns für etwas entscheiden.	veer mïs'-sen ųns fïr ąt'-vás ent-shī'-den.
I'm quite puzzled.	Ich bin in Verlegenheit.	ih bin in fer-lä'-gen-hīt'.
I don't know what to do.	Ich weiß nicht, was ich thun soll.	ih vīs niht, vás ih toon zoll.
I'm in a fix, in a great embarrassment.	Ich bin in einer großen Verlegenheit.	ih bin in ī'-ner grō'-ssen fer-lä'-gen-hīt'.
We are in a great perplexity.	Da sind wir in einer großen Verlegenheit.	dá zint veer in ī'-ner grō'-ssen fer-lä'-gen-hīt'.
Let us reflect.	Wir wollen überlegen.	veer vol'-len ü'-ber-lä'-gen.
Discretion is the word.	Es gilt Besonnenheit.	es gilt be-zon'-nen-hīt'.
We are in a very perplexing situation.	Wir sind in einer sehr heiklen Lage.	veer zint in ī'-ner zür hī'-klan lä'-ge.
This is very embarrassing.	Das ist um in Verlegenheit zu setzen.	dás ist ųm in fer-lä'-gen-hīt' tsoo ząt'-sen.
I think —	Ich glaube —	ih glou'-be —

Don't you think —	Glauben Sie —	glou'-ben zee —
You may try it.	Sie können es 'mal versuchen.	zee kĭn'-uen es 'mäl ferzoo'-chen.
If I were you —	Wäre ich wie Sie —	vai'-re iḣ vee zee —
If I were in your place —	Wenn ich an Ihrer Stelle wäre —	van iḣ an ee'-rer shtạl'-le vai'-re —
If you'll follow my advice —	Wollen Sie meinem Rathe folgen —	vol'-len zee mī'-nem rü'-te fol'-gen —
Just try.	Versuchen Sie es nur einmal.	fer-zoo'-chen zee es noor Inmäl'.
I am of opinion that —	Meine Meinung ist, daß —	mī'-ne mī'-nung ist, dȧs —
It is the only sensible way.	Es ist der einzige vernünftige Weg.	es ist där īn'-tsi-ge' fernünf'-ti-ge' vāg.
What else can you do?	Was können Sie sonst thun?	vȧs kĭn'-nen zee zoust toon?
An idea strikes me.	Ich habe einen Gedanken.	iḣ hä'-be Ī'-nen ge-dȧng'-ken.
It occurs to me; a thought strikes me.	Mir kommt ein Gedanke.	meer komt īn ge-dȧng'-ke.
Let me alone for that.	Lassen Sie mich machen.	lȧs'-sen zee miḣ mȧch'-en.
Let us do one thing.	Lassen Sie uns eins thun.	lȧs'-sen zee ųns Ins toon.
I've made up my mind.	Ich bin fest entschlossen.	iḣ bin fȧst ent-shlos'-sen.
I've changed my opinion.	Ich habe meine Meinung geändert.	iḣ hä'-be mī'-ne mī'-nung ge-ạn'-dert.
Let us try another experiment.	Lassen Sie uns etwas anderes probiren.	lȧs'-sen zee ųns ȧt'-vȧs ȧn'-de rȧs' prō-bee'-ren.
Change it.	Mach' es anders.	mȧch' es ȧn'-ders.
Let us go differently to work.	Wir wollen anders zu Werke gehen.	veer vol'-len ȧn'-ders tsoo vạr'-ke gäh'-en.
What do you say about it?	Was sagen Sie dazu?	vȧs zȧ'-gen zee dȧ-tsoo'?
I think as you do.	Ich denke wie Sie.	iḣ dạng'-ke vee zee.
It is very well thought.	Das ist sehr richtig gedacht.	dȧs ist zār riḣ'-tig ge-dȧcht'.
Nothing like it.	Es geht nichts darüber.	es gāt niḣts dür-ü'-ber.

EATING AND DRINKING.

Essen und Trinken.

(ạs'-sen ųnt tring'-ken)

Are you hungry?	Sind Sie hungrig?	zint zee hųng'-rig?
I have a very good appetite.	Ich habe einen sehr guten Appetit.	iḣ hä'-be Ī'-nen zār goo'-ten ȧp'-pe-teet'.
I am hungry.	Ich bin hungrig.	iḣ bin hųng'-rig.
I'm hungry and thirsty.	Ich bin hungrig und durstig.	iḣ bin hųng'-rig ųnt dųrs'-tig.
I could eat a bit of something.	Ich möchte wohl etwas essen.	iḣ miḣ'-te vōl ȧt'-vȧs ȧs'-sen.
Exercise in fresh air is a good appetizer.	Bewegung in freier Luft macht Appetit.	be-vā'-gųng in frī'-er lųft mȧcht ȧp'-pe-teet'.
Eat something.	Iß etwas.	iss ȧt'-vȧs.
You have not yet breakfasted.	Du hast noch nicht gefrühstückt.	doo hȧst noch niḣt ge-frü'-shtĭkt'.
What will you eat?	Was wollen Sie essen?	vȧs vol'-len zee ȧs'-sen?
What do you like [wish] to eat?	Was wünschen Sie zu essen?	vȧs vĭn'-shen zee tsoo ȧs'-sen?

I can eat anything.	Ich esse, was eben da ist.	ih as'-se, vås ā'-ben dä ist.
Will you have [do you wish for] some bread?	Wollen Sie etwas Brod haben?	vol'-len zee at'-vås bröt hä'-ben?
Will you take breakfast?	Willst Du frühstücken?	vilst doo frü'-shtĭk'-ken?
Yes, a cup of coffee and a slice of bread and butter.	Ja, eine Tasse Kaffee und ein Butterbrod.	yä, I'-ne tås'-se kaf'-fä unt In but'-ter-bröt'.
Nothing else?	Nichts weiter?	nihts vī'-ter?
No, more than that is not customary here.	Nein, mehr ist hier nicht gebräuchlich.	nīn, mär ist heer niht ge-broih'-lih.
Is it not too little?	Ist es nicht zu wenig?	ist es niht tsoo vā'-nig?
No, at 10 o'clock we take the second breakfast.	Nein, um 10 Uhr wird zum zweiten Mal gefrühstückt.	nīn, um tsān oor virt tsum tsvī'-ten mäl ge-frü'-shtĭkt'.
And dinner?	Und wann wird zu Mittag gegessen?	unt vån virt tsoo mit'-tüg ge-gas'-sen?
At 12 or 1 o'clock.	Um 12 oder 1 Uhr.	um tsvǐlf ō'-der īn oor.
Give me something to eat.	Geben Sie [gieb] mir etwas zu essen.	gā'-ben zee [geep] meer at'-vås tsoo as'-sen.
Eat something, a little bit.	Essen Sie [iß] etwas, ein bischen.	as'-sen zee [iss] at'-vås, īn bis'-hen.
What have you to eat, to drink?	Was haben Sie zu essen, zu trinken?	vås hä'-ben zee tsoo as'-sen, tsoo tring'-ken?
Will you have [do you wish for] more?	Wollen Sie mehr haben?	vol'-len zee mär hä'-ben?
You don't eat anything.	Sie essen nichts.	zee as'-sen nihts.
I beg your pardon, I make a good meal.	[Ich] bitte sehr, ich esse recht viel.	[ih] bit'-te zār, ih as'-se raht feel.
I did very well.	Ich habe sehr viel gegessen.	ih hä'-be zār feel ge-gas'-sen.
Will that do for you?	Ist das genug?	ist dås ge-noog'?
Eat another piece.	Essen Sie [iß] noch ein Stück.	as'-sen zee [iss] noch īn shtĭk.
Take an apple.	Nehmen Sie [nimm] einen Apfel.	nä'-men zee [nimm] I'-nen åp'-fel.
I have eaten enough, sufficient.	Ich habe genug [mich satt] gegessen.	ih hä'-be ge-noog' [mih zått] ge-gas'-sen.
I cannot take any more.	Ich kann nichts mehr genießen.	ih kån nihts mär ge-nee'-ssen.
Are you thirsty [dry]?	Sind Sie [bist Du] durstig?	zint zee [bist doo] durs'-tig?
Are you not thirsty?	Sind Sie nicht durstig? Haben Sie keinen Durst?	zint zee niht durs'-tig? hä'-ben zee kī'-nen durst?
I am very thirsty [dry].	Ich bin sehr durstig.	ih bin zār durs'-tig.
I am dying of thirst.	Ich komme um vor Durst.	ih kom'-me um for durst.
Having done eating, let us drink.	Da wir mit Essen fertig sind, wollen wir eins trinken.	dä veer mit as'-sen får'-tig zint, vol'-len veer Ins tring'-ken.
What will you drink?	Was wollen Sie trinken?	vås vol'-len zee tring'-ken?
A glass of wine, beer, [or] lemonade?	Ein Glas Wein, Bier, [oder] Limonade?	In glås vīn, beer [ō'-der] lim'-mo-nä'-de?
My thirst is quenched.	Mein Durst ist gelöscht.	mīn durst ist ge-lisht'.
I could drink a glass of sherry.	Ich möchte ein Glas Sherry trinken.	ih mih'-te In glås shar'-ry tring'-ken.
Take a glass of Culmbach beer.	Trinken Sie ein Glas Culmbacher.	tring'-ken zee In glås kulm'-båch'-er.

Drink another glass of wine.	Trinken Sie noch ein Glas Wein.	tring'-ken zee noch in gläs vīn.
My regards to you, Sir.	Mein Herr, ich trinke auf Ihre Gesundheit.	min harr, ih tring'-ke ouf ee'-re ge-zunt'-hīt'.
I drink your good health.	Ich habe die Ehre, auf Ihre Gesundheit zu trinken.	ih hä'-be dee ā'-re, ouf ee'-re ge-zunt'-hīt' tsoo tring'-ken.
Dinner is my best meal; I care very little about breakfast or supper.	Das Mittagessen ist meine beste Mahlzeit, ich mache mir wenig aus dem Frühstück oder Abendessen.	däs mit'-täg-as'-sen ist mī'-ne bäs'-te mäl'-tsīt, ih mäch'-e meer vä'-nig ous däm frü'-shtĭk ō'-der ä'-bent-as'-sen.
I like roast beef.	Ich esse gern Rindsbraten.	ih as'-se garn rints'-brä-ten.
I like German cookery.	Mir gefällt die deutsche Küche.	meer ge-falt' dee doit'-she kĭh'-he.
Has it not a peculiar taste?	Hat es nicht einen eigenthümlichen Geschmack?	hät es niht ī'-nen ī'-gentüm'-li-han ge-shmäk'?
I have eaten a good dinner.	Es hat mir sehr gut geschmeckt.	es hät meer zār goot geshmäkt'.
Taste this wine, do.	Kosten Sie diesen Wein einmal.	kos'-ten zee dee'-zen vīn īn-mäl'.
I'm not thirsty any more.	Ich habe keinen Durst mehr.	ih hä'-be kī'-nen durst mār.
It is excellent, indeed.	Er ist in der That vortrefflich.	är ist in där tät for-trąf'-lih.
I have no more appetite.	Ich habe keinen Appetit mehr.	ih hä'-be kī'-nen äp'-peteet' mār.
Your appetite will improve as you eat.	Der Appetit wird sich beim Essen einstellen.	där äp'-pe-teet' virt zih bīm as'-sen īn'-shtąl-len.
God bless the meal! Much good may it do you! (*Before or after meals.*)	Gesegnete Mahlzeit! Wohl bekomm's! (*Vor oder nach dem Essen.*)	ge-zāg'-ne-te' mäl'-tsīt'! vōl be-kom's'! (*Before or after meals.*)
The meals were very good there.	Die Mahlzeiten sind dort sehr gut.	dee mäl'-tsī'-ten zint dort zār goot.
Take something else, some more.	Nehmen Sie sonst etwas, noch etwas.	nā'-men zee zonst ąt'-väs, noch ąt'-väs.
For my part, I have quite done.	Ich, für mich, habe zur Genüge.	ih, fïr mih, hä'-be tsur genü'-ge.
Eat what you like, whatever you please.	Essen Sie, was Sie wollen.	as'-sen zee, väs zee vol'-len.
I'll take a little bit of cheese and butter.	Ich will ein bischen Käse und Butter essen.	ih vill īn bis'-hen kai'-ze unt but'-ter as'-sen.
I prefer some fruit [some confectionery].	Ich ziehe Obst [Conditorei] vor.	ih tseeh'-e ōpst [kon-dee'-to rī'] fōr.
I had rather not eat [drink] any more.	Ich will lieber nichts mehr essen [trinken].	ih vill lee'·ber nihts mār as'-sen [tring'-ken].
I will drink of this wine another time.	Ich will ein anderes Mal von diesem Wein trinken.	ih vill īn än'-de-rąs mäl fon dee'-zem vīn tring'-ken.
This meat looks very tempting.	Diese[s Fleisch] Speise sieht sehr einladend aus.	dee'-ze[s flĭsh] shpī'-ze zeet zār īn'-lä'-dent ous.
Only a little bit, just to taste it.	Nur ein wenig, blos um ihn [es] zu kosten.	nur īn vä'-nig, blōs um een [es] tsoo kos'-ten.
Very well; but you are a poor eater.	Sehr wohl; aber Sie essen [trinken] sehr wenig.	zār vōl; ü'·ber zee as'-sen [tring'-ken] zār vä'·nig.
You helped me to too much of everything.	Sie haben mir von Allem vorgelegt.	zee hä'-ben meer fon äl'-lem fōr'-ge-lägt'.

English	German	Pronunciation
I do not like a strong taug.	Ich mag keinen starken Beigeschmack.	iḫ mäg kī'-nen shtär'-ken bī'-ge-shmåk'.
But it whets the appetite.	Er schärft aber den Appetit.	är shärft ü'-ber dän åp'-pe-teet'.
Mix the wine with water.	Mische den Wein mit Wasser.	mish'-e dän vīn mit vås'-ser.
I like roast veal.	Ich esse gern Kalbsbraten.	iḫ as'-se garn kålps'-brä'-ten.
Give me some roast beef.	Geben Sie mir Rindsbraten.	gā'-ben zee meer rints'-brä'-ten.
I'll thank you for a piece of steak.	Bitte, geben Sie mir ein Stückchen Steak.	bit'-te, gā'-ben zee meer īn shtīk'-ḫen steak.
I like rump steak.	Vom dicken Theil des Hinterviertels.	fom dik'-ken tīl das hin'-ter-feer'-tels.
Here is a boiled leg of mutton.	Hier ist eine gekochte Hammelskeule.	heer ist ī'-ne ge-koch'-te häm'-mels-koi'-le.
Take some turnips, they are sweet.	Essen Sie Rüben, sie sind süß.	as'-sen zee rü'-ben, zee zint züs.
I like roast mutton with roasted potatoes and sweet turnips.	Ich esse gern Hammelsbraten mit gerösteten Kartoffeln und süßen Rüben.	iḫ as'-se garn häm'-mels-brä'-ten mit ge-rį'-sten' kår-tof'-feln ųnt sü'-ssen rü'-ben.
These mealy potatoes are delicious.	Diese mehligen Kartoffeln sind köstlich.	dee'-ze mä'-li-gen' kår-tof'-feln zint kĭst'-liḫ.
Let us have lamb and peas.	Lassen Sie uns Lammfleisch und Erbsen haben.	lås'-sen zee ųns låm'-flīsh' ųnt arp'-sen hä'-ben.
Roast pork and applesauce.	Schweinsbraten und Apfelcompot.	shvīns'-brä'-ten ųnt åp'-fel-kom-pō'.
A large head of cauliflower.	Ein großer Blumenkohlkopf.	īn grö'-sser bloo'-men-köl'-kopf'.
Cucumbers in thin slices.	Gurken in dünnen Scheibchen.	gur'-ken in dīn'-nen shīp'-ḫen.
An excellent salad.	Ein vortrefflicher Salat.	īn for-traf'-li-ḫer' zå-lät'.
Let me have some cold tongue.	Geben Sie mir kalte Ochsenzunge.	gā'-ben zee meer kål'-te ok'-sen-tsųng'-e.
Is the salad dressed?	Ist der Salat angemacht?	ist där zå-lät'än'-ge-mächt'?
Pepper, vinegar, olive oil and salt.	Pfeffer, Essig, Olivenöl und Salz.	pfaf'-fer, as'-sig, o-lee'-ven-īl' ųnt sålts.
I like onions, too.	Auch Zwiebeln esse ich gern.	ouch tsvee'-beln as'-se iḫ garn.
Is this ham well smoked?	Ist dieser Schinken gut geräuchert?	ist dee'-zer shing'-ken goot ge-roi'-ḫert?
Is this meat well cured?	Ist dieses Fleisch gut gepökelt?	ist dee'-zes flīsh goot ge-pį'-kelt?
White bacon with red streaks.	Weißer Speck mit rothen Streifen.	vī'-sser shpäk mit rō'-ten shtrī'-fen.
French beans and Lima beans.	Französische und Lima Bohnen.	från-tsį'-zi-she' ųnt lī'-må bō'-nen.
Slice some onions for me.	Schneiden Sie mir einige Zwiebeln.	shnī'-den zee meer ī'-ni-ge' tsvee'-beln.
What fine and white parsnips!	Welch' schöne und weiße Pastinaken!	valḫ' shį'-ne ųnt vī'-sse pås'-ti-nä'-ken!
They look like oyster-plants.	Sie sehen wie Schwarzwurz aus.	zee zäh'-en vee shvårts'-vurts' ous.
This savoy cabbage is not done yet.	Dieser Savoykohl ist noch nicht gahr.	dee'-zer zå-voi'-kōl ist noch niḫt gär.

6

English	German	Pronunciation
Will you take ham-bologna or beef-sausage?	Wollen Sie Schinken- oder Fleischwurst nehmen?	vol'-len zee shing'-ken- ö'-der flïsh'-vurst uä'-men?
Give us a calf's liver.	Geben Sie uns eine Kalbsleber.	gä'-ben zee uns ï'-ne kålps'-lä'-ber.
You have kept this venison too long.	Ihr habt dieses Wild zu lange liegen lassen.	eer hápt dee'-zes vilt tsoo láng'-e lee'-gen lás'-sen.
Do you like endive?	Essen Sie gern Endivien[salat]?	as'-sen zee garn au dee'-vi-e'[n-zá-lät']?
Here is a fine bed of asparagus.	Hier ist ein schönes Spargelbeet.	heer ist in shï'nes shpár'-gel-bät'.
Put some celery into the soup.	Thut Sellerie in die Suppe.	toot sal'-le ree' in dee zup'-pe.
Mix parsley and thyme in the stuffing.	Mischt Petersilie und Thymian in das Füllsel.	misht pä'-ter-zee'-li ye' unt tee'-mi-yán' in dás fïll'-sel.
Boil some mint with the peas.	Kocht Krausemünze mit den Erbsen.	kocht krou'-ze-mïn'-tse mit dän arp'-sen.
I like apples.	Ich esse gern Aepfel.	ih as'-se garn ap'-fel.
Bake some pears.	Schmort Birnen.	shmört bir'-nen.
Preserve some plums.	Machen Sie Pflaumen ein.	mách'-en zee pflou'-men in.
Give me some currant jelly.	Gebt mir Johannisbeersaft.	gäpt meer yo-hán'-nis-bär'-záft'.
Make a cherry pie.	Mache eine Kirschentorte.	mách'-e ï'-ne kir'-shen-tor'-te.
A basket of fine filberts.	Ein Korb mit schönen Lambertsnüssen.	in korp mit shï'-nen lám'-barts-nïs'-sen.
Look for blackberries.	Suche Brombeeren.	zoo'-che brom'-bä'-ren.
Take of this gooseberry jam.	Nehmen Sie von diesem Stachelbeerconserv.	nä'-men zee fon dee'-zem shtách'-el-bär'-kon-zarf'.
Here are huckleberries.	Hier sind Heidelbeeren.	heer zint hï'-del-bä'-ren.
Pick out the largest walnuts and the best hazelnuts.	Suchen Sie die größten Wallnüsse aus und die besten Haselnüsse.	zoo'-chen zee dee grïs'-ten vál'-nïs'-se ous unt dee bas'-ten hä'-zel-nïs'-se.
I should like some raspberry vinegar.	Ich möchte wohl etwas Himbeeressig haben.	ih nïh'-te völ at'-vás him'-bär-as'-sig hü'-ben.
Will you eat some apricots?	Wollen Sie Aprikosen essen?	vol'-len zee áp'-ri-kö'-zen as'-sen?
Have you any?	Haben Sie welche?	hü'-ben zee val'-he?
Give me a few peaches.	Geben Sie mir einige Pfirsiche.	gä'-ben zee meer ï'-ni-ge' pfir'-zi-he'.
Cut a pine-apple for me.	Zerschneiden Sie mir eine Ananas.	tser shnï'-den zee meer ï'-ne á'-ná-nás'.
I will take a glass of Niersteiner.	Ich will ein Glas Niersteiner trinken.	ih vill in glás neer'-shtï'-ner tring'-ken.
I will pledge you in a glass of Ahrwine.	Ich will Ihnen in einem Glase Ahrwein Bescheid thun.	ih vill ee'-nen iu ï'-nem glä'-ze är'-vïu be-shït' toon.
Will you take a cup of tea?	Wollen Sie eine Tasse Thee trinken?	vol'-len zee ï'-ne tás'-se tü tring'-ken?
A little more sugar, if you please.	Etwas mehr Zucker, wenn ich bitten darf.	at'-vás mär tsuk'-ker, van ih bit'-ten dárf.
Put plenty of rice in the broth.	Thun zee ge-noog' ris in die Fleischbrühe.	toon zee ge-noog' ris in dee flïsh'-brüh'-e.
Can you make the coffee stronger?	Können Sie den Kaffee stärker machen?	kïn'-nen zee dau káf'-fä shtar'-ker mách'-en?

English	German	Pronunciation
Chocolate is too rich for my stomach.	Schokolade ist für meinen Magen zu schwer.	shok'-kō lä'-de ist fïr mī'-nen mü'-gen tsoo shvär.
Do you like strawberries?	Essen Sie gern Erdbeeren?	as'-sen zee garn art'-bā'-ren?
I will take claret with my dinner.	Ich will beim Mittagessen Rothwein trinken.	iḣ vill bīm mit'-täg-as'-sen rōt'-vīn tring'-ken.
I prefer light Moselle wine.	Ich ziehe leichten Moselwein vor.	iḣ tsee'-e līḣ'-ten mō'-zel-vīn' fōr.
Don't you take a few drops of cognac in your coffee?	Nehmen Sie nicht einige Tropfen Cognac in Ihren Kaffee?	nä'-men zee niḣt ī'-ni-ge' trop'-fen kon'-yak in ee'-ren kaf'-fā'?
Will you try some cresses?	Wollen Sie etwas Kresse versuchen?	vol'-len zce at'-vas krus'-se fer-zoo'-chen?
This is genuine English mustard.	Dies ist echter englischer Senf.	dees ist aḣ'-ter ang'-li-sher' zanf.
There is no pepper in the caster.	Es ist kein Pfeffer in dem Flaschenstand.	es ist kīn pfaf'-fer in dam flash'-en-shtant'.
Give the man a glass of beer.	Gebt dem Mann ein Glas Bier.	gapt däm man in glas beer.
There are not raisins enough in the pudding.	Es sind nicht genug Rosinen in dem Pudding.	es zint niḣt ge-noog' ro-zee'-nen in dam pud'-ding.
Put a couple of cloves into the apple-pie.	Thut ein Paar Nelken in die Aepfelpastete.	toot in pär nal'-ken in dee ap'-fel-pas tä'-te.
Boil the barley with some lemon.	Kocht Graupen mit Zitronen.	kocht grou'-pen mit tsit-rō' nen.
Potatoes with the jacket.	Kartoffeln mit der Schale.	kár-tof'-feln mit där shä'-le.
Put plenty of allspice in the pickle.	Thut viel Piment [Nelkenpfeffer] in die Pökel.	toot feel pi-mant' [nal'-ken-pfaf'-fer] in dee pī'-kel.
I lunch on bread and cheese.	Ich nehme Brod und Käse zum zweiten Frühstück.	iḣ nä'-me brōt unt kai'-ze tsum tsvī'-ten frü'-shtïk'.
Will you have some bread and butter?	Wollen Sie Brod und Butter haben?	vol'-len zee brōt unt but'-ter hü'-ben?
Do you like potato salad?	Essen Sie gern Kartoffelsalat?	as'-sen zee garn kár-tof'-fel-zá-lät'?
I like corn [field] salad.	Ich esse Korn[Feld]-Salat gern.	iḣ as'-se korn[falt]-zá-lät' garn.
How do you like the meat?	Wie schmeckt Ihnen das Fleisch?	vee shmakt ee'-nen dás flīsh?
Did you ever taste vinegar-cured meat?	Haben Sie je Sauerfleisch versucht?	hü'-ben zee yä zou'-er-flīsh' fer-zoocht'?
It is a fine German dish.	Es ist ein feines deutsches Gericht.	es ist in fī'-nes doit'-shes ge-riḣt'.
Trout is a beautiful fish.	Die Forelle ist ein schöner Fisch.	dee fo-ral'-le ist in shī'-ner fish.
Buy a whole cod for me.	Kaufe mir einen ganzen Kabliau.	kou'-fe meer ī'-nen gàn'-tsen käb'-li-ou'.
Will you have the chickens boiled or roasted?	Wollen Sie die Küchlein gekocht oder gebraten haben?	vol'-len zee dee kïḣ'-līn ge-kocht' ō'-der ge brä'-ten hä'-ben?
Season the ducks with sage and onions.	Würzt die Enten mit Salbei und Zwiebeln.	virtst dee an'-ten mit zàl'-bī unt tsvee'-beln.
These partridges are for you.	Diese Rebhühner sind für Sie.	dee'-ze rup'-hü'-ner zint fïr zee.
I prefer Dutch herrings.	Ich ziehe holländische Häringe vor.	iḣ tsee'-e hol'-lan'-di-she' hai'-ring-e' fōr.

These are very fine eels.	Das sind sehr schöne Aale.	däs zint zār shī'-ne ü'-le.
When did you shoot this quail?	Wann haben Sie diese Wachtel geschossen?	vàn hü'-ben zee dee'-ze vách'-tel ge-shos'-sen?
I shot a brace of snipes.	Ich habe ein paar Schnepfen geschossen.	ih hü'-be īn pār shnap'-fen ge-shos'-sen.
Turkeys are delicious poultry.	Puter sind köstliches Geflügel.	poo'-ter zint kĭst'-li-ḥes ge-flü'-gel.
In Germany they eat the St. Martin's goose.	In Deutschland ißt man die Martinsgans.	in doitsh'-länt ist mán dee már'-teens-gànts'.
The pheasant's plumage is beautiful.	Das Gefieder des Fasans ist schön.	däs ge-fee'-der das fä-zäns' ist shīn.
My dog coursed a hare yesterday.	Mein Hund hat gestern einen Hasen aufgejagt.	mīn hunt hát gás'-tern ī'-nen ou''-ge-yägt'.
This turbot is not good.	Dieser Steinbutt [f.—bütte] ist nicht gut.	dee'-zer shtīn'-bụt [fem. –bĭt'-te] ist niht goot.
We will have the smelts fried.	Wir wollen die Stinten gebacken haben.	veer vol'-len dee shtin'-ten ge-bák'-ken hä'-ben.
You find tenches and carps in German rivers.	Schleien und Karpfen werden in deutschen Flüssen gefunden.	shlī'-en ụnt kárp'-fen vār'-den in doit'-shen flüs'-sen ge fụn'-den.
I have caught some large pikes.	Ich habe etliche große Hechte gefangen.	ih hü'-be ạt'-li-ḥe' grö'-sse hạh'-te ge-fáng'-en.
Wood-cocks are very scarce.	Waldschnepfen sind sehr selten.	vált'-shnap'-fen zint zār zạl'-ten.
I like pigeon pies.	Ich esse Taubenpasteten gern.	ih ạs'-se ton'-ben-pás-tā'-teu garn.
Boil the haddock well.	Kocht den Schellfisch gahr.	kocht dān shạl'-fish gär.
Codfish and new potatoes with butter and mustard-sauce.	Stockfisch und neue Kartoffeln mit Butter- und Senfsauce.	shtok'-fish ụnt noi'-e kár-tof'-feln mit bụt'-ter-ụnt zạnf'-zō'-se.
The meat is not yet well done.	Das Fleisch ist noch nicht gahr.	däs flīsh ist noch niht gär.
The lobsters are quite alive.	Die Hummer sind ganz lebendig.	dee hụm'-mer zint gánts le-bạn'-dig.
These crabs are not quite fresh.	Diese Krebse sind nicht ganz frisch.	dee'-ze krạp'-se zint niht gánts frish.
You find shell-fish in Germany, but oysters only on the coast of Holstein.	Man findet Schalenfische in Deutschland, aber Austern an der Küste von Holstein nur.	mán fin'-det shü'-len-fish'-she in doitsh'-länt, ü'-ber ous'-tern án där kīs'-te fon hol'-shtīn noor.
Let me have a few shrimps.	Lassen Sie mich einige Krabben haben.	läs'-sen zee mih ī'-ni-ge' krǎb'-ben hä'-ben.
The anchovies are palatable.	Diese Anchovis sind sehr schmackhaft.	dee'-ze än tshö'-vis zint zār shmák'-háft.
Give me a Dutch bloater.	Geben Sie mir einen holländischen Bückling.	gü'-ben zee meer ī'-nen hol'-lạn' di-shen' bĭk'-ling.
Soles are superior to plaice.	Seezungen sind den Schollen vorzuziehen.	zā'-tsụng'-en zint dān shol'-len för' tsoo-tsee' en.
Are you fond of buckwheat pancakes with bacon?	Essen Sie gern Buchweizenpfannkuchen mit Speck?	ạs'-sen zee gạrn booch'-vī'-tsen-pfán'-koo'-chen mit shpạk?
I am very fond of Westphalia rye-bread.	Ich esse Pumpernickel für mein Leben gern.	ih ạs'-se pụm'-per-nik'-kel f'ir mīn lā'-ben gạrn.
Mutton chops and rump steaks.	Hammelscotelets und Lendenschnitte.	hám'-mels- kot-lạts' ụnt lạn'-den-shnit'-te.
Cornbeef and cabbage.	Pökelfleisch und Weißkraut.	pī'-kel-flĭsh ụnt vīs' kront,

English	German	Pronunciation
This wine has a peculiar taste.	Dieser Wein hat einen eigenthümlichen Geschmack.	dee'-zer vīn hät ī'-nen ī'-gen-tüm'-li-ḥen' ge-shmäk'.
The dinners in this hotel consist of fish, beef, veal, lamb or mutton.	Zum Mittagessen in diesem Hotel hat man: Fisch, Rind-, Kalb-, Lamm- oder Hammelfleisch.	tsum mit'-täg-as'-sen in dee'-zem ho-tal hät män: fish, rint-, kälp-, läm- ō'-der häm'-mel-flīsh'.
All sorts of poultry, as: spring chickens, geese, ducks, turkeys, roast chickens, pigeons, partridges, field fares, pheasants and snipes.	Alle Arten Geflügel, wie: junge Hühner, Gänse, Enten, Puter, Brathühner, Tauben, Rebhühner, Krammetsvögel, Fasanen und Schnepfen.	äl'-le är'-ten ge-flü'-gel, vee: yung'-e hü'-ner, gan'-ze, an'-ten, poo'-ter, brät'-hü'-ner, tou'-ben, rup'-hü'-ner, kräm'-mets-fī'-gel, fä-zä'-nen unt shnap'-fen.
Potatoes, greens, vegetables and salads.	Kartoffeln, grünes und anderes Gemüse und allerlei Salat.	kär-tof'-feln, grü'-nes unt än'-de-res' ge-mü'-ze unt äl'-ler-lī' zä-lät'.
All kinds of puddings, sweet-meats, preserves, bread, cheese and butter.	Alle Arten Puddings, Confect, Eingemachtes, Brod, Käse und Butter.	äl'-le är'-ten pud'-dings, kon-fakt', īn'-ge-mäch'-tes, brōt, kai'-ze unt but'-ter.
Among the soups you'll find mock-turtle soup, sometimes also real turtle soup.	Unter den Suppen giebt's nachgemachte, zuweilen auch echte Schildkrötensuppe.	un'-ter dän zup'-pen gipt's näch'-ge-mäch'-te, tsoo-vī'-len ouch aḥ'-te shilt'-krī'-ten-zup'-pe.
Brain sausage and Brunswick pork sausage.	Cervelatwurst und Braunschweiger Mettwurst.	sar'-ve-lät'-vurst unt broun'-shvī'-ger mat'-vurst.
Do you like dumplings of flour or rice?	Essen Sie Mehl- oder Reisklöse gern?	as'-sen zee mäl- ō'-der rīs'-klī'-ze garn?
I am fond of dumplings of liver.	Ich esse Leberklöse gern.	iḥ as'-se lä'-ber-klī'-ze garn.
Slices of bread and butter with sardels.	Sardellen-Butterbrödchen.	zär-dal'-len-but'-ter-brīt'-hen.
Caviar mixed with onions.	Caviar mit Zwiebel gemischt.	kä'-vi-är mit tsvee'-bel ge-misht'.
Did you ever taste lampreys	Haben Sie je Neunaugen geschmeckt?	hä'-ben zee yā noin'-ou'-gen ge-shmakt'?

ADDRESSES. TITLES.

Anreden. Titulaturen.
(än'-rū'-den)   (ti'-too'-lä-too'-ren)

English	German	Pronunciation
Will you come [walk, step] in [enter], Sir?	Wollen Sie hereinkommen [eintreten], mein Herr?	vol'-len zee har-īn-kom'-men [īn'-trä'-ten], mīn harr?
Be seated, Madam.	Setzen Sie sich, Madame [mein Fräulein].	zat'-sen zee ziḥ, mä-däm' [mīn froi'-līn].
A gentleman wants you, Mr. A.	Herr A., ein Herr wünscht Sie zu sprechen.	harr A., īn harr vīnsht zee tsoo shpraḥ'-en.
May I offer you a fan, Miss B.	Fräulein B., darf ich Ihnen einen Fächer anbieten?	froi'-līn B., därf iḥ ee'-nen ī'-nen faḥ'-er än'-bee'-ten?

English	German	Pronunciation
Mr. and Mrs. C. are waiting for you, Sir.	Herr und Frau C. warten auf Sie, mein Herr.	harr unt frou C. vår'-ten ouf zee, mīn harr.
I had the pleasure of escorting the Misses D. to the theatre.	Ich hatte das Vergnügen, die Fräulein D. zum Theater zu führen.	ih hát'-te dås fer-gnü'-gen, dee froi'-līn D. tsum tā-ä'-ter tsoo fü'-ren.
Do you know this lady?	Kennen Sie diese Dame?	kan'-nen zee dee'-ze dä'-me?
There are several ladies, whom I know.	Da sind verschiedene Damen, die ich kenne.	då zint fer-shee'-de ne' dä'-men, dee ih kan'-ne.
Is Mrs. Schneider at home?	Ist Madame [Frau] Schneider zu Hause?	ist må-dåm' [frou] shnī'-der tsoo hou'-ze?
My mistress has gone out; but Mrs. Schneider, Junior, is at home.	Meine Herrin ist ausgegangen, aber die jüngere Frau Schneider ist zu Hause.	mī'-ne har'-rin ist ous'-ge-gång'-en, ü'-ber dee yīng'-e re' frou shnī'-der ist tsoo hou'-ze.
Where is young Mr. Becker?	Wo ist der junge Herr Becker?	vō ist där yung'-e harr bak'-ker?
The young gentleman is in his room.	Der junge Herr ist in seinem Zimmer.	där yung'-e harr ist in zī'-nem tsim'-mer.
Is anybody with him?	Ist Jemand bei ihm?	ist yā'-månt bī eem?
Three young gentlemen are with him, Sir.	Es sind drei junge Herren bei ihm [, mein Herr].	es zint drī yung'-e har'-ren bī eem [, mīn harr].
Ladies and Gentlemen!	Meine Damen und Herren!	mī'-ne dä'-men unt har'-ren!
This is Professor Hartmann.	Dies ist der Herr Professor Hartmann.	dees ist där harr pro-fas'-sor hårt-mån.
Please to introduce me to the professor's wife.	Stellen Sie mich gefälligst der Frau Professorin vor.	shtal'-len zee mih ge-fal'-ligst der frou pro-fes-so'-rin' fōr.
Who is that lady over there?	Wer ist jene Dame da drüben?	vär ist yā'-ne dä'-me dä drü'-ben?
That is Dr. Friedrich's good lady.	Das ist die Frau des Herrn Doctor's Friedrich.	dås ist dee frou das harrn dok'-tors free'-drih.
Here comes major Krieger.	Hier kommt Herr Major Krieger.	heer komt harr må-yōr kree'-ger.
And the major's wife, too.	Und die Frau Majorin auch.	unt dee frou må-yō'-rin ouch.
Do you see that young lady over there?	Sehen Sie jene junge Dame dort?	zāh'-en zee yā'-ne yung'-e dä'-me dort?
That's the lady, whose sister is engaged to the mayor.	Das ist das Fräulein, deren Schwester mit dem Herrn Bürgermeister verlobt ist.	dås ist dås froi'-līn, dā'-ren shvas'-ter mit däm harrn bīr'-ger-mīs'-ter fer-lōpt' ist.
She is a bride, and he is a bridegroom, until they are married.	Sie ist eine Braut und er ein Bräutigam, bis sie verheiratet sind.	zee ist ī'-ne brout' unt är īn broi'-ti-gåm', bis zee fer-hī'-rä'-tet zint.
And then they will call her Mrs. Mayoress.	Und dann wird man sie Frau Bürgermeisterin nennen.	unt dan virt mån zee frou bīr'-ger-mīs'-te-rin' nan'-nen.
Doctor, I am very ill.	Herr Doktor, ich bin sehr krank.	harr dok'-tor, ih bin zār kránk.
Madam, has the doctor returned?	Ist Ihr Herr Gemahl zurück, Frau Doktorin?	ist eer harr ge-mäl' tsoo-rīk', frou dok'-to-rin'?
Your son was my travelling companion.	Ihr Herr Sohn war mein Reisegesellschafter.	eer harr zōn vär mīn rī'-ze-ge-zall'-shåf'-ter.
Your father has asked for you.	Ihr Herr Vater hat nach Ihnen gefragt.	eer harr fä'-ter håt nåch ee'-nen ge-frägt.

English	German	Pronunciation
I saw your mother last night at the concert.	Ich habe Ihre Frau Mutter gestern Abend im Konzert gesehen.	iḥ hü'-be ee'-re frou mut'-ter gas'-tern ä'-bent im kon-tsart' ge-zäh'-en.
Give my kindest regards to your good lady.	Ueberbringen Sie Ihrer verehrten Gattin meine achtungsvollsten Grüße.	ü'-ber-bring'-en zee ee'-rer fer-är'-ten gát'-tin mī'-ne ách'-tungs-fol'-sten grü'-sse.
Remember me kindly to your daughter.	Empfehlen Sie mich Ihrer Fräulein Tochter.	emp-fā'-len zee miḥ ee'-rer froi'-lĭn toch'-ter.
You cannot intimidate me, Sir.	Sie, Herr, können mich nicht einschüchtern.	zee, harr, kĭn'-nen miḥ niḥt īn'-shiḥ'-tern.
How is the pastor, Mrs. Frommherz?	Was macht Herr Frommherz, Frau Pastorin?	vås mácht harr from'-harts, frou pás-tō'-rin?
Miss Kindlich is an excellent teacher.	Fräulein Kindlich ist eine vorzügliche Lehrerin.	froi'-līn kint'-liḥ ist ī'-ne for-tsüg'-li-ḥe'lā'-re-rin'.
My wife is the best cook imaginable.	Meine Frau ist die denkbar beste Köchin.	mī'-ne frou ist dee dạngk'-bär bas'-te kiḥ'-ḥin.
And my daughter an accomplished artiste.	Und meine Tochter eine vollkommene Virtuosin.	ụnt mī'-ne toch'-ter ī'-ne foll-kom'-ne vir'-too-ō'-zin.
The landlord and the landlady.	Der Hausbesitzer [-herr] und die Hausbesitzerin [-herrin].	där hous'-be-zit'-ser[-harr] ụnt dee hous'-be-zit' se-rin' [-har'-rin].
Mrs. Roth is chairman of the society.	Frau Roth ist die Präsidentin der Gesellschaft.	frou rōt ist dee praī'-zi-dạn'-tin där ge-zạll'-sháft.
Do you hear me, John [Gertrude]?	Hörst du mich, Johann [Gertrud]?	hịrst doo miḥ, yō'-hán' [gär'-troot]?
Yes, Sir [Madam]!	Ja, mein Herr [Madame]!	yü, mīn harr [má-dám']!
Have you been at church, my son?	Bist du zur Kirche gewesen, mein Sohn?	bist doo tsụr kir'-ḥe ge-vā'-zen, mīn zōn?
No, Sir [Madam]!	Nein!	nīn!
The author has been mistaken.	Der Herr Verfasser hat sich geirrt.	där harr fer-fás'-ser hát ziḥ ge-irrt'.
Here is the composer himself.	Hier ist der Herr Komponist selbst.	heer ist där harr kom'-pō-nist' zalpst.
Can I see the musician A.?	Kann ich den Herrn Musiker A. sehen?	kän iḥ dän harrn moo'-zi-ker' A. zäh'-en?

GOING AND COMING.

Gehen und Kommen.

(gāh'-en ụnt kom'-men)

English	German	Pronunciation
Where [whither] are you going?	Wohin gehen Sie [gehst Du]?	vō-hin' gäh'-en zee [gäst doo]?
I am going home.	Ich gehe nach Hause.	iḥ gäh'-e näch hou'-ze.
I was going to your house.	Ich wollte zu Ihnen gehen.	iḥ voll'-te tsoo ee'-nen gäh'-en.
Where are you coming from?	Woher kommen Sie [kommst Du]?	vo-här' kom'-men zee [komst doo]?
I come from my brother's; from school, church, the theatre.	Ich komme von meinem Bruder; aus der Schule, der Kirche, dem Theater.	iḥ kom'-me fon mī'-nem broo'-der; ous där shoo'-le, där kir'-ḥe, dụm tä-ä'-ter.

English	German	Pronunciation
I shall stay at home.	Ich bleibe zu Hause.	iḥ blī'-be tsoo hou'-ze.
I will not go out.	Ich will nicht ausgehen.	iḥ vill niḥt ous'-gäh'-en.
I expect a friend to call on me.	Ich erwarte den Besuch eines Freundes.	iḥ er-vâr'-te dän be-zooch' ī'-nes froin'-des.
Will you go with me?	Wollen Sie [willst Du] mit mir gehen?	vol'-len zee [villst doo] mit meer gäh'-en?
We will take a walk.	Wir wollen spazieren gehen.	veer vol'-len shpá·tsee'-ren gäh'-en.
Let us stroll for a while.	Lasse[n Sie] uns eine Weile herumschlendern.	lás'-se[n zee] uns ī'-ne vī'-le hạr-um'-shlạu'-dern.
Which way shall we go?	Welchen Weg wollen wir gehen?	vạl'-ḥen väg vol'-len veer gäh'-en?
We will go which ever way you please.	Wir wollen gehen, wo Sie wollen.	veer vol'-len gäh'-en, vō zee vol'-len.
Through the "Promenade?"	Durch die „Promenade?"	dụrḥ dee prom'-me·nü'-de?
Or do you prefer the Castle garden?	Oder ziehen Sie den Schloßgarten vor?	ō'-der tseeh'-en zee dän shlos'-gàr'-ten fōr?
I propose the drilling place.	Ich schlage den Exercirplatz vor.	iḥ shlü'-ge dän ạk'-sertseer'-pláts' fōr.
Let us stop for your brother on our way.	Wir wollen auf dem Wege Ihren Bruder mitnehmen.	veer vol'-len ouf däm vä'-ge ee'-ren broo'-der mit'-nä'-men.
As you please.	Wie Sie belieben.	vee zee be-lee'-ben.
Is Mr. Rabe at home?	Ist Herr Rabe zu Hause?	ist harr rä'-be tsoo hou'-ze?
He has just gone out.	Er ist soeben ausgegangen.	är ist zo-ā'-ben ous'-ge-gáng'-en.
He is not at home.	Er ist nicht zu Hause.	är ist niḥt tsoo hou'-ze.
Can you tell me where he has gone to?	Können Sie mir sagen, wohin er gegangen ist?	kín'-nen zee meer zä'-gen, vo-hin'är ge-gäng'-en ist?
I cannot tell you positively.	Ich kann es nicht bestimmt sagen.	iḥ kán es niḥt be-shtimt' zä'-gen.
Do you know when he will return?	Wissen Sie, wann er zurückkommen wird?	vis'-sen zee, vàn är tsoo-rïk'-kom'-men virt?
Do not walk so fast.	Gehe[n Sie] nicht so rasch.	gäh'-e[n zee] niḥt zō ràsh.
Stop a moment.	Warte[n Sie] einen Augenblick.	vár'-te[n zee] ī'-nen ou'-gen-blik'.
Let us proceed slowly.	Lasse[n Sie] uns langsam vorangehen.	lás'-se[n zee] uns láng'-sàm for-àn'-gäh'-en.
Go through that passage.	Gehe[n Sie] durch jenen Durchgang.	gäh'-e[n zee] dụrḥ yä'-nen dụrḥ'-gàng.
Walk straight on.	Gehe[n Sie] gerade aus.	gäh'-e[n zee] ge-rä'-de ous.
Turn to the right, left.	Wenden Sie sich rechts, links.	vạn'-den zee ziḥ ráḥts, links.
He is tired with running.	Er hat sich müde gelaufen.	är hàt ziḥ mü'-de ge-lou'-fen.
We ran our feet sore.	Wir haben uns die Füße wund gelaufen.	veer hü'-ben uns dee füsse vunt ge-lou'-fen.
My neighbor came running.	Mein Nachbar kam gelaufen.	mīn nàch'-bür käm ge-lou'-fen.
Lightly come, lightly go.	Wie du kommst, so gehst Du wieder.	vee doo komst, zo gäst doo vee'-der.
She came upon her unawares.	Sie war ihr unvermuthet auf den Hals gekommen.	zee vär eer un'-fer-moo'-tet ouf dän hàls ge-kom'-men.

I don't know, what has become of him.	Ich weiß nicht, wo er hingekommen ist.	ih vis niht, vō är hin'-ge-kom'-men ist.
The next steamer is bound for America.	Der nächste Dampfer geht nach Amerika.	där naih'-ste damp'-fer gäht näch ä-mā'-ri-kä.
Leave the world to take its course.	Laßt es gehen, wie es geht.	last es gäh'-en, vee es gäht.
Wait here, I will be with you again directly.	Warte hier, ich werde gleich wieder bei Dir sein.	vär'-te heer, ih vär'-de glīh vee'-der bī deer zīn.

SPEAKING.
Sprechen.
(shprah'-en)

A child begins to talk.	Ein Kind fängt an zu sprechen.	īn kint fangt än tsoo shprah'-en.
Or rather: to prattle.	Oder richtiger: babbeln.	ō'-der rih'-ti-ger': bäb'-beln.
It hears, and therefore it learns to speak.	Es hört, und darum lernt es sprechen.	es hirt, unt där'-um larnt es shprah'-en.
I am told that —	Man hat mir gesagt, daß —	män hät meer ge-zägt', däs
As I tell you.	Was ich Ihnen sage.	väs ih ee'-nen zä'-ge.
I speak the truth.	Ich sage die Wahrheit.	ih zä'-ge dee vär'-hīt.
We say "yes" or "no".	Wir sagen „ja" oder „nein".	veer zä'-gen yü ō'-der nīn.
What he said, was not worth hearing.	Was er sagte, war nicht hörenswerth.	väs är zäg'-te, vär niht hi'-rens-värt'.
He told him the plain truth.	Er sagte ihm die pure Wahrheit.	är zäg'-te eem dee poo'-re vär'-hīt.
They say, he told the untruth.	Man sagt, er habe die Unwahrheit gesprochen.	män zägt, är hü'-be dee un'-vär'-hīt ge-shproch'-en.
You talk nonsense.	Du sprichst Unsinn.	doo shprihst un'-zinn'.
We can talk while we walk.	Wir können während des Gehens sprechen.	veer kin'-nen vai'-rent däs gäh'-ens shprah'-en.
It is our turn to speak.	Die Reihe ist an uns, zu sprechen.	dee rī'-he ist än uns, tsoo shprah'-en.
You speak in vain.	Sie reden in den Wind.	zee rä'-den in dän vint.
He talks at random.	Er redet in den Tag hinein.	är rä'-det in dän täg hin-īn'.
He nearly lost his head for talking too freely.	Er hätte sich beinahe um den Kopf gesprochen.	är hat'-te zih bī'-näh'-e um dän kopf ge-shproch'-en.
Let us not talk of it any more.	Wir wollen nicht mehr davon sprechen.	veer vol'-len niht mär dä-fon' shprah'-en.
Parrots utter words, but they do not speak.	Papageien sprechen Wörter aus, aber sie reden nicht.	pä-pä-gī'-en shprah'-en vir'-ter ous, ä'-ber zee rä'-den niht.
Do not speak to me about it.	Reden Sie mir nicht davon.	rä'-den zee meer niht dä-fon'.
You talk so much about it.	Sie machen so viel Redens davon.	zee mäch'-en zō feel rä'-dens dä-fon'.
Didn't I tell you so?	Habe ich es Ihnen nicht gesagt?	hä'-be ih es ee'-nen niht ge-zägt'?
Wisdom keeps silence while folly talks.	Die Weisheit schweigt, während die Narrheit schwatzt.	dee vīs'-hīt shvīgt, vai'-rent dee närr'-hīt shvätst.

I have also to say a word.	Ich habe auch ein Wort mitzusprechen.	iḥ hä'-be ouch ĭn vort mit'-tsoo-shprạḥ'-en.
One word called for the other.	Ein Wort gab das andere.	ĭn vort gĭp das an'-de-re'.
I will not be amused with fair words.	Ich lasse mich nicht mit leeren Worten abspeisen.	iḥ lás'-se miḥ niḥt mit lä'-ren vor'-ten ap'-shpī-zen.
He has quick delivery.	Die Worte fließen ihm aus dem Munde.	dee vor'-te flee'-ssen eem ous dām mụn'-de.
He speaks German fluently.	Er spricht fließend deutsch.	är shpriḥt flee'-ssent doitsh.
You, too, speak German, I suppose.	Auch Sie sprechen deutsch, glaube ich.	ouch zee shprạḥ'-en doitsh, glou'-be iḥ.
Not very fluently, only enough to make myself understood.	Nicht sehr geläufig, blos genug, um mich verständlich zu machen.	niḥt zär ge-loi'-fig, blōs ge-noog' ụm miḥ fer-shtạnt'-liḥ tsoo mạch'-en.
I speak a broken German.	Ich spreche gebrochen deutsch.	iḥ shprạḥ'-e ge-broch'-en doitsh.
There are too many German dialects.	Es giebt der deutschen Dialekte zu viele.	es gipt där doit'-shen di'-ȧ-lạk'-te tsoo fee'-le.
But the educated man speaks a pure and correct German.	Aber der Gebildete spricht ein reines, richtiges Deutsch.	ä'-ber där ge-bil'-de-te' shpriḥt īn rī'-nes, riḥ'-ti-ges' doitsh.
The language is as beautiful, as it is difficult.	Die Sprache ist so schön, wie sie schwer ist.	dee shprä'-che ist zō shīn, vee zee shvär ist.
It is a mother-tongue of several daughters.	Es ist eine Muttersprache mehrerer Töchter.	es ist ī'-ne mụt'-ter-shprä'-che mä'-re-rer' tiḥ'-ter.
It is both an ancient and a modern language.	Sie ist sowohl eine alte, als moderne Sprache.	zee ist zo-vōl ī'-ne al'-te, als mo-dạr'-ne shprä'-che.
Let us speak German a little.	Sprechen wir ein wenig deutsch.	shprạḥ'-en veer īn vä'-nig doitsh.
You speak so sensibly.	Sie reden so vernünftig.	zee rä'-den zō fer-nĭnf'-tig.
I can talk all day.	Ich kann den ganzen Tag plaudern.	iḥ kạn dān gạn'-tsen täg plou'-dern.
But I can also be tacit.	Ich kann aber auch verschwiegen sein.	iḥ kạn ä'-ber ouch fer-shvee'-gen zīn.
He is very close, reserved.	Er ist sehr schweigsam.	är ist zär shvīg'-zäm.
I shall tell him.	Ich werde es ihm sagen.	iḥ vär'-de es eem zä'-gen.
Don't speak a word about it.	Sage kein Wort davon.	zä'-ge kīn vort dä-fon'.
About what shall we converse?	Worüber sollen wir uns unterhalten?	vor-ü'-ber zol'-len veer ụns ụn'-ter-häl'-ten?
About the speech of Mr. Mundstück.	Ueber die Rede des Herrn Mundstück.	ü'-ber dee rä'-de das hạrrn mụnt'-shtĭk.
He is a very good speaker.	Der ist ein sehr guter Redner.	där ist īn zär goo'-ter räd'-ner.
His speech was excellent.	Seine Rede war ausgezeichnet.	zī'-ne rä'-de vär ous-ge-tsīḥ'-net.
I call that speaking.	Das nenne ich noch reden.	däs nạn'-ne iḥ noch rä'-den.
What is the difference between speaking, saying and telling?	Was ist der Unterschied zwischen sprechen, sagen und reden?	vás ist där ụn'-ter-sheet tsvish'-en shprạḥ'-en, zä'-gen ụnt rä'-den?
When I spoke to you, you told me he had talked.	Als ich zu Dir sprach, sagtest Du mir, er habe geredet.	als iḥ tsoo deer shprüch, zäg'-test doo meer, är hä'-be ge-rä'-det.

English	German	Pronunciation
I have been told that you have something to tell [say to] me.	Man hat mir gesagt, Sie hätten mir etwas zu sagen.	män hät meer ge-zägt', zee hät'-ten meer ät'-väs tsoo zä'-gen.
He does not speak, he chatters.	Er redet nicht, er schwatzt.	är rā'-det niht, är shvätst.
I tell you for the second time: Speak!	Ich sage Dir zum zweiten Male: Sprich!	ih zä'-ge deer tsum tsvī'-ten mä'-le: shprih!
And the Lord spake to him, saying: Speak to them, conceal nothing.	Und der Herr sprach zu ihm und sagte: Rede zu ihnen, verschweige nichts.	unt där harr shpräch tsoo eem unt zäg'-te: rā'-de tsoo ee'-nen, fer-shvī'-ge nihts.
Say nothing but what you can answer for.	Sage nichts, was Du nicht verantworten kannst.	zä'-ge nihts, väs doo niht fer-änt'-vor'-ten känst.
People say — — So they say.	Die Leute sagen — — So sagen sie.	dee loi'-te zä'-gen — — zō zä'-gen zee.
He knows something of the matter.	Er versteht darüber zu sprechen.	är fer-shtāt' där-ü'-ber tsoo shpräh'-en.
The plain meaning of the long speech.	Der langen Rede kurzer Sinn.	där läng'-en rā'-de kur'-tser zinn.
Wisdom opens its mouth.	Die Weisheit öffnet ihren Mund.	dee vīs'-hīt iff'-net ee'-ren munt.
Pst! Silence! Be silent! Hush!	Pst! Schweigt! Seid stille!	pst! shvīgt! zīt shtil'-le!

DAYS, DATES, MONTHS.

Tage, Daten, Monate.

(tä'-ge)   (dä'-ten)   (mō'-nä'-te)

English	German	Pronunciation
I write every Monday.	Ich schreibe jeden Montag.	ih shrī'-be yä'-den mōn'-täg.
I paid him the money last Tuesday.	Ich zahlte ihm vorigen Dinstag das Geld.	ih tsül'-te eem fō'-ri-gen' deens'-täg däs galt.
We meet on the second Wednesday of every month.	Wir kommen am zweiten Mittwoch eines jeden Monats zusammen.	veer kom'-men äm tsvī'-ten mit'-voch ī'-nes yä'-den mō'-näts' tsoo-zäm'-men.
You shall have them without fail next Thursday.	Sie sollen sie unfehlbar nächsten Donnerstag haben.	zee zol'-len zee un'-fāl'-bär naih'-sten don'-ners-täg' hä'-ben.
The mail steamers from America arrive every day.	Die Post-Dampfer von Amerika kommen jeden Tag an.	dee post'-dämp'-fer fon ä-mā'-ri-kä' kom'-men yä'-den täg än.
Friday is fish day.	Freitag ist Fischtag.	frī'-täg ist fish'-täg.
I hope to see you next Saturday.	Ich hoffe, Sie nächsten Samstag zu sehen.	ih hof'-fe, zee naih-sten zäms'-täg tsoo zäh'-en.
The German Sunday is the people's holiday.	Der deutsche Sonntag ist ein Feiertag für's Volk.	där doit'-she zonn'-täg ist īn fī'-er-täg' fīr's folk.
I passed the day in sadness.	Ich verbrachte den Tag in Traurigkeit.	ih fer-bräch'-te dän täg in trou'-rig-kīt'.
To-day we have, yesterday we had, to-morrow we shall have.	Heute haben wir, gestern hatten wir, morgen werden wir haben.	hoi'-te hä'-ben veer, gäs'-tern hät'-ten veer, mor'-gen vār'-den veer hä'-ben.
He promised me last night to call to-morrow morning.	Er versprach mir gestern Abend, morgen früh vorzusprechen.	är fer-shpräch' meer gäs'-tern ä'-bent, mor'-gen frü fōr'-tsoo-shpräh'-en.

English	German	Pronunciation
There are three days between the day before yesterday and the day after to-morrow.	Es sind drei Tage zwischen vorgestern und übermorgen.	es zint drī tä'-ge tsvish'-en för-gns'-tern unt ü'-ber-mor'-gen.
I saw him only once, the next day he had left.	Ich sah ihn nur Ein Mal, am folgenden Tage war er abgereis't.	ih zāh een noor īn'-māl, ām fol'-gen-den' tä'-ge vār ār åp'-ge rīst'.
In the forenoon he talks, in the afternoon he sleeps, and in the evening he plays.	Vormittags schwatzt er, Nachmittags schläft er und Abends spielt er.	for'-mit'-tägs' shvåtst ār, nåch'-mit'-tägs' shlāift ār unt ü'-bents shpeelt ār.
How does he spend the night?	Wie verbringt er die Nacht?	vee fer-bringt' ār dee nåcht?
How would you like a hunting party every week and a ball every two weeks?	Wie würde Ihnen jede Woche eine Jagdpartie und alle 14 Tage ein Ball gefallen?	vee vīr'-de ee'-nen yā'-de voch'-e ī'-ne yächt'-pār-tee' unt ål'-le 14 tä'-ge īn båll ge-fål'-len?
That would be a hunting party and a ball every fortnight.	Das würde alle zwei Wochen eine Jagdpartie und ein Ball sein.	dås vīr'-de ål'-le tsvī voch'-en ī'-ne yächt'-pār-tee' unt īn båll zīn.
Please tell me, what day of the month it is.	Sagen Sie mir gefälligst, was für ein Datum heute ist.	zä'-gen zee meer ge-fål'-ligst, vås fīr īn dā'-tum hoi'-te ist.
You may expect me before the end of this month.	Erwarten Sie mich vor dem Ende dieses Monats.	er-vår'-ten zee mih för dām an'-de dee'-zes mō'-nāts.
His quarter will expire on the 30th of this month.	Sein Quartal läuft mit dem 30sten dieses Monats ab.	zīn kvár-täl' louft mit dām 30sten' dee'-zes mō'-nāts' åp.
He left on the 25th of last month.	Er reis'te am 25sten vorigen Monats ab.	ār rīz'-te ām 25sten' fō'-ri-gen' mō'-nāts' åp.
He died on the 27th of January 1858, in the prime of his life.	Er starb am 27. Januar 1858 in der Blüthe seines Lebens.	ār shtårp ām 27sten' yå'-nu-år' 1858 in dār blü'-te zī'-nes lā'-bens.
He was born the 15th of June, 1798.	Er war am 15ten Juni 1798 geboren.	ār vār ām 15ten yoo'-nee 1798 ge-bō'-ren.
Spring begins on the 21st of March, summer on the 22d of June, autumn on the 23d of September, and winter on the 22d of December.	Der Frühling beginnt am 21sten März, der Sommer am 22sten Juni, der Herbst am 23sten September und der Winter am 22. Dezember.	dār frü'-ling be-gint' ām 21. mårts, dār zom'-mer ām 22. yoo'-nee, dār harpst ām 23. zap'-tām'-ber unt dār vin'-ter ām 22. dā'-tsąm'-ber.
These are the four seasons of the year.	Das sind die vier Jahreszeiten.	dås zint dee feer yā'-res-tsī'-ten.
April is generally a rainy month.	Der April ist gewöhnlich ein regnerischer Monat.	dār åp-rill' ist ge-vȳn'-lih īn rūg'-ne-ri'-sher mō'-nåt'.
The country looks beautiful in the month of May —	Im Monat Mai sieht's auf dem Lande sehr schön aus —	im mō'-nåt' mī zeet's ouf dām lån'-de zār shȳn ous—
When early larks soar upward warbling.	Wenn frühe Lerchen trillernd aufwärts steigen.	van früh'-e lar'-hen tril'-larnt ouf'-vårts shtī'-gen.
August, September and October are the harvest months.	August, September und Oktober sind die Erntemonate.	ou-gust', zap'-tąm'-ber unt ok-tō'-ber zint dee arn'-te-mō'-nā'-te.

Such seed he sows, such harvest he'll find.	Wie er säet, so wird er ernten.	vee är zait, zō virt är ąrn'-ten.
The meadows are mowed in June.	Im Juni werden die Wiesen gemäht.	im yoo'-nee vŭr'-den dee vee'-zen ge-mait'.
A year has twelve months.	Ein Jahr besteht aus zwölf Monaten.	In yĭr be-shtāt ous tsvĭlf mō'-nä'-ten.
Charles the Great called the months by the following German names:	Karl der Große gab den Monaten folgende deutsche Namen:	kärl där grō'-sse gäp dän mō'-nä'-ten fol'-gen-de' doit'-she nä'-men:
January he called Wintermonth,	Den Januar nannte er Wintermonat,	dän yä'-nụ-är nån'-te är vĭn'-ter-mō'-nät',
February—Hornung,	den Februar Hornung [Hor, Koth],	dän fäb'-rụ ūr' hor'-nụng' [hōr, kōt],
March—Spring month,	den März Frühlingsmonat,	dän märts frü'-lings-mō'-nät',
April—Easter month,	den April Ostermonat,	dän äp'ril ō'-ster-mō'-nät',
May—Month of Delight,	den Mai Wonnemonat,	dän mī von'-ne-mō'-nät',
June—Hay month,	den Juni Heumonat,	dän yoo'-nee hoi'-mō'-nät',
July—Summer month,	den Juli Sommermonat,	dän yoo'-lee zom'-mer mō'-nät',
August—Harvest month,	den August Erntemonat,	dän ou-gụst' ąrn'-te-mō'-nät',
September — Autumn month,	den September Herbstmonat,	dän ząp'-tam-ber hąrpst'-mō'-nät',
October—Wine month,	den Oktober Weinmonat,	dän ok-tō'-ber vīn'-mō'-nät',
November — Hoar-frost month,	den November Reifmonat,	dän no-vąm'-ber rīf'-mō'-nät',
December — Salvation month.	den Dezember Heilmonat.	dän dā'-tsąm'-ber hīl'-mō'-nät'.
We had fine weather during the whole month.	Wir hatten diesen ganzen Monat schönes Wetter.	veer hät'-ten dee'-zen gän'-tsen mō'-nät' shį'-nes vąt'-ter.
We arrived in Bremen 8 days ago.	Wir kamen vor 8 Tagen in Bremen an.	veer kä'-men fōr ącht tä'-gen in brä'-men än.
Some almanacs contain weather prognostics.	Im Kalender stehen Wetterregeln.	im kä-ląn'-der shtäh'-en vet'-ter-rä'-geln.
Jews and Turks have their own computations of time.	Juden und Türken haben ihre eigenen Zeitrechnungen.	yoo'-den unt tĭr'-ken hä'-ben ee'-re ī'-ge-nen' tsīt'-rąh'-nụng'-en.
The Millennium is near.	Das tausendjährige Reich ist nahe.	däs tou'-zent-yai'-ri-ge' rīh ist näh'-e.
An Olympiad was a period of four years.	Eine Olympiade war ein Zeitraum von vier Jahren.	ī'-ne o-lim'-pi-ä'-de vär īn tsīt'-roum fon feer yä'-ren.
Seven years are a Sabbath year, and the 50th year is the year of Jubilee.	Sieben Jahre sind ein Sabbathjahr, und das 50ste Jahr ist ein Jubeljahr.	zee'-ben yä'-re zint īn ząb'-bät-yär', unt däs 50ste yär ist īn yoo' bel-yär'.
A leap-year has 366 days.	Ein Schaltjahr hat 366 Tage.	īn shält'-yär' hät 366 tä'-ge.
The German Empire was restored in Versailles on the 18th of January, 1871.	Am 18ten Januar 1871 wurde in Versailles das deutsche Kaiserreich wieder hergestellt.	ąm 18ten yä'-nụ-är' 1871 vụr'-de in vąr-zā'-y däs doit'-she kī'-zer-rīh vee'-der här'-ge-shtąllt'.

JOYS. SORROWS.
Freuden. Leiden.
(froi'-den) (lī'-den)

English	German	Pronunciation
Joy, gladness, mirth.	Freude, Fröhlichkeit, Lust.	froi'-de, frȳ'-liḥ-kīt', lust.
The former two lie more internal.	Die beiden ersten sind mehr innerlich.	dee bī'-den ärs'-ten zint mār in'-ner liḥ'.
The latter is more external.	Letztere zeigt sich mehr äußerlich.	lats'-te-re' tsīgt ziḥ mār oi'-sser-liḥ'.
It is temporary.	Sie ist vorübergehend.	zee ist for-ü'-ber-gāh'-ent.
What joy! What a pleasure!	Welche Freude! Welches Vergnügen!	val'-ḥe froi'-de, val'-ḥes fer-gnü'-gen.
What unexpected luck [fortune]!	Welch' unerwartetes Glück!	valḥ' un'-er-vâr'-te-tes' glik!
What a happy moment!	Welch' glücklicher Augenblick'!	valḥ' glïk'-li-ḥer' ou'-gen-blīk'!
How happy we are!	Wie glücklich sind wir!	vee glïk'-liḥ zint veer!
A pleasant chance brought you to us.	Ein freudiger Zufall führte Sie zu uns.	īn froi'-di-ger' tsoo'-fåll fīr'-te zee tsoo uns.
I am charmed, pleased, delighted.	Ich bin erfreut, entzückt, vergnügt.	iḥ bin er-froit', ent-tsïkt', fer-gnügt'.
I am very glad of it.	Es freut mich sehr.	es froit miḥ zār.
I am very happy.	Ich bin sehr glücklich.	iḥ bin zār glïk'-liḥ.
I am extremely glad.	Es freut mich außerordentlich; or, ich bin außerordentlich froh.	es froit miḥ ou'-sser-or'-dent-liḥ'; or, iḥ bin ou'-sser-or'-dent-liḥ' frō.
It gives me great pleasure to know that you returned safe and much improved in health.	Es macht mir viele Freude, Sie gesund, gestärkt und wohlbehalten zurückgekehrt zu sehen.	es mácht meer fee'le froi'-de, zee ge-zunt', ge-shtärkt' unt vōl'-he-häl'-ten tsu-rïk'-ge-kārt' tsoo zäh'-en.
It gives me a great deal of joy.	Es macht mir viel Freude.	es mácht meer feel froi'-de.
I wish you much pleasure.	Ich wünsche Ihnen viel Vergnügen.	iḥ vïn'-she ee'-nen feel fer-gnü'-gen.
I sincerely congratulate you on it.	Ich gratulire Ihnen aufrichtig dazu.	iḥ grå'-tu-lee'-re ee'-nen ouf'-riḥ'-tig då-tsoo'.
I am in a very good [bad] humor.	Ich bin in sehr guter [schlechter] Laune; or, sehr gut [schlecht] aufgelegt.	iḥ bin in zār goo'-ter [shlaḥ'-ter] lou'-ne; or, zār goot [shlaḥt] ouf'-ge-lägt'.
I am very sorry for your not accepting my offer.	Es thut mir leid, daß Sie mein Anerbieten nicht annehmen.	es toot meer līt, dås zee mīn án'-er-bee'-ten niḥt án'-nā'-men.
I am greatly afflicted.	Ich bin sehr betrübt.	iḥ bin zār be-trüpt'.
I am impatient, angry, that I might cry.	Ich bin ungeduldig, ärgerlich, traurig, daß ich weinen möchte.	iḥ bin un'-ge-dul'-dig, ạr'-ger-liḥ', trou'-rig, dås iḥ vī'-nen miḥ'-te.
He is low spirited at present.	Er ist jetzt ganz niedergeschlagen.	er ist yatst gånts nee'-der-ge-shlä'-gen.
His indifference is provoking.	Seine Gleichgültigkeit ist ärgerlich.	zī'-ne glīḥ'-gïl'-tig-kīt' ist ạr'-ger-liḥ'.
It grieves [vexes] me beyond expression.	Es verdrießt [ärgert] mich über alle Maßen.	es fer-dreest' [ạr'-gert] miḥ ü'-ber ål'-le mä'-ssen.

To my great regret.	Zu meinem großen Leibwesen.	tsoo mī'-nem grö'-ssen līt'-vā'-zen.
What misfortune [disaster]!	Welch' ein Unglück!	valh' īn ụn'-glĭk'!
Poor, unhappy, unfortunate man!	Armer, unglücklicher Mann!	ár'-mer, ụn'-glĭk'-li-her' män!
It is a pity, ever pitiful; a thousand pities.	Es ist Schade, ewig Schade; Jammer und Schade, [jammerschade]!	es ist shä'-de, ā'-vig shä'-de; yäm'-mer ụnt shä'-de [yäm'-mer-shä'-de]!
For God's sake!	Um Gottes Willen!	ụm got'-tes vil'-len!
It is terrible, provoking, shocking.	Das ist schrecklich, ärgerlich, anstößig.	däs ist shrak'-lih, ạr'-ger-lih, än'-shtī'-ssig.
It makes one's hair stand on end.	Da stehen Einem die Haare zu Berge.	dä shtūh'-en ī'-nem dee hü'-re tsoo bạr'-ge.
What a pity!	Wie Schade!	vee shü'-de!

SENTENCES WITH SPECIAL REFERENCE TO GRAMMAR.

Sätze mit besonderer Rücksicht auf die Grammatik.

(zạt'-se mit be-zon'-de-rer' rĭk'-ziht ouf dee gräm'-mät'-tik)

Adjectives, Adverbs, Conjunctions, Prepositions, etc., in their proper application.

Eigenschaftswörter (ī'-gen-shäfts-vīr'-ter), Neben= oder Umstandswörter (nä'-ben-ö'-der ụm'-shtánts-vīr'-ter), Bindewörter (bin'-de-vīr'-ter), Verhältniß= wörter (fer-hạlt'-nis-vīr'-ter) u. s. w. (ụnt zō vī'-ter) in ihrer richtigen Anwendung (in ee'-rer rih'-ti-gen' án'-vạn-dụng).

Half of the money will do.	Das halbe Geld reicht hin.	däs hál'-be gạlt rĭht hin.
He was here all the time.	Er war die ganze Zeit hier.	är vär dee gạn'-tse tsīt heer.
To the right and to the left.	Rechts und links.	rạhts ụnt links.
I know him by sight.	Ich kenne ihn von Ansehen.	ih kạn'-ne een fon án'-zāh'-en.
With your permission.	Mit Ihrer (dat.) Erlaubniß.	mit ee' rer er-loup'-niss.
Please give me a glass of sugared water.	Gieb mir ein Glas Zuckerwasser, bitte!	geep meer īn gläs tsụk'-ker-väs'-ser, hit'-te.
It is not worth mentioning.	Es ist nicht der (gen.) Erwähnung werth.	es ist niht där er-vai'-nụng värt.
I am greatly [extremely] indebted [obliged] to you.	Ich bin Ihnen sehr [außerordentlich] verbunden.	ih bin ee'-nen zär [ou'-sser-or'-dent-lih'] fer-bụn'-den.
You are joking, for it is not worth while.	Sie scherzen, denn es ist nicht der Mühe werth.	zee shạr'-tsen, dạnn es ist niht där müh'-e värt.

English	German	Pronunciation
I give you much trouble.	Ich mache Ihnen viele Mühe.	iḥ mách'-e ee'-nen fee'-le müh'-e.
You take [give yourself] a great deal of trouble.	Sie geben [machen] sich viele Mühe.	zee gä'-ben [mách'-en] ziḥ fee'-le müh'-e.
I am sorry to trouble you so much.	Es dauert mich [thut mir leid], Ihnen so viele Mühe zu machen.	es dou'-ert miḥ [toot meer līt], ee'-nen zō fee'-le müh'-e tsoo mách'-en.
I am ashamed, that I give you so much trouble.	Ich schäme mich, daß ich Ihnen so viele Mühe mache.	iḥ shai'-me miḥ, dás iḥ ee'-nen zō fee'-le müh'-e mách'-e.
No trouble at all.	Gar keine Mühe.	gär kī'-ne müh'-e.
I beg you not to mention it.	Bitte, dessen nicht zu erwähnen.	bit'-te, dás'-sen niḥt tsoo er-vai'-nen.
You are very kind [polite], Sir.	Sie sind sehr gütig [höflich], mein Herr.	zee zint zār gü'-tig [hȫf'-liḥ], mīn harr.
That is to say.	Das ist [das heißt].	dás ist [dás hīst].
You don't say so! Indeed! I declare!	Was Sie nicht sagen! Ei, das wäre! (In Leipzig:) Lieber gar!	vás zee niḥt zä'-gen! I, dás vai'-re! (in līp'-tsig): lee'-ber gär!
I say! The other day.	Hören Sie 'mal! Eines Tages.	hȫ'-ren zee 'mäl! I'-nes tä'-ges.
That is very unfortunate.	Das ist sehr unglücklich.	dás ist zār un'-glük'-liḥ.
They escaped without loss.	Sie kamen ohne Verlust davon.	zee kä'-men ō'-ne fer-lust' dá-fon'.
He borrowed a small sum from me to pay his debts.	Er borgte eine kleine Summe von mir, seine Schulden zu bezahlen.	är borg'-te ī'-ne klī'-ne zum'-me fon meer, zī'-ne shul'-den tsoo be-tsä'-len.
I am fully assured of it.	Ich bin völlig davon überzeugt.	iḥ bin fïl'-lig dá-fon ü'-ber-tsoigt'.
I saw him in the daytime.	Ich sah ihn bei Tage.	iḥ zäh een bī tä'-ge.
He desired to be introduced into the family.	Er wünschte, in die Familie eingeführt zu werden.	är vünsh'-te, in dee fá-mee'-li-ye īn'-ge-führt tsoo vär'-den.
I paid the money into your own hands.	Ich zahlte das Geld in Ihre eigenen Hände.	iḥ tsäl'-te dás galt in ee'-re I'-ge-nen' hän'-de.
You will find me in the restaurant at four o'clock.	Sie werden mich gegen vier Uhr im Restaurant treffen.	zee vär'-den miḥ gä'-gen feer oor im ras'-to-ráng' traf'-fen.
I hope to see you again.	Auf Wiedersehen.	ouf vee'-der-zäh'-en.
What do you want?	Was willst Du?	vás vilst doo?
What are you looking for?	Was suchst Du?	vás zoochst doo?
What are you looking at?	Wonach siehst Du?	vo-nách' zeest doo?
Where are you going to?	Wo gehst Du hin?	vō gāhst doo hin?
Are you fond of children, of music, of this or that dish, of shooting or fishing, playing at billiards or smoking?	Magst Du gern Kinder leiden, Musik hören, diese oder jene Speise essen, auf die Jagd oder auf den Fischfang gehen, Billard spielen, Tabak rauchen?	mägst doo gärn kin'-der lī'-den, mu-zeek' hȫ'-ren, dee'-ze ō'-der yä'-ne shpī'-ze as'-sen, ouf dee yácht ō'-der ouf dän fish'-fáng' gäh'-en, bil'-yárt shpee'-len, tä'-bák rou'-chen?
At all events you must call on me once more before you go on board.	Jedenfalls mußt Du noch einmal bei mir vorsprechen, ehe Du an Bord gehst.	yä'-den-fáls' musst doo noch īn'-mäl' bī meer fōr-shpreḥ'-en, äh'-e doo án bort gähst.

English	German	Pronunciation
The wife of the landlord is the landlady.	Die Frau des Wirthes heißt „Frau Wirthin."	dee frou das vir'-tes hist frou vir'-tin.
Two weeks ago you loaned me one hundred marks —	Vor 14 Tagen haben Sie mir 100 Marken geliehen —	för seer'-tsän tä'-gen hä'-ben zee meer hun'-dert mår'-ken ge-leeh'-en —
And a week ago fifty.	Und vor einer Woche 50.	unt för i'-ner voch'-e fïnf'-tsig.
I now return the whole sum to you with my best thanks.	Ich gebe Ihnen die ganze Summe mit meinem besten Danke zurück.	ih gä'-be ee'-nen dee gån'-tse zum'-me mit mi'-nem bås'-ten dång'-ke tsoo-rïk'.
You are very punctual.	Sie sind sehr pünktlich.	zee zint zür pïnkt'-lih'.
Don't mention it.	Keine Ursache.	kï'-ne ur'-zåch'-e.
This is the cause of it.	Das ist die Ursache davon.	dås ist dee ur'-zåch'-e då-fon'.
Never mind; no matter.	Thut nichts; macht nichts aus.	toot nihts; måcht nihts ous.
I got them at a very low price.	Ich bekam sie spottwohlfeil.	ih be-kåm' zee shpott'-völ'-fïl.
A bargain is a bargain.	Kauf ist Kauf.	kouf ist konf.
Into the bargain.	In den Kauf; or, oben drein.	in dän kouf; or, ō'-ben drin.
A chance bargain.	Ein [zufälliger] billiger Einkauf.	In [tsoo'-fål'-li-ger'] bil'-li-ger' ïn'-kouf.
This day two weeks.	Heute über vierzehn Tage.	hoi'-te ü'-ber feer'-tsän tä'-ge.
Delay it till this day week.	Verschiebe es bis heute über acht Tage.	fer-shee'-be es bis hoi'-te ü'-ber åcht tä'-ge.
We must now go straight ahead.	Jetzt müssen wir gerade vorwärts gehen.	yåtst müs'-sen veer ge-rä'-de för'-vårts gäh'-en.
We always find a cover laid for us.	Wir finden immer ein Gedeck für uns gelegt.	veer fïn'-den im'-mer In ge-dåk' für uns ge-lägt'.
I [he, she, etc.] did certainly not mean to offend you.	Es war durchaus nicht so böse gemeint.	es vür durh-ous' niht zō bȫ'-ze ge-mïnt'.
He had scarcely begun —	Kaum hatte er angefangen —	koum håt'-te är ån'-ge-fång'-en —
You must not sit too far apart.	Ihr müßt nicht zu weit auseinander sitzen.	eer mïsst niht tsoo vit ous'-ïn-ån'-der zit'-sen.
I was nowhere else.	Ich war sonst nirgends.	ih vår zonst nir'-gents.
She shall never see me again.	Niemals soll sie mich wiedersehen.	nee'-måls zoll zee mih vee'-der-zäh'-en.
You may accompany me on my walk to-morrow.	Morgen kannst Du mich auf meinem Spaziergang begleiten.	mor'-gen kånst doo mih ouf mï'-nem shpå-tseer'gång be-glï'-ten.
He nearly broke his neck.	Er brach sich beinahe das Genick.	är brüch zih bī-näh'e dås ge-nik'.
We had just received the news.	Wir hatten eben die Nachricht erhalten.	veer håt'-ten ä'-ben dee nåch'-riht er-hål'-ten.
She had expected her husband's arrival for a long time.	Sie hatte ihres Gatten Ankunft lange erwartet.	zee håt'-te ee'-res gåt'-ten ån'-kunft' läng'-e er-vår'-tet.
It must always have been forgotten.	Es muß immer vergessen worden sein.	es mus im'-mer fer-gås'-sen vor'-den zïn.
Our lamp never burns well.	Unsere Lampe brennt nie gut.	un'-ze-re' låm'-pe brant nee goot.

English	German	Pronunciation
We should always have been ready to loan it to you.	Wir wären stets bereit gewesen, es Ihnen zu leihen.	veer vai'-ren shtäts be-rīt'-ge-vä'-zen, es ee'-nen tsoo līh'-en.
He lives there.	Er wohnt dort.	är vönt dort.
Send him here.	Schicken Sie ihn her.	shik'-ken zee een här.
Come, let us go away from here, there are pickpockets here.	Kommen Sie, lassen Sie uns von hier weggeben, hier giebt's Taschendiebe.	kom'-men zee, lås'-sen zee uns fon heer vag'-gäh'-en, heer geept's täsh'-en-dee'-be.
Where have you put my umbrella?	Wo haben Sie meinen Regenschirm hingestellt?	vō hä'-ben zee mī'-nen rā'-gen-shirm' hin'-ge-shtalt?
You must not keep me here long.	Sie müssen mich hier nicht lange aufhalten.	zee müs'-sen mih heer niht lång'-e ouf'-häl'-ten.
I must go to Frankfort from there.	Ich muß von dort nach Frankfurt.	ih mus fon dort näch fränk'-furt.
Hence we sought in vain.	Daher suchten wir umsonst.	dä-här' zooch'-ten veer um-zonst'.
The sound comes from there.	Der Schall kommt von da her.	där shåll komt fon dä här.
You cannot start until I return.	Erst, wenn ich zurückkomme, wirst Du abreisen können.	ärst, van ih tsoo-rik'-kom'-me, virst doo äp'-rī'-zen kin'-nen.
He promised me that six years ago.	Das versprach er mir schon vor sechs Jahren.	dås fer-shpriich' är meer shōn fōr zäks yä'-ren.
I was here before you.	Ich war vor Ihnen hier.	ih vär fōr ee'-nen heer.
Thou art just in time.	Du kommst gerade zur rechten Zeit.	doo komst ge-rä'-de tsur rah'-ten tsīt.
I have done; I am ready to go.	Ich bin fertig; ich bin reisefertig.	ih bin får'-tig; ih bin rī'-ze-får'-tig.
I will try it, let the thing turn out as it may.	Wie die Sache auch ausfallen mag, ich werde es versuchen.	vee dee zäch'-e ouch ous'-fäl'-len mäg, ih vär'-de es fer-zoo'-chen.
Bring me some ice cream and a glass of wine.	Bringe mir ein Gefrornes und ein Glas Wein.	bring'-e meer īn ge-frōr'-nes unt īn glås vīn.
Has he also sold his white horse?	Hat er seinen Schimmel auch verkauft?	hät är zī'-nen shim'-mel ouch fer-kouft'?
These pears are ripe and very sweet.	Diese Birnen sind reif und auch sehr süß.	dee'-ze bir'-nen zint rīf unt ouch zār züss.
That's the very book I want.	Das ist gerade das Buch, das ich brauche.	dås ist ge-rä'-de dås booch, dås ih brou'-che.
It is just four o'clock.	Es ist gerade vier Uhr.	es ist ge-rä'-de feer oor.
He was so hungry that he actually ate the bones.	Er war so hungrig, daß er sogar die Knochen aß.	är vär zō hung'-rig, dås är zo-gär' dee knoch'-en üs.
He actually said so.	Das hat er wirklich gesagt.	dås hät är virk'-lih ge-zügt'.
The picture hangs above the table.	Das Bild hangt über dem Tische.	dås bilt hänkt ü'-ber dåm tish'-e.
It is now past [over].	Jetzt ist es vorüber.	yatst ist es fōr-ü'-ber.
He rides over the bridge.	Er reitet über die Brücke.	är rī'-tet ü'-ber dee brik'-ke.
She receives letter upon letter.	Sie bekommt Briefe über Briefe.	zee be-komt' bree'-fe ü'-ber bree'-fe.
It happened during the night time.	Es kam so über Nacht.	es küm zō ü'-ber nåcht.

English	German	Pronunciation
The clouds were over [above] our heads.	Die Wolken waren über unsern Köpfen.	dee vol'-ken vä'-ren ü'-ber un'-zern kip'-fen.
The balloon has risen above the clouds.	Der Luftballon ist bis über die Wolken gestiegen.	där luft'-bal-lon' ist bis ü'-ber dee vol'-ken ge-shtee'-gen.
He has [is] not come yet.	Er ist noch nicht gekommen.	är ist noch niht ge-kom'-men.
It is still cold.	Es ist noch immer kalt.	es ist noch im'-mer kält.
Say that once more.	Sagen Sie das noch einmal.	zä'-gen zee däs noch in'-mäl'.
I must learn German, be it ever so difficult.	Ich muß deutsch lernen, wenn es auch noch so schwer ist.	ih mus doitsh lär'-nen, van es ouch noch zō shvär ist.
Thou learnest neither German nor English.	Du lernst weder deutsch, noch englisch.	doo lärnst vä'-der doitsh noch äng'-lish.
The footstool is under the table.	Der Fußschemel steht unter dem Tische.	där foos'-shä'-mel shtät un'-ter däm tish'-e.
This school is for children not ten years old.	Diese Schule ist für Kinder unter zehn Jahren.	dee'-ze shoo'-le ist fir kin'-der un'-ter tsän yä'-ren.
Who will enlist as a soldier?	Wer will unter die Soldaten?	vär vill un'-ter dee zol-dä'-ten?
That is not beneath his dignity.	Das ist nicht unter seiner Würde.	däs ist niht un'-ter zī'-ner vir'-de.
The two students had one single coat between themselves.	Die beiden Studenten hatten nur einen Rock unter sich.	dee bī'-den shtoo-dän'-ten hät'-ten noor ī'-nen rokk un'-ter zih.
She was the only lady among the passengers.	Sie war unter den Reisenden die einzige Dame.	zee vär un'-ter dän rī'-zen-den' dee īn'-tsi ge' dä'-me.
The soldier wears a cravat about the neck.	Der Soldat trägt eine Binde um den Hals.	där zol-dät' trägt ī'-ne bin'-de um dän häls.
He goes to church every third [alternate] day.	Er geht einen Tag um den andern in die Kirche.	är gäht ī'-nen tüg um dän än'-dern in dee kir'-he.
The meeting is his object.	Es ist ihm um die Zusammenkunft zu thun.	es ist eem um dee tsoo-zäm'-men-kunft' tsoo toon.
He had not a single pfennig about him.	Er hatte nicht einen einzigen Pfennig bei sich.	är hät'-te niht ī'-nen īn'-tsi gen' pfän'-nig bī zih.
Here the battle of Leipsic was fought.	Hier wurde die Schlacht bei Leipzig geschlagen.	heer vur'-de dee shlächt bī līp'-tsig ge-shlä'-gen.
I sat close by him in a second-class railway carriage.	Ich saß bei ihm im Eisenbahnwagen zweiter Klasse.	ih säs bī eem im ī'-zen-bän-vä'-gen tsvī'-ter kläs'-se.
By no means praise Germany while you travel in France.	Wenn Sie in Frankreich reisen, loben Sie Deutschland bei Leibe nicht.	van zee in fränk'-rīh rī'-zen, lō'-ben zee doitsh'-länt bī lī'-be niht.
You put me beside my patience.	Bei Ihnen verliere ich die Geduld.	bī ee'-nen fer-lee'-re ih dee ge-dult'.
You must not try to swim against the stream.	Wider den Strom muß man nicht schwimmen wollen.	vee'-der dän shtröm mus män niht shvim'-men vol'-len.
That is not to be stomached.	Das geht einem wider den Mann.	däs güht ī'-nem vee'-der dän män.
We considered the pro and con of the question.	Wir erwogen das Für und Wider der Frage.	veer er-vō'-gen däs fir unt vee'-der där frä'-ge.
That happened altogether against my will.	Das geschah ganz und gar wider meinen Willen.	däs ge-shä' gänts unt gär vee'-der mī'-nen vil'-len.

English	German	Pronunciation
He is in a dilemma *or* strait.	Er steckt zwischen Thür und Angel.	ār shtäkt tsvish'-en tür ụnt ång'-el.
That weighs from 20 to 30 pounds.	Das wiegt zwischen 20 und 30 Pfund.	dås veegt tsvish'-en 20 ụnt 30 pfụnt.
During all this time I was in suspense, *or* floated between doubt and certainty.	Während dieser ganzen Zeit schwebte ich zwischen Himmel und Erde.	vai'-rent dee'-zer gån'-tsen tsīt shvūp'-te ih tsvish'-en him'-mel ụnt ār'-de.
Apply to your consul.	Wenden Sie sich an Ihren Konsul.	vẹn'-den zee zih ån ee'-ren kon'-zụl.
There is Frankfort on the Main and on the Oder.	Es giebt ein Frankfurt am Main und an der Oder.	es geept īn fränk'-fụrt åm mīn ụnt ån dār ō'-der.
Now it is your turn.	Jetzt ist die Reihe an Ihnen.	yạtst ist dee rīh'-e ån ee'-nen.
Yes, my time of going is near.	Ja, es ist an dem, daß ich fort muß.	yä, es ist ån dām, dås ih fort mụs.
I had to pay 100 marks for making.	Ich hatte 100 Mark an Macherlohn zu zahlen.	ih håt'-te 100 mårk ån mach'-er-lōn' tsoo tsü'-len.
My wife was laid up with an illness.	Meine Frau lag an einer Krankheit darnieder.	mī'-ne frou läg ån ī'-ner kränk'-hīt då'-nee'-der.
After his leaving they fell a-crying.	Als er fort war, ging es an ein Schreien.	åls ār fort vär, ging es ån īn shrī'-en.
While I lived in the country, he was at the university.	Während ich auf dem Lande lebte, war er auf der Universität.	vai'-rent ih ouf dām lån'-de läp'-te, vär ār ouf dār ụ'-ni-vạr'-zi-tait'.
I waited for you, when you were out hunting.	Ich wartete auf Sie, als Sie auf der Jagd waren.	ih vår'-te-te' ouf zee, åls zee ouf dār yächt vü'-ren.
In this manner it always goes up and down.	Auf dieser Welt geht's immer auf und ab.	ouf dee' zer vạlt gäht's im'-mer ouf ụnt åp.
He has taken to drinking, and you say it is no matter.	Er hat sich auf's Trinken gelegt, und Sie sagen, es hat nichts auf sich.	ār håt zih ouf's tring'-ken ge-lägt', ụnt zee zä'-gen, es håt nihts ouf zih.
I tell you it is of great importance, for he was surprised in the very act.	Ich sage Ihnen, es hat viel auf sich, denn er wurde auf frischer That ertappt.	ih zä'-ge ee'-nen, es håt feel ouf zih, dạn ār vụr'-de ouf frish'-er tāt er-täpt'.
That is in German: all at once.	Das heißt auf deutsch: auf einmal.	dås hīst ouf doitsh, ouf īn'-mäl'.
I never thought much of him, for he was proud of his birth.	Ich habe nie viel auf ihn gehalten, denn er war stolz auf seine Geburt.	ih hä'-be nee feel ouf een ge-häl'-ten, dạn ār vär shtolts ouf zī'-ne ge-bụrt'.
Out of love and respect to thee, I tell thee it is out of fashion.	Aus Achtung und Liebe für Dich sage ich Dir, es ist aus der Mode.	ous åch'-tụng ụnt lee'-be fīr dih zä'-ge ih deer, es ist ous dār mō'-de.
What shall I think of you? Of nothing comes nothing.	Was soll ich aus Dir machen? Aus nichts wird nichts.	vås zoll ih ous deer mäch'-en? ous nihts virt nihts.
I know by experience what you see by this letter.	Ich weiß aus Erfahrung, was Sie aus dem Briefe sehen.	ih vīs ous er-fü'-rụng, vås zee ous dām bree'-fe zäh'-en.
One sees by his behavior that he blames him through hatred.	Man sieht aus seinem Betragen, daß er ihn aus Haß tadelt.	mån zeet ous zī'-nem be-trä'-gen, dås ār een ous hås tü'-delt.

English	German	Pronunciation
For want of money, not in obedience to you, did he stay away from the theatre.	Aus Mangel an Geld, nicht aus Gehorsam gegen Sie, ist er aus dem Theater geblieben.	ous mäng'-el än gält, niht ous ge-hōr'-zäm gā'-gen zee, ist är ous däm tā-ä'-ter ge-blee'-ben.
He does not know how to help himself.	Er weiß weder aus noch ein.	är vis vā'-der ous noch īn.
He came home ten minutes after four.	Zehn Minuten nach vier kam er nach Hause.	tsān mi-noo'-ten näch feer käm är näch hou'-ze.
Immediately upon my arrival I shall have to go to Vienna.	Gleich nach meiner Ankunft werde ich nach Wien reisen müssen.	glīh näch mī'-ner än'-kunft vär'-de ih näch veen rī'-zen mĭs'-sen.
To travel eight days successively in a railway car is not according to my taste.	Acht Tage nach einander auf der Eisenbahn zu reisen, ist nicht nach meinem Geschmacke.	ächt tā'-ge näch īn'-än'-der ouf där ī'-zen-bān' tsoo rī'-zen, ist niht näch mī'-nem ge-shmäk'-ke.
He attempted his life, in my opinion.	Nach meiner Meinung hat er ihm nach dem Leben getrachtet.	näch mī'-ner mī'-nung hät är eem näch däm lā'-ben ge-träch'-tet.
By degrees they do everything after the English fashion.	Nach gerade thun sie Alles nach englischer Mode.	näch-ge-rä'-de toon zee äl'-les näch äng'-li-sher' mō'-de.
I have drawn this from nature after my own manner.	Ich habe dies nach meiner eigenen Art nach der Natur gezeichnet.	ih hä'-be dees näch mī'-ner ī'-ge-nen' ärt näch där nä-toor' ge-tsīh'-net.
Agreeably to his commands this was written in the year of our Lord eighteen hundred eighty-eight.	Dies ist nach seinem Befehle im Jahre achtzehnhundert acht und achtzig nach Christi Geburt geschrieben worden.	dees ist näch zī'-nem be-fā'-le im yä'-re ächt'-tsän-hun'-dert ächt unt ächt'-tsig näch kris'-tee ge-boort' ge-shree'-ben vor'-den.
The people around me come from afar.	Die Leute um mich her kommen weit her.	dee loi'-te um mih här kom'-men vīt här.
He went quietly to and fro on deck, while I turned over in my mind where I had put the money.	Er ging auf dem Verdecke ruhig hin und her, während ich hin und her überlegte, wo ich das Geld hingelegt hatte.	är ging ouf däm fer-dak'-ke rooh'-ig hin unt här, vai'-rent ih hin unt här ü'-ber-lāg'-te, vō ih däs galt hin'-ge-lāgt' hät'-te.
He came downstairs when I went upstairs.	Er kam herab, als ich die Treppe hinauf ging.	är käm har-äp', äls ih dee trap'-pe hin-ouf'-ging.
I come here, and he is off.	Ich komme her, und er ist fort.	ih kom'-me här, unt är ist fort.
Go thither and ask him from what country he comes.	Gehen Sie hin und fragen Sie ihn, wo er herkomme.	gāh'-en zee hin unt frä'-gen zee een, vō är här kom'-me.
The young man feels himself drawn toward the maiden; so it was from the beginning.	Der Jüngling fühlt sich zu der Jungfrau hingezogen; das war so vom Anfange her.	där yĭng'-ling fült zih tsoo där yung'-frou' hin'-ge-tsō'-gen; däs vär zō fom än'-fäng'-e här.
He went out of the gate to see the wagon that stood before it.	Er ging vor das Thor, um den Wagen zu sehen, der davor stand.	är ging för däs tōr, um dän vä'-gen tsoo zāh'-en, där dä-för shtänt.
Beware of that merchant, he is on the point of bankruptcy.	Hüten Sie sich vor dem Kaufmann B., er steht vor dem Bankerott.	hü'-ten zee zih för däm kouf'-män B., är shtāt för däm bäng'-ke-rot'.
Formerly he used to anticipate payment.	Sonst hat er immer vor der Zeit bezahlt.	zonst hät är im'-mer för där tsīt be-tsält'.

English	German	Pronunciation
I warned him not to stoop to him.	Ich habe ihn gewarnt, nicht vor ihm zu kriechen.	ih hā'-be een ge-várnt'. niht fōr eem tsoo kree'-hen.
But he sticks to it now as before, and is sure to die of humble submission.	Er bleibt aber vor wie nach dabei, und wird noch vor Unterwürfigkeit sterben.	är blīpt ä'-ber fōr vee nāch dā-bī', unt virt noch fōr un'-ter-vir'-fig-kīt shtar'-ben.
He swam across the river and ran through the town.	Er schwamm durch den Strom und lief durch die Stadt.	är shvám durh dän shtröm unt leef durh dee shtät.
By favorable rules and with your assistance I shall come off.	Durch günstige Regeln und Ihren Beistand werde ich durchkommen.	durh gin'-sti-ge' rä'-geln unt ee'-ren bī'-shtänt' vär'-de ih durh'-kom-men.
The whistling of the robbers was heard all night, in day-time they kept themselves concealed.	Man hörte das Pfeifen der Räuber die ganze Nacht hindurch, den Tag durch hielten sie sich versteckt.	män hīr'-te dás pfī'-fen där roi'-ber dee gán'-tse nächt hin-durh, dän tāg durh heel'-ten zee zih fer-shtäkt'.
Your shoes are worn out, and mine are quite wet.	Deine Schuhe sind durch, und die meinigen sind durch und durch naß.	dī'-ne shooh'-e zint durh, unt dee mī'-ni-gen' zint durh unt durh nás.
It is time for them to undergo a complete repair.	Es ist Zeit, daß sie durch und durch ausgebessert werden.	es ist tsīt, dás zee durh unt durh ous'-ge-bäs'-sert vär'-den.
I tell you once for all, she has a little property of her own.	Ich sage Ihnen ein für allemal, sie hat etwas Vermögen für sich.	ih zä'-ge ee'-nen īn für ál'-le-māl, zee hát at'-vás fer-mī'-gen für zih.
Well, that is plausible.	Ja wohl, das hat etwas für sich.	yä vōl, dás hát at'-vás für zih.
I take this in payment.	Ich nehme das für Bezahlung an.	ih nä'-me dás für be-tsä'-lung án.
I live at the rate of ten dollars a week.	Ich lebe wöchentlich für zehn Dollars.	ih lä'-be vīh'-ent-lih' für tsān dol'-lers.
I take this to be my duty.	Das halte ich für meine Pflicht.	dás hál'-te ih für mī'-ne pfliht.
Take care, lest he escape.	Gieb Acht, daß er nicht entwischt.	geep ácht, dás är niht entvisht'.
He was excited in such a degree as to be unable to speak.	Er war in einem solchen Grade aufgeregt, daß er nicht sprechen konnte.	är vär in ī'-nem zol'-hen grä'-de ouf'-ge-rägt', dás är niht shpräh'-en kon'-te.
It is not an hour since I saw him.	Es ist noch keine Stunde, daß ich ihn gesehen habe.	es ist noch kī'-ne shtun'-de, dás ih een ge-zäh'-en hä'-be.
I wonder at your being here.	Ich wundre mich, daß Sie hier sind.	ih vun'-dre mih, dás zee heer zint.
I see, he comes without our inviting him.	Ich sehe, daß er kommt, ohne daß wir ihn einladen.	ih zäh'-e, dás är komt, ō'-ne dás veer een īn'-lä-den.
Mercy!	Daß Gott erbarm!	dás gott er-bárm'.
I take it, however good or bad the style may be.	Ich nehme es, wie gut oder schlecht der Styl auch [immer] sein mag.	ih nä'-me es, vee goot ō'-der shlaht där shteel ouch [im'-mer] zīn mäg.
Be that as it may, he acted like a madman.	Es sei dem, wie ihm wolle, er benahm sich wie ein Rasender.	es zī däm, vee eem vol'-le, är be-nä́m' zih vee īn rä'-zen-der'.

He cannot match me; no, he cannot come up with me.	Er kann mir nicht gleich kommen; nein, er kann es mir nicht gleich thun.	ār kån meer niht glīh kom'-men; nīn, ār kån es meer niht glīh toon.
It is all one to me.	Es gilt mir alles gleich.	es gilt meer ål'-les glīh.
I quit scores.	Ich bezahle ihn mit gleicher Münze.	ih be-tsä'-le een mit glī'-her mīn'-tse.
That is all the same.	Das ist gleichviel.	dås ist glīh'-feel'.
As I said; just so.	Wie ich sagte; nicht anders.	vee ih zāg'-te; niht ån'-ders.
I will come, provided you be at home.	Ich komme, wenn Sie anders zu Hause sind.	ih kom'-me, vąn zee ån'-ders tsoo hou'-ze zint.
Continue virtuous, and it will go well with you.	Bleibe tugendhaft, so wird es Dir gut gehen.	blī'-be too'-gent-håft', zō virt es deer goot gāh'-en.
So goes the world.	So geht es in der Welt.	zō gāht es in dār vąlt.
You never scolded in such a manner.	So haben Sie noch nie gescholten.	zō hä'-ben zee noch nee geshol'-ten.
Yes, such was her virtue.	Ja, so groß war ihre Tugend.	yå, zō grōs vār ee'-re too'-gent.
He knows nothing, for aught I know.	So viel ich weiß, weiß er nichts.	zō feel ih vīss, vīss er nihts.
My neighbor on the left is a fool with a witness.	Mein Nachbar zur Linken ist ein rechter Narr.	mīn nåch'-bår tsųr linken ist īn rąh'-ter nårr.
You are the proper person for it.	Sie sind der rechte Mann dazu.	zee zint dār rąh'-te mån då-tsoo'.
For once I must set him right.	Ich muß ihm einmal den Kopf zurecht setzen.	ih mus eem īn'-mäl' dān kopf tsoo-rąht' ząt'-sen.
He cannot get on with it.	Er kann nicht damit zurecht kommen.	ār kån niht då-mit' tsoo-rąht' kom'-men.
Surely, he is a downright honest man.	Gewiß, er ist ein recht ehrlicher Mann.	ge-vis', ār ist īn rąht ār'-li-her' mån.
Are you not in your right senses?	Sie sind wohl nicht recht gescheidt.	zee zint vōl niht rąht geshīt'.
You mistake my meaning.	Sie verstehen mich nicht recht.	zee fer-shtāh'-en mih niht rąht.
You come just in time.	Sie kommen eben recht.	zee kom'-men ā'-ben rąht.
Nothing will satisfy him.	Man kann ihm nichts recht machen.	mån kån eem nihts rąht måch'-en.
I consent to everything.	Mir ist alles recht.	meer ist ål'-les rąht.
He commanded, hence I was obliged to act thus.	Er befahl, ich mußte also.	ār be-fäl', ih mųs'-te ål'-zō.
You have promised it me then?	Sie haben es mir also versprochen?	zee hä'-ben es meer ål'-zō fer-shproch'-en?
I hope we have now passed the danger.	Nun, hoffe ich, sind wir außer Gefahr.	noon, hof'-fe ih, zint veer ou'-sser ge-fär'.
Besides seeing the old world, you will also learn several languages.	Außerdem, daß Sie die alte Welt sehen, werden Sie auch mehrere Sprachen lernen.	ou'-sser-däm, dås zee dee ål'-te vąlt zāh'-en, vār'-den zee ouch mā'-re-re' shprå'-chen lar'-nen.
Let us take a walk along the river.	Gehen wir am Flusse spazieren.	gāh'-en veer åm flus'-se shpå-tsee'-ren.
Potatoes are sold in England by the pound, and cherries in Saxony by the number of fifteen.	In England werden die Kartoffeln pfundweise verkauft, in Sachsen die Kirschen mandelweise.	in ąng'-lånt vār'-den dee kår'-tof'-feln pfųnt'-vī'-ze fer-kouft', in zåk'-sen dee kir'-shen mån'-del-vī'-ze.

English	German	Pronunciation
The steamboat will be ready by June.	Das Dampfboot wird bis Juni fertig sein.	däs dämpf'-bōt virt bis yoo'-nee far'-tig zīn.
Did you see the sailor taking hold of the rope?	Sahen Sie den Matrosen, wie er sich am Stricke hielt?	zäh'-en zee dän mȧt-rō'-zen, vee är zih̡ ȧm shtrik'-ke heelt?
Tobacco chewing is not customary among the Germans.	Bei den Deutschen ist das Tabakkauen ungebräuchlich.	bī dān doit'-shen ist däs tä'-bȧk'-kou'-en un'-ge-broih̡'-lih̡.
Answer me by next mail.	Antworten Sie mir mit nächster Post.	ȧnt'-vor'-ten zee meer mit naih̡'-ster post.
I recognized her by her walk.	Ich erkannte sie am Gange.	ih̡ er-kȧn'-te zee ȧm gäng'-e.

DIALOGUES.—Gespräche.
(ge-shprai'-h̡e)

Of the State of Health.—Vom Befinden (fom be-fin'-den).

Good morning, Sir [Madam, Miss]; how do you do?	Guten Morgen, mein Herr [Madame, Fräulein]; wie befinden Sie sich?	goo'-ten mor'-gen, mīn harr [mȧ-däm', froi'-līn]; vee be-fin'-den zee zih̡?
I thank you, very well; and you?	Ich danke Ihnen, sehr wohl; und Sie?	ih̡ däng'-ke ee'-nen, zār völ; unt zee?
I was afraid, you might be ill; it is a very long time, indeed, since I had the pleasure of seeing you.	Ich fürchtete, Sie seien krank; es ist schon so lange, daß ich nicht das Vergnügen hatte, Sie zu sehen.	ih̡ fīrh̡'-te-te', zee zī'-en kränk; es ist shōn zō läng'-e, däs ih̡ nih̡t däs fer-gnü'-gen hȧt'-te, zee tsoo zäh'-en.
How is your wife [husband, daughter, son, etc.]?	Wie befindet sich Ihre Frau [Ihr Gatte, Ihr Fräulein Tochter, Ihr Sohn, u. s. w.]?	vee be-fin'-det zih̡ ee'-re frou [eer gȧt'-te, eer froi'-līn toch'-ter, eer zōn, unt zō vī'-ter]?
Remarkably well; but my — is not well.	Vortrefflich; aber mein[e] — ist unwohl.	for-trȧf'-lih̡; ä'-ber mīn[e] — ist un'-vōl'.
I am very sorry for it.	Das thut mir sehr leid.	däs toot meer zār līt.
How is your own health?	Wie steht's mit Ihrer Gesundheit?	vee shtāts mit ee'-rer ge-zunt'-hīt?
I am not very well.	Ich befinde mich nicht recht wohl.	ih̡ be-fin'-de mih̡ nih̡t rȧht vōl.
What ails you?	Was fehlt Ihnen?	vȧs fālt ee'-nen?
I suffer very much.	Ich leide sehr.	ih̡ lī'-de zār.
I caught a heavy cold.	Ich habe mich sehr erkältet.	ih̡ hü'-be mih̡ zār er-kȧl'-tet.
I have headache.	Ich habe Kopfschmerzen.	ih̡ hü'-be kopf'-shmȧr'-tsen.
I have a cold in my head.	Ich habe den Schnupfen.	ih̡ hü'-be dän shnup'-fen.
I hope it will not be serious.	Ich hoffe, daß es nicht schlimm sein wird.	ih̡ hof'-fe, däs es nih̡t shlim zīn virt.
I hope you will soon get over it.	Ich hoffe, es wird bald vorüber sein.	ih̡ hof'-fe, es virt bält for-ü'-ber zīn.
It comes quickly and goes slowly.	Es kommt rasch und geht langsam.	es komt räsh unt gāt läng'-zȧm'.

English	German	Pronunciation
There is indeed nothing like good health.	Gesundheit geht doch über Alles.	ge-zunt'-hīt' gāt doch ü'-ber ål'-les.
A sick man, a poor man.	Ein kranker Mensch, ein armer Mensch.	īn kräng'-ker mansh, īn år'-mer mansh.
Better poor and healthy, than rich and sick.	Besser arm und gesund, als reich und krank.	bas'-ser årm unt ge-zunt', åls rīh unt kränk.

Rising.—Vom Aufstehen (fom ouf'-shtäh'-en).

Early to bed and early to rise, makes a man healthy and wealthy and wise.	Morgenstunde hat Gold im Munde.	mor'-gen-shtun'-de hāt golt im mun'-de.
What! You are not up yet?	Wie? Sie sind noch nicht auf?	vee? zee zint noch niht ouf?
It is time to rise.	Es ist Zeit, aufzustehen.	es ist tsīt, ouf'-tsoo-shtäh'-en.
I am still sleepy.	Ich bin noch schläfrig.	ih bin noch shlaif'-rig.
You are an idler, a sluggard, a loiterer.	Du bist ein Faulenzer, ein Tagedieb.	doo bist īn foul'-lan'-tser, īn tä'-ge-deep'.
I am going to rise immediately.	Ich werde gleich aufstehen.	ih vār'-de glīh ouf'-shtäh'-en.
Sleep is so sweet in the morning.	Morgens schläft's sich so süß.	mor'-gens shlaift's zih zō züss.
May be; but sweets are not always wholesome.	Mag sein; aber Süßes ist nicht immer gesund.	mäg zīn, ü'-ber zü'-sses ist niht im'-mer ge-zunt'.
Londoners usually get up late.	Die Londoner stehen gewöhnlich spät auf.	dee lon'-don-er shtäh'-en ge-vĭn'-lih shpait ouf.
But they go to bed at a late hour.	Sie gehen auch spät zu Bette.	zee gäh'-en ouch shpait tsoo bat'-te.
Thou art not a Londoner, consequently —	Du bist aber kein Londoner, folglich —	doo bist ä'-ber kīn lon'-don-er, folg'-lih —
Very well, I am getting up; what time is it?	Nun ja, ich stehe auf; wie viel Uhr ist's?	noon yä, ih shtäh'-e ouf; vee feel oor ist's?
It just struck nine o'clock.	Es hat eben neun geschlagen.	es hät ä'-ben noin ge-shlä'-gen.
I did not know it is so late.	Ich wußte nicht, daß es so spät ist.	ih vust'-te niht, dås es zō shpait ist.
Did you sleep well?	Haben Sie gut geschlafen?	hü'-ben zee goot ge-shlä'-fen?
Very well, thank you.	Sehr gut, ich danke Ihnen.	zār goot, ih däng'-ke ee'-nen.
Not particularly; I was awake often.	Nicht besonders, ich war oft wach.	niht be-zon'-ders, ih vär oft vách.
Thus I slept longer than usual.	Darum schlief ich länger als gewöhnlich.	där'-um shleef ih lang'-er åls ge-vĭn'-lih.
I went to bed late last night.	Ich ging gestern Abend spät zu Bette.	ih ging gas'-teru ü'-bent shpait tsoo bat'-te.
Generally I rise at 6 o'clock.	Sonst stehe ich regelmäßig um 6 Uhr auf.	zonst shtäh'-e ih rā'-gel-mai'-ssig um zaks oor ouf.
At what time did you rise?	Wann sind Sie aufgestanden?	vån zint zee ouf'-ge-shtän'-den?
I got up before sunrise.	Ich stand vor Sonnenaufgang auf.	ih shtánt för zon'-nen-ouf'-gäng ouf.

Going to Bed.—Vom Schlafengehen (fom shlä'-fen-gäh'-en).

It begins to grow late.	Es fängt an, spät zu werden.	es fankt àn, shpait tsoo vär'-den.
Sing the child to sleep.	Singe das Kind in Schlaf.	zinkt dàs kint in shlïf.
Put the children to bed.	Bringe die Kinder zu Bette.	bring'-e dee kin'-der tsoo bat'-te.
It is time to go to bed.	Es ist Zeit, zu Bette zu gehen.	es ist tsīt, tsoo bat'-te tsoo gäh'-en.
It is not yet late, it is only 10 o'clock.	Es ist noch nicht spät, es ist erst 10 Uhr.	es ist noch niht shpait, es ist ārst tsāu oor.
I am quite sleepy; very tired.	Ich bin sehr schläfrig; müde.	ih bin zūr shlaif'-rig; mü'-de.
I will bid your father good night.	Ich will Ihrem Vater „gute Nacht" sagen.	ih vil ee'-rem fü'-ter goo'-te nàcht zä'-gen.
Don't trouble yourself, he is asleep.	Bemühen Sie sich nicht: er schläft.	be-müh'-en zee zih niht: är shlaift.
I feel that I fall asleep.	Ich fühle, daß ich einschlafe.	ih fü'-le, dàs ih īn'-shlä'-fe.
I am nearly dropping asleep.	Ich schlafe beinahe ein.	ih shlä'-fe bī'-näh'-e īn.
I shall go to bed.	Ich will zu Bette gehen.	ih vil tsoo bat'-te gäh'-en.
Do you take a night-cup?	Trinken Sie etwas vor dem Schlafengehen?	tring'-ken zee at'-vàs fōr dām shlä'-fen-gäh'-en?
No; yes; once in a while; now and then.	Nein; ja; selten; dann und wann.	nīn; yü; zal'-ten; dàn unt vàn.
I bid you good night; a good night's rest.	Ich wünsche Ihnen gute Nacht; angenehme Ruhe.	ih vīn'-she ee'-nen goo'-te nàcht; àn'-ge-nā'-me rooh'-e.
Thanks, I wish you the same.	Danke, ich wünsche Ihnen desgleichen.	dàng'-ke, ih vīn'-she ee'-nen des-glī'-hen.
Pleasant dreams.	Träumen Sie süß!	troi'-men zee züss!

Dressing.—Vom Ankleiden (fom àn'-klī'-den).

I will dress myself.	Ich will mich ankleiden.	ih vil mih àn'-klī'-den.
I am dressing.	Ich kleide mich an.	ih klī'-de mih àn.
Give me my morning gown.	Gieb mir meinen Schlafrock.	geep meer mī'-nen shlāf'-rok.
I need a pair of new slippers.	Ich brauche ein Paar neue Pantoffeln.	ih brou'-che īn pär noi'-e pàn-tof'-feln.
I must shave.	Ich muß mich rasiren.	ih mus mih rà-zee'-ren.
Get me some hot water.	Besorge mir heißes Wasser.	be-zor'-ge meer hī'-sses vàs'-ser.
Here is the soap and the brush.	Hier ist die Seife und der Pinsel.	heer ist dee zī'-fe unt dār pin'-zel.
The razor is not sharp.	Das Rasirmesser ist nicht scharf.	dàs rà-zeer'-mas'-ser ist niht shárf.
I wish for another towel.	Ich möchte ein anderes Handtuch haben.	ih mih'-te īn àn'-de-res' hàn'-tooch hä'-ben.
Give me my working clothes; my black suit; my dress-coat; my black silk waist-coat; my white necktie.	Gieb mir meine Arbeitskleider; meinen schwarzen Anzug; meinen Frack; meine schwarze seidene Weste; meine weiße Halsbinde.	geep meer mī'-ne àr'-bīts-klī'-der; mī'-nen shvàr'-tsen àn'-tsoog; mī'-nen fràk; mī'-ne shvàr'-tse zī'-de-ne' vas'-te; mī'-ne vī'-sse hàls'-bin'-de.

English	German	Pronunciation
My brown silk dress; my walking dress; my wrapper; my cloak and jacket; my velvet bonnet and straw hat; my linen collars and cuffs; my kid gloves and rubbers.	Mein braunseidenes Kleid; mein Promenadenkleid; mein Morgenkleid; mein Mantel und Jäckchen; mein Sammethut und Strohhut; meine leinenen Kragen und Manschetten; meine Glacéhandschuhe und Ueberschuhe.	mīn broun'-zī'-de-nes' klīt; mīn prom'-me-nä'-den-klīt'; mīn mor'-gen-klīt'; mīn măn'-tel unt yăk'-hen; mīn zăm'-met-hoot' unt shtrō'-hoot'; mī'-ne lī'-ne-nen' krä'-gen unt măn-shăt'-ten; mī'-ne glă-ssä'-hănt'-shooh'-e unt ü'-ber-shooh'-e.
Gaiters, shoes and boots.	Stiefelchen, Schuhe und Stiefeln.	shtee'-fel-hen', shooh'-e unt shtee'-feln.
I shall put on my new coat.	Ich will meinen neuen Rock anziehen.	ih vil mī'-nen noi'-en rok ăn'-tseeh'-en.
A lace and an embroidered handkerchief.	Ein Spitzen- und gesticktes Taschentuch.	īn shpit'-tsen unt ge-shtik'-tes tăsh'-en-tooch'.
A cane and an umbrella.	Ein Stock und ein Regenschirm.	īn shtok unt īn rä'-gen-shirm'.
Dress yourself quickly.	Ziehen Sie sich rasch an.	tseeh'-en zee zih răsh ăn.
I am not in a great hurry.	Ich bin nicht sehr eilig.	ih bin niht zär ī'-lig.

Breakfast.—Vom Frühstück (fom frü'-shtik').

Have you had your breakfast?	Haben Sie schon gefrühstückt?	hä'-ben zee shōn ge-frü'-shtĭkt'?
Breakfast is ready.	Das Frühstück ist bereit.	dăs frü'-shtĭk' ist be-rīt'.
Coffee, tea, chocolate, milk, rolls, cake, brown bread, honey and butter.	Kaffee, Thee, Chokolade, Milch, Semmel, Kuchen, Schwarzbrod, Honig und Butter.	kăf'-fä, tä, shok'-kō-lä'-de, milh, zăm'-mel, koo'-chen, shvărts'-brōt', hō'-nig unt but'-ter.
Eggs, boiled and poached eggs, fried or baked potatoes, beefsteak and chops, bacon, ham and sausage.	Eier, gesottene und Spiegeleier, gebratene oder gebackene Kartoffeln, Beefsteak und Cotelette, Speck, Schinken und Wurst.	ī'-er, ge-zot'-te-ne' unt shpee'-gel-ī'-er, ge-brä'-te-ne' ō'-der ge-băk'-ke-ne' kăr-tof'-feln, beef'-stäk' unt kot'-te-let', shpăk, shing'-ken unt vurst.
A cold collation.	Ein kaltes Frühstück.	īn kăl'-tes frü'-shtĭk'.
I like coffee in the morning.	Morgens trinke ich Kaffee gern.	mor'-gens tring'-ke ih kăf'-fä gărn.
Give me your cup, if you please.	Geben Sie mir gefälligst Ihre Tasse.	gä'-ben zee meer ge-făl'-ligst ee'-re tăs'-se.
Try my tea, it is delicious.	Versuchen Sie meinen Thee, er ist köstlich.	fer-zoo'-chen zee mī'-nen tä, er ist kĭst'-lih.
How do you like the chocolate?	Wie schmeckt Ihnen die Chokolade?	vee shmăkt ee'-nen dee shok'-ko-lä'-de?
Do you prefer cream or milk in your coffee [tea]?	Wollen Sie Rahm oder Milch in Ihren Kaffee [Thee]?	vol'-len zee räm ō'-der milh in ee'-ren kăf'-fä [tä]?
Is your coffee [tea] sweet enough?	Ist Ihr Kaffee [Thee] süß genug?	ist eer kăf'-fä [tä] züss ge-noog'?
Do you like Pumpernickel?	Essen Sie Pumpernickel gern?	ăs'-sen zee pum'-per-nik'-kel gărn?

These rolls are quite fresh.	Diese Semmel sind ganz frisch.	dee'-ze zam'-mel zint gants frish.
I had an excellent breakfast.	Ich habe vortrefflich gefrühstückt.	ih hü'-be för-traf'-lih ge-frü'-shtĭkt'.

Dinner.—Vom Mittagessen (fom mit'-tāg-as'-sen).

Will you take dinner with me?	Wollen Sie mit mir zu Mittag essen?	vol'-len zee mit meer tsoo mit'-tāg as'-sen?
With the greatest pleasure.	Mit dem größten Vergnügen.	mit dām grĭs'-ten fer-gnü'-gen.
We have, of course, but ordinary fare.	Wir haben allerdings nur Hausmannskost.	veer hä'-ben ăl'-ler-dings' noor hous'-măns-kost'.
You must be content with it.	Sie müssen damit fürlieb nehmen.	zee mĭs'-sen dă-mit' fĭr-leep nä'-men.
I know your meals are good.	Ich weiß, man speis't gut bei Ihnen.	ih vĭs, măn shpīst goot bī ee'-nen.
There is no occasion to excuse yourself.	Bitte, machen Sie keine Entschuldigungen.	bit'-te, măch'-en zee kī'-ne ent-shul'-di-gung-en.
Take of this soup, I am sure you will like it.	Nehmen Sie von dieser Suppe, sie wird Ihnen gewiß schmecken.	nä'-men zee fon dee'-zer zup'-pe, zee virt ee'-nen ge-vĭs' shmăk'-ken.
I will trouble you for a little of it.	Geben Sie mir davon, wenn ich bitten darf.	gü'-ben zee meer dă-fon', van ih bit'-ten dărf.
Here is soup meat and horse radish.	Hier ist Suppenfleisch und Meerrettig.	heer ist zup'-pen-flĭsh ŭnt mār'-rat'-tig.
Roast beef and cauliflower.	Rindsbraten und Blumenkohl.	rĭnts'-brä'-ten ŭnt bloo'-men-köl.
Roast veal and roast mutton.	Kalbs- und Hammelsbraten.	kălps- ŭnt hăm'-mels-brä'-ten.
Roast chicken and roast goose.	Gebratene Hähnchen, Gänsebraten.	ge-brä'-te-ne' hain'-hen, găn'-ze-brä'-ten.
Trout, pike, and carp.	Forellen, Hecht und Karpfen.	fo-ral'-len, haht ŭnt kărp'-fen.
Lettuce and endive salads.	Lattich- und Endiviensalat.	lăt'-tih- ŭnt en-dee'-vi-en-ză-lät'.
Tart, pie, and pudding.	Torte, Pastete und Pudding.	tor'-te, păs-tä'-te ŭnt pud'-ding.
White bread, butter, and cheese.	Weißbrod, Butter und Käse.	vīs'-bröt, but'-ter ŭnt kai'-ze.
May I help you to some potatoes?	Darf ich Ihnen Kartoffeln anbieten?	dărf ih ee'-nen kăr-tof'-feln ăn-bee'-ten?
I will thank you for a little more cabbage.	Ich bitte Sie noch um etwas Kohl.	ih bit'-te zee noch ŭm at'-văs köl.
Do you take rice and vermicelli?	Essen Sie Reis und Nudeln?	as'-seu zee rĭs ŭnt noo'-deln?
You have no gravy.	Sie haben keine Sauce.	zee hä'-ben kī'-ne zō'-ze.
Make yourself [do as] at home.	Thun Sie gerade wie zu Hause.	toou zee ge-rü'-de vee tsoo hou'-ze.
May I offer you a glass of wine?	Darf ich Ihnen ein Glas Wein einschenken?	dărf ih ee'-nen īn glăs vīn īn'-shang'-ken.
Try some of this salmon, it is very nice.	Versuchen Sie diesen Lachs, er ist sehr wohlschmeckend.	fer-zoo'-chen zee dee'-zen lăks, är ist zŭr völ-shmăk'-kent.

Help yourself to what you like best.	Bedienen Sie sich selbst, nach Ihrem Belieben.	be-dee'-nen zee zih zalpst, nüch ee'-rem be-lee'-ben.
You keep an excellent table.	Sie führen einen ausgezeichneten Tisch.	zee fü'-ren I'-nen ous'-ge-tsīh'-ne-ten' tish.
I thank you for your kind hospitality.	Ich danke Ihnen für Ihre gute Bewirthung.	ih dáng'-ke ee'-nen für ee'-re goo'-te be-vir'-tung.

The Time.—Von der Zeit (fon dār tsīt).

What time is it? Is it late?	Wie viel Uhr ist es? Ist es spät?	vee feel oor ist es? ist es shpait?
Yes, Sir, it is late, it is nearly ten.	Ja, es ist spät; es ist nahe an zehn.	yü, es ist shpait; es ist nä'-he ån tsān.
It is later than I thought.	Es ist später, als ich dachte.	es ist shpai'-ter, åls ih dách'-te.
It is early yet, only twelve o'clock.	Es ist noch früh, erst zwölf Uhr.	es ist noch frü', ārst tsvïlf oor.
It is almost one o'clock.	Es ist beinahe eins.	es ist bī'-näh'-e īns.
It struck just one o'clock.	Es hat eben eins geschlagen.	es hát ā'-ben īns ge-shlī'-gen.
It is a quarter past one; half past one; a quarter of two.	Es ist ein Viertel auf zwei; halb zwei; ein Viertel vor zwei.	es ist īn feer'-tel ouf tsvī; hålp tsvī; īn feer'-tel fōr tsvī.
It is after six o'clock.	Es ist sechs Uhr vorbei.	es ist zaks oor for-bī'.
What time is it by your watch?	Wie viel ist's nach Ihrer Uhr?	vee feel ist's nůch ee'-rer oor?
My watch is fast.	Meine Uhr geht vor.	mī'-ne oor gāt fōr.
And mine goes too slow.	Und die meinige geht nach.	unt dee mī'-ni-ge' gāt nåch.
It is twelve o'clock, noon; midnight.	Es ist Mittag; Mitternacht.	es ist mit'-tåg; mit'-ter-nácht'.
My watch does not go right.	Meine Uhr geht nicht richtig.	mī'-ne oor gāt niht rih'-tig.
It has run down; it is not wound up.	Sie ist abgelaufen; nicht aufgezogen.	zee ist áp'-ge-lou'-fen; niht ouf'-ge-tsō'-gen.
Wind it up.	Ziehen Sie sie auf.	tseeh'-en zee zee ouf.
Do you hear it strike?	Hören Sie es schlagen?	hȳ'-ren zee es shlü'-gen?
It struck five.	Es hat fünf geschlagen.	es hát finf ge-shlü'-gen.
What time do you think it is?	Wie viel Uhr denken Sie, daß es ist?	vee feel oor dảng'-ken zee, dås es ist?
It may be a quarter to four at the most.	Es kann höchstens drei Viertel auf vier sein.	es kån hīh'-stens drī feer'-tel ouf feer zīn.
It is going to strike six o'clock.	Es wird bald sechs schlagen.	es virt bålt zaks shlü'-gen.
What is the matter with your watch?	Was ist mit Ihrer Uhr los?	vås ist mit ee'-rer oor lōs?
It stopped.	Sie ist stehen geblieben.	zee ist shtäh'-en ge-blee'-ben.
Come to-morrow morning between nine and ten o'clock.	Kommen Sie morgen früh zwischen neun und zehn.	kom'-men zee mor'-gen frü tsvish'-en noin unt tsān.
The face, the hand, the key.	Das Zifferblatt, der Zeiger, der Schlüssel.	dås tsif'-fer-blåt', dār tsī'-ger, dār shlïs'-sel.

The Weather.—Vom Wetter (fom vat′-ter).

English	German	Pronunciation
How is the weather this morning?	Wie ist das Wetter heute Morgen?	vee ist vat′-ter hoi′-te mor′-gen?
The weather is fine [charming, uncertain, bad, disagreeable].	Es ist schönes [vortreffliches, unsicheres, schlechtes, unangenehmes] Wetter.	es ist shÿ′-nes [fōr-traf′-li-ћes′, un′-zih′-e-res′, shlah′-tes, un′-àn′-ge-nä′-mes] vat′-ter.
The sky is clear.	Der Himmel ist klar.	där him′-mel ist klär.
Does the sun shine?	Scheint die Sonne?	shīnt dee zon′-ne?
There is a sharp wind.	Es geht ein scharfer Wind.	es gāt in shàr′-fer vint.
How is the wind?	Woher kommt der Wind?	vo-här′ komt där vint?
The wind is [blows from the] north [south, west, east].	Der Wind kommt aus Norden [Süden, Westen, Osten]; or, es ist Nord- 2c., wind.	där vint komt ous nor′-den [zü′-den, vas′-ten, os′-ten]; or, es ist nort′-, etc., vint.
It is foggy.	Es ist neblig.	es ist näb′-lig.
The fog is falling [rising].	Der Nebel fällt [steigt].	där nä′-bel falt [shtīgt].
The sky is cloudy.	Der Himmel ist bewölkt.	där him′-mel ist be-vilkt′.
It threatens to rain.	Es droht zu regnen.	es drōt tsoo räg′-nen.
We shall have rain.	Wir werden Regen bekommen.	veer vär′-den rä′-gen bekom′-men.
It is raining.	Es regnet [schon].	es räg′-net [shōn].
The weather is very stormy.	Das Wetter ist sehr stürmisch.	däs vat′-ter ist zār shtīr′-mish.
It lightens [thunders].	Es blitzt [donnert].	es blitst [don′-nert].
The lightning struck.	Es hat eingeschlagen.	es hàt īn′-ge-shlä′-gen.
The rain begins to abate.	Der Regen fängt an nachzulassen.	där rä′-gen fankt än näch′-tsoo-läs′-sen.
The weather is clearing up.	Das Wetter klärt sich auf.	däs vat′-ter klairt ziħ ouf.
See, what a beautiful rainbow.	Sehen Sie: ein schöner Regenbogen.	zäh′-en zee: īn shÿ′-ner rä′-gen-bō′-gen.
The sun is very hot [burning].	Die Sonne scheint sehr warm [brennt].	dee zon′-ne shīnt zār vàrm [brant].
It is very dirty [slippery walking].	Es ist sehr schmutzig [geht sich schlüpfrig].	es ist zār shmut′-sig [gāt sih shlïpf′-rig].
There was a white frost last night.	Es hat vergangene Nacht gereift.	es hàt fer-gäng′-e-ne′ nächt ge-rīft′.
The days shorten visibly.	Die Tage nehmen zusehends ab.	dee tä′-ge nä′-men tsoo-zäh′-ents äp.
It is snowing.	Es schneit.	es shnīt.
It is freezing very hard.	Es friert sehr hart.	es freert zār hart.
I shiver with cold.	Ich zittre vor Kälte.	ih tsit′-re för kal′-te.
The ice bears [is thick].	Das Eis trägt [ist dick].	däs īs traigt [ist dik].
It is thawing.	Es thaut.	es tout.
The snow is melting.	Der Schnee schmilzt.	där shnä shmiltst.
It is hailing.	Es hagelt.	es hä′-gelt.
It is moonlight [new moon].	Es ist mondhell [Neumond].	es ist mōnt′-hal [noi′-mōnt′].
The moon is increasing [full].	Der Mond nimmt zu [ist voll].	där mōnt nimt tsoo [ist fol].
The moon is decreasing.	Der Mond nimmt ab.	där mōnt nimt äp.
Sleety weather; slushy; icicles.	Schnee- und Regenwetter; Schlackenwetter; Eiszapfen.	shnä- unt rä′-gen-vat′-ter; shlàk′-ken-vat′-ter; īs′-tsäp′-fen.

Age.—Vom Alter (fom äl'-ter).

English	German	Pronunciation
How old are you?	Wie alt sind Sie [bist Du]?	vee ålt zint zee [bist doo]?
I am twenty years old.	Ich bin zwanzig Jahre alt.	ih bin tsvån'-tsig yä'-re ålt.
You are still very young.	Sie sind [Du bist] noch sehr jung.	zee zint [doo bist] noch zūr' yungk.
My brother [sister] is — years old.	Mein[e Schwester] Bruder ist — Jahre alt.	min[e shvɐs'-ter] broo'-der ist — yä'-re ålt.
Your cousin must be nearly fifteen.	Ihr Vetter muß nahe an fünfzehn sein.	eer fɐt'-ter mus nüh'-e ån finf'-tsän zin.
He will be sixteen in two months.	Er wird in zwei Monaten sechzehn.	är virt in tsvī mō'-nä'-ten zạh'-tsän.
She enters her seventeenth year.	Sie tritt in ihr siebenzehntes Jahr.	zee trit in eer zee'-bentsän'-tes yīr.
Your uncle bears his age well.	Ihr Onkel sieht für sein Alter sehr gut aus.	eer ong'-kel zeet für zīn ål'-ter zūr goot ous.
How old do you think my father is?	Wie alt glauben Sie, daß mein Vater ist?	vee ålt glou'-ben zee, dås mīn fä'-ter ist?
He must be over fifty years old.	Er muß wohl über fünfzig sein.	är mus vōl ü'-ber finf'-tsig zīn.

Writing.—Vom Schreiben (fom shrī'-ben).

Can you lend me a sheet of paper?	Können Sie mir einen Bogen Papier leihen?	kin'-nen zee meer ī'-nen bō'-gen på-peer' līh'-en?
What kind of paper do you want?	Was für Papier wünschen Sie?	vås für på-peer' vin'-shen zee?
Some note paper.	Briefpapier.	breef'-på-peer'.
I have not a single sheet in my writing desk.	Ich habe nicht einen einzigen Bogen in meinem Schreibpulte.	ih hü'-be niht ī'-nen īn'-tsi-gen bō'-gen in mī'-nem shrīp'-pul-te.
I am going to send for some.	Ich werde etwas holen lassen.	ih vär'-de åt'-vås hō'-len lås'-sen.
I have a letter to write presently.	Ich muß sogleich einen Brief schreiben.	ih mus zo-glīh' ī'-nen breef shrī'-ben.
It must be immediately mailed.	Er muß sofort zur Post gebracht werden.	är mus zo-fort' tsur post ge-brăcht' vär'-den.
Here is the paper.	Hier ist das Papier.	heer ist dås på-peer'.
Thanks; one sheet will do.	Danke; ich brauche nur einen Bogen.	dång'-ke; ih brou'-che noor ī'-nen bō'-gen.
What day of the month is this?	Welches Datum haben wir heute?	vǎl'-hes dä'-tum hü'-ben veer hoi'-te?
To-day is the third.	Heute ist der dritte.	hoi'-te ist där drit'-te.
Here is an envelope.	Hier ist ein Briefumschlag.	heer ist īn breef'-um-shläg.
Just in time to write the address.	Gerade recht, um die Adresse zu schreiben.	ge-rä'-de rǎht, um dee åd-rǎs'-se tsoo shrī'-ben.
Take this letter to the post office.	Bringe diesen Brief auf die Post.	bring'-e dee'-zen breef ouf dee post.

Sea voyage.—Seereise (zā'-rī-ze).

Is this the first time you are at sea?	Sind Sie zum ersten Mal zur See?	zint zee tsum ärs'-ten mäl tsur zā?
Yes, it is my first voyage.	Ja, dies ist meine erste Reise.	yä, dees ist mī'-ne ärs'-te rī'-ze.

English	German	Pronunciation
Are you afraid of sea sickness?	Fürchten Sie sich vor der Seekrankheit?	fĭrh'-ten zee zĭh fōr dār zā'-krănk'-hīt'?
I think I am sick already.	Ich glaube, ich bin schon krank.	ĭh glou'-be, ĭh bin shōn krănk.
Resist it with all your power, and take a walk on deck.	Widersetzen Sie sich mit aller Macht und spazieren Sie auf dem Verdecke herum.	vee'-der-zăt'-sen zee zĭh mit ăl'-ler măcht ŭnt shpătsee'-ren zee ouf dăm ferdăk'-ke har-ŭm'.
Practice walking according to the motion of the steamer.	Ueben Sie sich, mit den Bewegungen des Dampfers zu gehen.	ü'-ben zee zĭh, mit dăn bevä'-gŭng'-en dăs dămp'fers tsoo gāh'-en.
The steamer moves steadily; it rolls, pitches.	Der Dampfer geht ruhig; er schaukelt, stampft.	dār dămp'-fer gāt rooh'-ig; ār shou'-kelt, shtămpft.
The wind is favorable [getting higher].	Der Wind ist günstig [wird etwas stärker].	dār vint ist gĭns'-tig [virt ăt'-văs shtar'-ker].
Is it not stormy?	Ist es nicht stürmisch?	ist es nĭht shtür'-mish?
This is merely a breeze.	Dies ist nur eine Briese.	dees ist noor ī'-ne bree'-ze.
A storm is quite a different thing.	Ein Sturm ist etwas ganz andres.	In shturm ist ăt'-văs gănts ăn'-dres.
And a gale, and a hurricane.	Und ein heftiger Wind, und ein Orkan.	ŭnt In hăf'-ti-ger' vint, ŭnt In or-kän'.
May be we shall have a little storm to-night.	Mag sein, daß wir heute Abend etwas Sturm bekommen.	măg zĭn, dăs veer hoi'-te ä'-bent ăt'-văs shtŭrm be-kom'-men.
But there is no danger.	Es ist aber keine Gefahr dabei.	es ist ä'-ber kī'-ne ge-făr' dă-bī'.
Did you see the waterspout there?	Haben Sie die Wasserhose da gesehen?	hä'-ben zee dee văs'-serhō'-ze dä ge-zäh'-en?
Is it dangerous for vessels?	Ist die den Schiffen gefährlich?	ist dee dăn shif'-fen gefăr'-lĭh?
O yes! Sometimes it takes away everything, sails and rigging.	O ja! Bisweilen nimmt sie Alles weg: Segel und Takelage.	o yä! bis-vī'-len nimt zee ăl'-les văg: zā'-gel ŭnt tä'-ke-lä'-je.
For God's sake, a gunshot—there is danger.	Um des Himmelswillen, ein Schuß—da ist Gefahr!	ŭm dăs him'-mels vil'-len, In shŭs—dä ist ge-făr'!
No danger; it is only to disperse the waterspout.	Keine Gefahr; er dient nur dazu, die Wasserhose zu zertheilen.	kī'-ne ge-făr'; ār deent noor dă-tsoo',dee văs'-serhō'-ze tsoo tser-tī'-len.
It is gone.	Sie ist fort.	zee ist fort.
Will there be a thunderstorm?	Wird es ein Gewitter geben?	virt es In ge-vit'-ter gā'-ben?
Perhaps.	Vielleicht.	feel-lĭht'.
Let us go down into the cabin.	Wir wollen in die Kajüte gehen.	veer vol'-len in dee kă-yī'te gāh'-en.
How many miles have we travelled?	Wie viele Meilen sind wir gereis't?	vee fee'-le mī'-len zint veer ge-rīst'?
Two thousand eight hundred.	Zwei tausend und achthundert.	tsvī tou'-zent ŭnt ăchthŭn'-dert.
I think I see land.	Ich glaube, ich sehe Laub.	ĭh glou'-be, ĭh zäh'-e lăut.
You are right; we shall disembark to-morrow.	Sie haben recht; wir werden morgen landen.	zee hä'-ben rȧht; veer vār'den mor'-gen lăn'-den.
Have you anything dutiable?	Haben Sie etwas Steuerbares?	hä'-ben zee ăt'-văs shtoi'er-bä'-res?
Not that I know of.	Nicht daß ich wüßte.	nĭht dăs ĭh vĭs'-te.
Now, thank God, we have arrived.	Nun, Gott sei Dank, wir sind angekommen.	noon, got zī dănk, veer zint ăn'-ge-kom'-men.

On the Railroad.—Auf der Eisenbahn (ouf där ī'-zen-bän').

English	German	Pronunciation
Have you made all your preparations for departure?	Haben Sie alle Ihre Vorbereitungen zur Abreise getroffen?	hā'-ben zee àl'-le ee'-re för-be-rī'-tung-en tsur àp'-rī'-ze ge-trof'-fen?
Everything is in readiness.	Alles ist bereit.	àl'-les ist be-rīt'.
Well, the hotel 'bus will bring you to the depot.	Der Omnibus des Gasthofes wird Sie an den Bahnhof bringen.	där om'-ni-bus' das gäst'-hō'-fes virt zee àn dän bän'-höf bring'-en.
We shall start immediately.	Wir werden sofort abfahren.	veer vär'-den zō-fort' áp'-fä'-ren.
Gentlemen, step in, if you please.	Meine Herren, steigen Sie gefälligst ein.	mī'-ne har'-ren, shtī'-gen zee ge-fäl'-ligst īn.
How soon shall we be at the depot?	Wann werden wir am Bahnhof sein?	vàn vär'-den veer àm bän'-höf zīn?
It will take us half an hour.	Es wird eine halbe Stunde dauern.	es virt ī'-ne hál'-be shtuu'-de dou'-ern.
I am afraid we shall be too late for the eight o'clock train.	Ich fürchte, wir werden für den Acht-Uhr-Zug zu spät sein.	ih firh'-te, veer vär'-den für dän àcht'-oor'-tsoog' tsoo shpait zīn.
Don't be uneasy, Sir, we always arrive in time.	Seien Sie unbesorgt, wir kommen immer zur rechten Zeit an.	zī'-en zee un'-be-zorgt', veer kom'-men im'-mer tsur rah'-ten tsīt àn.
Here you are at the depot.	Wir sind am Bahnhof.	veer zint àm bän'-höf.
The train will start in ten minutes.	In zehn Minuten geht der Zug ab.	in tsän mi-noo'-ten gät där tsoog áp.
What carriage do you take?	Welche Klasse fahren Sie?	vàl'-he kläs'-se fä'-ren zee?
Second class; the carriages of that class are very comfortable.	Zweite Klasse; die Wagen derselben sind sehr bequem.	tsvī'-te kläs'-se; dee vä'-gen där-zal'-ben zint zār be-kvām'.
Here is your ticket.	Hier ist Ihr Billet.	heer ist eer bil-yàt'.
Have you got your baggage ticket?	Haben Sie Ihren Gepäckschein?	hä'-ben zee ee'-ren ge-pak'-shīn'?
I have two trunks, a valise and a hat-box.	Ich habe zwei Koffer, eine Handtasche und eine Hutschachtel.	ih hä'-be tsvī kof'-fer, ī'-ne hànt'-tásh'-e unt ī'-ne hoot'-shách'-tel.
You have to pay overweight.	Sie haben Ueberfracht zu zahlen.	zee hü'-ben ü'-ber-fracht' tsoo tsä'-len.
I wish you a safe journey.	Ich wünsche Ihnen eine glückliche Reise.	ih vin'-she ee'-nen ī'-ne glik'-li-he' rī'-ze.
Take your seat, Sir.	Nehmen Sie Ihren Sitz, mein Herr.	nä'-men zee ee'-ren zits, mīn harr.
Make haste, the train will start directly.	Eilen Sie sich, der Zug wird sofort abgehen.	ī'-len zee zih, där tsoog virt zō-fort' áp'-gäh-en.
There you hear the signal for starting.	Da hören Sie das Zeichen zur Abfahrt.	dä hī'-ren zee däs tsī'-hen tsur áp'-fürt.
Isn't this quick traveling?	Heißt das nicht schnell reisen?	hīst däs niht shnàl rī'-zen?
The faster we go, the better I like it.	Je rascher es geht, besto lieber ist es mir.	yā ràsh'-er es gät, das'-tē lee'-ber ist es meer.
This is an express [limited, lightning] train.	Dies ist ein Schnell- [Expreß-] Zug.	dees ist īn shnàl- [ex-pràs'-] tsoog.
Accommodation trains are slower, of course.	Bummelzüge gehen natürlich langsamer.	bum'-mel-tsü'-ge gäh'-en nà-tür'-lih láng'-zä-mer.

8

English	German	Pronunciation
The road makes a sudden sharp curve at this place.	Die Bahn macht an dieser Stelle eine plötzliche Biegung.	dee bān mácht ān dee'-zer shtāl'-le ī'-ne plĭts'-li-he' bee'-gung.
I am afraid the engine will go off the rails.	Ich fürchte, die Lokomotive wird entgleisen.	ĭh fĭrh'-te, dee lō'-ko-mo-tee'-ve virt ant-glī'-zen.
Do not be afraid.	Seien Sie nicht bange.	zī'-en zee niht báng'-e.
It shakes somewhat.	Es schüttelt ein Bischen.	es shĭt'-telt ĭn bĭs'-hen.
That is to be expected.	Das ist zu erwarten.	dăs ist tsoo er-vâr'-ten.
Here comes a train.	Da kommt ein Zug.	dā komt ĭn tsoog.
It looks like coming toward us on our track.	Er scheint auf unserm Gleise auf uns zuzukommen.	är shīnt ouf ŭn'-zerm glī'-ze ouf ŭns tsoo'-tsu-kom'-men.
How long shall we stop at this station?	Wie lange halten wir uns an dieser Station auf?	vee lăng'-e hăl'-ten veer ŭns ăn dee'-zer shtăts'-yōn' ouf?
Only half a minute, Sir.	Nur eine halbe Minute, mein Herr!	noor ī'-ne hăl'-be mi-noo'-te, mīn harr.
There are a great many passengers waiting at the station.	Es warten hier viele Reisende auf dieser Station.	es vâr'-ten heer fee'-le rī'-zen-de' ouf dee'-zer shtăts'-yōn'.
Mostly third-class passengers.	Meistens Reisende dritter Klasse.	mī'-stens rī'-zen-de' drĭt'-ter klăs'-se.
We are off again.	Jetzt geht's schon wieder fort.	yatst gäts shōn vee'-der fort.
What do I see there at the end of this curve in front of us?	Was sehe ich da vor uns am Ende dieser Biegung?	văs zäh'-e ĭh dā fōr ŭns ăm ăn'-de dee'-zer bee'-gung?
It is a tunnel.	Das ist ein Tunnel.	dăs ist ĭn tŭn-năl'.
We shall be in the dark one minute only; the tunnel is not long.	Wir werden nur eine Minute im Dunkeln sein; der Tunnel ist nicht lang.	veer vär'-den noor ī'-ne mi-noo'-te im dŭng'-keln zīn; dăr tŭn-năl ist niht lăng.
Here we are at the last station.	Hier sind wir an der letzten Station.	heer zint veer ăn dăr lăts'-ten shtăts'-yōn'.
Ten minutes more, and we shall be at our journey's end.	Noch zehn Minuten, und wir sind am Ende unserer Reise.	noch tsūn mi-noo'-ten, ŭnt veer zint ăm ăn'-de ŭn'-ze-rer rī'-ze.
Thank God, we are at the depot.	Gottlob, wir sind am Bahnhof.	got-lōp', veer zint ăm bān'-hōf.
Let us go and see to our luggage.	Gehen wir, nach unserm Gepäck zu sehen.	gäh'-en veer, năch ŭn'-zerm ge-păk' tsoo zäh'-en.

In a Hotel.—**In einem Gasthofe** (in ī'-nem găst'-hō'-fe).

Have you a spare room?	Haben Sie ein Zimmer übrig?	hă'-ben zee ĭn tsĭm'-mer ü'-brig?
Of course with a good bed.	Natürlich mit einem guten Bette.	nă-tür'-lĭh mĭt ī'-nem goo'-ten băt'-te.
I leave my trunk down stairs, I only want my valise.	Ich lasse meinen Koffer unten, ich brauche blos meine Handtasche.	ĭh lăs'-se mī'-nen kof'-fer ŭn'-ten, ĭh brou'-che blōs mī'-ne hănt'-tăsh'-e.
I want some dinner [supper].	Ich möchte zu Mittag [Abend] essen.	ĭh mĭh'-te tsoo mĭt'-tăg [ā'-bent] ăs'-sen.
Give me the bill of fare.	Geben Sie mir die Speisekarte.	gă'-ben zee meer dee shpī'-ze-kâr'-te.

English	German	Pronunciation
I dine at the table d'hote.	Ich speise am Gast[hof]tische.	ih shpī'-ze am gåst'-[hōf'] tish'-e.
I take for supper — —	Zum Abendessen nehme ich — —	tsum ä'-bent-as'-sen nä'-me ih — —
Is my room heated? I want to retire.	Ist mein Zimmer geheizt? Ich will mich hinauf begeben.	ist mīn tsim'-mer ge-hītst? ih vil mih hin-ouf'-be-gä'-ben.
Don't forget to call me early enough to take my breakfast before leaving to-morrow morning.	Vergessen Sie nicht, mich morgen früh genug zu wecken, damit ich vor meiner Abreise noch frühstücken kann.	fer-gas'-sen zee niht, mih mor'-gen frü ge-noog' tsoo vak'-ken, dä-mit' ih för mī'-ner åp'-rī'-ze noch frü'-shtik'-ken kån.
Let me have my bill, please.	Geben Sie mir gefälligst meine Rechnung.	gū'-ben zee meer ge-fål'-ligst mī'-ne rah'-nung.

Renting Rooms.—Zimmer miethen (tsim'-mer mee'-ten).

Have you any rooms to let?	Haben Sie Zimmer zu vermiethen?	hä'-ben zee tsim'-mer tsoo fer-mee'-ten?
I want two furnished rooms; a sitting room and a bed room.	Ich brauche zwei möblirte Zimmer, nämlich: ein Wohn- und ein Schlafzimmer.	ih brou'-che tsvī mīb-leer'-te tsim'-mer, naim'-lih: īn vōn'- unt īn shläf'-tsim'-mer.
On the ground floor, if possible; or else on the second floor.	Parterre, womöglich, sonst im ersten Stock.	pår-tår', vō-mīg'-lih, zonst im ürs'-ten shtok.
A front sitting room.	Das Wohnzimmer vorne.	dås vōn'-tsim'-mer for'-ne.
The sitting room is rather small, but it is well furnished.	Das Wohnzimmer ist zwar klein, aber gut möblirt.	dås vōn'-tsim'-mer ist tsvår klīn, ü'-ber goot mīb-leert'.
The bed room suits me.	Das Schlafzimmer paßt mir.	dås shläf'-tsim'-mer påst meer.
I hope the bed is good and clean.	Ich hoffe, daß das Bett gut und rein ist.	ih hof'-fe, dås dås båt goot unt rīn ist.
Now let me hear about your terms.	Nun lassen Sie mich Ihre Bedingungen hören.	noon låssen zee mih ee'-re be-ding'-ung'-en hī'-ren.
How much do you ask for both rooms?	Wie viel verlangen Sie für beide Zimmer?	vee feel fer-lång'-en zee für bī'-de tsim'-mer?
Very well; I take them for twelve marks a week.	Wohlan, ich nehme sie für zwölf Marken wöchentlich.	vōl-ån', ih nä'-me zee für tsvilf mår'-ken vih'-ent-lih'.
Let them be ready to-night; I'll send my luggage within an hour.	Lassen Sie sie diesen Abend in Ordnung sein; ich werde mein Gepäck binnen einer Stunde schicken.	lås'-sen zee zee dee'-zen ä'-bent in ord'-nung zīn; ih vär'-de mīn ge-pak' bin'-nen ī'-ner shtun'-de shik'-ken.
We may also agree with regard to boarding.	Wir können uns auch zugleich über den Tisch einigen.	veer kin'-nen uns tsoo-glīh' ouch ü'-ber dån tish ī'-ni-gen'.
Full or partial board.	Ganz oder theilweise.	gånts ō'-der tīl'-vī'-ze.
We shall see about it later.	Das können wir später besprechen.	dås kin'-nen veer shpai'-ter be-shprah'-en.
Good morning.	Guten Morgen.	goo'-ten mor'-gen.

With a Physician.—Mit einem Arzte (mit i'-nem árts'-te).

English	German	Pronunciation
Doctor, I sent for you, for I need your assistance.	Herr Doctor, ich habe nach Ihnen geschickt, weil ich Ihres Beistandes bedarf.	harr dok'-tōr, ih hä'-be nach ee'-nen ge-shikt', vil ih ee'-res bī'-shtán'-des be-dárf'.
Yes, Sir, I myself am the patient.	Ja wohl, ich selbst bin der Patient.	yä vōl, ih zälpst bin dār pàts'-yant'.
I cannot explain how I feel [I don't know what's the matter with me].	Ich kann's nicht erklären, wie ich fühle [ich befinde mich, ich weiß nicht wie].	ih kán's niht er-klai'-ren, vee ih fü'-le [ih be-fin'-de mih, ih vĭs niht vee].
My head is giddy, and I can scarcely move about.	Mein Kopf ist mir ganz eingenommen und ich kann mich kaum herum bewegen.	mīn kopf ist meer gänts īn'-ge-nom'-men unt ih kán mih koum har-um'-be-vā'-gen.
I am not well at all.	Ich befinde mich gar nicht wohl.	ih be-fin'-de mih gär niht vōl.
I have been ailing for several weeks.	Ich leide seit mehreren Wochen.	ih lī'-de zīt mā'-re-ren' voch'-en.
I am very weak; feverish.	Ich bin sehr schwach; fieberisch.	ih bin zār shvách; fee'-brish.
Gout; rheumatism; influenza; a pain in my throat and neck; diarrhœa; tooth-ache; gripes; pain in my hip; colic; pain in my chest; constipation; violent head-ache; I can hardly breathe; I did not sleep for the last three nights.	Podagra; Rheumatismus; Grippe; Schmerz im Halse und Nacken; Abführen; Zahnschmerzen; Kneifen in den Eingeweiden; Hüftschmerzen; Kolik; Schmerzen in der Brust; Verstopfung; heftige Kopfschmerzen; ich kann kaum athmen; ich habe drei Nächte nicht schlafen können.	pō'-dä-grä'; rä'-oo-má-tis'-mus; grip'-pe; shmarts im hál'-ze unt näk'-ken; áp'-fü'-ren; tsän'-shmar'-tsen; knī'-fen in dän īn'-ge-vī'-den, hĭft'-shmar'-tsen; ko-leek'; shmar'-tsen in dār brust; fer-shtop'-fung, häf'-ti-ge' kopf'-shmar'-tsen; ih kán koum ät'-men; ih hä'-be drī nah'-te niht shlä'-fen kĭn'-nen.
I sometimes feel like vomiting, and I have a bitter taste in the morning.	Mir ist zuweilen, als sollte ich mich erbrechen, und Morgens habe ich einen bittern Geschmack.	meer ist tsoo-vī'-len, äls zol'-te ih mih er-brah'-en, unt mor'-gens hä'-be ih ī'-nen bit'-tern ge-shmák'.
I am always very thirsty.	Ich bin immer sehr durstig.	ih bin im'-mer zār dur'-stig.
I have the hiccough, an intolerable yawning.	Ich habe das Schlucken, ein unerträgliches Gähnen.	ih hä'-be dás shluk'-ken, īn un'-er-traig'-li-hes' gai'-nen.
Do you think the symptoms very bad?	Halten Sie die Symptome für sehr schlimm?	häl'-ten zee dee simp'-tō-me für zār shlim?
Of course I will be careful lest they become so.	Ich werde gewiß sehr vorsichtig sein, damit sie es nicht werden.	ih vär'-de ge-vis' zār för'-zih'-tig zīn, dä-mit' zee es niht vär'-den.
What am I to do?	Was soll ich thun?	vás zol ih toon?
What must I drink to quench my thirst?	Was soll ich trinken, um meinen Durst zu löschen?	vás zol ih tring'-ken, um mī'-nen durst tsoo lĭsh'-en?
When will you see me again, Doctor?	Wann werden Sie mich wieder besuchen, Herr Doctor?	ván vär'-den zee mih vee'-der be-zoo'-chen, harr dok'-tōr?

English	German	Pronunciation
I am very glad, Doctor, that you have come.	Ich freue mich sehr, Herr Doctor, daß Sie gekommen sind.	ih froi'-e mih zār, harr dok'-tōr, dás zee ge-kom'-men zint.
I perspired profusely; I slept very little; and I am now so giddy that I can scarcely stand on my legs.	Ich habe reichlich geschwitzt; wenig geschlafen; und bin jetzt so schwindelig, daß ich mich kaum auf den Beinen halten kann.	ih hā'-be rīh'-lih ge-shvitst; vā'-nig ge-shlā'-fen; unt bin yatst zō shvin'-de-lig', dás ih mih koum ouf dān bī'-nen hál'-ten kán.
I thought I could go to sleep again on the sofa.	Ich glaubte, auf dem Sopha wieder einschlafen zu können.	ih gloup'-te, ouf dām zō'-fā vee'-der īn'-shlā'-fen tsoo kīn'-nen.
What am I allowed to eat?	Was darf ich essen?	vás dárf ih as'-sen?
O yes, beef tea, oat meal and barley water.	O ja, Bouillon, Hafergrütze und Gerstenschleim.	o yä, bul-yong', hā'-fer-grīts'-e unt gār'-sten-shlīm'.
A little chicken in a few days. You think so?	Ein wenig von einem Küchlein in einigen Tagen. Glauben Sie?	In vā'-nig fon ī'-nem kīh'-līn in ī'-ni-gen' tā'-gen; glou'-ben zee?
Shall I see you to-morrow, Doctor?	Werde ich Sie morgen sehen, Herr Doctor?	vār'-de ih zee mor'-gen zāh'-en, harr dok'-tōr?

With a Tailor.—**Mit einem Schneider** (mit I'-nem shnī'-der).

I wish you to measure me for a coat.	Ich wünsche, daß Sie mir einen Rock anmessen.	ih vīn'-she, dás zee meer ī'-nen rok án'-mas'-sen.
I want to have it made according to fashion.	Ich will ihn nach der jetzigen Mode gemacht haben.	ih vil een nāch dār yat'-si-gen' mō'-de ge-mácht' hā'-ben.
Double breasted.	Mit doppelter Reihe Knöpfe.	mit dop'-pel-ter' rīh'-e knīp'-fe.
Single breasted.	Mit einer Reihe Knöpfe.	mit ī'-ner rīh'-e knīp'-fe.
A dress-coat.	Ein Frack.	In fråk.
I also want a waist-coat and pants.	Ich brauche auch eine Weste und ein Paar Hosen.	ih brou'-che ouch ī'-ne vas'-te unt īn pār hō'-zen.
Gilt buttons for the coat, and for the waist-coat silk ones.	Vergoldete Knöpfe für den Rock, und für die Weste seidene.	fer-gol'-de-te' knīp'-fe fūr dān rok, unt fūr dee vas'-te zī'-de-ne'.
Do not forget that I must have everything by Saturday next latest.	Vergessen Sie nicht, daß ich Alles spätestens bis nächsten Samstag haben muß.	fer-gas'-sen zee niht, dás ih ál'-les shpāi'-te-stens' bis naih'-sten zåms'-tāg hā'-ben mus.
The suit seems to be nicely done.	Der Anzug scheint hübsch gemacht zu sein.	dār án'-tsoog shīnt hīpsh ge-mácht' tsoo zīn.
Let us see how the coat fits me.	Wir wollen sehen, wie mir der Rock paßt.	veer vol'-len zāh'-en, vee meer dār rok påst.
Are the sleeves not too wide?	Sind die Aermel nicht zu weit?	zint dee ar'-mel niht tsoo vīt?
Is it not too tight?	Ist er nicht zu eng?	ist ār niht tsoo ang?
It pinches me under the arms.	Er kneift mich unter den Armen.	ār knīft mih un'-ter dān år'-men.
Does it not wrinkle between the shoulders?	Wirft er nicht Falten zwischen den Schultern?	virft ār niht fál'-ten tsvish'-en dān shul'-tern?

English	German	Pronunciation
Yes, the trousers are first rate.	Ja, die Hosen sind sehr gut.	yä, dee hō'-zen zint zār goot.
The waist-coat fits admirably.	Die Weste paßt ausgezeichnet.	dee vas'-te päst ous'-ge-tsĭh'-net.
I am pleased with your work.	Ihre Arbeit gefällt mir.	ee'-re är'-bīt ge-fạlt' meer.

In a Shoe Store.—In einem Schuhladen (in ī'-nem shoo'-lä'-den).

I want a pair of ready-made shoes.	Ich brauche ein Paar Schuhe; Sie haben ja fertige.	ih brou'-che īn pär shooh'-e; zee hä'-ben yä fạr'-ti-ge'.
Show me some good ones.	Zeigen Sie mir gute.	tsī'-gen zee meer goo'-te.
I wear number —	Ich trage Numero —	ih trä'-ge nụ'-me-rō' —
I will try them on myself.	Ich will sie mir selbst anprobiren.	ih vil zee meer zạlpst ȧn'-prō-bee'-ren.
They are too tight.	Sie sind zu eng.	dee zint tsoo ạng.
Let me have another pair.	Lassen Sie mich ein anderes Paar haben.	lȧs'-sen zee mih īn ȧn'-de-res' pär hä'-ben.
They hurt my toes.	Die thun mir an den Zehen weh.	dee toon meer ȧn dān tsäh'-en vū.
I cannot walk in them.	Ich kann nicht darin gehen.	ih kȧn niht dä-rin' gäh'-en.
Make a pair to order for me.	Machen Sie mir ein Paar.	mȧch'-en zee meer īn pär.
Take the measure.	Nehmen Sie das Maß.	nä'-men zee däs mäs.
I have a small foot.	Ich habe einen kleinen Fuß.	ih hä'-be ī'-nen klī'-nen foos.
The heels on these shoes are much too high.	Die Absätze an diesen Schuhen sind viel zu hoch.	dee ȧp'-zạts'-e ȧn dee'-zen shooh'-en zint feel tsoo hōch.
I never walked comfortably in them.	Ich konnte nie bequem darin gehen.	ih kon'-te nee be-kväm dä-rin' gäh'-en.
Show me this pair of kid, patent leather, calf leather.	Zeigen Sie mir das Paar von Glacé-, Glanz-, Kalbleder.	tsī'-gen zee meer däs pär fon glä-ssä', glȧnts-, kȧlp'-lä'-der.
No lacing and no buttons.	Kein Schnüren und keine Knöpfe.	kīn shnü'-ren ụnt kī'-ne knŏp'-fe.
Strong but not clumsy soles.	Starke, doch nicht plumpe Sohlen.	shtȧr'-ke, doch niht plụm'-pe zō'-len.
Let me have them tomorrow night.	Lassen Sie sie mich morgen Abend haben.	lȧs'-sen zee zee mih mor'-gen ü'-bent hä'-ben.

PHRASEOLOGY ALPHABETICALLY ARRANGED.

Phraseologie, alphabetisch geordnet.

(fră'-ze-ŏ-lo-gee' ăl'-fă-bā'-tish ge-ord'-net.)

A

English	German	Pronunciation
In the very act.	Auf frischer That.	ouf frish'-er tät.
Acts of the Apostles.	Apostelgeschichte.	ä-pos'-tel-ge-shiḫ'-te.
To bring an action against one.	Jemanden gerichtlich belangen.	yä'-män'-den ge-riḫt'-liḫ be-läng'-en.
To give advantage to.	Vorsprung [den Vortheil] geben.	för'-shprung [dän för'-tïl] gä'-ben.
To have advantage over.	Ueberlegen sein.	ü'-ber-lä'-gen zïn.
To have the advantage of one.	Im Vortheil sein.	im för'-tïl zïn.
To take advantage of.	Sich [etwas] zunutze machen.	ziḫ [ăt'-văs] tsoo-nuts'-e mäch'-en.
To the best advantage.	Auf das Vortheilhafteste.	ouf dăs för'-tïl-hăf'-te-ste'.
I cannot afford it so cheap.	Ich kann es nicht so billig geben.	iḫ kăn es niḫt zō bil'-lig gä'-ben.
Day after day.	Tag für Tag.	täg für täg.
What are you after?	Was hast Du vor?	văs hăst doo för?
As much again.	Noch einmal so viel.	noch ïn'-mäl zo feel.
Half as big again.	Um die Hälfte größer.	um dee hălf'-te grĕ'-sser.
Again and again.	Zu wiederholten Malen; hin und her; einmal über das andere.	tsoo vee'-der-hōl'-ten mäl'-len; hin unt här; ïn'-mäl ü'-ber dăs ăn'-de-re'.
To be of age.	Mündig [majorenn] sein.	mïn'-dig [mäy-yo-ran] zïn.
To come to age.	Mündig werden.	mïn'-dig vär'-den.
Under age.	Unmündig.	un'-mïn'-dig.
It is a thing agreed on.	Es ist eine abgethane Sache.	es ist ï'-ne ăp'-ge-tä'-ne zäch'-e.
To agree for the price.	Wegen des Preises einig werden.	vä'-gen das prī'-zes ï'-nig vär'-den.
To sound [give] alarm.	Lärm blasen [machen].	lärm blä'-zen [mäch'-en].
To take alarm.	Unruhig werden; Angst bekommen.	un-rooh'-ig vär'-den; ängst be-kom'-men.
By all means.	Schlechterdings; jedenfalls.	shlaḫ'-ter-dings'; yä'-den-făls'.
All at once.	Auf ein Mal.	ouf ïn mäl.
Once for all.	Ein für allemal.	ïn für ăl'-le mäl.
For good and all.	Auf immer; ganz und gar.	ouf im'-mer; gänts unt gär.
It is all one to me.	Es gilt mir Alles gleich.	es gilt meer ăl'-les glïḫ.
After all.	Am Ende; doch; dennoch; wohl gar noch; denn wohl gar; im Grunde betrachtet; reiflich erwogen.	ăm ăn'-de; doch; dăn'-noch; vōl gär noch; dan vōl gär; im grun'-de be-träch'-tet; rïf'-liḫ er-vō'-gen.
All the better.	Desto besser.	das'-tō bas'-ser.

My all is at stake.	Alles steht bei mir auf dem Spiele.	ál'-les shtāt bī meer ouf dām shpee'-le.
You are not alone in it.	Sie sind nicht der Einzige, Andere können es auch.	zee zint niht dār īn'-tsi-ge', án'-de-re' kīn'-nen es ouch.
Let me alone.	Lassen Sie mich gehen [in Ruhe, in Frieden].	lás'-sen zee miḥ gāh'-en [in rooh'-e, in free'-den].
Let me alone for [with] that.	Lassen Sie mich dafür sorgen.	lás'-sen zee miḥ dā-für' zor'-gen.
To take amiss.	Uebel nehmen; übel auslegen; verdenken.	ü'-bel nā'-men; ü'-bel ous'-lā-gen; fer-dạng'-ken.
If anything should happen amiss.	Wenn es etwa schief ginge [mißrathen sollte].	van es ạt'-vā sheef gịng'-e [mis-rū'-ten zol'-te].
Nothing comes amiss to him.	Er nimmt mit Allem fürlieb; er schickt sich in Alles.	ār nimt mit ál'-lem fürleep'; ūr shikt ziḥ in ál'-les.
To give animation.	In Bewegung setzen; beseelen.	in be-vā'-gụng zạts'-en; be-zā'-len.
To keep one at arm's end [length].	Jemanden von sich abhalten; nicht auf den Leib kommen lassen.	yā'-man-den' fon ziḥ áp'-hál'-ten; niht ouf dān līp kom'-men lás'-sen.
On an average.	Im Durchschnitt; Eins in's Andere gerechnet.	im dụrḥ'-shnit; īns iu's án'-de-re' ge-raḥ'-net.

B

I will bail him.	Ich will für ihn bürgen.	iḥ vil für een bīr'-gen.
Bailed [out of prison].	Los gebürgt; durch gestellte Bürgschaft auf freiem Fuß.	lōs ge-bīrgt'; dụrḥ ge-shtál'-te bīrg'-shaft ouf frī'-em foos.
To strike a balance.	Eine Rechnung ausgleichen; aufgehen lassen.	ī'-ne raḥ'-nụng ous'-glī'-ḥen; ouf'-gūh'-en lás'-sen.
He has had a sad balk.	Er hat sich sehr geirrt; hat einen Bock gemacht; ist mit einer langen Nase abgezogen.	ār hát ziḥ zūr ge-irt'; hát ī'-nen bok ge-mácht'; ist mit ī'-ner láng'-en nā'-ze áp'-ge-tsō'-gen.
A chance bargain.	Ein zufälliger [billiger] Einkauf.	īn tsoo'-fạl'-li-ger [bil'-li-ger'] īn'-kouf.
Into the bargain.	In den Kauf; obendrein.	in dān kouf; ō-ben-drīn'.
To make [buy or strike] a bargain.	Einen Kauf oder Handel schließen.	ī'-nen kouf ō'-der hán'-del shlee'-ssen.
To have hard bargains with.	Es genau nehmen mit; streng handeln mit.	es ge-nou' nā'-men mit, shtrạng hán'-deln mit.
He will not bait an inch of it.	Er will nicht das Geringste nachlassen; nicht ein Haarbreit nachgeben.	ār vil niht dás ge-ring'-ste náḥ'-lás'-sen, niht īn hār'-brīt náḥ'-gā'-ben.
To stand at bay.	In der größten Noth sein; in letzten Zügen liegen; sich widersetzen; die Spitze bieten.	in dār grīs'-ten nōt zīn; in lạts'-ten tsū'-gen lee'-gen; ziḥ vee'-der-zạt'-sen; dee shpit'-se bee'-ten.
To keep at bay.	Aufhalten; abhalten; hinhalten; sich vom Leibe halten.	ouf'-hál'-ten; áp'-hál'-ten; hin'-hál'-ten; ziḥ fom lī'-be hál'-ten.
It beggars description.	Es ist über alle Beschreibung.	es ist ü'-ber ál'-le be-shrī'-bụng.

To beg the question.	Die Frage zum Satze machen; etwas Unerwiesenes als erwiesen voraussetzen.	dee frā'-ge tsum zāt'-se mách'-en; át'-vás ŭn'-er-vee'-ze-nes' áls er-vee'-zen fōr-ous'-zats'-en.
To be bound to one's good behavior.	Rechenschaft wegen seines Verhaltens geben müssen.	rạh'-en-shàft' vā'-gen zī'-nes fer-hál'-tens gā'-ben mĭs'-sen.
To be behind.	Rückstände zu bezahlen haben.	rĭk'-shtạn'-de tsoo be-tsā'-len hā'-ben.
To be behind time.	Sich verspätet haben; über die Zeit ausgeblieben sein.	zih fer-shpāi'-tet hā'-ben; ü-ber dee tsīt ous'-ge-blee'-ben zīn.
Beside the purpose.	Nicht zweckmäßig.	niht tsvạk'-mai-ssig.
To be beside one's self.	Außer sich sein; nicht bei Verstande sein.	ou'-sser zih zīn; niht bī fer-shtán'-de zīn.
The bias of interest.	Die Macht des Eigennutzes.	dee mácht dạs Ī'-gen-nụts'-es.
Not a bit.	Ganz und gar nicht; nicht im Geringsten.	gạnts ụnt gär niht; niht im ge-ring'-sten.
To bite the dust.	In's Gras beißen.	in's grás bī'-ssen.
To blast one's reputation.	Einen um seinen guten Namen bringen.	Ī'-nen ụm zī'-nen goo'-ten nā'-men bring'-en.
Bless me!	Sieh da! Wie? Ist es möglich?	zee dü! vee? ist es mĭg'-lih?
A blind alley.	Eine Sackgasse.	Ī'-ne zạk'-gás'-se.
A blind wall.	Eine Wand ohne Fenster.	Ī'-ne vánt ō'-ne fạn'-ster.
His blood is up.	Er ist aufgebracht [heftig].	ār ist ouf'-ge-brácht' [hạf'-tig].
To breed ill blood.	Die Gemüther erbittern.	dee ge-mü'-ter er-bit'-tern.
A distemper that runs in the blood.	Ein Erb-[Familien-]übel.	In arp'-[fá-mee'-li-yen']-ü'-bel.
At a blow.	Plötzlich; auf ein Mal.	plĭts'-lih; ouf īn mäl.
'Tis but a word and a blow with him.	Er schlägt sofort aus [um sich].	ār shlạigt zo-fort' ous [ụm zih].
To make bold.	Sich erkühnen; die Freiheit nehmen.	zih er-kü'-nen; dee frī'-hīt' nā'-men.
To put on a bold face.	Ein Herz fassen; Muth schöpfen.	In harts fás'-sen; moot shĭp'-fen.
It is a bold word.	Das ist viel gesagt.	dás ist feel ge-zägt'.
Bona fide.	Aus redlicher Meinung; auf Treu' und Glauben.	ous rät'-li-her mī'-nụng; ouf troi ụnt glou'-ben.
To bounce a person out of a thing.	Jemanden durch Einschüchterung berauben.	yā'-mán-den dụrh In'-shĭh'-te-rụng' be-rou'-ben.
I must have a bout with him.	Wir haben ein Ei mit einander zu schälen; ich muß mich mit ihm schlagen.	veer hā'-ben In I mit In-án'-der tsoo shai'-len; ih nụss mih mit eem shlü'-gen.
To have two strings to one's bow.	Mehr Mittel haben, um sich zu helfen.	mār mit'-tel hā'-ben, ụm zih tsoo hạl'-fen.
To have no bowels of compassion.	Kein Mitleid haben; gefühllos sein.	kīn mit-līt' hā'-ben; ge-fü̈l'-lös zīn.
To puzzle one's brain about a thing.	Sich den Kopf über Etwas zerbrechen.	zih dān kopf ü'-ber ạt'-vás tser-brạh'-en.
Cracked brain [brain-cracked].	Nicht bei Verstand.	niht bī fer-shtánt'.

To branch out upon a thing.	Viel Redens von Etwas machen.	feel rū'-dens fon at'-vás mäch'-en.
There is a storm brewing.	Es zieht ein Ungewitter auf.	es tseet in un'-ge-vit'-ter ouf.
To bring about.	Bewerkstelligen; zu Stande bringen.	be-vark'-shtal'-li-gen'; tsoo shtän'-de bring'-en.
A brisk sale.	Ein schneller Absatz.	in shnal'-ler äp'-zäts.
We gave them a brisk charge.	Wir feuerten wacker auf sie los; griffen sie muthig an.	veer foi'-er-ten' väk'-ker ouf zee lōs; grif'-fen zee moo'-tig än.
To make a bubble of one.	Einen zum Narren haben.	i'-nen tsum när'-ren hü'-ben.

C

To be ready at a call.	Auf jeden Wink bereit sein.	ouf yā'-den vink be-rīt' zīn.
To mount a cannon.	Eine Kanone auf die Laffette bringen.	i'-ne kä-nō'-ne ouf dee läf-fat'-te bring'-en.
What do I care?	Was kümmert's mich? Was geht's mich an?	vás kim'-mert's mih? vás gāt's mih än?
She cares for nobody [nothing].	Sie kümmert sich um Niemanden [Nichts].	zee kim'-mert zih um nee-män'-den [nihts].
For aught I care.	Meinetwegen.	mī'-net-vā'-gen.
To carry one's self.	Sich betragen, benehmen, verhalten.	zih be-trä'-gen, be-nā'-men, fer-häl'-ten.
To carry the cause.	Einen Prozeß gewinnen.	i'-nen pro-tsas ge-vin'-nen.
To carry the day.	Eine Schlacht gewinnen; siegen.	i'-ne shlächt ge-vin'-nen; zee'-gen.
It was carried.	Es wurde beschlossen; ging durch.	es vur'-de be-shlos'-sen; ging durh.
Carried away with admiration.	Von Bewunderung fortgerissen.	fon be-vun'-de-rung' fort'-ge-ris-sen.
To carry out.	Durchsetzen; ausführen.	durh'-zat'-sen; ous'-fü'-ren.
To be upon the catch.	Auf der Lauer liegen.	ouf der lou'-er lee'-gen.
To look to the main chance.	Auf die Hauptsache sehen.	ouf dee houpt'-zäch'-e zäh'-en.
You must stand the chance of it.	Sie müssen es darauf ankommen lassen.	zee mis'-sen es där-ouf' än'-kom-men läs'-sen.
To check one's appetite.	Seine Begierde überwinden.	zī'-ne be-geer'-de ü'-ber-vin'-den.
To make good cheer.	Einen guten Tisch führen.	i'-nen goo'-ten tish fü'-ren.
A clean trick.	Ein sauberer Streich.	in zou'-be-rer' shtrīh.
Clear coast.	Freies Feld; Niemand nahe.	frī'-es falt; nee'-mänt näh'-e.
To turn coat.	Abtrünnig werden.	äp'-trin'-nig vār'-den.
You will come off a loser.	Sie werden dabei verlieren.	zee vār'-den dä-bī' fer-lee'-ren.
It is none of my concern.	Es geht mich nichts an.	es gāt mih nihts än.
I will not be concerned with him any more.	Ich will nichts mehr mit ihm zu thun haben.	ih vil nihts mār mit eem tsoo toon hä'-ben.
By constitution.	Von Natur [aus].	fon nä-toor' [ous].
To couch in writing.	Schriftlich aufsetzen.	shrift'-lih ouf'-zat'-sen.
To keep countenance.	Die Fassung behalten; ruhig bleiben.	dee fäs'-sung be-häl'-ten; rooh'-ig blī'-ben.
To put out of countenance.	Aus der Fassung bringen; verblüffen.	ous dār fäs'-sung bring'-en; fer-blif'-fen.

D

He dabbles in physic.	Er pfuſcht in der Medizin.	är pfusht in där mä′-di-tseen′.
To cast a damp upon one's spirit.	Einem allen Muth benehmen.	I′-nem äl′-len moot be-nä′-men.
I have no dealings with him.	Ich habe nichts mit ihm zu thun.	iḥ hü′-be niḥts mit eem tsoo toon.
To give the devil his due.	Jedem Recht thun.	yä′-dem raḥt toon.
The devil rebukes sin.	Der Teufel predigt Buße.	där toi′-fel prä′-digt boo′-sse.
To hold a candle to the devil.	Aus Furcht höflich ſein.	ous furḥt hĩf′-liḥ zĩn.
Diamond cuts diamond.	Auf einen groben Kloß gehört ein grober Keil.	ouf I′-nen grö′-ben klots ge-hĩrt′ In grö′-ber kĩl.
To discharge the conscience.	Ein gutes Gewiſſen behalten.	In goo′-tes ge-vis′-sen be-hàl′-ten.
To discharge from duty.	Der Pflicht entlaſſen; ablöſen.	där pfliḥt ent-làs′-sen; àp′-lĩ′-zen.
To be distracted with passion.	Vor Zorn außer ſich ſein.	fōr tsorn ou′-sser ziḥ zĩn.
I doubled the fist.	Ich ballte die Fauſt.	iḥ bàl′-te dee foust.
To drop a courtesy.	Sich neigen, verbeugen; einen Knix machen.	ziḥ nī′-gen, fer-boi′-gen; I′-nen knix mách′-en.

E

To set together by the ears.	Zuſammenhetzen.	tsoo-zàm′-men-hat′-sen.
Up to the ears.	Bis an [über] die Ohren [den Hals].	bis àn [ü′-ber] dee ö′-ren [dän hàls].
Over head and ears.	Ueber Hals und Kopf; ganz und gar.	ü′-ber hàls unt kopf; gànts unt gàr.
To make both ends meet.	Ausgabe und Einnahme gleich machen; eben auskommen.	ous′-gä-be unt In′-nà′-me gliḥ mách′-en; ä′-ben ous′-kom′-men.
To engage one's self to —	Sich verpflichten oder verbindlich machen, zu —	ziḥ fer-pfliḥ′-ten ö′-der fer-bint′-liḥ mách′-en, tsoo
Enough is as good as a feast.	Der Zufriedene hat immer genug [iſt reich].	där tsoo-free′-de-ne′ hàt im′-mer ge-noog′[ist riḥ].
To enter a minute.	Eine Note [Anmerkung] machen.	I′-ne nō′-te[àn′-mar′-kung] mách′-en.
To be even with one.	Einem Gleiches mit Gleichem vergelten.	I′-nem glī′-ḥes mit glī′-ḥem fer-gàl′-ten.
To play at even or odd.	Gerade oder ungerade ſpielen.	ge-rü′-de ö′-der un′-ge-rü′-de shpee′-len.
To be exhausted for want of breath.	Außer Athem ſein.	ou′-sser ü′-tem zĩn.
Extravagancies.	Närriſche Streiche.	nàr′-ri-she′ shtrī′-ḥe.

F

To fly into one's face.	Einem zu Leibe gehen.	I′-nem tsoo lī′-be gŭh′-en.
How can you have the face?	Wie kannſt Du ſo unverſchämt ſein?	vee kànst doo zō un′-fer-shaimt′ zĩn?
Put a bold face upon the matter.	Nimm Dir die Sache nicht ſehr zu Herzen.	nim deer dee zách′-e niḥt zūr tsoo hạr′-tsen.

To be very fair with one.	Einem reinen Wein einschenken.	I'-nem rī'-nen vīn īn'-shang'-ken.
To bid fair.	Anlagen haben; zu Hoffnungen berechtigen.	ån'-lā-gen hā'-ben; tsoo hoff'-nung'-en be-raḥ'-ti-gen.
To fall in love with —	Sich in — verlieben.	ziḥ in — fer-lee'-ben.
To fall short of.	Nicht zureichen; das Gewicht nicht haben.	niḥt tsoo'-rī'-ḥen; dås ge-viḥt' niḥt hā'-ben.
The day was far spent.	Es war schon spät am Tage.	es vär shōn shpait åm tā'-ge.
Far fetched.	Mit den Haaren herbeigezogen.	mit dān hā'-ren her-bī'-ge-tsō'-gen.
To find fault [with].	Tadeln; auszusetzen haben an.	tā'-deln; ous'-tsoo-zåt'-sen hā'-ben ån.
May I be favored with—?	Darf ich mir — ausbitten?	dårf iḥ meer — ous'-bit'-ten?
Birds of a feather [will] flock together.	Gleich und Gleich gesellt sich gern.	glīḥ unt glīḥ ge-zålt' ziḥ garn.
I am not of that feather.	Ich bin nicht von dieser Art.	iḥ bin niḥt fon dee'-zer ärt.
A good fellow.	Ein guter Kerl; ein fideles Haus.	īn goo'-ter kårl; īn fi-dā'-les hous.
Not a fig.	Nicht einen Pfifferling.	niḥt I'-nen pfif'-fer-ling'.
To fight one's way.	Sich durchschlagen.	ziḥ durḥ-shlā'-gen.
To double the file.	Die Glieder schließen.	dee glee'-der shlee'-ssen.
To have a thing at one's finger's ends.	Etwas an den Fingern hersagen können.	åt'-vås ån dān fing'-ern hār'-zā'-gen kön'-nen.
To have a finger in the pie.	Die Hand im Spiele haben.	dee hånt im shpee'-le hā'-ben.
First come first served.	Wer zuerst kommt, mahlt zuerst.	vār tsoo-ārst komt, mält tsoo-ārst'.
Skin flint.	Geizhals.	gīts'-håls.
To roll on a flood of wealth.	Im Gelde schwimmen.	im gål'-de shvim'-men.
To make a fool of one.	Einen zum Besten haben.	I'-nen tsum bås'-ten hā'-ben.
To make free with one.	Sich mit einem gemein machen.	ziḥ mit I'-nem ge-mīn' måch'-en.
To make free with one's constitution.	Seine Gesundheit auf's Spiel setzen.	zī'-ne ge-zunt'-hīt' ouf's shpeel zåts'-en.
To be too free.	Sich zu viel Freiheit herausnehmen.	ziḥ tsoo feel frī'-hīt' her-ous'-nā'-men.
To frighten one out of his wits.	Einen durch Furcht außer sich bringen; in's Bockshorn jagen.	I'-nen durḥ furḥt ou'-sser ziḥ bring'-en; in's boks'-horn yā'-gen.

G

I have a great game to play.	Ich habe große Dinge vor.	iḥ hā'-be grö'-sse ding'-e för.
To make [a] game of —	Scherz treiben mit —; zum Besten haben.	shårts trī'-ben mit —; tsum bås'-ten hā'-ben.
His genius does not run that way.	Dazu hat er keine Anlage.	då-tsoo' håt ār kī'-ne ån'-lā-ge.
Give me a republic.	Da lobe ich mir eine Republik.	dā lō'-be iḥ meer I'-ne ra-pub-lik'.
To set a fine gloss upon a thing.	Einer Sache einen schönen Anstrich geben.	I'-ner zåch'-e I'-nen shī'-nen ån'-shtriḥ gā'-ben.

The report goes —	Man sagt, daß —	mån zügt, dås —
For good.	Ganz und gar.	gånts unt går.
To buy the good will of a house.	Eine Firma [mit der Kundschaft] käuflich übernehmen.	Ī'-ne fīr'-mä [mit dār kunt'-shåft] koif'-lih ü'-ber-nä'-men.
Much good may it do you.	Wohl bekomme es Ihnen.	vōl be-kom'-me es ee'-nen.
I can do no good in it.	Ich kann hierin nichts ausrichten.	ih kån heer-in' nihts ous'-rih'-ten.
Goods and chattels.	Bewegliches und unbewegliches Hab und Gut.	be-vāg'-li-hes' unt un'-be-vāg'-li-hes' håp unt goot.
God grant.	Gott gebe.	got gā'-be.
I take it for granted.	Ich nehme es als ausgemacht an.	ih nā'-me es åls ous'-ge-måcht' ån.
To put beside one's gravity.	Außer Fassung bringen.	ou'-sser fås'-sung bring'-en.
To go a great way with one.	Viel bei einem gelten.	feel bī ī'-nem gål'-ten.
To give one cross language.	Jemanden grob anfahren.	yā'-mån'-den grōp ån'-fä'-ren.
To dispute the ground.	Das Feld streitig machen.	dås fålt shtrī'-tig måch'-en.

H

Within a hair's breadth.	Auf ein Haar —; es fehlte nicht viel, so —	ouf īn hår —; es fāl'-te niht feel, zō —
To hammer a thing into one's head.	Jemandem etwas einbläuen.	yā'-mån-dem åt'-vås īn'-bloi'-en.
To have a good hand.	Glück im Spiele [gute Karten] haben.	glik im shpee'-le [goo'-te kår'-ten] hä'-ben.
To have a hand in a thing.	Die Hand mit im Spiele haben.	dee hånt mit im shpee'-le hä'-ben.
Hard drinking.	Unmäßiges Trinken; Saufen.	un'-mai'-ssi-ges' tring'-ken; zou'-fen.
The more haste, the less speed.	Eilen thut kein gut.	ī'-len toot kīn goot.
Make hay while the sun shines.	Man muß das Eisen schmieden, weil es heiß ist.	mån mus dås ī'-zen shmee'-den, vīl es hīs ist.
My head turns.	Mir schwindelt.	meer shvin'-delt.
To be on the wrong side of the hedge.	Vor die unrechte Schmiede gehen; fehl schießen; sich irren.	för dee un'-rah'-te shmee'-de gāh'-en; fāl shee'-ssen; zih ir'-ren.
To betake one's self to one's heels.	Fersengeld geben; das Hasenpanier ergreifen; durch die Lappen geben; ausreißen; durchbrennen.	fär'-zen-gålt' gā'-ben; dås hä'-zen-på-neer' er-grī'-fen; durh dee låp'-pen gāh'-en; ous'-rī'-ssen; durh'-bran'-nen.
To be out at the heels.	Löcher im Strumpfe haben; in elenden Umständen sein.	līh'-er im shtrump'-fe hä'-ben; in ā'-lån'-den um'-shtån'-den zīn.
I cannot help [it].	Ich kann nicht umhin [es nicht hindern].	ih kån niht um-hin' [es niht hin'-dern].
Helter-skelter.	Ueber Hals und Kopf; holterpolter.	ü'-ber håls unt kopf; hol'-ter-pol'-ter.
To hit one home.	Einen gehörig treffen; heimleuchten.	ī'-nen ge-hī'-rig tråf'-fen; hīm'-loih'-ten.

Hit or miss.	Es gerathe oder nicht; wohl oder übel.	es ge-rā'-te ō'-der niht; vōl ō'-der ü'-bel.
Home is home, let it be ever so homely.	Eigener Herd ist Goldes werth.	ī'-ge-ner' härt ist gol'-des värt.
To be off the hooks.	Mißlaunig, böse, aufgebracht sein.	mis'-lou'-nig, bĭ'-ze, ouf'-ge brächt' zīn.
To reckon without one's host.	Die Rechnung ohne den Wirth machen.	dee räh'-nung ō'-ne dän virt mäch'-en.
To keep good [bad, late] hours.	Abends rechtzeitig [spät] nach Hause kommen.	ä'-bents räht'-tsī'-tig [shpait] näch hou'-ze kom'-men.
To be out of humor.	Nicht bei [guter] Laune [verstimmt] sein.	niht bī [goo'-ter] lou'-ne [fer-shtĭmt'] zīn.
To do a thing for the humor of it.	Etwas aus guter Laune, zum Spaß thun.	ąt'-väs ous goo'-ter lou'-ne, tsum shpäs toon.

I

Ill weeds grow apace.	Unkraut vergeht nicht.	un'-krout fer-gāt niht.
Give him an inch, and he'll take an ell.	Zeig' ihm den Finger, und er wird die ganze Hand nehmen wollen.	tsīg eem dän fĭng'-er, unt är virt dee gän'-tse hänt nā'-men vol'-len.
In the first instance.	Erstens; zum ersten Male.	är'-stens; tsum är'-sten mä'-le.
For the best of your interest.	Zu Ihrem Besten.	tsoo ee'-rem bąs'-ten.

J

Jack will never make a gentleman.	Hans bleibt Hans.	häns blīpt häns.
Jack of all trades.	In allen Sätteln gerecht.	in äl'-len ząt'-teln ge-raht'.
To be Jack of all trades, but master of none.	Etwas von Allem, aber nichts gründlich wissen.	ąt'-väs fon äl'-lem, ä'-ber nihts grünt'-lih vis'-sen.

L

To be lame at a thing.	In einer Sache unerfahren, ein Stümper sein.	in ī'-ner zäch'-e un'-er-fä'-ren, īn shtĭm'-per zīn.
To talk at large.	Weitläufig [ein Langes und Breites] reden.	vīt'-loi'-fig [īn läng'-es unt brī'-tes] rä'-den.
He has breathed his last.	Er hat den Geist aufgegeben.	är hät dän gīst ouf'-ge-gä'-ben.
My way lay just by him.	Mein Weg führte mich an ihm vorbei.	mīn väg für'-te mih än eem fōr-bī'.
To lay on the shelf.	Bei Seite legen.	bī zī'-te lā'-gen.
To have the lead.	Der Erste sein; die Vorhand haben.	där är'-ste zīn; dee fōr'-hänt hä'-ben.
To have the leading hand.	Am Ausspielen sein.	äm ous'-shpee'-len zīn.
To stand on one's own legs.	Sich selbst forthelfen.	zih ząlpst fort'-hal'-fen.
To have the length of one's foot.	Jemanden sehr genau kennen.	yā'-män'-den zār ge-nou' kąn'-nen.
Festina lente.	Eile mit Weile.	ī'-le mit vī'-le.
To help one at a dead lift.	Einem aus der Noth helfen.	ī'-nem ous där nōt hąl'-fen.

To go one's long home.	In die Ewigkeit gehen; sterben.	in dee ā'-vig-kīt' gäh'-en; shtar'-ben.
To look in upon one.	Jemandem einen kurzen Besuch machen.	yä'-man-dem ī'-nen kur'-tsen be-zooch' mách'-en.
To be on the look out.	Auf der Lauer liegen.	ouf där lou'-er lee'-gen.
To keep a good look out.	Ein wachsames Auge haben; sich wohl vorsehen.	īn vách'-zä'-mes ou'-ge hä'-ben; zih vōl fōr'-zäh-en.
To make one lose.	Einen um — bringen.	ī'-nen um — bring'-en.
To be in love with —	In — verliebt sein.	in — fer-leept' zīn.

M

Mad as a march hare.	Fuchswild.	fux'-vilt'.
With might and main.	Mit aller Macht.	mit äl'-ler mácht.
To offer a fair margin of —	Einen schönen Nutzen von — bieten.	ī'-nen shī'-nen nut'-sen fon — bee'-ten.
He is not his match.	Er ist ihm nicht gewachsen.	är ist eem niht ge-vák'-sen.
She is not his match.	Sie paßt nicht zu ihm [für ihn].	zee pást niht tsoo eem [für een].
He has met [with] his match.	Er hat seinen Mann gefunden.	är hát zī'-nen mán ge-fun'-den.
To have hard measures.	Einen harten Stand haben; schlecht behandelt werden.	ī'-nen här'-ten shtánt hä'-ben; shláht be-hán'-delt vär'-den.
Measure for measure.	Gleiches für Gleiches; Wurst wider Wurst.	glī'-hes für glī'-hes; vurst vee'-der vurst.
It is meat and drink to me.	Ich lebe ganz davon.	ih lā'-be gánts dá-fon'.
To be at one's mercy.	In Jemandes Gewalt sein.	in yä'-mán'-des ge-vált' zīn.
At the mercy of the waves.	Den Wellen preisgegeben.	dän vál'-len prīs-ge-gā'-ben.
Merry Andrew.	Der Hanswurst; Lustigmacher.	där háns'-vurst; lus'-tig-mách'-er.
Mind your own business.	Bekümmere Dich um Deine Sachen.	be-kim'-me-re' dih um dī'-ne zách'-en.
I don't mind it.	Ich mache mir nichts daraus.	ih mách'-e meer nihts där-ous'.
Never mind [it].	Laß' es gut sein; es macht nichts aus; erwähne es nicht weiter.	lás es goot zīn; es mácht nihts ous; er-vai'-ne es niht vī'-ter.
Never mind him.	Kehre Dich nicht an ihn; sorge für den nicht, für den ist mir nicht bange.	kā'-re dih niht án een; zor'-ge für dän niht, für dän ist meer niht báng'-e.
You mistake me for another.	Sie sehen mich für einen Andern an.	zee zäh'-en nih für ī'-nen án'-dern án.
I second the motion.	Ich unterstütze den Vorschlag; pflichte ihm bei.	ih un-ter-shtit'-se dän fōr'-shläg; pflih'-te eem bī.

N

It is next to impossible.	Es ist fast unmöglich.	es ist fást un'-mig'-lih.
He is more nice than wise.	Er übertreibt die Vorsicht.	är ü'-ber-trīpt' dee fōr'-ziht.
In the very nick of time.	Zur rechten Zeit; auf den Punkt.	tsur ráh'-ten tsīt; ouf dän punkt.

I took no notice of her.	Ich kümmerte mich um sie nicht; ich that, als sähe ich sie nicht.	ih küm'-mer-te' mih um zee niht; ih tät, äls zaih'-e ih zee niht.
To avoid notice.	Um Aufsehen zu vermeiden.	um ouf'-zäh'-en tsoo fer-mī'-den.
Upon notice given.	Auf ein gegebenes Zeichen.	ouf īn ge-gā'-be-nes' tsī'-hen.
To come to nought.	Mißlingen; verunglücken.	mis-ling'-en; fer-un'-glïk'-ken.
To set at nought.	In den Wind schlagen; verachten.	in dän vint sblä'-gen; fer-ách'-ten.
Now and then.	Dann und wann; hier und da.	dän unt vän; beer unt dä.
Now for them.	Nun mögen sie kommen.	nun mī'-gen zee kom'-men.

O

There is no objection to it.	Es ist nichts dagegen einzuwenden.	es ist nihts dä-gā'-gen īn'-tsoo-van'-den.
I am under no such obligation.	Ich bin gar nicht dazu verpflichtet.	ih bin gär niht dä-tsoo' fer-pflih'-tet.
To obscure one's self.	Sich versteckt halten; eingezogen leben.	zih fer-shtäkt' häl'-ten; īn'-ge-tsō'-gen lā'-ben.
To have occasion for.	[Etwas] nöthig haben, brauchen.	[ąt'-väs] nī'-tig hä'-ben, brou'-chen.
There is no occasion.	Es ist nicht nöthig.	es ist niht nī'-tig.
There is some odd money.	Es ist noch etwas Geld mehr [übrig].	es ist noch ąt'-väs galt mär [üb'-rig].
Odd money.	Ueberzähliges Geld.	ü'-ber-tsäi'-li-ges' galt.
There are great odds.	Es ist ein großer Unterschied.	es ist īn grō'-sser un'-ter-sheet'.
On which side do the odds lie?	Wer hat das Uebergewicht?	vär hät däs ü'-ber-ge-viht'?
They are ever at odds.	Sie zanken sich beständig; sind stets uneinig.	zee tsäng'-ken zih be-shtän-dig, zint shtäts un'-ī'-nig.
I am off.	Ich mache, daß ich fortkomme.	ih mäch'-e, däs ih fort'-kom'-me.
Well off.	In guten Umständen.	in gōo'-ten um'-shtąn'-den.
Ill off.	Uebel daran.	ü'-bel där-än'.
To be off one's legs.	Schlecht zu Fuße sein.	shläht tsoo foo'-sse zīn.
No offence.	Nichts für ungut.	nihts für ụu'-goot.
No offence, I hope.	Es nimmt doch Niemand übel.	es nimt doch nee'-mänt ü'-bel.
To be in office.	Ein Amt bekleiden.	īn ämt be-klī'-den.
Old birds are not caught with chaff.	Alte Füchse fängt man nicht.	äl'-te fïk'-se fąnkt män niht.
Omnium gatherum.	Alles durcheinander.	äl'-les durh'-īn-än'-der.
To have an open account with —	In Rechnung stehen mit —	in rah'-nung shtāh'-en mit —
I have a high opinion of —	Ich schätze — sehr hoch; halte viel auf —	ih shąt'-se — zär boch; häl'-te feel ouf —
To give an order.	Bestellen.	be-shtąl'-len.
Overcast.	Ueberzogen; trübe; getrübt.	ü'-ber-tsō'-gen; trü'-be; ge-trüpt'.
This smell overcomes me.	Dieser Geruch nimmt mir den Kopf ein.	dee'-zer ge-ruch' nimt meer dän kopf īn.

P

For my part.	Ich meines Theils; was mich betrifft.	ih mī'-nes tīls; vás mih be-trift'.
In part payment.	Auf Abschlag; abschlägliche Zahlung.	ouf áp'-shlág; áp'-shlaig'-li-he' tsä'-lung.
To take in good part.	Nicht übel nehmen.	niht ü'-bel nä'-men.
To part with.	Sich von — trennen.	zih fon — trąn'-nen.
To be a party in.	Theil haben oder nehmen an —	tīl hā'-ben ō'-der nä'-men án —
Will you be of the party?	Wollen Sie dabei sein?	vol'-len zee dā-bī' zīn?
To pass current.	Für voll anbringen.	für fol án'-bring'-en.
To pass for —	Gehalten werden für —; gelten als —	ge-hál'-ten vär'-den für —; gąl'-ten áls —.
To pass a trick upon one.	Jemandem einen Streich spielen.	yā'-mán'-dem ī'-nen shtrih shpee'-len.
To have a passion for.	Einen starken Hang zu etwas haben.	ī'-nen shtár'-ken háng tsoo ąt'-vás hā'-ben.
Peal of laughter.	Schallendes Gelächter.	shál'-len-des' ge-lah'-ter.
To be perfect in a thing.	Etwas gründlich verstehen.	ąt'-vás grínt'-lih fer-shtäh'-en.
At the peril of —	Bei Vermeidung von —	bī fer-mī'-dung fon —
To be petrified with horror.	Vor Schrecken außer sich sein.	för shrąk'-ken ou'-sser zih zīn.
To pin one's opinion upon another man's sleeve.	Eines Andern Meinung blindlings folgen.	ī'-nes án'-dern mī'-nung blint'-lings fol'-gen.
It is a thousand pities.	Es ist ewig Schade.	es ist ā'-vig shā'-de.
To play the hypocrite.	Heucheln.	hoi'-heln.
To keep at sword's point.	Abwehren; entfernt halten.	áp'-vā'-ren; ent-fąrnt' hál'-ten.
Principal and charges.	Die volle Summe einer Forderung.	dee fol'-le zum'-me ī'-ner for'-de-rung'.
I am privy to it.	Man hat es mir anvertraut.	mán hát es meer án'-fer-trout'.
Purchase money.	Kaufpreis; Kaufgeld[er].	kouf'-prīs; kouf'-gąld[er].

Q

To qualify one's self.	Sich eignen; sich für etwas schicken.	zih īg'-nen; zih für ąt'-vás shik'-ken.
The question is —	Die Rede [Frage] ist —; es betrifft —	dee rä'-de [frä'-ge] ist —; es be-trift' —
The point in question.	Die vorliegende Frage; der Streitpunkt.	dee för'-lee'-gen-de' frä'-ge; där shtrīt'-punkt.
To be out of question.	Nicht in Betracht kommen.	niht in be-tráht' kom'-men.
I don't question it.	Ich zweifle nicht daran.	ih tsvīf'-le niht dār-án'.
To quit one's self like —	Sich benehmen, wie —	zih be-nä'-men vee —
To quit a situation.	Eine Stelle aufgeben; abdanken.	ī'-ne shtál'-le ouf'-gā'-ben; áp'-dáng'-ken.
To quit [scores] with one.	Mit Jemandem abrechnen; ihn ausbezahlen.	mit yā'-mán'-dem áp'-rąh'-nen; een ous'-be-tsä'-len.
Quit claim.	Verzicht, Verzichtleistung.	fer-tsiht', fer-tsiht'-līs'-tung.
To be quoted at —	Im Curse stehen zu —	im kur'-ze shtäh'-en tsoo —

9

R

To keep a racket.	Einen Lärm machen.	ī'-nen larm mách'-en.
For ready cash.	Für [gegen] baares Geld.	für [gā'-geu] bā'-res galt.
To meet with ready purchasers.	Willige Käufer finden.	vil'-li-ge' koi'-fer fin'-den.
Ready payment.	Baarzahlung.	bār'-tsā'-lung.
Ready sale.	Schneller Verkauf.	shnąl'-ler fer-kouf'.
To make reckoning without the host.	Die Rechnung ohne den Wirth machen.	dee rąh'-nung ō'-ne dän virt mách'-en.
To give the rein.	Den Zügel schießen lassen.	dän tsü'-gel shee'-ssen läs'-sen.
Well remembered.	Gut, daß Sie mich daran erinnern.	goot, dás zee mih där-án'-er-in'-nern.
To remove the cloth.	Den Tisch abdecken.	dän tish áp'-dąk-ken.
Out of repair.	Baufällig.	bou'-fąl'-lig.
It rests upon a testimony.	Es beruht auf einem Zeugnisse.	es be-root' ouf ī'-nem tsoig'-nis'-se.
It rests with me.	Es bleibt mir überlassen.	es blīpt meer ü'-ber-lás'-sen.
The fault rests with her.	Die Schuld liegt an ihr.	dee shųlt leegt án eer.
To make round abouts.	Umschweife machen.	ųm'-shvī'-fe mách'-en.
To put to [the] rout.	Auf's Haupt [in die Flucht] schlagen.	ouf's houpt [in dee flųcht] shlä'-gen.
To rub through the world.	Sich durch die Welt helfen; sich durchschlagen.	zih dųrh dee valt hąl'-fen; zih dųrh'-shlä'-gen.

S

Hunger is the best sauce.	Hunger ist der beste Koch.	hųng'-er ist där bąs'-te koch.
Sweet meat and sour sauce.	Gutes und Böses durcheinander.	goo'-tes ųnt bĭ'-zes dųrh'-īn-án'-der.
I will serve him the same sauce.	Ich werde ihn mit gleicher Münze bezahlen.	ih vär'-de een mit glī'-her mįn'-tse be-tsä'-len.
You don't say so!	Was Sie nicht sagen! Ei, das wäre!	vás zee niht zü'-gen! ī, dás vai'-re!
Every second year.	Ein Jahr um's andere.	īn yür ųm's án'-de-re'.
He is second to none.	Er steht Keinem nach.	är shtāt kī'-nem näch.
To send in [up] one's name.	Sich melden lassen.	zih mąl'-den läs'-sen.
To serve one a trick.	Einem einen Possen spielen.	ī'-nem ī'-nen pos'-sen shpee'-len.
It serves my turn.	Das ist mir recht [genug]; so will ich es.	dás ist meer rąht [ge-noog']; zō vil ih es.
To set up for one's self.	Sein eigenes Hauswesen anfangen.	zīn ī'-ge-nes' hous'-vā-zen án'-fáng'-en.
To shift for one's self.	Für sich selbst sorgen; sich selbst helfen; sich aus dem Staube machen.	für zih ząlpst zor'-gen; zih ząlpst hąl'-fen; zih ous däm shtou'-be mách'-en.
To be at shilly-shally.	Unschlüssig sein; nicht wissen, was man thun soll.	ųn'-shlīs'-sig zīn; niht vis'-sen, vás mán toon zol.
To strive against the stream.	Gegen den Strom schwimmen.	gā'-gen dän shtröm shvim'-men.

T

She is made a common talk.	Die Welt spricht von ihr.	dee vȧlt shpriḥt fon eer.
Never tell me.	Keine Entschuldigung.	kī'-ne ent-shul'-di-gung'.
Tell it in a word.	Mache es kurz.	mȧch'-e es kurts.
To tell fortunes by the cards.	Die Karte schlagen.	dee kȧr'-te shlä'-gen.
To tell stories.	Geschichtchen erzählen; lügen.	ge-shiḥt'-ḥen er-tsai'-len; lü'-gen.
Tell-tale.	Der Zuträger, Zwischenträger, Ohrenbläser.	dār tsoo'-trai'-ger, tsvish'-en-trai'-ger, ö'-ren-blai'-zer.
To make [come to] terms.	Uebereinkommen; sich abfinden; vergleichen.	ü'ber-īn'-kom'-men; ziḥ ȧp'-fin'-den; fer-glī'-ḥen.
To be on good terms with —	Mit — in gutem Einvernehmen stehen.	mit — in goo'-tem īn'-fer-nä'-men shtäh'-en.
To touch the glasses.	[Auf Jemandes Gesundheit] anstoßen.	[ouf yā'-mȧn'-des ge-zunt'-hīt] ȧn'-shtö'-ssen.
Trickster.	Gauner; feiner Betrüger.	gou'-ner, fī'-ner be-trü'-ger.
Don't trouble my head with it.	Macht mir den Kopf nicht warm damit.	mȧcht meer dān kopf niḥt vȧrm dȧ-mit'.

U

My blood is up.	Das Blut kocht mir in den Adern.	dȧs bloot kocht meer in dān ü'-dern.
To come up with —	— einholen.	— īn'-hō'-len.

V

At [for] a venture.	Auf gut Glück; auf Gerathewohl; in den Tag hinein; blindlings.	ouf goot glik; ouf ge-rä'-te-völ; in dān tȧg hin-īn'; blint'-lings.
His very picture.	Sein wahres Ebenbild.	zīn vä'-res ā'-ben-bilt'.
To cut to the very bone.	Bis auf den Knochen schneiden.	bis ouf dān knoch'-en shnī-den.
In the very air you breathe.	Selbst die Luft, die man athmet.	zȧlpst dee luft, dee mȧn ät'-met.
The very next morning.	Schon den folgenden Morgen.	shōn dān fol'-gen-den' mor'-gen.
She did violence on herself.	Sie that sich ein Leides.	zee tät ziḥ īn lī'-des.
To do violence to —	— Gewalt anthun.	— ge-vȧlt' ȧn'-toon'.
To vote an address.	Ueber eine Adresse abstimmen.	ü'-ber ī'-ne ȧd-rȧs'-se ȧp'-shtim'-men.

W

To walk a horse.	Ein Pferd spazieren reiten [am Zaume führen].	īn pfȧrt shpȧ-tsee'-ren rī'-ten [ȧm tsou'-me fü'-ren].
Who wants you to do it?	Wer verlangt das von Ihnen?	vār fer-lȧnkt' dȧs fon ee'-nen?
Which way?	Wohin? Auf welche Art?	vo-hin'? ouf vȧl'-ḥe ärt?

He is of my way of thinking.	Er ist meiner Meinung; hat meine Ansichten.	är ist mī'-ner mī'-nung; hät mī'-ne än'-zih'-ten.
This is a thing out of my way.	Davon verstehe ich nichts; das steht nicht in meiner Gewalt.	dä-fon' fer-shtäh'-e ih nihts; däs shtät niht in mī'-ner ge-vält'.
To stand out of, *or* clear the way.	Aus dem Wege gehen; Platz machen.	ous däm vä'-ge gäh'-en; pläts mäch'-en.
Lead the way.	Gehen Sie voran.	gäh'-en zee for-än'.
He must have his own way.	Er will es nach seinem Sinne haben.	är vil es näch zī'-nem zin'-ne hä'-ben.
To be weighed down with —	Mit — niedergebeugt sein.	mit — nee'-der-ge-boigt' zīn.
What though?	Und wenn auch?	unt van ouch?
I gave him what money I had.	Ich gab ihm alles Geld, was ich hatte.	ih gäp eem äl'-les galt, väs ih hät'-te.
What with his conduct, what with his courage.	Theils durch seine Aufführung, theils durch seinen Muth.	tīls durh zī'-ne ouf'-fü'-rung, tīls durh zī'-nen moot.
What a Goth!	Wie ausländisch er sich benimmt!	vee ous'-län'-dish är zih be-nimt'.
Mr. what's his name.	Der Herr So-und-So.	där harr zō-unt-zō.
To have one's will.	Jemandes Zustimmung haben.	yä'-män'-des tsoo'-shtim'-mung hä'-ben.
To have all things at will.	Alles nach Wunsch [zu Gebote] haben.	äl'-les näch vunsh [tsoo ge-bō'-te] hä'-ben.
I wish to God —	Wollte Gott —	vol'-te got —
To learn wit.	Durch Schaden klug werden.	durh shä'-den kloog vär'-den.
He frightened him out of his wits.	Er hat ihn zu Tode erschreckt.	är hät een tsoo tō'-de er-shrakt'.
To be at one's wits' ends.	In Verlegenheit sein.	in fer-lā'-gen-hīt' zīn.
It is a usual thing with him.	Es ist so sein Gebrauch.	es ist zō zīn ge-brouch'.
He parted with everything he had.	Er gab Alles hin, was er hatte.	är gäp äl'-les hin, väs er hät'-te.
One with another.	Eins in's Andere gerechnet.	ins in's än'-de-rè' ge-rah'-net.
So goes the world.	So geht's in der Welt.	zō gāt's in där valt.
Not for all the world.	Um keinen Preis.	um kī'-nen prīs.
What is he worth?	Wie viel [Geld] hat er?	vee feel [galt] hät är?

WORDS SIMILAR IN SOUND.

Aehnlich lautende Wörter.

(ain'-liḥ lou'-ten-de' vīr'-ter)

Aale (ü'-le), *pl.* of **Aal** (ül), *m.*, eel; **Ahle** (ü'-le), *f.*, awl; **Allee** (ȧl-lä'), *f.*, alley, avenue, walk.

Aas (ȧs), *n.*, carrion; **aß** (ȧs), ate; **As** (ȧs), *n.*, ace.

Achse (ȧk'-se), *f.*, axle; **Axt** (ȧkst), *f.*, ax, axe.

acht (ȧcht), eight; **Acht haben** (ȧcht hä'-ben), to watch, to be attentive; **in die Acht erklären** (in dee ȧcht er-klai'-ren), to proscribe.

Aehre (ai'-re), *f.*, ear of corn; **Ehre** (ä'-re), *f.*, honor; **Oehre** (ī'-re), *f.*, also **Oehr** (īr), *n.*, eye of a needle.

ändern (ạn'-dern), to change; **entern** (ạn'-tern), to board [a vessel].

äußern (oi'-ssern), to utter; **eisern** (ī'-zern), of iron.

ahmen (ü'-men), to imitate; **Amen** (ä'-men), amen; **Ammen** (ȧm'-men), *pl.*, female nurses.

Ahnen (ü'-nen), *m. pl.*, ancestors; **ahnen**, to have a presentiment; **ahnden** (än'-den), to resent, punish.

aichen (ī'-ḥen), to gauge; **Eichen** (ī'-ḥen), *f. pl.*, oak trees; **eigen** (ī'-gen), own, proper, peculiar.

Anger (ȧng'-er), *m.*, grassy place; **Anker** (ȧng'-ker), *m.*, anchor; anker, a liquid measure.

anshträngen (ȧn'-shtrạng'-en), to fasten horses with cords; **anstrengen**, to exert, strain.

Arm (ȧrm), *m.*, arm; **arm**, poor; **Arme** (ȧr'-me), *m. sing.* and *pl.* of **Arm**, *m.*, and **arm**, poor, *pl.* poor; **Armee** (ȧr-mä'), *f.*, army.

Baal (bäl), *m.*, an idol; **Ball** (bȧl), *m.*, ball [globe and dancing]; **Ballen** (bȧl'-len), *m.*, bale, pack, palm of the hand; Typ. T. ball.

Backen (bȧk'-ken), *m.*, cheek, buttock; **backen**, to bake; **packen** (pȧk'-ken), to pack, pack up.

Bad (bät), *n.*, bath; **bat**, prayed, asked, *past perf.*; **Pathe** (pä'-te), *m.*, godfather, *f.* godmother.

Bahn (bän), *f.*, way, road; **Bann** (bȧn), *m.*, ban, excommunication; **Pan** (pän), god of the shepherds.

bald (bȧlt), soon; **ballt** (bȧlt), *3d person, pres. perf.*, balls into forms, clinches [the fist].

balgen (bál'-gen), *refl.*, to romp, wrestle; **Balken** (bál'-ken), *m.*, beam, rafter.
Band (bánt), *m., pl.* **Bände** (bąn'-de), volume; *n., pl.* **Bänder** (bąu'-der), ribbon, string; *pl.* **Bande** (bán'-de), fetters.
bang (báng), anxious, uneasy; **Bank** (bánk), *f.*, bench, *pl.* **Bänke** (bąng'-ke); bank, *pl.* **Banken** (báng'-ken).
bar (bär), without; **baar**, cash; **Bahre** (bä'-re), *f.*, barrow, bier; **Paar** (pär), *n.*, pair, couple.
Baß (bás), *m.*, bass; **Paß** (pás), *m.*, pass.
Bast (bást), *m.*, bark of a tree; **paßt** (pást), *3d person, pres. perf.* of **passen** (pàs'-sen), to fit, suit.
Bauer (bou'-er), *m.*, farmer, *pl.* **Bauern** (bou'-ern); *n.*, a bird-cage, *pl.* **Bauer**.
bedacht (be-dácht'), *part. past*, considered, considerate; **betagt** (be-tägt'), aged, stricken in years.
Beeren (bä'-ren), *f. pl.*, berries; **Bären** (bai'-ren), *m. pl.*, bears; *m. sing.*, rammer.
Beet (bät), *n.*, [flower] bed; **Bett** (bąt), *n.*, bed [to sleep in]; **ich bete** (iḥ bä'-te), I pray, worship; **Bete** (bä'-te), *f.*, beet; **ich bäte** (iḥ bai'-te), *imp. subj.* of **bitten** (bit'-ten), to pray, ask for.
begleiten (be-gli'-ten), to accompany; **bekleiden** (be-kli'-den), to clothe.
Beil (bīl), *n.*, hatchet; **Beule** (boi'-le), *f.*, a boil.
Bein (bīn), *n.*, leg, bone; **Pein** (pīn), *f.*, pain.
bereichern (be-ri'-hern), to enrich; **beräuchern** (be-roi'-heru), to fumigate.
berichtigt (be-riḥ'-tigt), adjusted, corrected, settled; **berüchtigt** (be-riḥ'-tigt), ill-famed.
berücken (be-rik'-ken), to entrap; **Perrücken** (per-rïk'-ken), *f. pl.*, periwigs.
bewährt (be-vairt'), approved, proof against; **bewehrt**, armed; wind- or weather-bound.
bei (bī), near, with; **Bey** (bī), *m.*, Turkish officer; **Bai** (bī), *f.*, bay.
bescheren (be-shä'-ren), (1) to shave, apply shears; (2) to give a present, a Christmas box, a share.
beschweren (be-shvä'-ren), to burden, trouble, importune, clog, load [the stomach]; **sich** (ziḥ) **beschweren**, to complain; **beschwören** (be-shvī'-ren), to confirm by oath, conjure, swear.
Besen (bä'-zen), *m.*, broom; **die Bösen** (dee bī'-zen), *pl.*, the bad [people].
bezeigen (be-tsī'-gen), to show, express; **bezeugen** (be-tsoi'-gen), to attest, bear witness, testify.
beuchen (boi'-hen), to buck [linen]; **beugen** (boi'-gen), to bend, bow, depress.
Beute (boi'-te), *f.*, (1) booty, spoil, prey; (2) a large trough; **beide** (bī'-de), both.
Biene (bee'-ne), *f.*, bee; **Bühne** (bü'-ne), *f.*, scaffolding, gallery, stage, scene.
bieten (bee'-ten), to offer, bid, wish; **bitten** (bit'-ten), to request, pray; of which the noun **Bitte** (bit'-te), *f.*; **Bütte** (bït'-te), *f.*, tub, wooden vessel.
Bissen (bis'-sen), *m.*, bit; with p instead of b, to urinate; **büßen** (bü'-ssen), to atone for, expiate.
Biß (bis), *m.*, bite; **bis**, till, until.
blank (blánk), blank, polished; **Planke** (pláng'-ke), *f.*, plank, board.
Blässe (blás'-se), *f.*, paleness; **Blöße** (blī'-sse), *f.*, nakedness.
Blasen (blä'-zen), *f. pl.*, bubbles, bladders, blisters; **blasen**, to blow; **blaß** (blás), pale.

𝕭𝖑𝖆𝖙𝖙 (blåt), *n.*, sheet, leaf; 𝕻𝖑𝖆𝖙𝖙𝖊 (plåt′-te), *f.*, plate, bald pate; 𝖕𝖑𝖆𝖙𝖙 (plåt), flat, plain.

𝖇𝖑ö𝖐𝖊𝖓 (blī′-ken), to bleat; 𝖇𝖑𝖊𝖐𝖊𝖓 (blǖ′-ken), to show the teeth, tongue.

𝕭𝖑ü𝖙𝖊 (blü′-te), *f.*, blossom; 𝖇𝖑ü𝖍𝖙𝖊 (blü′-te), *past perf.* of 𝖇𝖑ü𝖍𝖊𝖓 (blüh′-en), to bloom; 𝕲𝖊𝖇𝖑ü𝖙 (ge-blüt′), blood, the mass of it in the animal body; 𝖌𝖊𝖇𝖑ü𝖍𝖙 (ge-blüt′), *past part.* of 𝖇𝖑ü𝖍𝖊𝖓.

𝕭𝖔𝖉𝖊𝖓 (bō′-den), *m.*, ground, bottom, floor, garret; 𝕭𝖔𝖙𝖊𝖓 (bō′-ten), *m. pl.*, messengers; 𝖋𝖎𝖊 𝖇𝖔𝖙𝖊𝖓 (zee bō′-ten), they offered; 𝕭𝖔𝖔𝖙 (bōt), *n.*, boat.

𝕭𝖔𝖍𝖑𝖊 (bō′-le), *f.*, a strong board; 𝕻𝖔𝖑𝖊 (pō′-le), *m.*, a Polander; 𝕻𝖔𝖑 (pōl), *m.*, pole; 𝕭𝖔𝖜𝖑𝖊 (bō′-le), *f.*, bowl [of punch].

𝕭𝖔𝖗𝖙 (bort), *m.* and *n.*, board, brim; shelf, *n.*; 𝕭𝖔𝖗𝖙𝖊 (bor′-te), *f.*, border, lace; 𝕻𝖔𝖗𝖙 (port), *m.*, harbor; 𝖊𝖗 𝖇𝖔𝖍𝖗𝖙 (är bört), he perforates, bores.

𝖇𝖗𝖆𝖈𝖍 (brächt), fallow, unplonghed; 𝖊𝖗 𝖇𝖗𝖆𝖈𝖍 (är bräch), he broke; 𝕻𝖗𝖆𝖌 (präg), Prague.

𝕭𝖗ä𝖚𝖙𝖊 (broi′-te), *f. pl.*, brides; 𝕭𝖗𝖊𝖎𝖙𝖊 (brī′-te), *f.*, breadth.

𝕭𝖗𝖎𝖈𝖐𝖊 (brik′-ke), *f.*, lamprey; 𝕭𝖗ü𝖈𝖐𝖊 (brǖk′-ke), *f.*, bridge.

𝕭𝖗𝖎𝖑𝖑𝖊 (bril′-le), *f.*, spectacles; 𝖎𝖈𝖍 𝖇𝖗ü𝖑𝖑𝖊 (iḫ brǖl′-le), I roar.

𝕭𝖗𝖚𝖈𝖍 (bruch), *m.*, breach, fraction, rupture; 𝕭𝖗𝖚𝖈𝖍 (brooch), *m.*, marshground.

𝕭𝖚𝖈𝖍 (booch), *n.*, (1) book; (2) quire, *pl.* 𝕭𝖚𝖈𝖍; 𝕭𝖚𝖈𝖍𝖊 (boo′-che), *f.*, beach tree; 𝕭𝖚𝖌 (boog), *m.*, flexure, bow, bent; shoulder of animal.

𝕭𝖚𝖉𝖊 (boo′-de), *f.*, booth, stall, shop; 𝕭𝖚𝖙𝖙𝖊 (but′-te), *f.*, (1) tub; (2) flounder.

𝕭𝖚𝖓𝖉 (bunt), *m.*, band, league, alliance; *n.*, bunch, bundle; 𝖇𝖚𝖓𝖙 (bunt), variegated, colored.

ℭ𝖍𝖎𝖋𝖋𝖗𝖊 (shif′-fer), *f.*, cipher; 𝕾𝖈𝖍𝖎𝖋𝖋𝖊𝖗 (shif′-fer), *m.*, mariner; 𝕾𝖈𝖍𝖎𝖊𝖋𝖊𝖗 (shee′-fer), *m.*, slate, splinter; 𝖘𝖈𝖍𝖎𝖊𝖋𝖊𝖗 (shee′-fer), *comp.* of 𝖘𝖈𝖍𝖎𝖊𝖋 (sheef), oblique.

ℭ𝖍𝖔𝖗 (kōr), *m.*, chorus, choir; *n.*, choir of a church; ℭ𝖔𝖗𝖕𝖘 (kōr), *n.*, corps.

ℭ𝖍𝖚𝖗 (koor), *f.*, O. G., election, hence ℭ𝖍𝖚𝖗𝖋ü𝖗𝖘𝖙 (koor′-fīrst′), elector; ℭ𝖚𝖗 (koor), *f.*, cure;. ℭ𝖔𝖚𝖗 (koor), *f.*, originally French, proper German: 𝕳𝖔𝖋 (hōf), *m.*, hence: court;—𝖊𝖎𝖓𝖊𝖗 𝕯𝖆𝖒𝖊 𝖉𝖎𝖊 ℭ𝖔𝖚𝖗 [𝖉𝖊𝖓 𝕳𝖔𝖋] 𝖒𝖆𝖈𝖍𝖊𝖓 (ī′-ner dü′-me dee koor [dān hōf] mách′-en), to court a lady.

ℭ𝖎𝖉𝖊𝖗 (tsee′-der), *m.*, cider; 𝖅𝖎𝖙𝖍𝖊𝖗 (tsit′-ter), *f.*, guitar.

𝕯𝖆𝖈𝖍 (dách), *n.*, roof; 𝕿𝖆𝖌 (täg), *m.*, day.

𝕯𝖆𝖈𝖍𝖘 (däks), *m.*, badger; 𝕿𝖆𝖗 (täks), *m.*, yew; 𝕿𝖆𝖝𝖊 (täk′-se), *f.*, taxe.

𝕯ä𝖓𝖊𝖓 (dai′-něn), *pl.* Danes; 𝖉𝖊𝖓𝖊𝖓 (dā′-nen), *rel. pron.*, to whom; 𝖉𝖊𝖍𝖓𝖊𝖓 (dā′-nen), to stretch, extend.

𝖉𝖆𝖘 (dás), (1) *n.*, the; (2) instead of 𝖜𝖊𝖑𝖈𝖍𝖊𝖘 (val′-ḫes), *rel. pron.*, *n.*, which; (3) this *or* that [this *or* that is good]; (4) instead of 𝖏𝖊𝖓𝖊𝖘, *demonst. pron.*, *n.*, that, opposite to this; 𝖉𝖆𝖘 (dás), *conj.*, that.

𝕯𝖆𝖚𝖇𝖊 (dou′-be), *f.*, stave [of a cask]; 𝕿𝖆𝖚𝖇𝖊 (tou′-be), *f.*, dove, pigeon; *m.*, deaf person.

𝖉𝖆𝖚𝖊𝖗𝖓 (dou′-ern), *impers. verb*, (1) to last; (2) to grieve, to make sorry, to be sorry for; 𝖊𝖘 𝖉𝖆𝖚𝖊𝖗𝖙 𝖒𝖎𝖈𝖍 (es dou′-ert miḫ), I am sorry for it.

𝕯𝖊𝖎𝖈𝖍 (diḫ), *m.*, dike; 𝕿𝖊𝖎𝖈𝖍 (tīḫ), *m.*, pond; 𝕿𝖊𝖎𝖌 (tīg *or* tīḫ), *m.*, dough.

𝖉𝖎𝖈𝖍𝖙𝖊𝖓 (diḫ′-ten), (1) to make close, tight; (2) to meditate, write poetry, invent.

Dicke (dik'-ke), *f.*, thickness; Tücke (tĭk'-ke), *f.*, malice.

Dingen (ding'-en), *dat. pl.* of Ding, *n.*, thing; dingen, to bargain for, hire; düngen (dĭng'-en), to dung.

Docke (dok'-ke), *f.*, (1) bull dog [Dogge]; (2) rail, little pillar; (3) *mus. term*, jack; (4) plug, peg; (5) doll; (6) dock, dock yard.

Dorf (dorf), *n.*, village; Torf (torf), *m.*, turf, peat.

drei (drī), three; treu (troi), faithful.

Draht (drät), *m.*, wire; trat (trät), *past perf.* of treten (trä'-ten), to tread.

Drang (dräng), *m.*, throng, pressure, strong desire; Trank (tränk), *m.*, drink; trank, *past perf.* of trinken (tring'-ken), to drink.

Dritte (drit'-te), *m., f., n*, third; Tritte (trit'-te), *m. pl.*, steps.

Dünste (dĭns'-te), *pl.* of Dunst (dunst), *m.*, vapor, mist, damp; dünnste, *superl.* of dünn (dĭn), thin; Dienste (deens'-te), *pl.* of Dienst (deenst), *m.*, service.

Ecke (ak'-ke), *f.*, corner, edge; Egge (ag'-ge), *f.*, harrow.

Ehe (äh'-e), *f.*, marriage, matrimony; ehe, before, prior to, ere.

Eider (ī'-der), (1) a fowl; Eidergans (ī'-der-gäns'), *f.*, eider duck; Eiderbunen (ī'-der-doo'-nen), *pl.*, eider down; (2) *f.*, the name of a river in Danemark, where the fowl comes from; Eiter (ī'-ter), *m.*, pus, suppuration; Euter (oi'-ter), *n.*, udder, dug.

Eigen, see Aichen.

Ende (an'-de), *n.*, end; Ente (an'-te), *f.*, duck.

Engel (ang'-el), *m.*, angel; Enkel (ang'-kel), *m.*, (1) grandchild, grandson; (2) ankle.

Erbe (ar'-be), *n.*, inheritance, heritage; *m.*, heir.

Erkenntniß (er-kant'-nis), *f.*, knowledge, perception; *n.*, judicial decision.

Essen (as'-sen), *n.*, meal; *pl.* of Esse (as'-se), *f.*, forge.

euer (oi'-er), your; Eier (ī'-er), *pl.* of Ei (ī), *n.*, egg.

Eule (oi'-le), *f.*, owl; Eile (ī'-le), *f.*, haste, speed.

fade (fä'-de), insipid, dull; Pfade (pfä'-de), *pl.* of Pfad (pfät), *m.*, path; Faden (fä'-den), *m.*, thread.

fahl (fäl), fallow; Pfahl (pfäl), *m.*, pale, post stake.

Falz (fälts), *m.*, furrow; Pfalz (pfälts), *f.*, Palatinate.

Farre (fär'-re), *m.*, bullock; Pfarre (pfär'-re), *f.*, parsonage.

Feige (fī'-ge), *f.*, fig; feige, cowardly.

Feilchen (fīl'-hen), *n.*, a small file; Veilchen (fīl'-hen), *n.*, violet.

Feld (falt), *n.*, field; fällt (falt), *indic. pres.* of fallen (fäl'-len), to fall, and fällen (fal'-len), to fell.

Felle (fal'-le), *pl.* of Fell (fal), *n.*, skin, hide; Fälle (fal'-le), *pl.* of Fall (fäl), *m.*, fall, ruin, case, cataract; fälle, *imperative* and *1st person pres. indic.* of fällen [see the preceding].

Ferse (fär'-ze), *f.*, heel; Verse, *pl.* of Vers (färs), *m.*, verse.

Fest (fast), *n.*, feast, festival; fest, firm.

fetter (fat'-ter), *comp.* of fett, fat; Vetter (fat'-ter), *m.*, cousin; Väter (fai'-ter), fathers; Feder (fä'-der), *f.*, pen, feather.

𝔉𝔢𝔲𝔢𝔯 (foi'-er), *n.*, fire; 𝔉𝔢𝔦𝔢𝔯 (fī'-er), *f.*, celebration, feast.
𝔉𝔦𝔟𝔢𝔯 (fee'-ber), *f.*, fibre; 𝔉𝔦𝔢𝔟𝔢𝔯, *n.*, fever; 𝔙𝔦𝔭𝔢𝔯 (fee'-per), *f.*, viper.
𝔣𝔦𝔢𝔩 (feel), *past perf.* of 𝔣𝔞𝔩𝔩𝔢𝔫 (fál'-len), to fall; 𝔳𝔦𝔢𝔩 (feel), much; 𝔓𝔣ü𝔥𝔩 (pfül), *m.*, pillow, bolster.
𝔉𝔦𝔩𝔷 (filts), *m.*, (1) felt; (2) blanket, *typ. term*; (3) miser.
𝔉𝔦𝔫𝔨 (fingk), *m.*, finch; 𝔣𝔦𝔫𝔤, *past perf.* of 𝔣𝔞𝔫𝔤𝔢𝔫 (fàng'-en), to catch.
𝔉𝔩𝔞𝔲𝔪 (floum), *m.*, down; 𝔓𝔣𝔩𝔞𝔲𝔪𝔢 (pflou'-me), *f.*, plum.
𝔉𝔩𝔢𝔠𝔨𝔢𝔫 (flak'-ken), *m.*, (1) borough, market-place; (2) spot, stain; 𝔉𝔩𝔢𝔠𝔨 (flak), *m.*, botch, piece.
𝔣𝔩𝔦𝔠𝔨𝔢𝔫 (flik'-ken), to botch, cobble, mend, repair; 𝔭𝔣𝔩ü𝔠𝔨𝔢𝔫 (pflïk'-ken), to pluck.
𝔉𝔩𝔦𝔢ß (flees), *radical* of 𝔣𝔩𝔦𝔢ß𝔢𝔫 (flee'-ssen), to flow; 𝔙𝔩𝔦𝔢ß (flees), *n.*, skin of a lamb or sheep, fleece; 𝔡𝔞𝔰 𝔤𝔬𝔩𝔡𝔢𝔫𝔢 (däs gol'-de-ne') 𝔙𝔩𝔦𝔢ß, the golden fleece.
𝔉𝔩𝔬𝔯 (flōr), *m.*, [*pl.* 𝔢 and 𝔢𝔫] (1) bloom, blossom; (2) gauze, crape, veil; (3) *f.*, see 𝔉𝔩𝔲𝔯.
𝔉𝔩ö𝔥𝔢 (flïh'-e), *m. pl.*, flees; 𝔣𝔩ö𝔥𝔢, *subjunc.*, would fly; 𝔣𝔩𝔢𝔥𝔢 (fläh'-e), *1st person sing. pres.* of 𝔣𝔩𝔢𝔥𝔢𝔫 (fläh'-en), to implore.
𝔉𝔩𝔲𝔠𝔥 (flooch), *m.*, curse; 𝔉𝔩𝔲𝔤 (floog *or* flooch), *m.*, the act of flying, flight; 𝔓𝔣𝔩𝔲𝔤 (pfloog), *m.*, plough; *prov.*, a troop of people.
𝔉𝔩𝔲𝔯 (floor), *m.*, floor, flooring; *f.*, field, plain, plot of ground.
𝔉𝔯𝔞𝔠𝔥𝔱 (frächt), *f.*, freight; 𝔣𝔯𝔞𝔤𝔱 (frägt *or* frächt), *3d person sing. pres.* of 𝔣𝔯𝔞𝔤𝔢𝔫 (frä'-gen), to ask.
𝔉𝔯𝔞𝔠𝔨 (fräk), *m.*, dress coat; 𝔚𝔯𝔞𝔨 (vräk), *n.*, wreck.
𝔣𝔯𝔢𝔦𝔢𝔫 (frī'-en), to woo, marry; 𝔣𝔯𝔢𝔲𝔢𝔫 (froi'-en), to be glad; 𝔣𝔯𝔢𝔦 (frī), free; 𝔟𝔢=𝔣𝔯𝔢𝔦𝔢𝔫 (be-frī'-en), to free, liberate.
𝔉𝔯𝔦𝔰𝔱 (frist), *f.*, space of time, term; 𝔣𝔯𝔦ß𝔱 (frist), *3d person sing. pres.* of 𝔣𝔯𝔢𝔰𝔰𝔢𝔫 (fräs'-sen), to eat [said of animals], to eat greedily [vulgar of man].
𝔉𝔲𝔡𝔢𝔯 (foo'-der), *n.*, (1) cart load; (2) measure for wine; 𝔉𝔲𝔱𝔱𝔢𝔯 (fut'-ter), *n.*, (1) case, lining; (2) food.
𝔉ü𝔩𝔩𝔢𝔫 (fül'-len), *n.*, foal; 𝔣ü𝔩𝔩𝔢𝔫, to fill; 𝔣ü𝔥𝔩𝔢𝔫 (fü'-len), to feel.
𝔉𝔲𝔫𝔡 (funt), *m.*, finding, thing found; 𝔓𝔣𝔲𝔫𝔡 (pfunt), *n.*, pound.
𝔣ü𝔯 (fūr), for; 𝔳𝔦𝔢𝔯 (feer), four.

𝔤ä𝔥𝔫𝔢𝔫 (gai'-nen), to yawn; 𝔤ö𝔫𝔫𝔢𝔫 (gïn'-nen), not to grudge.
𝔤ä𝔥𝔯𝔢𝔫 (gai'-ren), to ferment; 𝔟𝔢𝔤𝔢𝔥𝔯𝔢𝔫 (be-gä'-ren), to covet, desire, crave.
𝔊𝔞𝔫𝔰 (gäns), *f.*, goose; 𝔤𝔞𝔫𝔷 (gänts), whole, all, entire.
𝔊𝔞𝔯𝔡𝔢𝔫 (gär'-den), *f. pl.*, guards; 𝔤𝔞𝔯𝔡𝔢𝔫, to go begging; 𝔊𝔞𝔯𝔱𝔢𝔫 (gär'-ten), *m.*, garden; 𝔎𝔞𝔯𝔱𝔢𝔫 (kär'-ten), *f. pl.*, cards.
𝔊𝔞𝔰𝔢 (gä'-ze), *n. pl.* of 𝔊𝔞𝔰; 𝔊𝔞𝔰𝔰𝔢 (gäs'-se), *f.*, street, lane; 𝔎𝔞𝔰𝔰𝔢 (käs'-se), *f.*, money box.
𝔊𝔢𝔡𝔯ä𝔫𝔤𝔢 (ge-dräng'-e), *n.*, throng, crowd; *figuratively*, dilemma; 𝔊𝔢𝔱𝔯ä𝔫𝔨 (ge-tränk'), *n.*, beverage.
𝔊𝔢𝔣ü𝔥𝔩 (ge-fül'), *n.*, feeling, sensation; 𝔤𝔢𝔣𝔦𝔢𝔩 (ge-feel'), *past perf.* of 𝔤𝔢𝔣𝔞𝔩𝔩𝔢𝔫 (ge-fäl'-len), to please.
𝔊𝔢𝔥𝔢𝔦ß (ge-hīs), *n.*, order, command; 𝔊𝔢𝔥ä𝔲𝔰𝔢 (ge-hoi'-ze), *n.*, case [of a watch].
𝔊𝔢𝔦𝔰𝔢𝔩 (gī'-zel), *f.*, hostage; 𝔊𝔢𝔦ß𝔢𝔩 (gī'-ssel), *f.*, whip, scourge.

𝕲𝖊𝖑𝖆𝖈𝖍 (ge-lách′), n., (1) puddle, bog; (2) continued laughter; 𝕲𝖊𝖑𝖆𝖌 (ge-lüg′), n., feast, banquet.

𝕲𝖊𝖑ä𝖚𝖙𝖊 (ge-loi′-te), n., ringing of bells; 𝕲𝖊𝖑𝖊𝖎𝖙𝖊 (ge-lī′-te), n., accompanying, escort.

𝕲𝖊𝖑𝖇 (galt), n., money; 𝖌𝖊𝖑𝖙 (galt), interj., true! is it not true? 𝖌𝖊𝖑𝖑𝖙 (galt), 3d person sing. pres. of 𝖌𝖊𝖑𝖑𝖊𝖓 (gal′-len), to yell.

𝖌𝖊𝖑𝖊𝖊𝖗𝖙 (ge-lärt′), emptied; 𝖌𝖊𝖑𝖊𝖍𝖗𝖙 (ge-lärt′), learned, skilled, informed.

𝕲𝖊𝖑ü𝖇𝖇𝖊 (ge-lĭb′-de), n., vow; 𝕲𝖊𝖑𝖎𝖊𝖇𝖙𝖊 (ge-leep′-te), m. and f., (1) lover; (2) sweetheart.

𝖌𝖊𝖒𝖆𝖈𝖍 (ge-mách′), adv., softly, gently; 𝕲𝖊𝖒𝖆𝖈𝖍, n., (1) room, chamber; (2) something not well made.

𝖌𝖊𝖗𝖆𝖉𝖊 (ge-rä′-de), straight, plain; 𝖌𝖊𝖗𝖆𝖙𝖍𝖊 (ge-rü′-te), 1st person pres. indic. and imperative of 𝖌𝖊𝖗𝖆𝖙𝖍𝖊𝖓, to come upon; to prosper; 𝕲𝖗𝖆𝖉𝖊 (grü′-de), m. pl., degrees.

𝖌𝖊𝖗ä𝖙𝖍 (ge-rait′), 3d person sing. pres. of 𝖌𝖊𝖗𝖆𝖙𝖍𝖊𝖓 [see the preceding]; 𝕲𝖊𝖗ä𝖙𝖍𝖊 (ge-rai′-te), n. pl., tools, implements; 𝕲𝖊𝖗𝖊𝖉𝖊 (ge-rü′-de), n., talk, report, rumor.

𝖌𝖊𝖗𝖊𝖈𝖍𝖙 (ge-raht′), just; 𝖌𝖊𝖗ä𝖈𝖍𝖙 (ge-raiht′), revenged.

𝕲𝖊𝖗𝖎𝖈𝖍𝖙 (ge-riht′), n., (1) judgment, court, tribunal; (2) dish [of fish, etc.]; 𝕲𝖊𝖗ü𝖈𝖍𝖙 (ge-rīht′), n., report, fame.

𝕲𝖊𝖗𝖙𝖊𝖓 (gar′-ten), f. pl., switches; 𝕲ä𝖗𝖙𝖊𝖓 (gar′-ten), m. pl. of 𝕲𝖆𝖗𝖙𝖊𝖓 (gar′-ten), garden.

𝕲𝖊𝖘𝖎𝖈𝖍𝖙 (ge-ziht′), n., (1) eye sight; (2) face, countenance; (3) [pl. 𝖊] apparition.

𝕲𝖊𝖘𝖙𝖆𝖉𝖊 (ge-shtä′-de), n., shore, coast; 𝖌𝖊𝖘𝖙𝖆𝖙𝖙𝖊 (ge-shtàt′-te), 1st person pres. indic. and imperative sing. of 𝖌𝖊𝖘𝖙𝖆𝖙𝖙𝖊𝖓, to permit, grant.

𝕲𝖊𝖛𝖎𝖊𝖗𝖙 (ge-feert′), n., square; 𝖌𝖊𝖋ü𝖍𝖗𝖙 (ge-fürt′), part. past. of 𝖋ü𝖍𝖗𝖊𝖓 (fü′-ren), to guide, conduct.

𝕲𝖊𝖜ä𝖍𝖗 (ge-vair′), f., vouch, pledge; 𝕲𝖊𝖜𝖊𝖍𝖗 (ge-vär′), n., weapon [any kind of weapon].

𝕲𝖊𝖜𝖆𝖓𝖉 (ge-vànt′), n., garment; 𝖌𝖊𝖜𝖆𝖓𝖉𝖙 (1) part. past of 𝖜𝖊𝖓𝖉𝖊𝖓 (vau′-den), to turn; (2) quick, nimble, adroit, clever, smart.

𝕲𝖑𝖎𝖊𝖉 (gleet), n., member, limb, joint; 𝖌𝖑ü𝖍𝖙 (glüt), 3d person sing. pres. of 𝖌𝖑ü𝖍𝖊𝖓 (glüh′-en), to glow; 𝖌𝖑𝖎𝖙𝖙 (glit), past perf. of 𝖌𝖑𝖊𝖎𝖙𝖊𝖓 (glī′-ten), to glide, slip.

𝖌𝖑𝖎𝖒𝖒𝖊𝖓 (glim′-men), to glimmer; 𝖐𝖑𝖎𝖒𝖒𝖊𝖓 (klim′-men), to climb.

𝕲𝖗𝖆𝖒 (grüm), m., grief; 𝕶𝖗𝖆𝖒 (krüm), m., trade, shop, stuff.

𝕲𝖗𝖆𝖘 (grás), n., herb, grass; 𝖌𝖗𝖆𝖘 (grass), horrible, ghastly.

𝕲𝖗𝖆𝖚𝖊𝖓 (grou′-en), n., horror; 𝖌𝖗𝖆𝖚𝖊𝖓, (1) to have horror; (2) to dawn; 𝖐𝖗𝖆𝖚𝖊𝖓 (krou′-en), to scratch softly.

𝕲𝖗𝖊𝖓𝖟𝖊 (gran′-tse), f., limit, boundary; 𝕶𝖗ä𝖓𝖟𝖊 (kran′-tse), pl. of 𝕶𝖗𝖆𝖓𝖟 (kránts), m., wreath.

𝕲𝖗𝖎𝖊𝖈𝖍𝖊 (gree′-he), m., a Greek; 𝖐𝖗𝖎𝖊𝖈𝖍𝖊𝖓 (kree′-hen), to creep, crawl, cringe; 𝖐𝖗𝖎𝖊𝖌𝖊𝖓 (kree′-gen), to seize, to make war, to get; 𝕶𝖗𝖎𝖊𝖌𝖊 (kree′-ge), m. pl., wars; 𝕶𝖗ü𝖌𝖊 (krü′-ge), m. pl., pitchers; 𝕶𝖗ü𝖈𝖐𝖊 (krik′-ke), f., crutch; 𝕶𝖗𝖎𝖊𝖌𝖊𝖗 (kree′-ger), m., warrior; 𝕶𝖗ü𝖌𝖊𝖗 (krü′-ger), m., tapper.

𝕲ü𝖙𝖊𝖗 (gü′-ter), pl. of 𝕲𝖚𝖙 (goot), n., estate; 𝕲𝖎𝖙𝖙𝖊𝖗 (git′-ter), n., grate, railing.

haart (härt), *3d person sing. pres.* of haaren (hü'-ren), to shed *or* lose the hair; harrt (hárrt), *3d person sing. pres.* of harren (hár'-ren), to abide, wait for, hope; hart (hárt), hard.

hacken (hák'-ken), to chop; Hacken, *noun pl., prov.*, heels; Haken (hü'-ken), *m.*, hook.

Hader (hü'-der), *m.*, (1) rag; (2) quarrel, brawl.

Hafen (hü'-fen), *m.*, (1) harbor; (2) pot.

Häfen (hai'-fen), *pl.* of Hafen; Hefen (hä'-fen), *pl.*, dregs, yeast.

Haft (háft), *m. & n.*, hold, firmness; clasp; *f.*, prison, arrest; *n.*, ephemera.

Hai (hī), *m.*, shark; Heu (hoi), *n.*, hay.

Hain (hīn), *m.*, grove; Hein (hīn), *term for* death.

hält (halt), *3d person sing. pres.* of halten (hál'-ten), to hold, keep; Held (halt), *m.*, hero.

hängst (hangst), *2d person sing. pres.* of hängen (hang'-en), to suspend; Hengst (hangst), *m.*, stallion.

Hasen (hü'-zen), *pl.* of Hase, *m.*, hare; hassen (hás'-sen), to hate.

Häuser (hoi'-zer), *pl.* of Haus (hous), *n.*, house; heiser (hī'-zer), hoarse; heißer (hī'-sser), hotter.

Häute (hoi'-te), *pl.* of Haut (hout), *f.*, skin, hide; heute (hoi'-te), to-day.

Hecke (hák'-ke), [*pl.* n] *f.*, (1) hedge, enclosure; (2) brood, breed, and the verb hecken, to hatch.

heilen (hī'-len), to cure; heulen (hoi'-len), to howl.

Helle (hal'-le), *f.*, brightness, clearness; Hölle (hīl'-le), *f.*, hell.

Heller (hal'-ler), *m.*, small copper coin worth about a sixth of a cent; heller, clearer, lighter; Hehler (hä'-ler), *m.*, receiver of stolen goods.

Henne (han'-ne), *f.*, chicken; Hähne (hai'-ne), *pl.* of Hahn (hän), *m.*, rooster, cock.

her (här), here, hither; Heer (här), *n.*, host, army; hehr, sublime, high, holy; Herr (harr), *m.*, lord, master.

Herde (här'-de), *f.*, herd, flock, drove; *dative* of Herb (härt), *m.*, hearth; Härte (har'-te), *f.*, hardness; hörte (hīr'-te), *3d person past perf.* of hören (hī'-ren), to hear.

Hindin (hin'-din), *f.*, hind; Hündin (hīn'-din), *f.*, bitch.

Hofstaat (hōf'-shtät), *m.*, court, household of a prince; Hofstatt (hōf'-shtät), *f.*, place and buildings of a farm.

holen (hō'-len), to fetch; hohl (hōl), hollow.

holzicht (hol'-tsiht), wood-like; holzig (hol'-tsig), woody.

Hut (hoot), *m.*, hat; *f.*, heed, guard, care.

hüten (hü'-ten), to watch, guard; Hütten (hīt'-ten), *pl.* of Hütte, *f.*, hut, cottage.

jener (yā'-ner), that one; Jänner (yan'-ner), *m.*, January.

ihm (eem), to him; im (im), contracted from in (in) and dem (dām), in the.

ihre (eeh'-re), hers, theirs; Ihre, yours; irre (ir'-re), astray; ich irre mich, *1st person pres. indic.* of sich irren (zih ir'-ren), to be mistaken.

ist (ist), is; ißt (ist), *3d person sing. pres.* of essen (as'-sen), to eat.

Kahm (käm), *m.*, mould [on liquids]; **kam** (käm), *1st* and *3d person sing. past* of **kommen** (kom′-men), to come; **Kamm** (kämm), *m.*, comb.
Kammrad (käm′-rät′), *n.*, cog-wheel; **Kamerad** (käm-rät′), *m.*, comrade; **Kammerrath** (käm′-mer-rät′), *m.*, chamber counselor.
kann (kän), *1st* and *3d person sing. pres.* of **können** (kin′-nen), to be able; **Kahn** (kän), *m.*, boat; **Kanne** (kän′-ne), *f.*, measure of liquid, quart.
Kaper (kä′-per), *m.*, privateer; *f.*, caper.
Karbätsche (kär-dät′-she), *f.*, horse-brush; **Kartätsche** (kär-tät′-she), *f.*, cartridge.
Kärrner (kär′-ner), *m.*, carter; **Körner** (kir′-ner), *pl.* of **Korn** (korn), *n.*, grain.
Kehle (kä′-le), *f.*, throat, gutter; **Kelle** (käl′-le), *f.*, trowel, ladle.
Keil (kil), *m.*, wedge; **Keule** (koi′-le), *f.*, club; **Keiler** (ki′-ler), *m.*, wild boar.
Keller (käl′-ler), *m.*, cellar; **Köhler** (ki′-ler), *m.*, collier; **Kellner** (käl′-ner), *m.*, butler, waiter.
Kelter (käl′-ter), *f.*, wine press; **kälter**, *comparative* of **kalt** (kält), cold.
kennen (kän′-nen), to know; **können** (kin′-nen), to be able.
Kerbe (kär′-be), *f.*, notch, indent; **Körbe** (kir′-be), *pl.* of **Korb** (korp), *m.*, basket.
kernicht (kär′-niht), like a kernel *or* granule; **kernig** (kär′-nig), pithy, solid; **körnig** (kir′-nig), granulous.
Kichern (kih′-hern), *pl.* of **Kicher**, *f.*, chick-pea; **kichern**, to titter.
Kiefer (kee′-fer), *f.*, pine, fir; *m.*, jaw, jaw-bone.
Kiel (keel), *m.*, quill; keel; bulb of a plant; **kühl** (kül), cool.
Kien (keen), *m.*, pine wood; **Kinn** (kin), *n.*, chin; **kühn** (kün), bold.
Kissen (kis′-sen), *n.*, cushion, pillow; **küssen** (kis′-sen), to kiss.
Kiste (kis′-te), *f.*, chest, trunk; **Küste** (kis′-te), *f.*, coast; **küßte**, *1st* and *3d person sing. past* of **küssen** [see the preceding].
Klette (klät′-te), *f.*, burdock; **Glätte** (glät′-te), *f.*, smoothness.
kleiden (kli′-den), to dress, to sit well; **gleiten** (gli′-ten), to glide, slide.
Klinge (kling′-e), *f.*, blade, sword; **klinge**, *imperative* of **klingen**, to sound, to tingle; **Klinke** (kling′-ke), *f.*, latch.
Knappe (knäp′-pe), *m.*, shield bearer, adherent; **Knabe** (knä′-be), *m.*, boy; **knapp** (knäp), close, strait, tight, narrow.
Kobalt (kō′-bält), *m.*, cobalt; **Kobold** (kō′-bolt), *m.*, goblin.
Koppel (kop′-pel), *f.*, tie; band *or* belt [for a sword]; pack of hounds; **Kuppel** (kup′-pel), *f.*, cupola, dome.
Kreis (kris), *m.*, circle; **Greis** (gris), *m.*, aged man.
kreischen (kri′-shen), to shriek, screech; **kreisen** (kri′-zen), to turn, spin, whirl round; **kreißen** (kri′-ssen), to cry out, to be in labor.
Krippe (krip′-pe), *f.*, crib, manger; **Grippe** (grip′-pe), *f.*, influenza.
Kröte (krī′-te), *f.*, toad; **Gräte** (grai′-te), *f.*, fish bone.
Kunde (kun′-de), *m.*, customer; *f.*, news, notice, intelligence.
Kur, see **Cur**.

Lache (lách′-e), *f.*, slough, puddle, lake; **Lage** (lä′-ge), *f.*, lying, situation, site; **Lake** (lä′-ke), *f.*, brine, pickle; **Laken**, *n.*, cloth, sheet.
Laden (lä′-den), *pl.* of **Labe**, *f.*, chest, press; *m.*, shutter; shop, stall; **laden**, to load; to summon; to charge *or* load a gun; **Latten** (lät′-ten), *pl.* of **Latte**, *f.*, lath.

𝔏aien (lī'-en), *pl.* of 𝔏aie, *m.*, layman; leihen (līh'-en), to lend, borrow.
𝔏amm (lăm), *n.*, lamb; lahm (lăm), lame.
𝔏ärche (lair'-he), *f.*, larch [tree]; 𝔏erche (lạr'-he), *f.*, lark.
𝔏appen (láp'-pen), *m.*, flap, patch, tatter; *pl.* of 𝔏appe, Laplander, and instead of 𝔏affen (láf'-fen), *m.*, fops.
𝔏asen (lă'-zen), *pl.* of 𝔏ase, *f.*, pitcher; lasen, *3d person pl. past* of lesen (lă'-zen), to read; lassen (lás'-sen), to let, leave.
𝔏ast (lăst), *f.*, burden; laßt, *imperative* and *2d person pl.* of lassen [see the preceding].
𝔏äuse (loi'-ze), *pl.* of 𝔏aus (lous), *f.*, louse; leise (lī'-ze), low, not loud, soft, gentle.
läuten (loi'-ten), to ring, toll [bells]; 𝔏euten, *dative* of 𝔏eute (loi'-te), people, folks; leiten (lī'-ten), to conduct, guide; leiden (lī'-den), to suffer.
lecken (lăk'-ken), (1) to lick; (2) to spring a leak.
leeren (lă'-ren), to empty; lehren, to teach; 𝔏ehren, *pl.* of 𝔏ehre, *f.*, teaching, instruction, doctrine.
𝔏ehm (lăm), *m.*, clay; 𝔏eim (līm), *m.*, lime, glue; 𝔏ein (līn), *m.*, flax, linseed.
𝔏eib (līp), *m.*, body [human]; 𝔏aib (līp), *m.*, loaf.
𝔏eich, also 𝔏aich (līh), *m.* and *n.*, spawn; 𝔏eiche (lī'-he), *f.*, dead human body, corpse.
leichter (līh'-ter), *compar.* of leicht, easy, light; 𝔏euchter (loih'-ter), *m.*, chandelier.
leiden, see läuten.
lesen (lă'-zen), (1) to gather, to pick out; (2) to read; lösen (lȳ'-zen), to loosen, solve, redeem.
𝔏iebe (lee'-be), *f.*, love; 𝔏ippe (lip'-pe), *f.*, lip.
𝔏ied (leet), *n.*, (1) song, air, ditty; (2) lid [of the eye]; litt (lit), *1st* and *2d person sing. past* of leiden (lī'-den), to suffer.
liegen (lee'-gen), to lie; lügen (lü'-gen), to tell a falsehood.
lies (lees), *imperative sing.* of lesen [see above]; ließ, *1st* and *2d person sing. past* of lassen [see above].
𝔏inse (lin'-ze), *f.*, lens; lentil; 𝔏ünse (lǐn'-ze), *f.*, linch-pin.
𝔏iste (lis'-te), *f.*, list; 𝔏üste (lǐs'-te), *pl.* of 𝔏ust (lust), *f.*, lust.
𝔏ocken (lok'-ken), *pl.* of 𝔏ocke, *f.*, curl; locken, to allure, induce, decoy.
𝔏ose (lō'-ze), *pl.* of 𝔏oos (lōs), *n.*, lot, ticket; lose, loose, unsettled, wanton.

𝔐aas (mäs), *f.*, the river Meuse; 𝔐aß, *n.*, measure; maß, *1st* and *3d person sing. past* of messen (más'-sen), to measure; 𝔐asse (más'-se), *f.*, mass, bulk, stock.
𝔐agd (măgt), *f.*, maid-servant; 𝔐acht (măcht), *f.*, power; macht, *3d person pres. indic.* of machen (măch'-en), to make.
mahnen (mă'-nen), to remind; 𝔐anen, *pl.*, departed spirits.
man (măn), *pron.*, one, they; 𝔐ann, *m.*, man.
𝔐andel (măn'-del), *f.*, (1) almond; (2) number of fifteen [in measure]; 𝔐antel (măn'-tel), *m.*, cloak.
𝔐arder (măr'-der), *m.*, marten; 𝔐arter (măr'-ter), *f.*, torment, torture.
𝔐ark (mărk), *m.*, marrow [in bones]; pith [in wood]; juice, pulp [in fruits]; *f.*, march, boundary, mark; mark [weight of silver]; German coin, worth a quarter of a dollar.

Märkte (mark'-te), *pl.* of Markt (màrkt), *m.*, market; merkte, *1st* and *2d person sing. past* of merken (mar'-ken), to notice, observe.

Mast (màst), *m.*, (1) mast [of a ship] ; (2) mast, feeding and fattening pigs, poultry, etc.; food.

Mäuler (moi'-ler), *pl.* of Maul (moul), *n.*, mouth [of animals] ; Meiler (mī'-ler), *m.*, charcoal kiln.

Mäuse (moi'-ze), *pl.* of Maus (mous), *f.*, mouse; Meise (mī'-ze), *f.*, titmouse; Meißen (mī'-ssen), name of a city in Saxony.

mein (mīn), my ; Main, name of a river [Frankfort on the Main].

messen (mas'-sen), *pl.* of Messe, *f.*, mass, fair; messen, to measure.

Meth (màt), *m.*, mead ; Mett (mat), *n.*, the lean of meat.

Mieder (mee'-der), *n.*, bodice ; müder (mü'-der), *compar.* of müde, tired, fatigued.

Miene (mee'-ne), *f.*, mien, air, look; Mine, *f.*, mine [of ore, metal, etc.].

missen (mis'-sen), to miss; müssen (mīs'-sen), to be obliged, compelled, bound.

Mist (mist), *m.*, manure; mißt, *3d person sing. pres.* of messen [see above] ; müßt (mīst), *2d person pl. pres.* of müssen [see the preceding].

Mode (mō'-de), *f.*, fashion ; Motte (mot'-te), *f.*, moth.

Möhre (mī'-re), *f.*, carrot ; Mähre (mai'-re), *f.*, mare, tiding.

Moor (mōr), *n.*, moor; Mohr, *m.*, negro, African.

Muse (moo'-ze), *f.*, Muse; banana tree ; Muße (moo'-sse), *f.*, leisure, spare time.

Mus (moos), *n.*, pap; muß (muss), *1st* and *3d person sing. pres.* of müssen [see missen].

Nachen (nách'-en), *m.*, boat, skiff ; nagen (nä'-gen), to gnaw; Nacken (nák'-ken), *m.*, neck.

Nacht (nácht), *f.*, night; nagt (nügt), *3d person sing. pres.* of nagen [which see]; nackt (nákt), naked.

nein (nīn), no ; neun (noin), nine.

niesen (nee'-zen), to sneeze ; genießen (ge-nee'-ssen), to enjoy.

Nisse (nis'-se), *pl.* of Niß, *f.*, nit, bee's egg ; Nüsse (nīs'-se), *pl.* of Nuß (nuss), *f.*, nut.

Ofen (ō'-fen), *m.*, oven, stove, furnace ; offen (of'-fen), open.

Orden (or'-den), *m.*, order, decoration ; Orten (or'-ten), *dat. pl.* of Ort, *m.*, place.

Palast (pà'-làst), *m.*, palace ; Ballast (bál'-làst), *m.*, ballast.

Patron (pàt-rōn), *m.*, patron ; Patrone (pàt-rō'-ne), *f.*, cartridge.

Perrücken (par-rīk'-ken), *pl.* of Perrücke, *f.*, periwig; berücken (be-rīk'-ken), to ensnare, to take in.

pflügen (pflū'-gen), to plough ; pflücken (pflīk'-ken), to pluck.

Pfund (pfunt), *n.*, pound ; Fund (funt), *m.*, finding.

picken (pik'-ken), to pick ; Pieken (pee'-ken), *pl.* of Pieke, *f.*, pike, spade.

Posten (pos'-ten), *m.*, (1) post, station ; (2) item [in an account] ; (3) *pl.* of Post, *f.*, mail, post office.

prahlen (prū'-len), to brag, boast ; prallen (pràl'-len), to bounce, bound.

Preise (prī'-ze), *pl.* of Preis (prīs), *m.*, price, prize ; Preuße (proi'-sse), *m.*, Prussian.

Puder (poo'-der), *m.*, hair powder; Puter (poo'-ter), *m.*, turkey.

Quellen (kvąl'-len), *pl.* of Quelle, *f.*, source, well, spring; quellen, to gush, spring, swell, soak · quälen (kvai'-len), to torment.

Rad (rät), *n.*, wheel; Rath (rät), *m.*, council, counsel, counselor, advice.
Rain (rin), *m.*, green strip of land, boundary, ridge; Rhein, *m.*, Rhine [river]; rein, pure, clean.
Räuber (roi'-ber), *m.*, robber; Reiber (rī'-ber), *m.*, grater.
Rahm (räm), *m.*, cream; Rahmen (rä'-men), *m.*, frame; rammen (räm'-men), to ram, to drive *or* thrust into.
Rang (räng), *m.*, (1) rank, order, rate [of a vessel], quality; (2) precedence; (3) row [of boxes in theatre]; Rank (ränk), *m.*, intrigue, crookedness, trick.
Rangen (räng'-en), (1) *pl.* of Range, *m.*, good-for-nothing boy; (2) ridge of a hill; Ranken (räng'-ken), *pl.* of Ranke, *f.*, tendril, clasper, vine.
Rappe (räp'-pe), *m.*, black horse; Rappee (räp-pā'), *m.*, rappee, coarse snuff; Rabe (rä'-be), *m.*, raven.
Rasen (rä'-zen), *m.*, turf, sod; rasen, to rave, rage.
Ratten (rät'-ten), *pl.* of Ratte, *f.*, rat; rathen (rä'-ten), to guess, advise.
rauch (rouch), *adj.*, hairy, furred, rough [mostly rauh]; Rauch, *m.*, smoke, soot.
Raupen (rou'-pen), *pl.* of Raupe, *f.*, caterpillar; rauben (rou'-ben), to rob.
Recken (rek'-ken), *pl.* of Recke, *m.*, giant, hero; recken, to stretch, strain, rack; regen (rä'-gen), to stir, move, excite; Regen, *m.*, rain; rächen (rah'-hen), to revenge; Rechen (rah'-hen), *m.*, rake.
rechnen (rah'-nen), to reckon, cipher, esteem; regnen (räg'-nen), to rain.
Rede (rä'-de), *f.*, speech, discourse, oration; Rhede, *f.*, road, road-stead [of vessels]; Röthe (rī'-te), *f.*, redness, madder; Räthe (rai'-te), *pl.* of Rath [see above].
redlich (rät'-lih), honest, fair; räthlich (rait'-lih), advisable; röthlich (rīt'-lih), reddish.
Reich (rīh), *n.*, reign, empire, realm; reich, *adj.*, rich.
Reif (rīf), *m.*, (1) hoar frost; (2) ring, hoop; reif, *adj.*, ripe, mature.
Reihe (rīh-e), *f.*, row, rank, range, order, succession; Reue (roi'-e), *f.*, repentance.
Reime (rī'-me), *pl.* of Reim, *m.*, rhyme; Räume (roi'-me), *pl.* of Raum, *m.*, space.
Reis (rīs), *m.*, rice; *n.*, twig.
reisen (rī'-zen), to travel; reißen (rī'-ssen), to tear, pull; Reusen (roi'-zen), *pl.* of Reuse, *f.*, bow-net.
reiten (rī'-ten), to ride on horseback; reuten (roi'-ten), to root out.
retten (rät'-ten), to save; reden (rä'-den), to speak; röthen (rī'-ten), to redden.
Riemen (ree'-men), *m.*, thong, strap of leather; rühmen (rü'-men), to commend, praise, extol.
Ries (rees), *n.*, ream; Riß (riss), *m.*, (1) rent, cleft, crack; (2) draught, plan, sketch, design.
Riese (ree'-ze), *m.*, giant; *f.*, gutter *or* channel down a mountain.
Rocken (rok'-ken), *m.*, distaff, rock, rack; Roggen (rog'-gen), *m.*, rye; Rogen (rō'-gen), *m.*, roe, spawn.
Rose (rō'-ze), *f.*, rose; rosette; erysipelas; a name; Rosse (ros'-se), *pl.* of Roß (ross), *n.*, horse.
Rost (rost), *m.*, rust; gridiron.

Rotten (rot'-ten), *pl.* of **Rotte**, *f.*, troop, band, flock, gang; **rotten**, to root out, rot.
Rübe (rü'-be), *f.*, turnip; **Rippe** (rip'-pe), *f.*, rib; timberwork of an arched roof.
Rücken (rik'-ken), *m.*, back; **rücken**, to move, proceed, march; **rügen** (rü'-gen), to resent, to reprove; **Rügen**, name of an island in Pomerania; **riechen** (ree'-hen), to smell.
Ruhm (room), *m.*, glory, praise; **Rum** (rum), *m.*, rum.
Ruthe (roo'-te), *f.*, (1) rod, wand, verge; (2) switch; (3) perch; (4) rod [as measure]; **ruhte** (rooh'-te), *1st* and *3d person past perf.* of **ruhen** (rooh'-en), to rest.

Saat (zät), *f.*, seed, [act of] sowing, green and standing grain; **satt** (zät), satiated.
sachte (zäch'-te), soft, gentle, slow; **sagte** (zäg'-te), *1st* and *3d person sing. past perf.* of **sagen** (zä'-gen), to say.
Sache (zäch'-e), *f.*, thing, matter; **Sage** (zä'-ge), saying, tale, legend.
säen (zai'-en), to sow; **sehen** (zäh'-en), to see; **Seen** (zä'-en), *pl.* of **See**, *f.*, sea; *m.*, lake.
Sägen (zai'-gen), *pl.* of **Säge**, *f.*, saw; **Segen** (zä'-gen), *m.*, blessing.
säugen (zoi'-gen), to suckle; **Seuchen** (zoi'-hen), *pl.* of **Seuche**, *f.*, pestilence, plague.
Saite (zi'-te), *f.*, string [fiddle— or lute—]; **Seite** (zi'-te), *f.*, side, flank; page [of a book]; **Seide** (zi'-de), *f.*, silk.
Sammt (zämt), also **Sammet** (zäm'-met), *m.*, velvet; **sammt**, *prepos.*, together with; *adv.*, **sammt und sonders** (zämt unt zon'-ders), all together.
Sang (zäng), *m.*, song; **sang** (zäng), *1st* and *3d person sing. past perf.* of **singen** [see below]; **sank** (zänk), the same of **sinken** [see below].
Sangen (zäng'-en), *pl.* of **Sange**, *f.*, roasted corn; **sangen**, *3d person pl. past perf.* of **singen** [see below].
Schaben (shä'-ben), *pl.* of **Schabe**, *f.*, kind of insects; **schaben**, to scrape, shave.
Schaden (shä'-den), *m.*, loss, damage, harm; sore; **Schatten** (shät'-ten), *m.*, shadow, shade, phantom.
Schaft (shäft), *m.*, shaft, shank, stock, handle; **schafft**, *3d person sing. pres.* of **schaffen** (shäf'-fen), to do, make, work, furnish, convey, order.
schal (shäl), stale, flat; **Schale** (shä'-le), *f.*, shell, peel; **Schall** (shäll), *m.*, sound.
schälen (shai'-len), to pare, peel, shell; **schellen** (shäl'-len), to ring, ring the bell, tingle; **Schellen**, *pl.* of **Schelle** (shäl'-le), *f.*, bell.
schalt (shält), *1st* and *3d person sing. past perf.* of **schelten** (shäl'-ten), to scold; **schallt**, *3d person sing. pres.* of **schallen** (shäl'-len), to sound.
Scharen (shä'-ren), *pl.* of **Schar**, *f.*, troop, host, band, multitude; **scharren** (shär'-ren), to scrape, rake.
Schärfe (shär'-fe), *f.*, edge; **Schärpe** (shär'-pe), *f.*, scarf, sash.
Scheune (shoi'-ne), *f.*, barn, shed; **Scheine** (shi'-ne), *pl.* of **Schein**, *m.*, bond, certificate.
schief (sheef), oblique, crooked; **Schiff** (shiff), *n.*, ship; nave [of a church]; shuttle [of weavers].
Schiefer, see **Chiffre**.
Schild (shilt), *m.*, shield, buckler; *n.*, sign board, firm; **schilt**, *3d person sing. pres.* of **schelten** (shäl'-ten), to scold; **schielt** (sheelt), *3d person sing. pres.* of **schielen**, to squint.

Schlächter (shlăh'-ter), *m.*, butcher; schlechter, *comparative* of schlecht, bad.
Schlaf (shläf), *m.*, sleep; also instead of Schläfe (shlai'-fe), *f.*, temple; schlaff (shläff), slack, loose, flabby.
schlief (shleef), *1st* and *3d person sing. past perf.* of schlafen (shlä'-fen), to sleep; schliff (shliff), the same of schleifen (shlī'-fen), to grind, polish.
Schnur (shnoor), *f.*, lace, string; O. G., daughter-in-law; Schnurre (shnur'-re), *f.*, drollery, farce.
Schoos (shōs), *m.*, lap; Schoß (shoss), *m.*, shoot, sprig; schoß, *1st* and *3d person sing. past perf.* of schießen (shee'-ssen), to shoot.
Schote (shō'-te), *f.*, husk, shell; Schotte (shot'-te), *m.*, Scotchman.
Schute (shoo'-te), *f.*, skute, barge, sloop; Schutte (shut'-te), bundle, truss, heap.
Schwämme (shvăm'-me), *pl.* of Schwamm (shvămm), *m.*, sponge, mushroom; Schwemme, *f.*, horse pond, watering.
Schwären (shvai'-ren), *m.*, abscess; schwören (shvī'-ren), to swear, to take an oath; Schwere (shvā'-re), *f.*, weight, heaviness.
Seile (zī'-le), *pl.* of Seil, *n.*, rope; Säule (zoi'-le), *f.*, column, pillar.
seimen (zī'-men), to strain honey; säumen (zoi'-men), to hem, tarry.
seit (zīt), since; seid, *2d person pl. pres.* of sein (zīn), to be.
sengen (zăng'-en), to singe; senken (zăng'-ken), to let down, sink, lower.
siech (zeech), sick; Sieg (zeeg), *m.*, victory; sich (zih), *refl. acc.*, one's self.
sieden (zee'-den), to seethe, boil; Süden (zü'-den), *m.*, South; Sitten (zit'-ten), *pl.* of Sitte, *f.*, manner, custom, mode.
Siegel (zee'-gel), *n.*, seal; Sichel (zih'-el), *f.*, sickle.
Sohle (zō'-le), *f.*, sole; Sole, *f.*, salt water, salt spring.
Sold (zolt), *m.*, pay; sollt, *2d person pl. imperative* of sollen (zol'-len), to be bound, obliged to do.
sparen (shpä'-ren), to save, husband, spare, economize; Sparren (shpăr'-ren), *m.*, spar, rafter.
spielen (shpee'-len), to play; spülen (shpü'-len), to rinse, wash.
Spötter (shpĭt'-ter), *m.*, mocker; später (shpai'-ter), *comparative* of spät, late.
Sprengel (shpră̆ng'-el), *m.*, diocese; Sprenkel (shpră̆ng'-kel), *m.*, springe, noose, spots.
Sprosse (shpros'-se), also Sproß, *m.*, sprig, scion; *f.*, step; freckle.
Staar (shtär), *m.*, (1) disease of the eye; (2) starling; starr (shtărr), stiff, numb, inflexible.
Staat (shtät), *m.*, (1) State; (2) pomp, parade; (3) great retinue, train; (4) finery, dress; Stadt (shtătt), *f.*, city, town; Statt, *f.*, place, stead.
stählen (shtai'-len), to steel, harden, temper; stehlen (shtä'-len), to steal.
Ställe (shtăl'-le), *pl.* of Stall (shtăll), *m.*, stable; Stelle, *f.*, place, spot.
stäuben (shtoi'-ben), to dust; stäupen (shtoi'-pen), to flog, whip.
Stift (shtift), *m.*, tag, peg, pencil, stump; *n.*, [charitable] foundation, monastery, chapter.
Stiel (shteel), *m.*, handle, stalk; Stil, *m.*, style; still (shtill), still, quiet; Stühle (shtü'-le), *pl.* of Stuhl (shtool), *m.*, chair.
sticken (shtik'-ken), to stitch, embroider; choke; Stücken (shtĭk'-ken), *dative pl.* of Stück, *n.*, piece, fragment [of music], trick.

10

Strauß (shtrous), *m.*; (1) ostrich ; (2) bunch, nosegay.
Sträuche (shtroi'-he), *pl.* of Strauch (shtrouch), *m.*, shrub, bush; Streiche (shtrī'-he), *pl.* of Streich, *m.*, stroke, blow, trick.
Streit (shtrīt), *m.*, fight, war, quarrel, strife; streut (shtroit), *3d person sing. pres.* of streuen, to strew, scatter.
Strenge (shtrang'-e), *f.*, harshness, severity, strictness; Stränge, *pl.* of Strang (shtrāng), *m.*, rope.

Takt (täkt), *m.*, tact, time, measure; tagt (tägt), *pres.* of tagen (tä'-gen), to grow light, dawn.
tadeln (tä'-deln), to blame, to find fault with; Datteln (dät'-teln), *pl.* of Dattel, *f.*, palm fruit.
Tau (tou), *n.*, tow, cable; Thau, *m.*, dew.
Taube, see Daube.
tauchen (tou'-chen), to dive, dip; taugen (tou'-gen), to be fit for, good, proper.
Teich (tīh), *m.*, pond; Teig (tīg), *m.*, dough, paste.
Thier (teer), *n.*, animal, beast; Thür (tür), *f.*, door.
Thor (tōr), *m.*, [*pl.* en] fool; *n.*, [*pl.* e] gate.
Thränen (trai'-nen), *pl.* of Thräne, *f.*, tear; trennen (tran'-nen), to separate, sever.
Thon (tōn), *m.*, clay; Ton (tōn), *m.*, tune, strain, tone.
Tracht (trächt), *f.*, load, carriage, costume; tragt (trägt), *imperative pl.* of tragen, to carry.
Träger (trai'-ger), *m.*, bearer, carrier; träger, *comparative* of träge (trai'-ge), lazy, idle.
Trieb (treep), *m.*, drift, drove; instinct, impulse; young shoots; inclination; trüb (trüp), properly trübe, troubled, muddled, dull; trieb, *1st* and *3d person sing. past perf.* of treiben (trī'-ben), to drive, carry on.
trieft (treeft), *3d person sing. pres.* of triefen, to drip, trickle; trifft (trifft), *3d person sing. pres.* of treffen (traf'-fen), to hit; Trift, *f.*, passage for cattle ; drove.

Verband (fer-bänt'), *m.*, dressing, bandage; verband, *1st* and *3d per. sing. past perf.* of verbinden, to bind, to dress a wound, join, oblige; verbannt, exiled.
verbirgt (fer-birgt'), *3d person sing. pres.* of verbergen (fer-bar'-gen), to hide; verbürgt (fer-bïrgt'), the same of verbürgen (fer-bīr'-gen), to bail, warrant, to stand security for.
verdienen (fer-dee'-nen), to gain, earn, deserve; verdünnen (fer-dïn'-nen), to dilute.
Verdienst (fer deenst'), *m.*, gain, profit ; *n.*, merit.
vergießt (fer-geest'), *3d person sing. pres.* of vergießen (fer-gee'-ssen), to shed, spill ; vergißt (fer-gisst'), the same of vergessen (fer-gas'-sen), to forget.
verheeren (fer-hä'-ren), to devastate; verhören (fer-hï'-ren), to interrogate, to try [judicially].
verwaisen (fer-vī'-zen), to become an orphan; verweisen, to refer to; to banish, to rebuke.

Waare (vä'-re), *f.*, goods, ware, merchandise; wahre, eine wahre Geschichte (ī'-ne vä'-re ge-shih'-te), of wahr, true; war (vär), was.
Waden (vä'-den), *pl.* of Wade, *f.*, calf of the leg; waten (vä'-ten), to wade.

𝔚𝔞𝔥𝔫 (vän), *m.*, delusion; 𝔴𝔞𝔫𝔫 (vån), when; 𝔚𝔞𝔫𝔫𝔢 (vån'-ne), *f.*, fan, van.
𝔚𝔞𝔦𝔡 (vīt), *m.*, woad; weld; 𝔚𝔢𝔦𝔡, *f.*, chase; 𝔴𝔢𝔦𝔱, far, wide.
𝔚𝔞𝔦𝔰𝔢 (vī'-ze), *f.*, orphan; 𝔚𝔢𝔦𝔰𝔢, *f.*, manner, mode; *m.*, wise man, sage.
𝔚𝔞𝔥𝔩 (väl), *f.*, choice, election; 𝔚𝔞𝔩𝔩 (våll), *m.*, rampart, dam.
𝔚𝔞𝔫𝔡 (vånt), *f.*, wall; 𝔴𝔞𝔫𝔡, *1st* and *3d person sing. past perf.* of 𝔴𝔦𝔫𝔡𝔢𝔫 (vin'-den), to wind.
𝔚ä𝔩𝔩𝔢 (vạl'-le), *pl.* of 𝔚𝔞𝔩𝔩 [see above]; 𝔚𝔢𝔩𝔩𝔢, *f.*, wave, billow.
𝔚𝔞𝔫𝔤𝔢𝔫 (vång'-en), *pl.* of 𝔚𝔞𝔫𝔤𝔢, *f.*, cheek; 𝔴𝔞𝔫𝔨𝔢𝔫 (vång'-ken), to stagger, reel.
𝔚𝔢𝔤𝔢𝔫 (vä'-gen), *dative pl.* of 𝔚𝔢𝔤, *m.*, way; 𝔴𝔢𝔤𝔢𝔫, *prep.*, on account of; 𝔴𝔢𝔠𝔨𝔢𝔫 (vạk'-ken), to awake.
𝔴ä𝔥𝔯𝔢𝔫 (vai'-ren), to last, to hold out; 𝔴𝔢𝔥𝔯𝔢𝔫 (vä'-ren), to check, restrain, defend.
𝔴𝔦𝔡𝔢𝔯 (vee'-der), against; 𝔚𝔦𝔡𝔡𝔢𝔯 (vid'-der), *m.*, ram; 𝔴𝔦𝔢𝔡𝔢𝔯 (vee'-der), again.
𝔴𝔦𝔯𝔡 (virt), *3d person sing. pres.* of 𝔴𝔢𝔯𝔟𝔢𝔫 (vär'-den), to be, become; 𝔚𝔦𝔯𝔱𝔥, *m.*, host, landlord; 𝔚ü𝔯𝔡𝔢 (vïr'-de), *f.*, dignity.
𝔴𝔦𝔰𝔰𝔢𝔫 (vis'-sen), to know; 𝔚𝔦𝔢𝔰𝔢𝔫 (vee'-zen), *pl.* of 𝔚𝔦𝔢𝔰𝔢, *f.*, meadow; 𝔴𝔦𝔢𝔰𝔢𝔫, *1st* and *3d person pl. past perf.* of 𝔴𝔢𝔦𝔰𝔢𝔫 (vī'-zen), to show.
𝔚𝔬𝔫𝔫𝔢 (von'-ne), *f.*, delight; 𝔦𝔠𝔥 𝔴𝔬𝔥𝔫𝔢 (iḥ vö'-ne), I reside, dwell.
𝔚ü𝔰𝔱𝔢 (vüs'-te), *f.*, desert; 𝔴ü𝔰𝔰𝔱𝔢 (vīs'-te), *1st* and *3d person sing., subj.* of 𝔴𝔦𝔰𝔰𝔢𝔫 [see above].

𝔷ä𝔥𝔢 (tsaih'-e), tough; 𝔷𝔢𝔥𝔢 (tsäh'-e), *f.*, toe.
𝔷ä𝔥𝔯𝔢𝔫 (tsai'-ren), *pl.* of 𝔷ä𝔥𝔯𝔢, *f.*, tear; 𝔷𝔢𝔥𝔯𝔢𝔫 (tsäh'-ren), to consume, spend; 𝔷𝔢𝔯𝔯𝔢𝔫 (tsạr'-ren), to pull, haul, tug.
𝔷𝔞𝔫𝔤𝔢𝔫 (tsång'-en), *pl.* of 𝔷𝔞𝔫𝔤𝔢, *f.*, tongs, a pair of tongs; 𝔷𝔞𝔫𝔨𝔢𝔫 (tsång'-ken), to quarrel.
𝔷𝔞𝔲𝔪 (tsoum), *m.*, bridle; 𝔷𝔞𝔲𝔫 (tsoun), *m.*, fence.
𝔷𝔢𝔦𝔠𝔥𝔢𝔫 (tsī'-ḥen), *n.*, token, sign; 𝔷𝔢𝔦𝔤𝔢𝔫 (tsī'-gen), to show; 𝔷𝔢𝔲𝔤𝔢𝔫 (tsoi'-gen), to testify, generate.
𝔷𝔦𝔢𝔤𝔢 (tsee'-ge), *f.*, she-goat; 𝔷ü𝔤𝔢 (tsü'-ge), *pl.* of 𝔷𝔲𝔤 (tsoog), feature; train.
𝔷𝔦𝔢𝔤𝔢𝔩 (tsee'-gel), *m.*, brick; 𝔷ü𝔤𝔢𝔩 (tsü'-gel), *m.*, rein.
𝔷𝔦𝔢𝔪𝔢𝔯 (tsee'-mer), *m.*, a kind of field fare; buttock-piece; 𝔷𝔦𝔪𝔪𝔢𝔯 (tsim'-mer), *n.*, room.
𝔷𝔬𝔩𝔩 (tsoll), *m.*, (1) inch [*pl.* 𝔢]; (2) toll, custom, duty [*pl.* ö𝔰𝔰𝔢].
𝔷𝔲𝔫𝔞𝔥𝔪𝔢 (tsoo'-nä-me), *f.*, increase, growth; 𝔷𝔲𝔫𝔞𝔪𝔢, *m.*, family name, surname.

𝔑𝔞𝔠𝔥𝔱𝔯𝔞𝔤:

𝔞𝔲𝔣𝔣𝔞𝔩𝔩𔢫𝔡 (ouf'-fål'-lent), striking, strange; 𝔞𝔲𝔣𝔴𝔞𝔩𝔩𝔢𝔫𝔡 (ouf'-vål'-lent), *part. pres.* of 𝔞𝔲𝔣𝔴𝔞𝔩𝔩𝔢𝔫, to bubble, effervesce.
𝔊𝔢𝔣ä𝔥𝔯𝔱𝔢 (ge-fair'-te), *m.*, companion; 𝔊𝔢𝔣ä𝔥𝔯𝔱 (ge-fairt'), *n.*, vehicle, wagon.
𝔊𝔢𝔰𝔠𝔥𝔬ß (ge-shos'), *n.*, shot, arrow, dart, fire-arm; floor, story [of a house].
𝔊𝔢𝔰𝔦𝔠𝔥𝔱 (ge-ziḥt'), *n.*, sight, eye-sight; face; vision; visor of a rifle; 𝔊𝔢𝔷ü𝔠𝔥𝔱 (ge-tsīht'), *n.*, brood, breed.
𝔊𝔢𝔴ä𝔥𝔯 (ge-vair'), *f.*, vouch, warrant, guaranty; 𝔊𝔢𝔴𝔢𝔥𝔯 (ge vär'), *n.*, weapon, gun.
𝔤𝔢𝔴𝔦𝔱𝔱𝔢𝔯𝔱 (ge-vit'-tert), *past part.* of 𝔤𝔢𝔴𝔦𝔱𝔱𝔢𝔯𝔫, to thunder; *past part.* of 𝔴𝔦𝔱𝔱𝔢𝔯𝔫, to scent, smell.
𝔯𝔞𝔫𝔤 (rång), see 𝔑𝔞𝔫𝔤; *1st* and *3d person sing. past perf.* of 𝔯𝔦𝔫𝔤𝔢𝔫, to wrestle.
𝔳𝔢𝔯𝔯ü𝔠𝔨𝔱 (fer-rïkt'), crazed, mad; *past part.* of 𝔳𝔢𝔯𝔯ü𝔠𝔨𝔢𝔫, to displace, derange.

148

VOCABULARY WITH THE NOUNS CLASSIFIED ACCORDING TO GENDER.

(Compare Rules to determine the Gender, page 216.)

Masculine Nouns. Männliche Hauptwörter. (man'-li-he' houpt'-vir'-ter)	Feminine Nouns. Weibliche Hauptwörter. (vīp'-li-he' houpt'-vir'-ter)	Neuter Nouns. Sächliche Hauptwörter. (zäh'-lih-e' houpt'-vir'-ter)
Abode, Aufenthalt, ouf'-ent-hält'.	Abbacy, Abtei, äp-tī'.	Ace, Aß, äs.
Abundance, Ueberfluß, ü'-ber-flus'.	Ability, Fähigkeit, faih'-ig-kīt'.	Adage, Sprichwort, shprih'-vort.
Abuse, Mißbrauch, mis'-brouch'.	Absence, Abwesenheit, äp'-vā'-zen-hīt'.	Age, Alter, äl'-ter.
Access, Zutritt, tsoo'-trit'.	Account, Rechnung, rah'-nung; Rechenschaft, rah'-en-shaft'.	Agio, Aufgeld, ouf'-gelt.
Accident, Zufall, tsoo'-[un]-fäl'.		Ague, kalte Fieber, käl'-te fee'-ber.
Accord, Einklang, īn'-kläng.	Accuracy, Genauigkeit, ge-nou'-ig-kīt'.	Aisle, Seitenschiff, zī'-ten-shif'.
Acre, Acker, äk'-ker.	Ache, Wein, pīn.	Alley, Gäßchen, gäs'-hen.
Advantage, Vortheil, for'-tīl'.	Adder, Natter, nät'-ter.	Allspice, Piment, pi-mänt'.
Adversary, Gegner, gaig'-ner; Feind, fīnt.	Adulation, Schmeichelei, shmī'-he-lī'.	Amulet, Amulet, ä'-mu-lęt'.
Advice, Rath, rät.	Affability, Leutseligkeit, loit'-zā'-lg-kīt'.	Animal, Thier, teer.
Agriculture, Ackerbau, äk'-ker-bou'.	Affection, Zuneigung, tsoo'-nī'-gung.	Anteroom, Vorzimmer, fōr'-tsim'-mer.
Aid, Beistand, bī'-shtänt.	Affinity, Aehnlichkeit, ain'-lih-kīt'.	Apartment, Zimmer, tsim'-mer; Gemach, ge-mach'.
Alarm, Lärm, lärm.	Affirmation, Bejahung, be-yä'-ung.	
Alien, Ausländer, ous'-län'-der.	Affront, Beleidigung, be-lī'-di-gung.	Aqua fortis, Scheidewasser, shī'-de-vas'-ser.
Almighty, Allmächtige, äl-mäh'-ti-ge'.	Aliment, Nahrung, nä'-rung.	Arcanum, Geheimniß, ge-hīm'-nis.
Amateur, Dilettant, dī'-let-tänt'.	Allegiance, Loyalität, lo'-yä'-li-tait'.	Arsenal, Arsenal, är'-ze-näl'.
Amber, Bernstein, barn'-shtīn.	Allocution, Anrede, än'-rā'-de.	Arsenic, Arsenik, är-zā'-nik.
Ancestor, Vorfahr, fōr'-fär'.	Almond, Mandel, män'-del.	Assize, Geschworneugricht, ge-shvōr'-nen-ge-riht'.
Angle, Winkel, ving'-kel.	Anecdote, Anekote, ä'-nek-dō'-te.	
Anvil, Amboß, äm'-bos.	Anguish, Angst, ängst.	Atom, Atom, ä-tōm'.
Apothecary, Apotheker, ä'-po-tā'-ker.	Answer, Antwort, änt'-vort.	Attest, Zeugniß, tsoig'-niss.
Appetite, Appetit, äp'-pe-tīt'.	Ant, Ameise, ä'-mī'-ze.	Awning, leinene Schirmbach, lī'-ne-ne' shirm'-dach'.
Apple, Apfel, äp'-fel.	Aperture, Oeffnung, ö'-nung.	
Apprentice, Lehrling, lär'-ling.	Apology, Entschuldigung, ent-shul'-di-gung'.	Axe, Beil, bīl.
Arc, Bogen, bō'-gen.		

149

Archer, Bogenschütze, bō'-gen-shtǐ'-se.
Arm, Arm, ärm.
Arrest, Verhaft, fer-haft'.
Arrow, Pfeil, pfīl.
Article, Artikel, är-tī'-kel.
Artisan, Handwerker, hänt'-var'-ker.
Attack, Angriff, än'-grif.
Attorney, Anwalt, än'-vält.
Average, Durchschnitt, durh'-shnit.

Babe, baby, Säugling, zoig'-ling.
Bachelor, Junggeselle, yung'-ge-zal'-le.
Back, Rücken, rīk'-ken.
Bacon, Speck, shpak.
Badger, Dachs, däks.
Bag, Sack, zäk; Beutel, boi'-tel.
Bail, Bürge, bir'-ge.
Ball, Ball, bäl.
Balm, Balsam, bäl'-zäm.
Barrier, Schlagbaum, shläg'-boum.
Basket, Korb, korp.
Battoon, Kommandostab, kom-män'-dō-shtäp.
Beach, Strand, shtränt.
Beam, Balken, bäl'-ken; Strahl, shträl.
Bear, Bär, bair.
Beard, Bart, bärt.
Beau, Stutzer, shtut'-ser; Hofmacher, hōf'-mäch-er.

Apron, Schürze, shir'-tse.
Arbor, Laube, lou'-be.
Area, Fläche, flah'-e.
Aristocracy, Aristokratie, ä'-ris-tō'-krä-tee'.
Arm, Waffe, väf'-fe.
Arrival, Ankunft, än'-kunft.
Arson, Mordbrennerei, mort'-brǔn'-ne-[rī'.
Art, Kunst, kunst.
Assemblage, Versammlung, fer-zäm'-lung.
Assurance, Versicherung, fer-zih'-e-rung'.
Audience, Zuhörerschaft, tsoo'-hǐ'-rer-shäft'.
Awe, Furcht, furht; Ehrfurcht, är'-furht; Schrecken, shrǐk'-ken.

Bail, Bürgschaft, bǐrg'-shäft.
Bait, Lockspeise, lok'-shpī'-ze.
Balance, Wage, vā'-ge; Bilanz, bi-länts'. Glatze,
Baldness, Kahlheit, käl'-hīt; Glatze, glät'-se.
Ballot, Wahlstimme, väl'-shtim'-me.
Baluster, Geländersäule, ge-län'-der-zoi'-le.
Bank, Bank, bängk; Sandbank, zänt'-bängk.
Baptism, Taufe, tou'-fe.
Bar, Barre, bär'-re; Schranke, shräng'-ke, Saubbank.
Barn, Scheune, shoi'-ne; Scheuer, shoi'-er.
Barrack, Hütte, hǐt'-te; Kaserne, kä-zar'-ne.
Barrel, Tonne, ton'-ne.
Basis, Basis, bā'-zis; Stütze, shtǐt'-se.

Babe, baby, Kindchen, kint'-hen.
Badge, Zeichen, tsī'-hen; Kennzeichen, kǎn'-tsī'-hen.
Bane, Verderben, fer-dar'-ben; Gift, gift.
Barrel, Fass, fäs.
Basin, Becken, bak'-ken.
Basis, Fundament, fun'-dä-mant'.
Bath, Bad, bät.
Battalion, Bataillon, bät'-täl-yōn'.
Bed, Bett, bat.
Bed-chamber, bedroom, Schlafzimmer, shläf'-tsim'-mer.
Beer, Bier, beer.
Bishopric, Bisthum, bis'-toom.
Bitumen, Erdharz, art'-härts.
Black lead, Reissblei, rīs'-blī.
Blast, Gebläse, ge-blai'-ze.
Blood, Blut, bloot.
Board, Brett, brat.

M.

Beaver, Biber, boo'-ber.
Bee-hive, Bienenstock, bee'-nen-shtok'.
Belt, Gürtel, gir'-tel.
Besom, broom, Besen, bä'-zen.
Bird, Vogel, fō'-gel.
Biscuit, Zwieback, tsvee'-bak.
Block, Block, blok; Floß, klots.
Blunder, Mißgriff, mis'-grif; Schnitzer, shnit'-ser.
Board, Tisch, tish.
Body, Leib, lip; Körper, kir'-per.
Bog, Sumpf, zumpf; Morast, mo-räst'.
Bolster, Pfühl, pfül.
Bolt, Riegel, ree'-gel; Bolzen, bol'-tsen; Pfeil, pfīl.
Border, Rand, rant.
Bosom, Busen, boo'-zen.
Branch, Zweig, tsvīg; Ast, ást; Arm, arm; Flügel, flü'-gel.
Break, Bruch, bruch.
Bridle, Zaum, tsoum; Zügel, tsü'-gel.
Brim, Rand, ránt.
Bugbear, Popanz, pō'-pánts'.
Burglar, Einbrecher, īn'-brah'-er.

F.

Battle, Schlacht, shlácht.
Beech, Buche, boo'-che.
Bench, Bank, bángk; Gerichtsbank, gerihts'-bángk'.
Bible, Bibel, bee'-bel.
Bile, Galle, gál'-le.
Billow, Welle, vál'-le; Woge, vō'-ge.
Birch, Birke, bir'-ke.
Birth, Geburt, ge-boort'.
Blade, Klinge, kling'-e.
Blister, Blatter, blát'-ter.
Bloom, Blüte, blü'-te.
Board, Tafel, tä'-fel; Koft, kost.
Bodice, Schnürbrust, shnür'-brust.
Boil, Beule, boi'-le.
Boon, Gabe, gä'-be.
Booty, Beute, boi'-te.
Bower, Laube, lou'-be; Hütte, hüt'-te.
Bow-saw, Schweifsäge, shvīf'-zai'-ge.
Brake, Bremse, brém'-ze.
Breast, Brust, brust.
Bribe, Bestechung, be-shtah'-ung.
Bristle, Borste, bors'-te.
Bristol-board, gefirnißte Pappe, ge-firn'-te [páp'-pe.
Broach, Lochnadel, tooch'-nä'-del; Brosche, brosh'-e.
Broth, Brühe, brü'-e.
Brow, Augenbraue, ou'-gen-brou'-e; Stirn, shtirn. [boi'-le.
Bruise, Quetschung, kvát'-stung; Beule, Brush, Bürste, bürs'-te.
Bubble, Blase, blä'-ze. [boi'-le.
Bump, Schwellung, shvál'-lung; Beule, Buttery, Speisekammer, shpī'-se-käm'-mer.

N.

Boat, Boot, bōt.
Bonfire, Freudenfeuer, froi'-den-foi'-er.
Book, Buch, booch.
Boorishness, bäurisches Wesen, boi'-ri-shes' vä'-zen.
Botch, Flickwerf, flik'-várk.
Bracelet, Armband, ärm'-bant.
Brain, Gehirn, ge-hirn'.
Brake, Hemmschuh, ham'-shoo.
Brawl, Geschrei, ge-shrī'; Gezänk, getsángk'.
Bread, Brot, brōt.
Breakfast, Frühstück, frü'-shtük.
Breeze, Lüftchen, lift'-hen.
Brisket, Bruststück, brust'-shtük.
Budge, Lammfell, lámm'-fäl.
Buff, Büffelleder, bif'-fel-lä'-der.
Bull-fight, Stiergefecht, shteer-ge-facht'.
Bulwark, Bollwerk, bol'-várk.
Bundle, Bündel, bün'-del; Packet, päk-kät'.
Burial, Begräbniß, be-graip'-nis.
Busket, Gebüsch, ge-bish'.
Bust, Brustbild, brust'-bilt.
Buttock, Hintertheil, hin'-ter-tīl'.
Buzz, Gesumm, ge-zum'; Geflüster, ge-flis'-ter.

Cabbage, Kohl, kōl.
Cactus, Kaktus, kȧk'-tŭs.
Cadaver, Leichnam, lĭh'-nȧm.
Cage, Käfig, kāi'-fĭg.
Cake, Kuchen, koo'-chen.
Cakiron, Kessel, kȧs'-sel.
Calendar, Kalender, kȧ-lĕn'-der.
Caliber, Kaliber, kȧ-lee'-ber.
Calix, Blumenkelch, bloo'-men-kolh'.
Canal, Kanal, kȧ-nȧl'.
Canary bird, Kanarienvogel, kȧ-nāi'-ryȧn-fō'-gel.
Cancer, Krebs, kraps.
Cane, Stock, shtok.
Canopy, Tragehimmel, trāg'-him'-mel.
Canton, Kanton, kȧn-tōn'; Bezirk, be-tsĭrk'.
Capias, Verhaftsbefehl, fer-hȧfts'-be-fāl'.
Capon, Kapaun, kȧ-poun'.
Captain, Kapitän, kȧ'-pi-tāin'.
Car, Karren, kȧr'-ren; Wagen, vā'-gen.
Carbine, Karabiner, kȧ'-rȧ-bee'-ner.
Carbon, Kohlenstoff, kō'-len-shtof'.
Carbuncle, Karfunkel, kȧr-fŭng'-kel.
Caries, Beinfraß, bīn'-frās.
Carpet, Teppich, tĕp'-pih.
Cart, Karren, kȧr'-ren.
Cartilage, Knorpel, knor'-pel.
Cascade, Wasserfall, vȧs'-ser-fȧl'.
Catarrh, Katarrh, kȧ-tȧrr'; Schnupfen, shnŭp'-fen.
Cauliflower, Blumenkohl, bloo'-men-kōl'.
Causeway, Damm, dȧm.
Cellar, Keller, kȧl'-ler.
Cemetery, Todtenacker, tō'-ten-ȧk'-ker.
Cent, Zent, tsȧnt.

Cabal, Kabale, kȧ-bā'-le.
Cabin, Hütte, hĭt'-te; Kajüte, kȧ-yĭt'-te.
Calamity, Kalamität, kȧ-lȧ'-mi-tait'.
Calm, Ruhe, rooh'-e.
Caloric, Wärme, vȧr'-me.
Camomile, Kamille, kȧ-mĭl'-le.
Cancellation, Aufhebung, ouf'-hāi'-bŭng.
Candidness, Offenheit, of'-fen-hīt'.
Candle, Kerze, kȧr'-tse.
Canvass, Wahlbewerbung, vāl'-be-vȧr'-bŭng.
Cap, Kappe, kȧp'-pe; Mütze, mĭt'-se.
Capability, Fähigkeit, fāi'-ĭg-kīt'.
Caprice, Laune, lou'-ne; Grille, grĭl'-le.
Care, Sorge, zor'-ge; Vorsicht, fōr'-zĭht.
Caress, Liebkosung, leep'-kō'-zŭng.
Carrot, Möhre, mō'-re.
Cart-load, Karrenladung, kȧr'-ren-lā'-dŭng.
Cartoon, Musterzeichnung, mŭs'-ter-tsīh'-nŭng.
Cartridge, Patrone, pȧt-rō'-ne.
Cat, Katze, kȧt'-se.
Caterpillar, Raupe, rou'-pe.
Cell, Zelle, tsȧl'-le.
Chain, Kette, kȧt'-te.
Chalk, Kreide, krī'-de.
Chamois, Gemse, gȧm'-ze.
Charcoal, Holzkohle, holts'-kō'-le.
Chasm, Kluft, klŭft; Lücke, lĭk'-ke.
Check [for money], Anweisung, ȧn'-vī'-zŭng.
Cheek, Wange, vȧng'-e.
Cherry, Kirsche, kĭr'-she.
Chest, Brust, brŭst; Kiste, kĭs'-te.
Chocolate, Chokolade, shok'-kō-lā'-de.
Choice, Wahl, vāl.

Cabbage, Kraut, krout.
Calf, Kalb, kȧlp.
Camel, Kameel, kȧ-māl'.
Camp, [Feld] Lager, [fȧlt] lā'-ger.
Candle, Licht, lĭht.
Candy, Zuckerwerk, tsŭk'-ker-vȧrk'.
Cane, Rohr, rōr.
Carouse, Zechgelag, tsȧh'-ge-lāg'.
Cash, baares Geld, bā'-res gȧlt.
Chat, Geschwätz, ge-shvȧts'.
Cheese, Schachspiel, shȧch'-shpeel'.
Chicken, Huhn, hoon; Küchlein, kĭh'-līn.
Child, Kind, kĭnt.
Chin, Kinn, kĭnn.
Chump, Stück, shtĕk.
Climate, Klima, klee'-mȧ.
Cloister, Kloster, klō'-ster.
Cloth, Tuch, tooch; Zeug, tsoih.
Coat, Seerrock, zāi'-oo'-ĕr.
Cockloat, Beischiff, bī'-shĭff.
College, Gymnasium, grĭm-nāi'-zi-ŭm'.
Cologne, Kölnisches Wasser, kĭl'-nĭ-shes vȧs'-ser.
Colt, Füllen, fĭl'-len.
Comma, Komma, kom'-mȧ.
Commissariat, Kommissariat, kom'-mĭs-sȧ'-ri-āt'.
Compassion, Mitleiden, mĭt-lī'-den.
Compliment, Kompliment, kom'-pli-mȧnt'.
Conplot, Komplott, kom-plot'.
Concern, Geschäft, ge-shȧft'.
Concert, Konzert, kon-tsȧrt'.
Conclave, Conclave, kon-klāv'.
Conscience, Gewissen, ge-vĭs'-sen.
Convent, Kloster, klō'-ster.

152

M.

Chair, Stuhl, shtool; Sessel, zas'-sel.
Chant, Kirchengesang, kir'-hen-ge-zang'.
Character, Karakter, kå-råk'-ter.
Chariot, Wagen, vä'-gen.
Charlatan, Marktschreier, mårkt'-shrī'-er.
Check, Einhalt, In'-hålt.
Cheese, Käse, kai'-ze.
Chief, Häuptling, hoipt'-ling.
Chum, Kumpan, kum-pån'.
Circle, Zirkel, tsir'-kel; Kreis, kris.
Circumstance, Umstand, um'-shtånt.
Clay, Lehm, lām; Thon, tōn.
Clergyman, Geistlicher, gīst'-li-her'.
Clerk, Gehilfe, ge-hil'-fe.
Cloak, Mantel, mån'-tel.
Coat, Rock, rok; Pelz, palts.
Coffee, Kaffee, kåf-fä'.
Coffer, Koffer, kof'-fer.
Comb, Kamm, kåm.
Commerce, Handel, hån'-del.
Conceit, Eigendünkel, I'-gen-düng-kel.
Concept, Begriff, be-grif'.
Conclusion, Schluß, shluss. [See Fem.]
Connoisseur, Kenner, kan'-ner.
Contention, Streit, shtrīt.
Context, Zusammenhang, tsoo-zåm'-men-häng'.
Cook, Koch, koch.
Court, Hof, hōf.
Crater, Krater, krå'-ter.
Cream, Rahm, råm.
Credit, Kredit, kre-dīt'.
Creditor, Gläubiger, gloi'-bi-ger'.
Crest, Kamm, kåm.
Cripple, Krüppel, krüp'-pel.

F.

Cholera, Cholera, kol'-le-rä'.
Chord, Saite, zī'-te; Sehne, zā'-ne.
Church, Kirche, kir'-he.
Cinder, Kohlasche, kōl'-ash'-e.
Cipher, Ziffer, tsif'-fer; Null, nul; Chiffre, shif'-fer.
Civet, Zibethkatze, tsī'-bet-kåt'-se.
Claim, Forderung, for'-de-rung'.
Clarionet, Klarinette, klå'-ri-yō-nåt'-te.
Class, Klasse, klås'-se.
Claw, Klaue, klou'-e; Kralle, krål'-le.
Clemency, Milde, mil'-de; Huld, hult.
Clergy, Geistlichkeit, gīst'-lih-kīt.
Clock, Wand-[Thurm-]Uhr, vånt'-[turm'-]oor.
Clove, [garlic] Zehe, tsā'-e.
Clove, Gewürznelke, ge-vīrts'-nal'-ke.
Coach, Kutsche, kut'-she.
Coast, Küste, kūs'-te.
Comfort, Bequemlichkeit, be-kvām'-lih-kīt'.
Compliment, Empfehlung, emp-fā'-lung.
Composition, Komposition, kom'-po-zits'-yōn'.
Conjunction, Reue, roi'-e.
Conclusion, Folgerung, fol'-ge-rung'.
Considerateness, Besonnenheit, be-zon'-nen-hīt'.
Conversation, Konversation, kon'-ver-zåts'-yōn'.
Cook, Köchin, köh'-in.
Cotton, Baumwolle, boum'-vol'-le.
Cow, Kuh, koo.
Crumb, Krume, kroo'-me.
Crust, Kruste, krus'-te; Rinde, rin'-de.
Crutch, Krücke, krük'-ke.

N.

Copper, Kupfer[geld], kup'-fer[gålt].
Copse, Gebüsch, ge-büsh'; Unterholz, un'-ter-holts'.
Core, Herz, harts; Inneres, in'-ne-res'.
Corn, Hühnerauge, hü'-ner-ou'-ge.
Corn, Korn, korn; Getreide, ge-trī'-de.
Cornet, Horn, horn.
Corps, Korps, kōr'.
Corpuscle, Körperchen, kö'-per-hen'.
Couch, Ruhebett, roo'-e-båt'.
Counterpoise, Gegengewicht, gä'-gen-ge-viht'.
Crackle, Gekrach, ge-kråch'; Geknister, ge-knis'-ter.
Creosote, Kreosot, krī'-o-zōt'.
Crime, Verbrechen, fer-brah'-en.
Crocodile, Krokodil, kro'-kō-dil'.
Crone, altes Schaf, ål'-tes shüf; altes Weib, ål'-tes vīp.
Cross, Kreuz, kroits.
Croup [of a horse], Kreuz.
Crout [sour], [Sauer- zou'-er-]kraut, krout.
Cruor, geronnenes Blut, ge-ron'-ne-nes' bloot.
Currency, Papiergeld, på-peer'-gålt'.
Cutlet, Rippchen, rip'-hen.

153

Cuirass, Harnisch, hār'-nish.
Cup, Becher, bah'-er; Kelch, kęlh.
Curtain, Verhang, for'-hăng.
Cylinder, Cylinder, tsi-lin'-der.

Dad, Daddy, Papa, pă-pit'; Vater, fä'-ter.
Dagger, Dolch, dolh.
Dam, Damm, dăm.
Damage, Schaden, shä'-den.
Damask, Damast, dä-măst'.
Dance, Tanz, tănts.
Dandelion, Löwenzahn, lī'-ven-tsăn'.
Dandy, Stutzer, shtųt'-ser.
Darling, Liebling, leep'-ling.
Dastard, Feigling, fīg'-lĭng.
Day, Tag, täg.
Dean, Dekan, de-kăn'.
Dear, Theurer, toi'-rer.
Death, Tod, tōt.
Debtor, Schuldner, shųlt'-ner.
Debut, erster öffentlicher Auftritt, ārs'-ter iǐ'-fent-lǐ'-her oŭf'-trit.
Decay, Verfall, fer-făl'.
Deceit, Betrug, be-troog'.
Decency, Anstand, ăn'-shtănt. [See Fem.]
Deception, Betrug, be-troog'.
Decorum, Anstand, ăn'-shtănt.
Decoy, Köder, kǐ'-der.
Deer [red], Hirsch, hirsh.
Default, Fehler, fā'-ler.
Delegate, Abgeordneter, ăp'-ge-ord'-ne-ter.
Demagogue, Demagog, de'-mä-gōg'.
Demon, Dämon, daǐ'-mon.
Denizen, freier Bürger, frī'-er bir'-ger.

Cucumber, Gurke, gųr'-ke.
Curve, krumme Linie, krųm'-melee'-n-ye.
Custom, Gewohnheit, ge-vōn'-hīt; Kundschaft, kųnt'-shăft.

Dairy, Melkerei, măl'-ke-rī'; Meierei, mī'-e-rī'.
Daisy, Gänseblume, găn'-ze-bloo'-me.
Dam [of animals], Mutter, mųt'-ter; Alte, äl'-te.
Danger, Gefahr, ge-fär'.
Dark, Dunkelheit, dųng'-kel-hīt'.
Date, Dattel, dät'-tel.
Daw, Dohle, dō'-le.
Dawn, Dämmerung, dăm'-me-rųng'.
Deal, Dorenstille, tō'-des-shtil'-le.
Deal, Diele, deo'-le.
Dear, Theure, toi'-re.
Debt, Schuld, shųlt.
Deceit, List, list.
Decency, Schicklichkeit, shik'-lĭh-kīt'.
Decision, Entscheidung, ent-shī'-dųng.
Decree, Verordnung, fer-ord'-nųng.
Dedication, Zueignung, tsoo'-īg'-nųng.
Deed, That, tät; Handlung, hănd'-lųng; Urkunde, oor'-kųn'-de.
Deep, Tiefe, tee'-fe. [rųng'.
Defamation, Verläſterung, fer-las'-te-
Defeat, Niederlage, nee'-der-lä'-ge.
Defence, Vertheidigung, fer-tī'-di-gųng'.
Deference, Ehrerbietung, är'-er-bee'-tųng.
Degradation, Herabsetzung, her-ăp'-zųt'-tsųng.
Deliberation, Ueberlegung, ü'-ber-lä'-gųng.
Delusion, Täuschung, toi'-shųng.

Dale, Thal, täl.
Damsel, Mädchen, mait'-hen; Fräulein, froi'-līn.
Dark, Dunkel, dųng'-kel.
Date, Datum, dä'-tųm.
Daylight, Tageslicht, tä'-ges-lįht'.
Day's work, Tagewerf, tä'-ge-vark'.
Dead light, Schrickt, shī'-lįht.
Dead lock, Riegelschloß, ree'-gel-shlos'.
Dead water, Kielwasser, keel'-văs'-ser.
Deal [of cards], Ausstheilen, ous'-tī'-len.
Debit, [Debit], Soll, zoll.
Decoction, Desost, de-kokt'.
Decree, Defret, dąk-rāt'.
Deed, Instrument, in'-shtrų-mant'.
Deer, Rothwild, rōt'-vįlt.
Default, Defect, dą-fį-tsit'.
Deficit, Deficit, dą'-fi-tsit'.
Delicateness, Zartgefühl, tsärt'-ge-fül'.
Deliriousness, Delirium, de-lee'-ri-ųm'.
Dell, Thal, täl.
Demain [for domain], Landeigenthum, länt'-ī'-gen-toom'.
Demand, Begehren, be-gā'-ren.
Demeanor, Betragen, be-trä'-gen; Verhalten, fer-hăl'-ten.
Denerit, Verschulden, fer-shųl'-den.
Denise, Ablehen, ăp'-lā'-ben.
Denial, Leugnen, loig'-nen.
Dentifrice, Zahnpulver, tsän'-pųl'-fer.

M.

Depth, Abgrund, äp'-grunt.
Derider, Spötter, shpït'-ter.
Desertcr, Ausreißer, ous'-rī'-sser.
Design, Abriß, äp'-ris; Entwurf, ent-vurf' [*See Fem.*]
Desperado, Wagehals, vii'-ge-hals'.
Despot, Despot, des-pot'.
Dessert, Nachtisch, nächt'-tish.
Detriment, Nachtheil, nächt'-tīl.
Devil, Teufel, toi'-fel.
Dew, Thau, tou.
Diagram, Abriß, äp'-ris.
Diamond, Diamant, dee-ä-mänt'.
Die, Würfel, vïr'-fel.
Dignitary, Würdenträger, vïr'-den-trai'-ger.
Dilettant, Kunstfreund, kunst'-froint.
Din, Lärm, larm; Schall, shäl.
Disadvantage, Nachtheil, näch'-tīl.
Disciple, Schüler, shü'-ler; Jünger, yïng'-er.
Disgust, Ekel, ā'-kel.
Disobedience, Ungehorsam, un'-ge-hōr'-zām.
Dissonance, Mißton, mis'-tōn.
Distaff, Rocken, rok'-ken.
Distress, Beschlag, be-shlāg'; Arrest, ārrest'.
Ditch, Graben, grä'-ben.
Divan, Divan, dī'-vän; [Turk.] Staatsrath, shtäts'-rät.
Dizziness, Schwindel, shvint'-del.
Doe, Damhirsch, däm'-hirsh.
Dog, Hund, hunt.

F.

Demand, Forderung, for'-de-rung; Bitte, bit'-te. [*See Neut.*]
Democracy, Demokratie, dä-mok'-rä-tee'.
Demoralization, Entsittlichung, ent-zit'-li-hung; Entmuthigung, ent-mōō'-ti-gung'.
Demureness, Sittsamkeit, zit'-zäm-kīt'.
Den, Höhle, hī'-le.
Denunciation, Anzeige, än'-tsī'-ge; Anflage, än'-klä'-ge.
Departure, Abreise, äp'-rī'-ze. [syng.
Depreciation, Herabsetzung, her-äp-zät'-
Depth, Tiefe, tee'-fe.
Derision, Verspottung, fer-shpot'-tung.
Derivation, Ableitung, äp'-lī'-tung.
Derogation, Entwerthung, ent-vär'-tung.
Desecration, Entweihung, ent-vī'-ung.
Design, Absicht, äp'-ziht. [*See Neut.*]
Despair, Verzweiflung, fer-tsvīf'-lung.
Destruction, Zerstörung, tser-shtï'-rung.
Detection, Entdeckung, ent-lak'-kung.
Detestation, Verabscheuung, fer-äp'-shoi'-ung. [tung.
Development, Entwickelung, ent-vik'-ke-
Deviation, Abweichung, äp'-vī'-hung.
Devotedness, Ergebenheit, er-gā'-ben-hīt'.
Devotion, Andacht, än'-däcḥt; Aufopferung, ouf'-op'-fe-rung'.
Digestion, Verdauung, fer-dou'-ung.
Direction, Richtung, rih'-tung; Adresse, äd'-räs'-se.
Disappointment, Täuschung, toi'-shung.
Disapprobation, Mißbilligung, mis'-bil'-li-gung'.

N.

Deposit, Depositum, de-pō'-zi-tum'; Pfand, pfänt.
Derivative, Abgeleitetes, äp'-ge-lī'-te-tes'.
Desert, Verdienst, fer-deenst'.
Design, Vorhaben, fōr'-hä'-ben.
Desire, Verlangen, fer-läng'-en.
Destiny, Schicksal, shik'-zäl.
Devise, [legacy] Vermächtniß, fer-mäht'- [nis.
Dialem, Diadem, dee-ä-däm'.
Dialogue, Gespräch, ge-shpraih'.
Diary, Tagebuch, tä'-ge-booch'.
Dicing, Würfelspiel, vïr'-fel-shpeel'.
Dictation, Geheiß, ge-hīss'.
Dictionary, Wörterbuch, vïr'-ter-booch'.
Diffidence, Mißtrauen, mis'-trou'-en.
Dilemma, Dilemma.
Diluvium, angeschwemmtes Erdreich, än'-ge-shvam'-tes ärt'-rīh.
Dimension, Maß, mäs.
Diminutive, Verkleinerungswort, fer-klī'-ne-rungs'-vort'.
Dimple, Grübchen, grüp'-hen.
Din, Getöse, ge-tī'-ze.
Dingle, Thal, täl.
Dinner, Mittagessen, mit' täg-äs'-sen.
Diploma, Diplom, dip-lōm'.
Directory, Adreßbuch, äd-räs'-booch; Directorium, dee'-rak-tō'-ri-um'.
Dirge, Klagelied, klä'-ge-leet'.
Disaster, Mißgeschick, mis'-ge-shik'.
Discount, Disconto, dis-kon'-tō.
Discourse, Gespräch, ge-shpraih'.
Disease, Unwohlsein, un'-vol-zīn'.
Disorder, do. do.

Doge [Venice], Doge, dō'je.
Dogstar, Hundsstern, hunts'-shtqrn.
Donne, Dem, dēm.
Donkey, Esel, ā'-zel.
Donor, Geber, gā'-ber.
Dormouse, Hamster, häm'-ster.
Doubt, Zweifel, tsvī'-fel.
Dragon, Drache, dräch'-e.
Drake, Enterich, an'-te-rih'.
Draper, Tuchhändler, tooch'-hand'-ler.
Dread, Schrecken, shrak'-ken.
Dream, Traum, troum.
Dudgeon, Unwille, un'-vil'-le.
Duke, Herzog, har'-tsōg.
Dung, Dünger, ding'-er; Mist, mist.
Dungeon, Kerker, kar'-ker.
Dust, Staub, shtoup.
Dutchman, Holländer, hol'-lan-der.

Discontent, Unzufriedenheit, un'-tsoo-free'-den-hīt'.
Discourse, Rede, rā'-de.
Discrepancy, Verschiedenheit, fer-shee'-den-hīt'.
Disease, Krankheit, krank'-hīt.
Disfiguration, Entstellung, ent-shtql'-lung.
Disgrace, Schande, shän'-de; Unehre, un'-ā'-re; Ungnade, un'-gnā'-de.
Disguise, Verstellung, fer-shtql'-lung
Dishonesty, Unehrlichkeit, un'-ār'-lih-kīt'.
Disinclination, Abneigung, äp'-nī'-gung.
Display, Schaustellung, shou'-shtql'-lung.
Dispatch, Abfertigung, äp'-fer'-ti-gung'; Depesche, de-pash'-e.
Disproportion, Ungleichheit, un'-glīh'-hīt.
Disrespect, Geringschätzung, ge-ring'-shqt'-tsung.
Dissension, Uneinigkeit, un'-ī'-nig-kīt'.
Distemper, Verstimmung, fer-shtim'-mung.
Distinction, Unterscheidung, un'-ter-shī'-dung.
Distress [at sea], Angst, ängst; Noth, nōt.
Distribution, Vertheilung, fer-tī'-lung.
Divination, Ahnung, ä'-nung.
Divinity, Gottheit, got'-hīt.
Divorce, Ehescheidung, ā-e-shī'-dung.
Document, Urkunde, oor'-kun'de.
Doe, Hindin, hin'-din.
Door, Thür, tür.
Dotage, zweite Kindheit, tsvī'-te kint'-hīt.
Dove, Taube, tou'-be.
Drive, Spazierfahrt, shpä-tseer'-färt.

Disproportion, Mißverhältniß, mis'-fer-hqlt'-nis.
Dissolvent, Auflösungsmittel, ouf'-lē'-zungs-mit'-tel.
Distress [signal of], Nothzeichen, nōt'-tsī'-hen.
Distrust, Mißtrauen, mis'-trou'-en.
Ditty, Liedchen, leet'-hen.
Document, Dokument, do'-ku-ment'.
Domain, Gebiet, ge-beet'.
Doom, Urtheil, ur'-tīl; Loos, lōs; Schicksal, shik'-zäl.
Dozen, Dutzend, dut'-sent.   [gen.
Drainage, Trockenlegen, trok'-ken-lā'-
Draughtboard, Damenbrett, dä'-men-brqt'.
Dredge, Mischform, mish'-korn.
Duel, Duell, du-ql'.
Dukedom, Herzogthum, har'-tsōg-toom'.
Dungeon, Gefängniß, ge-fqng'-nis.
Dusk, Dunkel, dung'-kel.

156

M.

Eagle, Abler, ád'-ler.
Earl, Graf, gráf.
Earnest, Ernst, ərnst.
East, Osten, os'-ten.
Eclat, Glanz, glants; Eclat, ec-lä'.
Edge, Rand, ront; Schnitt, shnit.
Effect, Effect, ef-fäkt'; Erfolg, er-folg'.
Effort, Versuch, fer-zooch'. [See Neut.]
Elbow, Ellbogen, äl'-bō'-gen.
Elder, Kirchenvorsteher, kir'-ḥen-for-shtä'-er.
Element, Urstoff, oor'-shtoff. [See Neut.]
Embryo, Embryo, äm'-bri-ō.
Emerald, Smaragd, sma-rägt'.
Emery, Schmirgel, shmir'-gel.
Emigrant, Auswanderer, ous'-vän'-de-rer'.
Emissary, Emissär, e'-mis'-sär'.
Emperor, Kaiser, kī'-zer.
Emphasis, Nachdruck, näch'-drųk.
Employer, Principal, prin'-tsi-päl'.
Emporium Stapelplatz, shtä'-pel-pläts'.
Emption, Kauf, kouf.
Emulation, Wetteifer, vät'-ī'-fer.
Emanuel, Schmelz[arbeit], shmälts'-[är-bīt].
End, Zweck, tsvęk; Endzweck, ęnt'-tsvęk.
Enemy, Feind, fīnt.
Energy, Nachdruck, näch'-drųk.

F.

Drone, Drohne, drō'-ne.
Dropsy, Wassersucht, vàs'-ser-zucht'.
Drug, Arzneiwaare, ärts-nī'-vä'-re.
Duck, Ente, ąn'-te.
Duckling, junge Ente, yung'-e ąn'-te.

Ear [of corn], Aehre, ai'-re.
Earldom, Grafschaft, gräf'-shäft.
Earth, Erde, ār'-de.
Ease, Gemächlichkeit, ge-mäh'-liḥ-kīt';
  Ruhe, roo'-e.
Easel, Staffelei, shtäf'-fel-lī'.
Eaves, Dachtraufe, däch'-trou'-fe.
Ebriety, Trunkenheit, trųng'-ken-hīt'.
Eclipse, Eklipse, ek-lip'-se.
Ecstasy, Estase, eks-tä'-ze.
Edge, Schärfe, shar'-fe; Schneide, shnī'-de.
Education, Erziehung, er-tsee'-ung.
Effect, Wirkung, vir'-kųng; Leistung, lī'-stųng.
Effort, Anstrengung, än'-shtręng-ųng;
  Bemühung, be-mü'-ung.
Egoism, Selbstsucht, zalpst'-zųcht'.
Eiderdown, Eiderdaune, I'-der-dou'-ne.
Eiderduck, Eidergans, I'-der-gäns.
Elegance, Eleganz, ä'-le-gänts'.
Emancipation, Emancipation, e-män'-tsi-päts-yōn'.
Embassy, Gesandtschaft, ge-zänt'-shäft.
Ember, heiße Asche, hī'-sse äsh'-e.
Embezzlement, Unterschlagung, ųn'-ter-shlä'-gųng.
Embrasure, Schießscharte, shees'-shär'-te.
Embroilment, Verwirrung, fer-vir'-rųng.

N.

Ear, Ohr, ōr; Gehör, ge-hr'.
Earlap, Ohrläppchen, ōr'-läp'-ḥen.
Earth, Land, länt.
Earthquake, Erdbeben, ārt'-bā'-ben.
Ease, Behagen, be-hä'-gen.
Ebony, Ebenholz, ā'-ben-holts'.
Echo, Echo, ą'-ḥō.
Effigy, Bildniß, bilt'-nis.
Effort, Streben, shträ'-ben.
Egg, Ei, I.
Element, Element, ą'-le-mant'.
Elk, Muletthier, moo' ze-teer'.
Emblem, Emblem, em-blām'; Sinnbild, zin'-bilt.
Empire, Reich, rīḥ; Kaiserreich, kī'-zer-rīḥ'.
End, Ende, ąn'-de.
Enigma, Räthsel, rait'-sel.
Entertainment, Gastmahl, gäst'-mäl.
Epigram, Epigramm, e-pi-gräm'.
Epistle, Sendschreiben, zänt'-shrī'-ben.
Escort, Schutzgleit, shųts'-ge-līt'
Esponsal, Verlöbniß, fer-lip'-nis.
Essence, Wesen, vā'-zen.
Eucharist, das heilige Abendmahl, das hī'-li-ge' ä'-bent-mäl'.
Eulogy, Lob, lōp.
Evil, Uebel, ü'-bel.
Excess, Uebermaß, ü'-ber-mäs'.

Engineer, Ingenieur, in'-jen-yīr'; Maschinist, măˈ-shi-nist'.
Engrosser, Aufkäufer, ouf'-koi'-fer.
Enthusiasm, Enthusiasmus, en-too'-zi-ăs'-mus.
Enthusiast, Enthusiast, en-too'-zi-ăst'; Schwärmer, shvär'-mer.
Entrance, Eintritt, īn'-tritt'; Eingang, īn'-gäng.
Envelope, Umschlag, um'-shläg.
Envoy, Gesandter, ge-zăn'-ter.
Envy, Neid, nīt.
Epicure, Epikuräer, e-pĭ'-ku-rai'-er; Sinnenmensch, zin'-nen-mănsh'.
Epilogue, Epilog, a'-pĭ-lŏg'.
Epistle, Brief, breef.
Epitome, Auszug, ous'-tsug.
Equator, Äquator, ek-vä'-tor.
Error, Irrtum, ir'-tum.
Eruption, Ausbruch, ous'-bruch; Ausschlag, ous'-shlăg.
Ether, Äther, ai'-ter.
Excess, Exceß.
Exchange, Wechsel, vek'-sel; Tausch, toush.
Excise, Accise, ak-tsee'-ze.
Executioner, Vollstrecker, foll'-shtrěk'-ker; Scharfrichter, sharf'-rĭh'-ter.
Exigence, Drang, dräng.
Exit, Abgang, ap'-gäng; Ausgang, ous'-gäng.
Exodus, Auszug, ous'-tsoog.
Expectoration, Schleimauswurf, shlīm'-ous'-vurf.
Exponent, Exponent, ex-po-nănt'.
Expositor, Erklärer, er-klai'-rer.
Expression, Ausdruck, ous'-druk.

Eminence, Eminenz, a-mi-nănts'; Erhabenheit, er-hä'-ben-hīt'; Anhöhe, än'-hĭ'-e.
Emmet, Ameis, ä'-mī'-ze.
Empress, Kaiserin, kĭ'-ze-rin'.
Enactment, Verordnung, fer-ord'-nung.
Encouragement, Ermutigung, er-moo'-ti-gung'; Aufmunterung, ouf'-mun'-te-rung'.
Endeavor, Bestrebung, be-shträ'-bung.
Energy, Energie, en-ner-gee'; Kraft, kraft.
Engine, Maschine, mä-shee'-ne; Feuerspritze, foi'-er-shprĭt'-se; Lokomotive, lō'-kō-mō-tee'-ve.
Engrossment, Reinschrift, rīn'-shrift.
Ennui, Langweile, läng'-vī'-le.
Entertainment, Unterhaltung, un'-ter-häl'-tung.
Epistle, Epistel, e-pis'-tel.
Equinox, Tag- und Nachtgleiche, täg'-unt-nacht' glī'-he.
Equity, Billigkeit, bil'-lig-kīt'.
Escort, Bedeckung, be-dek'-kung.
Essence, Kraft, kraft.
Excellence, Vortrefflichkeit, for-trăf'-lih-kīt'.
Exchange [building], Börse, bĭr'-ze.
Excommunication, Ausschließung, ous'-shlee'-ssung.
Execution, Ausführung, ous'-fü'-rung; Hinrichtung, hin'-rih'-tung.
Exhibition, Dar[Aus]stellung, där[ous']-shtäl'-lung.
Exile, Verbannung, fer-bän'-nung.
Expedition, Schnelligkeit, shnăl'-lig kīt'; Expedition, ăks-pe-dits'-yōn'.

Expectoration, Aushusten, ous'-hoo'-sten.
Exterior, Äußerliche, oi'-sser-li'-he.
Extinguisher, Auslöschhütchen, ous'-lĭsh'-hüt'-hen.
Extreme, Extrem, ex-trām'.
Exudation, Ausschwitzen, ous'-slvit'-sen.
Eye, Auge, ou'-ge; Gesicht, ge-zĭht'; Ohr, īr.
Eyeglass, Augenglas, on'-gen-gläs'.
Eyelid, Augenlid, on'-gen-leet'.
Eyesight, Sehvermögen, zā'-fer-mĭ'-gen.
Eyesore, Augenschmür, ou'-gen-ge-shvür'; Gerstenkorn, gär'-sten-korn'.

M.

Exterminator, Vertilger, fer-til'-ger.
Extinguisher, Auslöscher, ous'-lish'-er.
Extortioner, Erpresser, er-prßs'-ser.

Factor, Faktor, fäk-tōr'.
Failure, Fehler, fā'-ler; Mangel, mäng'-el; Bankerott, bängk-rot'.
Fair, Jahrmarkt, yär'-märkt.
Faith, Glaube, glou'-be.
Falcon, Falke, fäl'-ke.
Fall, Fall, fäl; Sturz, shtųrts.
Fame, Ruf, roof.
Fan, Fächer, fäh'-er.
Fanatic, Fanatiker, fä-nä'-ti-ker'.
Fang, Fangzahn, fäng'-tsäin.
Farewell, Abschied, äp'-sheet.
Fathom, Faden, fā'-den.
Fault, Fehler, fā'-ler.
Fawn, Faun, foun; Waldgott, vält'-got.
Feature, Gesichtszug, ge-zihts'-tsoog; Zug, tsoog.
Fellow, Kerl, kąrl; Bursche, bur'-she; Geselle, ge-zµl'-le; Gefährte, ge-fair'-te.
Felt, Filz, filts; Filzhut, filts'-hoot.
Fig tree, Feigenbaum, fī'-gen-boum'.
Filibuster, Flibustier, flī'-bųs-teer'; Freibeuter, frī'-boi'-ter.
Filth, Unflat, ųn'-flāt; Schmutz, shmųts.
Finger, Finger, fing'-er.
Fish, Fisch, fish.
Flavor, Wohlgeruch, vōl'-ge-rųch'; Wohlgeschmack, vōl'-ge-shmäk'.

F.

Explosion, Explosion, äks-plō'-zi-yōn'.
Extenuation, Milderung, mil'-de-rųng'.
Extinction, Auslöschung, ous'-lish'-ųng.
Extravagance, Ausschweifung, ous'-shvī'-fųng.

Fable, Fabel, fä'-bel.
Fac-simile, genaue Nachahmung, ge-nou'-e näch'-ä'-mųng.
Faction, Faktion, fäk-tsyōn'; Partei, pär-tī'.
Faculty, Fähigkeit, fai'ig-kīt'; Kraft, kräft.
Fair, Messe, mąs'-se; Ausstellung, ous'-shtąl'-lung.
Fairy, Fee, fā.
Faith, Treue, troi'-e; Redlichkeit, rāt'-lih-kīt'.
Falsification, Fälschung, fäl'-shung; Verfälschung, fer-fäl'-shung.
Family, Familie, fä-mee'-li-ye'.
Famine, Hungersnoth, hųng'-ers-nōt'.
Fang, Kralle, kräl'-le.
Farce, Farce, fär'-sse; Posse, pos'-se.
Fashion, Mode, mō'-de; Tracht, trächt; Façon, fä-ssong'.
Fatigue, Ermüdung, er-mü'-dung; Beschwerde, be-shvär'-de.
Fatness, Fettigkeit, fąt'-tig-kīt'.
Favor, Gunst, gųnst; Gefälligkeit, gefäl'-lig-kīt'.
Fear, Furcht, fųrcht.
Feat, That, tāt.
Feature, Gesichtsbildung, ge-zihts'-bil'-dung.

N.

Fabric, Gebäude, ge-boi'-de.
Factotum, Faktotum, fäk-tō'-tųm.
Failure, Mißlingen, mis-ling'-en; Fehlschlagen, fāl'-shlä'-gen.
Fame, Gerücht, ge-riht'.
Farm, Pachtgut, pächt'-goot.
Farrow, Ferkel, fär'-kel.
Fascicle, Bündel, bin'-del.
Feast, Fest, fąst.
Feat, Kunststück, kųnst'-shtïk.
Fellow, Mitglied, mit'-gleet.
Fern, Farrenkraut, fär'-ren-krout'.
Farret, Frettchen, frąt'-hen.
Fever, Fieber, fee'-ber.
Fief, Lehen, lā'-en.
Field, Feld, fąlt.
Fiend, Feind, fīnt.
File, Glied, gleet.
Fire, Feuer, foi'-er.
Floor, Geschoß, ge-shoss'; Stockwerk, shtok'-vąrk.
Flour, Mehl, mäl.
Fodder, Viehfutter, fee'-fųt'-ter.
Font, Taufstecken, touf'-bąk'-ken.
Forecastle, Vorderkastel, for'-der-käs-tąl'.
Forelock, Stirnhaar, shtirn'-hār.
Forerank, erstes Glied, ār'-stes gleet.
Forestay, Fockstag, fok'-stäg.
Fother, Futter, fųt'-ter.

Flax, Flachs, flaks.
Flea, Floh, flō.
Floor, Fußboden, foos'-bō-den.
Florin, Gulden, gŭl'-den.
Flue, Rauchfang, rouch'-fáng; Feuerjug, foi'-er-tsoog'.
Foam, Schaum, shoum.
Fog, Nebel, nā'-bel.
Fool, Narr, när; Thor, tōr.
Foot, Fuß, foos.
Football, Fußball, foos'-bal.
Footfall, Fußtapfen, foos'-shtäp'-fen.
Footman, Lakei, lā-kī'.
Footstool, Fußschemel, foos'-shā'-mel.
Fop, Geck, gek; Laffe, läf'-fe.
Foreigner, Ausländer, ous'-lęn'-der.
Foreman, Obergesell, ō'-ber-ge-sęl'; Vormann, fōr'-man; Vorsitzer, fōr'-zitser.
Forester, Förster, fir'-ster.
Foretaste, Vorschmack, fōr'-shmäk.
Forum, Gerichtsstand, ge-rihts'-shtänt'.
Founder, Gründer, grün'-der; Stifter, shtif'-ter.
Fowl, Vogel, fō'-gel.
Fraction, Bruch, bruch.
Fragrance, Wohlgeruch, vōl-ge-ruch'.
Frame, Rahmen, rä'-men.
Fraud, Betrug, be-troog'.
Friar, Mönch, mönh.
Friend, Freund, froint.
Frock, Rock, rok; Kinderrock, kin'-der-rok'.
Frost, Frost, frost.
Froth, Schaum, shoum; Geifer, gī'-fer.
Fulgency, Glanz, glänts.

Ferment, Gährung, gai'-rung.
Ferry, Fähre, fai'-re.
Fertility, Fruchtbarkeit, frucht'-bär-kīt'.
Feud, Fehde, fā'-de.
Fib, Lüge, lü'-ge.
Fiction, Erdichtung, er-dih'-tung.
Fiddle, Geige, gī'-ge.
Fidelity, Treue, troi'-e.
Fife, Querpfeife, kvär-pfī'-fe.
Figure, Figur, fi-goor'; Gestalt, ge-shtält'; Ziffer, tsif'-fer.
Filbert, Haselnuß, hä'-zel-nuß'.
Fine, Geldbuße, gęlt'-boo'-sse.
Firm, Firma, fir'-mä.
Fistula, Fistel, fis'-tel.
Fit, Anwandlung, än'-vän'-dlung; Laune, lou'-ne.
Fitness, Schicklichkeit, shik'-lih-kīt'; Tüchtigkeit, tüh'-tig-kīt'.
Fix, Klemme, klęm'-me.
Flame, Flamme, fläm'-me.
Flank, Flanke, fläng'-ke; Seite, zī'-te.
Flask, Flasche, fläsh'-e.
Fleet, Flotte, flot'-te.
Flight, Flucht, flucht.
Flock, Herde, här'-de.
Flood, Fluth, floot; Ueberschwemmung, ü'-ber-shvęm'-mung.
Floor, Flur, floor.
Flower, Blume, bloo'-me.
Flute, Flöte, flī'-te.
Font, Quelle, kvąl'-le.
Food, Speise, shpī'-ze.
Force, Kraft, kräft; Gewalt, ge-vält'.
Forfeit, Verwirkung, fer-vir'-kung; Geldbuße, gęlt'-boo'-sse.

Fowl, Geflügel, ge-flü'-gel.
Frame, Gestell, ge-shtäl'; Gebäude, ge-boi'-de.
Freehold, Freilehn, frī'-lān.
Fright, Entsetzen, ent-ząt'-sen.
Frontlet, Stirnband, shtirn'-bänt.
Fruit, Obst, ōpst.
Fulminating powder, Knallpulver, knäl'-pul'-fer.
Function, Amt, ämpt.
Fund, Kapital, kä-pi-täl'.
Funds, Fonds, fongs; Stocks, stoks.
Funeral, Leichenbegängniß, lī'-hen-be-gęng'-nis.
Fungate, funginsaures Salz, fun-geen'-zou'-res zälts.
Fungin, Fungin, fun-geen'.
Fur, Fell, fäl.
Furbelow, Gebräme, ge-brai'-me.
Furniture, Möbel, mī'-bel; Geräth, ge-rait'.

160

M.

Fume, Rauch, ronch; Dampf; Dunst, dunst.
Fun, Scherz, sharts; Spaß, shpas.
Funnel, Trichter, trih'-ter.
Furlough, Urlaub, oor'-loup.
Fuse, Zünder, tsin'-der.
Fust, muffiger Geruch, muf'-fi-ger ge'-ruch'.

F.

Forge, Schmiede, shmee'-de.
Fork, Gabel, gä'-bel.
Form, Form, form; Gestalt, ge-shtält'; Formel, for'-mel.
Fort, Feste, fas'-te.
Fortification, Befestigung, be-fas'-ti-gung'.
Frankness, Freimüthigkeit, frī'-mü'-tig-kīt'.
Fraternization, Verbrüderung, fer-brü'-de-rung'.
Freight, Fracht, fracht.
Friction, Reibung, rī'-bung.
Front, Stirn, shtirn; Front.
Fruit, Frucht, frucht.
Fulness, Fülle, fil'-le.
Function, Funktion, funk'-tsyōn'.
Future, Zukunft, tsoo'-kunft.

G.

Gable, Giebel, gee'-bel.
Gag, Knebel, knā'-bel.
Gait, Gang, gäng.
Gala, Staat, shtāt.
Gale, Wind, vint; Sturm, shturm.
Galena, Bleiglanz, blī'-glänts.
Gallows, Galgen, gäl'-gen.
Gallop, Galopp, gä-lop'.
Gambler, Spieler, shpee'-ler.
Gander, Gänserich, gan'-ze-rih'.
Gangrene, Knochenfraß, knoch'-en-fräs; kalter Brand, käl'-ter bränt.
Gaol, Kerker, kar'-ker.
Garbage, Auswurf, ous'-vurf.
Garden, Garten, gar'-ten.
Garlic, Knoblauch, knoly'-louch.

Gaiter, Gamasche, gä-mäsh'-e.
Gallery, Gallerie, gäl-le-ree'.
Galley, Galeere, gä-lā'-re.
Gallon, Gallone, gäl-lō'-ne.
Gang, Bande, bän'-de; Rotte, rot'-te.
Gap, Lücke, lük'-ke; Bresche, brash'-e.
Garb, Kleidung, klī'-dung.
Garland, Guirlande, gir'-län'-de.
Garrison, Garnison, gär'-ni-zōn'.
Gasconade, Prahlerei, prā'-le-rī'.
Gaspipe, Gasröhre, gäs-rö'-re.
Gazette, Zeitung, tsī'-tung.
Gear, Tracht, trächt.
Genealogy, Geschlechtsfolge, ge-shläts'-fol'-ge.

N.

Gabble, Geschnatter, ge-shnät'-ter.
Gable roof, Giebeldach, gee'-bel-däch'.
Gage, Pfand, pfänt.
Gage, Maß, Richmaß, rī̌ -mäs.
Game, Spiel, shpeel.
Ganglion, Ueberbein, ü'-ber-bīn'.
Gaol, Gefängniß, ge-fängʹ-nis.
Gargle, Gurgelwasser, gur'-gel-väs'-ser.
Garment, Gewand, ge-vänt'; Kleid, klīt.
Garter, Strumpfband, shtrumpf'-bant.
Gas, Gas, gäs; —light, —licht, —'-liht; —works, —werk, —'-vark.
Gate, Thor, tōr.
Gaze, Angaffen, än'-gaf'-fen.
Gear, Geschirr, ge-shir'.
Gender, Geschlecht, ge-shlaht'.

Garnet, Granat, gra-nät'.
Gasometer, Gasometer, gä'-zo-mä'-ter.
Gaud, Pus, puts; Staat, shtät.
Gauze, Seidenflor, zī'-den-flōr'.
Gear, Anzug, än'-tsoog.
Gem, Edelstein, ā'-del-shtīn'.
Generator, Erzeuger, er-tsoi'-ger.
Ghost, Geist, gīst.
Giant, Riese, ree'-ze.
Gibbet, Hochgericht, hōch'-ge-riht'.
Giddiness, Schwindel, shvin'-del
Gin, Wachholderbranntwein, vach-hol'-der-brant'-vīn.
Ginger, Ingwer, ing'-ver.
Gingerbread, Pfefferkuchen, pfăf'-fer-koo'-chen.
Gipsy, Zigeuner, tsi-goi'-ner.
Girdle, Gürtel, gir'-tel.
Gizzard, Kropf, kropf.
Glass [mirror], Spiegel, shpee'-gel.
Gleam, Glanz, glants; Schimmer, shim'-mer.
Glitter, do. do. do.
Gloss, äußerer Schein, oi'-sse-rer' shīn; Glanz, glants.
Glove, Handschuh, hänt'-shoo.
Glow worm, Johannniswurm, yo-hän'-nis-vurm'.
Glutton, Vielfraß, feel'-frās.
Gnome, Gnom, gnōm; Erdgeist, ārt'-gīst.
Gnostic, Gnostiker, gnos'-ti-ker.
Goad, Stachel, shtäch'-el.
Goat, Ziegenbock, tsee'-gen-bok'.
Goblet, Becher, bäh'-er.
Goblin, Kobold, kō'-bolt.
God, Gott, got.

Genus, Gattung, gät'-tung; Art, ärt.
Giantess, Riesin, ree'-zin.
Gill, Bierweinte, fir'-tel-pin'-te.
Giraffe, Giraffe, gi-räf'-fe.
Gland, Drüse, drü'-ze.
Glee, Lustigkeit, lus'-tig-kīt'.
Globe, [Erd-]Kugel, [ārt'-]koo'-gel.
Glorification, Verherrlichung, fer-hār'-li-hung.
Glow, Glut, gloot.
Goat, Ziege, tsee'-ge; Geis, gīs.
Goblin, Elfe, al'-fe.
Goddess, Göttin, gőt'-tin.
Gondola, Gondel, gon'-del.
Goose, Gans, gäns.
Gout, Gicht, giht.
Grace, Grazie, grä'-tsye'; Anmuth, än'-moot.
Gradation, Steigerung, shti-ge-rung'.
Grammar, Grammatif, gräm-mät'-tik.
Grange, Farm, farm.
Grape, Weintraube, vīn'-trou'-be.
Gratification, Befriedigung, be-free'-di-gung.
Gravity, Schwerkraft, shvār'-kräft.
Gravy, Brühe, brü'-e; Sauce, zō'-ze.
Grease, Schmiere, shmee'-re. [de.
Greed, Sucht, zucht; Begierde, be-geer'-
Grit, Grütze, grūt'-se.
Grocery, Spezereien, shpā'-tse-rī'-en.
Grotto, Grotte, grot'-te.
Group, Gruppe, grup'-pe.
Guard, Wache, väch'-e; Garde, gär'-de; Hut, hoot.
Guesswork, Vermuthung, fer-moo'-tung.
Guidance, Führung, fü'-rung.

Genius, Genie, je-nee'.
Ghastliness, geisterhaftes Ansehen, gīs'-ter-häf'-tes än-zā'-en.
Ghost, Gespenst, ge-shpanst'.
Gibberish, Kauderwälsch, kou'-der-valsh'.
Giblets, Gänseklein, gan'-ze-klīn'.
Gig, Gig; Cabriolet, käb'-ri-o-lā'.
Glair, Eiweiß, ī'-vīs.
Glass, Glas, gläs.
Glauber salt, Glaubersalz, glou'-ber-zälts'.
Gloom, Dunkel, dung'-kel.
Glottis, Zäpfchen, tsapf'-hen.
Glycerine, Glycerin, glit'-se-reen'.
Gold, Gold, golt.
Gosling, Gänschen, gans'-hen.
Gospel, Evangelium, ā'-van-gā'-li-um'.
Gossip, Matschmaul, klätsh'-moul; Geschwätz, ge-shvats'.
Gown, Gewand, ge-vänt'; Amtskleid, ämts'-klīt.
Graft, Pfropfreis, pfropf'-rīs.
Grain, Korn, korn; Saatenforn, zā'-men-korn'.
Graphite, Reisblei, rīs'-blī.
Grass, Gras, gräs.
Grate, Gitter, git'-ter.
Grating, Gitterwerk, git'-ter-vark'.
Grave, Grab, gräp.
Graving, Schnitzwerk, shnits'-vark.
Grease, Fett, fat.
Greenhouse, Gewächshaus, ge-vaks'-hous.
Greyhound, Windspiel, vint'-shpeel.
Grief, Leiden, lī'-den; Leid, līt; Elend, ā'-lent.

M.

Godsend, unerwarteter Glücksfall, ŭn'-er-vär'-te-ter' glĭks'-fŭl.
Gourd, Kürbiß, kïr'-bĭs.
Graphite, Graphit, grä'-fĭt.
Gravel, Kies, kees; Gries, grees; grober Sand, grō'-ber zănt.
Gravestone, Grust, arnst.
Gravestone, Grabstein, gräp'-shtīn.
Green grocer, Gemüsehändler, ge-mü'-ze-hund'-ler.
Greyhound, Windhund, vĭnt'-hŭnt.
Gridiron, Rost, rost.
Grief, Kummer, kŭm'-mer; Gram, grăm; Schmerz, shmarts.
Griffin, Greif, grĭf.
Grig, kleiner Aal, klī'-ner āl.
Grip, Griff, grĭf.
Grocer, Spezereihändler, shpā'-tse-rī'-hănd'-ler.
Groom, Knecht, knaht; Stallknecht, shtäl'-knaht; Bräutigam, broi'-tĭ-gäm'; junger Ehemann, yŭng'-er ā'-e-män'.
Ground, Grund, grunt; Boden, bō'-den; Erdboden, ärd'-bō'-den.
Grove, Hain, hīn.
Grudge, Groll, groll; Neid, nīt.
Guerilla, Guerilla, gŭ'-e-rĭl'-lä.
Guest, Gast, găst.
Guide, Führer, fü'-rer.
Guilder, Gulden, gŭl'-den.
Gulf, Golf, golf; Abgrund, äp'-grŭnt.

F.

Guillotine, Guillotine, gĭl'-yo-teē'-ne.
Guilt, Schuld, shŭlt.
Guinea, Guinee, gĭ-nä'.
Guitar, Guitarre, gĭ-tăr'-re.
Gun, Kanone, kă-nō'-ne; Flinte, flĭn'-te.
Gun carriage, Lafette, lă-făt'-te.
Gunnery, Geschützkunde, ge-shĭts'-kŭn'-de.
Gutter, Rinne, rĭn'-ne.
Gymnastics, Turnkunst, tŭrn'-kunst.
Gypsy, Zigeunerin, tsi-goi'-ne-rĭn'.

N.

Grimness, grimmiges Aussehen, grĭm'-mĭ-ges' ous'-zā'-en.
Grin, Grinsen, grĭn'-zen.
Griping, Bauchgrimmen, bouch'-grĭm'-men.
Grist, Mahlkorn, mäl'-korn.
Groan, Stöhnen, shtī'-nen.
Gross [12 dozen], Groß, grōs.
Gross, Ganzes, găn'-tses.
Ground, Land, länt.
Ground floor, Erdgeschoß, ärt'-ge-shos'.
Grouse, Waldhuhn, vălt'-hoon; Birkhuhn, bĭrk'-hoon.
Grub, Futter, fŭt'-ter.
Guard-ship, Wachtschiff, văcht'-shĭf.
Gum-resin, Schleimharz, shlīm'-härts.
Gun, Feuergewehr, foi'-er-ge-vär'; Geschütz, ge-shĭts'.
Gunboat, Kanonenboot, kă-nō'-nen-bōt'.
Gymnasium, Gymnasium, gĭm-nä'-zĭ-ŭm'.

Habiliment, Kleidung, klī'-dŭng.
Habitation, Wohnung, vō'-nŭng.
Hack, Miethkutsche, meet'-kŭt'-she.
Hack[ney], Miethpferd, meet-pfärt'.
Hair, Haar, hār. [fast'.
Halfmass, Allerseelenfest, äl'-ler-zā'-len-zĭ-

Hall, Saal, zäl.
Ham, Schinken, shing'-ken.
Hammer, Hammer, häm'-mer.
Hamster, Hamfter, häm'-ster.
Hangeron, Schmarotzer, shmä-rot'-ser.
Hangman, Henker, hang'-ker.
Harbor, Hafen, hä'-ze.
Hare, Hafe, hä'-ze.
Harm, Schaden, shä'-den; Harm, härm.
Harness, Harnisch, här'-nish.
Hart, Hirsch, hirsh.
Hat, Hut, hoot.
Hate, Haß, hus.
Hatter, Hutmacher, hoot'-mäch'-er.
Haughtiness, Hochmuth, hoch'-moot.
Haunch, Schenkel, shang'-kel.
Haven, Hafen, hä'-fen.
Haversack, Proviantsack, prō'-vi-änt'-zäk.
Hawk, Habicht, hä'-biht.
Hawker, Höker, hī'-ker; Hausirer, hou-zee'-rer.
Hawthorn, Hagdorn, hä'-ge-dorn'.
Hazard, Zufall, tsoo'-fäl.
Haze, Dunst, dunst; Nebel, nā'-bel.
Head, Kopf, kopf; Gipfel, gip'-fel.
Heap, Haufen, hou'-fen.
Hearse, Leichenwagen, lī'-hen-vä'-gen.
Hearth, Herd, härt.
Heathen, Heide, hī'-de.
Heaven, Himmel, him'-mel.
Heaver, Hebel, hā'-bel; Heber, hā'-ber.
Heir, Erbe, är'-be.
Helm[et], Helm, hälm.
Hen, Saum, zoum.
Hemlock, Schierling, sheer'-ling.

Hag, Here, häx'.
Halibut, Scholle, shol'-le.
Hallucination, Hallucination, häl-loo'-tsi-näts-yōn'.
Hammock, Hängematte, häng'-e-mät'-te.
Hamstring, Kniefleche, knee'-lähk'-se.
Hand, Hand, hänt.
Harangue, Anrede, än'-rā'-de.
Harbor, Herberge, hār'-bār'-ge; Zuflucht, tsoo'-flucht.
Hardship, Strapaze, shträ-pät'-se.
Hardware, Eisen[Stahl-]waare, ī'-zen-[shtāl'-]vā'-re.
Harmony, Harmonie, här'-mo-nee'.
Harness, Rüstung, rüs'-tung.
Harp, Harfe, här'-fe.
Harpoon, Harpune, här-poo'-ne.
Harvest, Ernte, ärn'-te.
Haste, Eile, ī'-le.
Hatch, Brut, broot; Hecke, häk'-ke.
Hatch, Luke, loo'-ke; Fallthüre, fäl'-tü'-re.
Hazel, Gefahr, ge-fär'.
Hazel, Hasel[staude] hā'-zel[shtou'-de].
Head, Größe, shpit'-se.
Health, Gesundheit, ge-zunt'-hīt.
Heartiness, Herzlichkeit, härts'-lih-kīt'.
Heat, Hitze, hit'-se; Wärme, vār'-me.
Heath, Haide, hī'-de.
Heaviness, Schwere, shvā'-re.
Hedge, Hecke, häk'-ke.
Heed, Hut, hoot; Acht, ächt.
Heel, Ferse, fär'-se; Hacke, häk'-ke.
Heifer, junge Kuh, yung'-e koo; Rind, rint.
Height, Höhe, hī'-e.

Halyard, Ziehtau, tsee'-tou.
Hamlet, Dörfchen, dirf'-hen.
Handbook, Handbuch, hänt'-booch.
Handkerchief, Schnupftuch, shnupf'-tooch; Halstuch, häls'-tooch.
Harls, Berg, varg.
Harm, Unrecht, un'-reht; Leid, līt.
Harness [horses], Geschirr, ge-shir'.
Harpsichord, Klavier, klä-veer'.
Hartshorn, Hirschhorn, hirsh'-horn.
Hash, gehacktes Fleisch, ge-häk'-tes flīsh; Ragout, rä-goo'.
Hatchet, Beil, bīl.
Haw, Gehäge, ge-hai'-ge.
Hay, Heu, hoi.
Hazard, Ungefähr, un'-ge-fair'.
Head, Haupt, houpt.
Headache, Kopfweh, kopf'-vā'.
Heart, Herz, harts; Gemüth, ge-müt'.
Heartburn, Sodbrennen, zōt'-brän'-nen.
Heather, Haidekraut, hī'-de-krout'.
Heirloom, Erbstück, ärp'-shtük.
Heirship, Erbschaft[srecht], ärp'-shäft[s-reht'].
Helm [in a ship], Steuerruder, shtoi'-er-roo'-der.
Herb, Kraut, krout; Gras, gräs.
Herbal, Kräuterbuch, kroi'-ter-booch'.
Heritage, Erbe, är'-be; Erbgut, ärp'-goot.
Hide, Fell, fäl.
Hilt, Heft, häft.
Hippopotamus, Fluß-[Nil-]Pferd, flus'-[neel'-]pfärt.
Hobby-horse, Steckenpferd, shtäk'-ken-pfärt'.

164

M.

Hemorrhage, Blutfluŗ, bloot'-shturts.
Hemp, Hanf, hänf.
Hermit, Einſiedler, In'-zeed-ler.
Hernea, Bruch, bruch.
Heron, Helb, halt.
Herring, Häring, hai'-ring.
Hiding place, Schlupfwinkel, shlupf'-ving'-kel.
Hint, Wink, vink.
Hit, Stoß, shtōs; Schlag, shläg; Hieb, heep.
Hive, Bienenſtock, bee'-nen-shtok'; Bienenſchwarm, bee'-nen-shvärm'.
Hoarfrost, Reif, rīf.
Hoax, Schwank, shvänk.
Hobnail, Hufnagel, hoof'-nä'-gel.
Hock, Hochbeiner, höch'-hī-mer.
Hold, Griff.
Holiday, Feſttag, fęst'-täg.
Homicide, Todtſchläger, tōt'-schlai'-ger.
Honey, Honig, hö'-nig.
Hoof, Huf.
Hoop, Reif[rod], rīf'-[rok].
Hop, Lanz, tänts.
Hop [plant], Hopfen, hop'-fen.
Horizon, Horizont, hō'-ri-tsont'.
Horse-radish, Meerrettig, mär'-ręt'-tig.
Horticulture, Gartenbau, gär'-ten-bou'.
Host, Wirth, virt.
Hostler, Stallknecht, shtäl'-knąht.
Hound, Hund, hunt; Jagdhund, yächt'-hunt.
Huckster, Höfer, hö'-ker.
Humor, Einfall, īn'-fäl.

F.

Hell, Hölle, hil'-le.
Help, Hilfe, hil'-fe.
Hemisphere, Demiſphäre, hą'-mi-sfai'-re; Halbkugel, hälp'-koo'-gel.
Hen, Henne, hąn'-ne.
Herd, Herde, här'-de.
Heroine, Heldin, hąl'-din.
Hesitancy, Unſchlüſſigkeit, un'-shlüs'-sig-kīt'.
Hide, Haut, hout.
Hierarchy, Hierarchie, lee'-rär-hee'.
Hinge, Thürangel, tür'-äng'-el.
Hip, Hüfte, hif'-te.
Hirse, Hirſe, hir'-ze.
History, Geſchichte, ge-shih'-te.
Hoax, Ereichung, er-dih'-tung.
Homage, Huldigung, hul'-di-gung.
Homoeopathy, Homöopathie, hō'-mi-ō-pä-tee'.
Honor, Ehre, ä'-re; Würde, vir'-de.
Hood, Haube, hou'-be; Kapuŗe, kä-put'-se.
Hoof, Klaue klou'-e.
Hope, Hoffnung, hof'-nung.
Horde, Horde, hor'-de.
Hornet, Horniß, hor'-nis.
Hosiery, Strumpfwirkeri, shtrumpf'-vir'-ke-rī'.
Host, Hoſtie, hos'-ti-e'.
Hour, Stunde, shtun'-de.
Huckleberry, Heidelbeere, hī'-del-bä'-re.
Hull, Hülſe, hil'-ze; Schale, shä'-le.
Humanity, Menſchlichkeit, mąnsh'-lih-kīt'.
Humbug, Schwindelei, shvin'-de-lī'.

N.

Hobgoblin, Geſpenſt, ge-shpąnst'.
Hog, Schwein, shvīn.
Hogshead, Orhoft, oks'-hoft.
Holding, Pachtgut, pącht'-goot; Lehngut, lān'-goot.
Home, Heim, hīm.
Honey, Liebchen, leep'-hen.
Hoot, Geſchrei, ge-shrī'.
Horn, Horn, horn.
Horologe, Stuntenglas, shtun'-den-gläs.
Horror, Grauen, grou'-en; Entſeŗen, ent-ząt'-sen.
Horse, Pferd, pfärt.
Horse-shoe, Hufeiſen, hoof'-ī'-zen.
Host [many], Heer, här.
Hostry, Gaſthaus, gäst'-hous'.
Hot-bed, Miſtbeet, mist'-bāt.
Hot-blast, Gebläſe, ge-blai'-ze.
Hotel, Gaſthaus, gast'-hous; Wohnhaus, vōn'-hous [elegant].
Hot-house, Treibhaus, trīp'-hous.
House, Haus, hous.
Housing [of goods], Lagern, lä'-gęrn.
Howl, Geheul, ge-hoil'.
Huddle, Gewirr, ge-vir'.
Hunting, Jagen, yä'-gen.
Hunting horn, Hüfthorn, hift'-horn.
Huntsmanship, Waidwerf, vīt'-vąrk.
Hurly-burly, Getümmel, ge-tim'-mel.
Hush money, Schweiggelb, shvī'-ser-shtof-gąlt'.
Hydrogen, Waſſerſtoffgas, vąs'-ser-shtof-gąs'.

Hump, Höcker, hik'-ker; Buckel, buk'-kel.
Hunger, Hunger, hung'-er.
Huntsman, Jäger, yai'-ger.
Hurricane, Orkan, or-kän'; Sturmwind, shturm'-vint.
Husband, Landwirth, länt'-virt.
Hussar, Husar, hu-zär'.

Humor, Laune, lou'-ne.
Husk, Hülse, hil'-ze; Schale, shä'-le.
Hyacinth, Hyacinthe, hee'-ä-tsin'-te.
Hydrophobia, Wasserscheu, väs'-ser-shoi'.
Hymn, Hymne, him'-ne.
Hypocricy, Heuchelei, hoi'-he-li'.
Hypothesis, Hypothese, hi'-po-tä'-ze.
Hysterics, Hysterie, his-tä'-ri-e'.

Ibex, Steinbock, shtin'-lok.
Ibis, Ibis, ee'-bis.
Iceberg, Eisberg, is'-barg.
Icicle, Eiszapfen, is'-tsapf'-fen.
Idiot, Blödsinniger, blit'-zin'-ni-ger.
Idol, Abgott, äp'-got.
Idolatry, Götzendienst, git'-sen-deenst'.
[See Fem.]
Ignoramus, Ignorant, ig'-no-ränt';
Dummkopf, dum'-kopf.
Immigrant, Einwanderer, In'-vän'-de-rer'.
Impetuosity, Ungestümheit, un'-ge-shtüm-hit.
Imperative, Imperativ, im'-pe-rä-teef'.
Impostor, Betrüger, be-trü'-ger.
Impression [print], Abdruck, äp'-druk.
Impulse, Impuls, im-puls'; Antrieb, än'-treep.
Imputation, Tadel, tä'-del; Vorwurf, for'-vurf.
Incendiary, Brandstifter, bränt'-shtif'-ter.
Incentive, Reiz, rits; Antrieb, än'-treep; Sporn, shporn.
Inception, Anfang, än'-fäng.

Idea, Idee, i-dä'; Vorstellung, for'-shtäl'-lung.
Identity, Identität, i-dän'-ti-tait'.
Idiocy, Blödsinn, blit'-zin.
Idolatry, Abgötterei, äp'-git-te-ri'. [See Masc.]
Illiteracy, Ungelehrtheit, un'-ge-lärt'-hit.
Illmination, Erleuchtung, er-[be-loih'-tung.
Illusion, Illusion, il-loo'-zi-ōn'; Täu-schung, toi'-shung.
Illustration, Erläuterung, er-loi'-te-[rung.
Imagination, Einbildung, In'-bil'-dung.
Imbecility, Schwachsinnigkeit, shväch'-zin'-nig-kit'.
Immensity, Unermeßlichkeit, un'-er-mäs'-lih-kit'.
Immigration, Einwanderung, In'-vän'-de-rung'.
Immorality, Unsittlichkeit, un'-zit'-lih-[kit'.
Immortality, Unsterblichkeit, un'-shtarp'-lih-kit'.
Immunity, Befreiung von —, be-fri'-ung fon —.
Impeachment, Anklage, än'-klä'-ge.
Imperfection, Unvollkommenheit, un'-fol-kom'-men-hit'.

Ice, Eis, Is.
Ice-cellar [-house], Eiskeller [-haus], Is-kal'-ler [-hous].
Ideal, Ideal, i'-de-äl'; Musterbild, mus'-ter-bilt'.
Idiom, Idiom, i'-di-ōm'.
Idol, Götzenbild, git'-sen-bilt'.
Ignis fatuus, Irrlicht, ir'-liht.
Image, Bild, bilt.
Immunity, Vorrecht, för'-ruht.
Imperfect, Imperfectum, un'-per-fak'-tum.
Import [of goods], Einfuhren, In'-fü'-ren.
Impotence, Unvermögen, un'-fer-mī'-gen.
Impression, Gepräge, ge-prai'-ge.
Incensory, Rauchfaß, rouch'-fäs.
Indecorum, unanständiges Benehmen, un'-än-shtan'-di-ges' be-nä'-men.
Index, Inhaltsverzeichniß, in'-hälts-fer-tsih'-nis.
Indian corn, Mälschkorn, valsh'-korn.
Infantry, Fußvolk, foos'-folk.
Inn, Wirthshaus, virts'-hous.
Inquest, Verhör, fer-hir'.
Insect, Insekt, in-zakt'.
Inside, Innere[s], in'-ne-re[s].

M.

Inch, Zoll, tsol.
Incidence, Zufall, tsoo'-fál.
Incisor, Schneidezahn, shnī'-de-tsäin'.
Increment, Zuwachs, tsoo'-väks.
Indenture, Vertrag, fer-träg'; Kontrakt, kon-träkt'.
Industry, Fleiß, flīs.
Infanticide, Kindesmord, kin'-des-mort'; —mörder, —mir'-der.
Influence, Einfluß, īn'-flus.
Informer, Ankläger, än'-klai'-ger.
Ingress, Eintritt, īn'-trit; Zutritt, tsoo'-trit.
Initial, Anfangsbuchstabe, än'-fängs-booch'-shtā'-be.
Inkling, Wink, vink.
Innovator, Neuerer, noi'-e-rer'.
Inspector, Aufseher, ouf'-zāi'-er.
Insurgent, Aufgereut, in'-sur-gnut'; Aufrührer, ouf'-rü'-rer.
Intercourse, Verkehr, fer-kār'.
Interdict, Kirchenbann, kir'-hen-bän'.
Interpreter, Dolmetscher, dol'-mat'-sher.
Intrigue, Liebeshandel, lee'-bes-hän'-del. [See Next.]
Invalid, Invalide, in'-vä-lee'-de.
Isle [of building], Flügel, flü'-gel; Gang, gäng.
Item, neuer Artikel, noi'-er är-ti'-kel.

F.

Impertinence, Zudringlichkeit, tsoo'-dring'-lih-kīt'; Unverschämtheit, un'-fer-shaimt'-hīt.
Impiety, Gottlosigkeit, got'-lō'-zig-kīt'.
Implication, Verflechtung, fer-flah'-tung.
Importance, Wichtigkeit, vih'-tig-kīt'.
Impossibility, Unmöglichkeit, un'-mäg'-lih-kīt'.
Impracticability, Unausführbarkeit, un'-ous-für'-bair-kīt'.
Improvidence, Unvorsichtigkeit, un'-fōr-ziḥ'-tig-kīt'.
Impudence, Schamlosigkeit, shäm'-lō'-zig-kīt'. [kīt'.
Impunity, Straflosigkeit, shtrāf'-lō'-zig-
Imputation, Zurechnung, tsoo'-reh'-nung.
Inauguration, Einweihung, īn'-vī'-nng.
Incarnation, Menschwerdung, mansh'-vär'-dung. [lih-kīt'.
Inclemency, Unfreundlichkeit, un'-froint'-
Indolence, Trägheit, träg'-hīt.
Inferiority, Folgerung, fol'-ge-rung'; Inferiorität, in'-fā'-ri-ō'-ri-tait'. [dyng.
Inflammation, Entzündung, ent'-tsün'-
Inheritance, Erbschaft, arp'-shaft.
Ink, Dinte, din'-te.
Inn, Schenke, shang'-ke; Kneipe, knī'-pe.
Innocence, Unschuld, un'-shylt. [yōn'.
Inquisition, Inquisition, in'-kvi-zits-
Insult, Beschimpfung, be-shimp'-fung.
Intercourse, Gemeinschaft, ge-mīn'-shaft.
Intrigue, Intrigue, in-tree'-ge.
Itch, Krätze, krat'-se.

N.

Instrument, Werkzeug, vark'-tsoig.
Interdict, Verbot, fer-bōt'.
Interest, Interesse, in'-te-ras'-se.
Intrigue, Truggewebe, troog'-ge-vā'-be.
Islet, Inselchen, in'-zel-ḥen'.
Item, Item, ee'-tem.
Ivory, Elfenbein, äl'-fen-bīn'.
Ivy, Ephen, ā'-foi.

Jack, Burſche, bur'-she.
Juckass, Eſel, ä'-zel; Dummkopf, dum'-kopf.
Jaguar, Jaguar, yä'-gṳ-är'.
Janitor, Pförtner, pfirt'-ner.
Jar, irdener Krug, ir'-de-ner' kroog.
Jasmin, Jasmin, yäs-meen'.
Jasper, Jaspis, yäs'-pis.
Jaw, Kinnbacken, kin'-bäk'-ken.
Jest, Scherz, shärts; Spaß, shpäs.
Jester, Spaßvogel, shpäs'-fō'-gel.
Jesuit, Jeſuit, yä'-zṳ-eet'.
Jew, Jude, yoo'-de.
Jewel, Liebling, leep'-ling. [See Fem.]
Jobber, Mäkler, mäik'-ler.
Joiner, Schreiner, shrī'-ner; Tiſchler, tish'-ler.
Joist, Querbalken, kvär'-bäl'-ken.
Joke, Spaß, shpäs; Scherz, shärts.
Journeyman, Geſelle, ge-zäl'-le.
Judge, Richter, rih'-ter.
Jug, Krug, kroog.
Juggler, Gaukler, gouk'-ler; Taſchenſpieler, tash'-en-shpee'-ler.
Juice, Saft, zäft.
Julep, Kühltrank, kūl'-tränk.
Junction, Anſchlußort, än'-shlus-ort'; Zeitpunkt, tsīt'-punkt. [See Fem.]
Junior, Jüngerer, yüng'-e-rer'.
Juniper, Wachholter, vaeh-hol'-der.
Jurist, Juriſt, yṳ-rist'.
Juror, Geſchworner, ge-shvör'-ner.

Jack, Jugmütze, tsoog'-vin'-de.
Jalap, Jalappe, yä-läp'-pe.
Jam, Marmelade, mär'-me-lä'-de.
Jaundice, Gelbſucht, gelp'-zṳeht.
Jaw, Kinnlate, kin'-lä'-te.
Jealousy, Eiferſucht, ī'-fer-zṳeht'. [See Neut.]
Jewel, Juwele, yṳ-vā'-le. [See M. & N.]
Jewess, Jüdin, yü'-din.
Jews-harp, Maultrommel, moul'-trom'-mel.
Jilt, Coquette, ko-kat'-te.
Jocularity, Joeundity, Luſtigkeit, lus'-tig-kīt'.
Joint, Keule, koi'-le.
Journey, Reiſe, rī'-ze; Tagereiſe, tä'-ge-rī'-ze.
Jovialness, Heiterkeit, hī'-ter-kīt'.
Joy, Freude, froi'-de; Fröhlichkeit, frö'-lih-kīt'.
Judiciousness, Einſicht, īn'-ziht.
Jugglery, Gaukelei, gou'-ke-lī'.
Jugular vein, Gurgelader, gṳr'-gel-ä'-der.
Juiciness, Saftigkeit, zäf'-tig-kīt'.
Junction, Verbindung, fer-bin'-dung. [See Masc.]
Jurisdiction, Gerichtsbarkeit, ge-rihts'-bär-kīt'.
Justice, Gerechtigkeit, ge-reh'-tig-kīt'.
Justification, Rechtfertigung, reht'-fər-ti-gung'.
Justness, Richtigkeit, rih'-tig-kīt'; Genauigkeit, ge-nou'-ig-kīt'.
Juvenility, Jugendlichkeit, yoo'-gent-lih-kīt'; Jugend, yoo'-gent.

Jail, Gefängniß, ge-fäng'-nis.
Jam, Gedränge, ge-drṳng'-e.
Jargon, Rauderwälſch, kou'-der-vɐlsh'.
Jealousy, Mißtrauen, mis'-trou'-en.
Jelly, Gelée, je-lä'.
Jeopardy, Wagefluck, vä'-ge-shtūk'.
Jewel, Kleinod, klī'-nōt.
Jigger [maritime], Windzug, vin'-de-tsoog'.
Jingle, Geklapper, ge-kläp'-per.
Job, Geſchäft, ge-shaft'.
Joint, Gelenk, ge-lank'.
Jointure, Leibgeding, līp'-ge-ding'.
Jot, Jota, yō'-tä; Pünktchen, pṳnkt'-hen.
Journal, Journal, jur-näl'.
Journey work, Tagewerk, tä'-ge-vɐrk'.
Judaism, Judenthum, yoo'-den-tum'.
Judgment, Gericht, ge-riht'; Urtheil, ur'-tīl.
Judiciary, Gerichtsweſen, ge-rihts'-vā'-zen.
Jungle, Dickicht, dik'-kiht.
Jury, Schwurgericht, shvoor'-ge-riht'.

M.

Kale, Kohl, kōl; Krauskohl, krous'-kōl.
Kalendar, Kalender, kā-lạn'-der.
Keel, Kiel, keel.
Keeper, Aufseher, ouf'-zāh'-er; Hüter, hū'-ter.
Kennel, Hundestall, hụn'-de-shtäl'. [See Fem.]
Kermes, Kermes, kạr'-mes.
Kernel, Kern, kạrn. [See Fem.]
Kettle, Kessel, kẹs'-sel.
Key, Schlüssel, shlịs'-sel.
Kick, Fußtritt[-tes], foos'-trit'[shtōs'].
King, König, kị'-nig.
Kiss, Kuß, kụs.
Kite, Papierdrache, pa-peer'-drach'e.
Knapsack, Tornister, tor-nis'-ter. [ke.
Knave, Schelm, shạlm; Schurke, shụr'-
Knight, Ritter, rit'-ter.
Knob, Knopf, knopf.
Knock, Schlag, shlạg.
Knocker, Thürklöpfel, tür'-klip'-fel.
Know-nothing, Fremdenhasser, frạm'-den-hȧs'-ser.
Knuckle, Knöchel, knīh'-el. [See Neut.]

L.

Label, Zettel, tsạt'-tel.
Laborer, Arbeiter, ȧr'-bī'-ter.
Lack, Mangel, mȧng'-el.
Ladle, Schöpflöffel, shipf'-lịf'-fel.
Laic, Laie, lī'-e.
Lair, Lagerplatz, lä'-ger-plạts'.
Lairl, Gutsherr, goots'-hạr'.
Lake, See, zā.
Lake, Lack, lȧk.
Landbreeze, Landwind, lȧnt'-vint'.

F.

Keenness, Schärfe, shạr'-fe.
Kennel, Gosse, gos'-se.
Kernel, Pinie, pee-ni-e'. [See Neut.]
Kettle drum, Pauke, pou'-ke.
Key, Taste, tȧs'-te.
Kidney, Niere, nee'-re.
Kin, Verwandtschaft, fer-vȧnt'-shȧft. [See Neut.]
Kind, Gattung, gȧt'-tung; Art, ȧrt.
Kindness, Güte, gü'-te.
Kinsfolk, Verwandte, fer-vȧn'-te.
Kirk, Kirche, kir'-he.
Kitchen, Küche, kịh'-e.
Knighthood, Ritterschaft, rit'-ter-shȧft'.
Knitting needle, Stricknadel, shtrik'-nā'-del.
Knot, Schleife, shlī'-fe.
Knout, Knute, knoo'-te.
Knowledge, Wissenschaft, vis'-sen-shȧft'; Kenntniß, kạnt'-nis.

Label, Aufschrift, ouf'-shrift.
Labor, Arbeit, ȧr-bīt'; Mühe, mü'-e.
Ladder, Leiter, lī'-ter.
Lading, Ladung, lā'-dung.
Lady, Dame, dā'-me; Gebieterin, ge-bee'-te-rin'.
Lamp, Lampe, lȧm'-pe.
Lampoon, Satyre, zȧ-tee'-re.
Lamprey, Lamprete, lȧm-prē'-te.
Lance, Lanze, lȧn'-tse.

N.

Keel, Schiff, shif.
Keeping, Halten, hȧl'-ten.
Keepsake, Andenken, ȧn'-dạng'-ken.
Kernel, Korn, korn.
Keyhole, Schlüsselloch, shlịs'-sel-loch'.
Kin, Geschlecht, ge-shlạht'. [See Fem.]
Kingdom, Königreich, kī'-nig-rīh'.
Kitten, Fäschen, kȧts'-hen.
Knag, Spielzeug, shpeel'-tsoig.
Knee, Knie, knee.
Knell, Geläute, ge-loi'-te.
Knife, Messer, mạs'-ser.
Knowledge, Wissen, vis'-sen.
Knuckle, Gelenk, ge-lạnk'.
Kreosote, Kreosot, krī-o-zōt',

Label, Anhängsel, ȧn'-hȧng'-sel.
Labyrinth, Labyrinth, lȧ'-bi-rint'.
Lactate, milchsaures Salz, milh'-zou'-res sȧlts.
Lager beer, deutsches Bier, doit'-shes beer.
Lair, Lager, lā'-ger. [See Masc.]
Lamb, Lamm, lȧm.
Land, Land, lȧnt.
Lane, Gäßchen, gạs'-hen.

169

Landing, Landungsplaß, lăn'-dŭngs-pläts'.
Languisher, Schmachtlappen, shmäeht'-läp'-pen.
Lap, Schoos, shōs.
Larceny, Diebstahl, deep'-shtāil.
Larch, Lärchenbaum, lair'-hen-boum'.
Larynx, Kehlkopf, kāl'-kopf.
Lash, Hieb, heep; Streich, shtrīh.
Last [shoemaker's], Leisten, lī'-sten.
Latch, Schlüssel, shlüs'-sel.
Lather, Seifenschaum, zī'-fen-shoum'.
Latitude, Umfang, ŭm'-fäng; Spielraum, shpeel'-roum.
Laurel, Lorbeer[baum], lor'-bār[boum'].
Lavender, Lavendel, lä-van'-del.
Lawn, Grasplaß, gräs'-pläts.
Layman, Laie, lī'-e.
Leader, Anführer, än'-fü'-rer.
Leap, Sprung, shprŭng.
Learned, Gelehrter, ge-lār'-ter.
Learner, Einer der lernt, ī'-ner dār lạrnt. [See Fem.]
Lecturer, Borleser, fōr'-lā'-zer.
Leech, Blutegel, bloot'-ā'-gel.
Leek, Lauch, louch.
Legerdemain, Taschenspielerstreich, täsh'-en-shpee'-ler-shtrīh'.
Leopard, Leopard, lā'-o-pärt'.
Leper, Aussäßiger, ous'-zạt'-si-ger'.
Lessee, Pächter, pạch'-ter.
Lesson, Unterricht, ŭn'-ter-riht'.
Letter, Buchstabe, booch'-shtä'-be; Brief, breef.
Lettuce, Salat, zä-lät'.
Leven, Sauerteig, zou'-er-tīg'.

Landlady, Haushelsherin, hous'-be-zit'-se-rin'.
Landscape, Landschaft, länt'-shäft.
Language, Sprache, shprä'-che.
Lantern, Laterne, lä-tạr'-ne.
Lathe, Drehbank, drā'-bänk'.
Latitude, Breite, brī'-te.
Laundress, Wäscherin, vạsh'-e-rin'.
Law, Rechtswissenschaft, rạhts'-vis'-sen-shäft'.
Leanness, Magerkeit, mä'-ger-kīt'.
Lease, Verpachtung, fer-pạch'-tŭng.
Lecture, Vorlesung, fōr'-lā'-zŭng. [See Mase.]
Left, linke Seite [Hand], ling'-ke zī'-te [hänt].
Legality, Gesetzlichkeit, ge-zạts'-lih-kīt'.
Legend, Legende, le-gạn'-de.
Legibility, Leserlichkeit, lā'-zer-lih'-kīt'.
Legislation, Gesetzgebung, ge-zạts'-gā'-bŭng.
Legitimacy, Rechtmäßigkeit, rạht'-mai'-ssig-kīt'.
Leisure, Muße, moo'-sse. [rū'-ne.
Lemon, Limone, limō'-ne; Zitrone, tsit-
Lemonade, Limonade, li'-mo-nā'-de.
Length, Länge, lạng'-e.
Lenience, Milde, mil'-de.
Lens, Linse, lin'-ze.
Lent, Fastenzeit, fäs'-ten-tsīt'.
Lethargy, Schlafsucht, shläf'-zŭcht.
Letter, Schrift, shrift.
Levity, Leichtigkeit, līh'-tig-kīt'.
Libel, Schmähschrift, shmai'-shrift.
Liberality, Freigebigkeit, frī'-gā'-big-kīt'; Freisinnigkeit, frī'-zin' nig-kīt'.

Lantern wheel, Treibrad, trīp'-rāt.
Lard, Schweinschmalz, shvī'-ne-shmälts'.
Lass, Mädchen, mait'-hen.
Latch, Schloß, shlos.
Latin, Latein, lä-tīn'.
Lattice, Gitter, git'-ter.
Laugh, Laughter, Lachen, lạch'-en; Gelächter, ge-lạh'-ter.
Laundry, Waschhaus, vạsh'-hous'.
Law, Gesetz, ge-zạts'; Recht, rạht.
Laxative, Absührungsmittel, äp'-fü'-rŭngs-mit'-tel.
Lazaret, Krankenhaus, kräng'-ken-hous'.
Lead, Blei, blī.
Lead ore, Bleierz, blī'-ạrts.
Leaf, Blatt, blät.
Leaflet, Blättchen, blạt'-hen.
League, Bündniß, bünt'-nis.
Leakage, Leckcin, lạk'-zīn; Rinnen, rin'-nen.
Leap-year, Schaltjahr, shält'-yār'.
Leather, Leder, lā'-der.
Leave-taking, Abschiednahme, äp'-sheet'-nā'-me.
Ledger, Hauptbuch, houpt'-booch.
Leg, Bein, bīn.
Legacy, Vermächtniß, fer-mạht'-nis.
Letter paper, Briefpapier, breef'-pä-peer'.
Levant, Morgenland, mor'-gen-länt'.
Leveling, Nivelliren, ni'-vel-lee'-ren.
Leveret, Häschen, hais'-hen.
Lichen, Leberkraut, lā'-ber-krout'.
Lien, Retentionsrecht, rạ'-tạns-yōns'-rạht'.
Life, Leben, lā'-ben.
Lifeboat, Rettungsboot, rạt'-tŭngs-bōt'.

M.

Liar, Lügner, līg'-ner.
Libertine, Wüstling, vüst'-ling.
Librarian, Bibliothekar, bib'-li-ō-tā-kūr'.
Licorice, Süßholzsaft, zūs'-holts-zaft'.
Liege, Basall, vȧ-ssȧl'.
Lieutenant, Lieutenant, loi'-te-nȧnt'.
Light-house, Leuchtturm, loiht'-turm.
Lightning, Blitz, blits.
Lineament, Gesichtszug, ge-zihts'-tsoog'.
Linguist, Sprachkenner, shprȧch'-kan'-ner.
Lion, Löwe, lī'-ve.
Liquor, Liqueur, lik'-kir'. [See F. & N.]
Lithographer, Lithograph, lit'-to-grȧf'.
Litigation, Rechtsstreit, rahts'-shtrīt.
Litmus, Lackmus, lȧk'-mus.
Livelihood, Unterhalt, un'-ter-hȧlt'.
Loadstar, Polarstern, po-lȧr'-shtärn'.
Loadstone, Magnet, mȧg-nāt'.
Loaf, Laib, līp.
Loft, Boden, bō'-den; Söller, zil'-ler.
Loiterer, Zauberer, tsou'-de-rer'.
Loss, Verlust, fer-lust'. [See Fem.]
Lover, Liebhaber, leep'-hȧī'-ber.
Lucre, Gewinn, ge-vin'.
Luminary, leuchtender Körper, loih'-ten-der' kir'-per. [See Neut.]
Lunatic, Wahnsinniger, vȧn'-zin'-ni-ger'.
Lunch, Zwischenimbiß, tsvish'-en-im'-bis.
Lusern, Lynx, Luchs, luks.

F.

License, Erlaubniß, er-loup'-nis.
Licentiousness, Zügellosigkeit, tsū'-gel-lō'-zig-kīt'.
Life insurance, Lebensversicherung, lā'-bens-fer-zih'-e-rung'.
Likelihood, Wahrscheinlichkeit, vȧr'-shīn'-lih-kīt'.
Lilac, Lilafarbe, lī'-lȧ-far'-be. [kung.
Limitation, Beschränkung, be-shrȧng'-
Linden, Linde, lin'-de.
Linen, Leinwand, līn'-vȧnt. [See Neut.]
Lip, Lippe, lip'-pe.
Liquor, Flüssigkeit, flūs'-sig-kīt'.
Literature, Litteratur, lit'-te-rȧ-toor'.
Litter, Sänfte, zȧnf'-te. [klt'.
Liveliness, Lebhaftigkeit, lāp'-hȧf'-tig-
Liver, Leber, lā'-ber.
Livery, Livree, liv-rā'.
Lizard, Eidechse, ī'-dak'-se.
Lobby, Vorhalle, fōr'-hȧl'-le.
Locality, Oertlichkeit, irt'-lih-kīt'. [ve.
Locomotive, Lokomotive, lō'-ko-mo-tee'-
Lodge, Loge, lō'-jo.
Lodging, Wohnung, vō'-nung.
Longitude, Länge, lȧng'-e.
Loss, Verlegenheit, fer-lā'-gen-hīt'.
Love, Liebe, lee'-be.
Loyalty, Loyalität, lo-yȧ'-li-tait'.
Lozenge, Pastille, pȧs-til'-le.
Lunacy, Mondsucht, mōnt'-zucht.
Lung, Lunge, lung'-e.
Lurch, Patsche, pȧt'-she. [geer'-de.
Lust, Wollust, vol'-lust'; Begierde, be-
Lute, Laute, lou'-te.
Lyre, Leier, lī'-er; Lyra, lee'-rȧ.

N.

Ligament, Ligature, Band, bȧnt.
Light, Licht, liht.
Liking, Gefallen, ge-fȧl'-len.
Limb, Glied, gleet.
Lineage, Geschlecht, ge-shlaht'.
Linen, Leinzug, līn'-tsoig.
Lining, Futter, fut'-ter.
Liquor, starkes Getränk, shtȧr'-kes ge-trȧngk'.
Liquorice, Süßholz, zūs'-holts.
Livelihood, Auskommen, ous'-kom'-men.
Loan, Darlehen, dȧr'-lā'-en.
Loan office, Leihhaus, lī'-hous.
Lock, Schloß, shlos.
Log cabin, Blockhaus, blok'-hous.
Loin, Lendenstück, lan'-den-shtük'.
Look, Aussehen, ous'-zā'-en.
Loop, Schlupfloch, shlupf'-loch.
Lordliness, herrisches Wesen, hȧr'-ri-shes vā'-zen.
Lounge, Canapee, kȧ'-nȧ-pā'.
Love, Liebchen, leep'-hen.
Love song, Liebeslied, lee'-bes-leet'.
Love-token, Liebespfand, lee'-bes-pfȧnt'.
Lowing, Brüllen, brül'-len.
Luck, Glück, glik.
Luggage, Gepäck, ge-pȧk'.
Lullaby, Wiegenlied, vee'-gen-leet'.
Lumber, Bauholz, bou'-holts.
Luminary, Licht, liht. [See Masc.]
Lump, Stück, stūk.
Lymph, Blutwasser, bloot'-vȧs'-ser.
Lymphatic, Blutwassergefäß, bloot'-vȧs'-ser-ge-fäs'.

Machinist, Maschinist, mä'-shi-nist'.
Madder, Krapp, kräp.
Madman, Wahnsinniger, vän'-zin'-ni-ger'.
Magician, Schwarzkünstler, shvärts'-kinst'-ler.
Magistrate, Beamter, be-äm'-ter.
Magnet, Magnet, mäg-nāt'.
Magnetism, Magnetismus, mäg'-ne-tis'-mus.
Mail [coat of], Panzer, pän'-tser.
Main-mast, Mittelmast, mit'-tel-mäst'.
Major, Major, mä-yōr'.
Malefactor, Uebelthäter, ü'-bel-tai'-ter.
Mallet, Hammer, häm'-mer.
Mammon, Reichthum, rīh'-tum.
Manager, Verwalter, fer-väl'-ter.
Mandatary, Bevollmächtigter, bo-fol'-maḥ'-tig-ter'.
Manganese, Braunstein, broun'-shtīn.
Maniac, Wahnsinniger, vän'-zin'-ni-ger'.
Manslaughter, Todtschlag, tōt'-shläg.
Manure, Dünger, düng'-er.
Maple, Ahorn, ä'-horn.
Marble, Marmor, mär'-mōr.
March, Marsch, marsh.
Margin, Rand, ränt.
Market, Markt[platz], märkt'-[pläts].
Marl, Mergel, mär'-gel.
Marsh, Sumpf, zumpf; Morast, mo-räst'.
Martyr, Märtyrer, mär'-ti-rer'.
Mason, [Frei-]Maurer, [frī'-]mour'-rer.
Master, Meister, mī'-ster; Herr, här; Lehrer, lā'-rer.
Mastic, Mastix, mäs'-tiks.
Mastiff, Bullenbeisser, bul'-len-bī'-sser.

Mace, Muskatblüte, mus-kät'-blü'-te.
Machination, Anstiftung, än'-shtif'-tung.
Mackerel, Makrele, mäk-rā'-le.
Madness, Tollheit, tol'-hīt; Wuth, voot.
Magnanimity, Grossmuth, grōs'-moot.
Magnificence, Pracht, präht; Herrlichkeit, här'-liḥ-kīt'.
Magpie, Elster, al'-ster.
Mail, Post, post; Briefpost, breef'-post.
Majesty, Majestät, mä'-yes-tait'.
Malady, Krankheit, kränk'-hīt.
Malediction, Verfluchung, fer-floo'-chung.
Maleficence, Bösartigkeit, bös'-är'-tig-kīt'.
Malice, Bosheit, bōs'-hīt.
Mane, Mähne, mai'-ne.
Mange, Räude, roi'-de.
Manger, Krippe, krip'-pe.
Mania, Manie, mä-nee'; Wuth, voot; Sucht, zuḥt.
Manipulation, Manipulation, mä'-ni-poo'-läts-yōn'.
Manner, Manier, mä-neer'; Sitte, zit'-te; Weise, vī'-ze.
Manufactory, Fabrik, fäb'-rik'.
Map, Landkarte, länt'-kär'-te.
Marigold, Ringelblume, ring'-el-bloo'-me.
Marmelade, Marmelade, mär'-me-lä'-de.
Marriage, Heirat, hī'-rāt; Ehe, ā'-e.
Martin, Hausschwalbe, hous'-shväl'-be.
Mash, Maische, mī'-she.
Masquerade, Maskerade, mäs'-ke-rä'-de.
Mass, Messe, mäs'-se.
Match, Partie, pär-tee',

Mad-house, Tollhaus, tol'-hous.
Madrigal, Hirtenlied, hir'-ten-leet'.
Magazine, Magazin, mä'-gä-tseen'.
Magnifier, Vergrösserungsglas, fer-grī'-sse-rungs'-gläs'.
Mahogany, Mahagoniholz, mä'-hä-gō'-ni-holts'.
Mainland, Festland, fäst'-länt.
Making, Machwerk, mäch'-värk.
Malaria, Miasma, mi-äs'-mä.
Malpractice, gesetzwidriges Verfahren, ge-zats'-vee'-dri-ges' fer-fä'-ren.
Malt, Malz, mälts.
Mammal, Säugetier, zoi'-ge-teer'.
Mammoth, Mammut, mäm'-put.
Mandate, Mandat, män-dāt'.
Manganese, Mangan, män'-gän'.
Manifesto, Manifest, mä'-ni-fäst'.
Mankind, Menschengeschlecht, mar'-shen-ge-shläḥt.
Manoeuvre, Manöver, mä-nö'-ver.
Manor, Landgut, länt'-goot.
Mansion, Herrnhaus, härn'-hous.
Mantelet, Mäntelchen, män'-tel-hen'.
Manual, Handbuch, hänt'-booch.
Manufacture, Fabrikat, fäb'-ri-kät'.
Murk, Merkmal, märk'-mäl.
Martyrdom, Märtyrerthum, mar'-ti-rer'-tum'.
Marvel, Wunder, vun'-der.
Massacre, Gemetzel, ge-mät'-sel.
Massicot, Bleigelb, blī'-gälp.
Match, Zündholz, tsint'-holts; Gleiches, glī'-hes. [See Fem.]
Mate [check], Schachmatt, shäch'-mät.
Matter, Geschäft, ge-shäft'.

M.

Mate, Genosse, ge-nos'-se. [See Neut.]
Matter, Stoff, shtof; Gitter, l'-ter.
Mayor, Bürgermeister, bir'-ger-mī'-ster.
Mead, Meth, māt.
Mediator, Vermittler, fer-mit'-ler.
Meerschaum, Meerschaum[kopf], mār'-shoum-[kopf'].
Mendicant, Bettler, bet'-ler.
Mercury, Merkur, mer-koor'.
Mestizo, Mestize, mas-tī'-tse.
Meter, Messer, mas'-ser.
Midday, Mittag, mit'-tāg.
Migrant, Zugvogel, tsoog'-fō'-gel.
Mind, Sinn, zin; Verstand, fer-shtänt'.
Miner, Bergmann, bärg'-män.
Minister, Diener, dee'-ner; Minister, mi-nis'-ter; Geistlicher, gīst-li-her'.
Minor, Unmündiger, un'-mīn'-di-ger.
Minstrel, Meistersänger, mī'-ster-seng'-er.
Mire, Schlamm, shläm; Koth, kōt.
Misanthrope, Menschenfeind, män'-shen-fīnt'.
Mischief, Irrglaube, ir'-glou'-be.
Mischance, Unfall, un'-fäl.
Miscreant, Bösewicht, bī'-ze-viht'.
Miser, Geizhals, gīts'-häls.
Mishap, Unfall, un'-fäl.
Misprint, Druckfehler, drŭk'-fā'-ler.
Missionary, Missionär, mis'-yō-nair'.
Mist, Nebel, nā'-bel; Staubregen, stoup'-rā'-gen.
Mistake, Irrthum, ir'-tum.
Mister, Herr, här.
Mole, Maulwurf, moul'-vŭrf.
Moment, Augenblick, ou'-gen-blik'.

M. F.

Mathematics, Mathematik, mä'-te-mä-tik'.
Matins, Frühmesse, frü'-mäs'-se.
Matter, Materie, mä-tā'-ry-e'; Sache, zäch'-e.
Mattress, Matratze, mät-rät'-se.
Meanness, Gemeinheit, ge-mīn'-hīt.
Meat, [Fleisch-]Speise, [flīsh-]spīs[l'-ze.
Medicine, Medizin, ma'-di-tseen'.
Meditation, Betrachtung, be-träch'-tŭng.
Mediar, Mispel, mis'-pel.
Meeting, Versammlung, fer-zäm'-lŭng.
Melancholy, Schwermuth, shvār'-moot.
Melioration, Verbesserung, fer-bas'-se-rŭng.
Melon, Melone, me-lō'-ne.
Memorandum, Anmerkung, än'-mär'-kŭng; Note, nō'-te.
Merchandise, Waare, vä'-re.
Mercy, Gnade, gnā'-de; Barmherzigkeit, bärm-her'-tsig-kīt'.
Mermaid, Wasserniye, väs'-ser-niks'-e.
Merriment, Lustigkeit, lus'-tig-kīt'.
Mess, Schüssel, shis'-sel; Portion, ports-yōn'. [See Neut.]
Message, Botschaft, bōt'-shäft.
Method, Methode, me-tō'-de.
Mica, Glimmererde, glim'-mer-är'-de.
Midnight, Mitternacht, mit'-ter-nächt'.
Midwife, Hebamme, hāb'-äm'-me.
Mile, Meile, mī'-le.
Milk, Milch, milh.
Mill, Mühle, mü'-le.
Milliner, Putzmacherin, puts'-mäch'-e-rin'.

N.

Matting, Mattenwerf, mät'-ten-vark'.
Meal, Mahl, mäl.
Mean, Mittel, mit'-tel.
Measure, Verhältniß, fer-halt'-nis.
Medal, Schaustück, shou'-shtik.
Medicament, Arzuei[mittel], arts-nī'-[mit'-tel].
Mediterranean, Mittelmeer, mit'-tel-mār'.
Medium, Mittel, mit'-tel.
Medley, Gemisch, ge-mish'.
Melodeon, Melodeon.
Melodrama, Melodrama.
Member, Glied, gleet.
Memento, Andenken, än'-dang'-ken.
Memorandum book, Notizbuch, no-tits'-booch. [See Fem.]
Memorial, Denkmal, dänk'-mäl.
Memory, Gedächtniß, ge-daht'-nis; Andenken, än'-dang'-ken.
Mercury, Quecksilber, kvak'-zĭl'-ber.
Merit, Mitleid, mit'-līt. [See Fem.]
Merit, Verdienst, fer-deenst'.
Mess, Gericht, ge-riht'.
Metal, Metall, me-täl'.
Metre, Versmaß, färs'-mäs.
Microscope, Mikroskop, mik-ro-skōp'.
Midrif, Zwergfell, tsvarg'-fęl.
Mien, Aussehen, ous'-zā'-en.
Military, Militär, mī'-li-tair'.
Mind, Gemüth, ge-müt'.
Mine, Bergwerf, barg'-vark.
Mineral, Mineral, mī'-ne-räl'.
Mink, Wiesel, vee'-zel.
Miracle, Wunder, vŭn'-der.

Monarch, Monarch, mo-närch'.
Mongrel, Zwitter, tsvit'-ter.
Monitor, Monitor, mo'-ni-tŏr'.
Monk, Mönch, münh.
Monkey, Affe, äf'-fe.
Monotheism, Ein-Gott-Glaube, In'-gŏt'-glou'-be.
Month, Monat, mō'-nät.
Mood, Modus, mō'-dŭs.
Moon, Mond, mônt.
Morass, Sumpf, zumpf.
Morn[ing], Morgen, mor'-gen.
Mortar, Mörtel, mir'-tel.
Mount[ain], Berg, barg.
Mouth, Mund, munt'.
Mud, Schlamm, shläm.
Muff, Muff, muf.
Mug, Becher, bäh'-er.
Mulberry[tree], Maulbeer[baum], moul'-bār-[boum'].
Murderer, Mörder, mir'-der.
Murder, Mord, mort.
Muscadel, Muskateller, mus'-kä-tal'-ler.
Muscle, Muskel, mus'-kel. [See Fem.]
Musician, Musiker, mu'-zi-ker'.
Musk, Moschus, mosh'-us; Bisam, bee'-zäm.
Musk-ox, Bisamochse, bee'-zäm-ok'-se.
Must, Most, most.
Mustache, Schnurrbart, shnur'-bärt.
Mustard, Senf, zänf.
Muzzle, Maulkorb, moul'-korp.

Milt, Milz, milts.
Mind, Meinung, mī'-nung; Gesinnung, ge-zin'-nung.
Mine, Mine, mee'-ne. [See Neut.]
Miniature, Miniatur, min'-ni-yä-toor'.
Mint, Münze, min'-tse; Pfeffermünze, pfäf'-fer-mīn'-tse.
Minute, Minute, mi-noo'-te.
Mirage, Fata Morgana, fä'-tä mor-gä'-nä.
Mirth, Fröhlichkeit, frī'-lih-kīt'.
Mis-alliance, Mißheirat, mis'-hī'-rät.
Mistletoe, Mistel, mis'-tel.
Mismanagement, schlechte Verwaltung, shlah'-te fer-väl'-tung.
Mission, Mission, mis-yōn'.
Mistress, Frau, frou; Herrin, har'-rin.
Moan, Wehklage, vā'-klä'-ge.
Mockery, Spötterei, shpit'-te-rī'.
Moderation, Mäßigung, mai'-ssi-gung'.
Modesty, Bescheidenheit, be-shī'-den-hīt'.
Modulation, Modulation, mo'-du-lats-yōn'.
Moisture, Feuchtigkeit, foih'-tig-kīt'.
Monotony, Eintönigkeit, īn'-tī'-nig-kīt'.
Morality, Moralität, mo-rä'-li-tait'.
Mortgage, Hypothek, hi'-po-tāk'.
Moth, Motte, mot'-te.
Mouse, Maus, mous.
Mulct, Geldstrafe, galt'-shträ'-fe.
Multitude, Menge, mang'-e.
Murrain, Viehseuche, fee'-zoi'-he.
Musle [shell], Muschel, mush'-el.
Music, Musik, mу'-zeek.
Musket, Muskete, mus-kā'-te.

Missal, Meßbuch, mas'-booch.
Mistrust, Mißtrauen, mis'-trou'-en.
Misunderstanding, Mißverständniß, mis'-fer-shtänt'-nis.
Mite, Scherflein, sharf'-līn.
Mob, Gesindel, ge-zin'-del.
Monastery, Kloster, klō'-ster.
Money, Geld, galt.
Monopoly, Monopol, mō-no-pōl'.
Monster, Ungeheuer, un'-ge-hoi'-er.
Monument, Denkmal, dank'-mäl.
Morse, Walroß, väl'-ros.
Morsel, Stück[chen], shtük'-[hen].
Moss, Moos, mos.
Mould, Model, mo-dal'.
Mouth-piece, Mundstück, munt'-shtük.
Mule, Maultier, moul'-teer.
Mnn, Stillschweigen, shtil' shvī'-gen.
Museum, Museum, mу-zā'-ŭm.
Muslin, Nesseltuch, näs'-sel-tooch'.
Mustang, wildes Pferd, vil'-des pfärt.
Mystery, Geheimniß, ge-hīm'-nis.

M.

Nabob, reicher Mann, rī′-ḥer mȧn.
Nag, Klepper, kläp′-per.
Nail, Nagel, nā′-gel.
Name, Name, nā′-me; Ruf, roof.
Namesake, Namensvetter, nā′-mens-fĕt′-ter.
Nasal sound, Nasenlaut, nā′-zen-lout′.
Native, Eingeborner, īn′-ge-bōr′-ner.
Nebula, Nebelstern, nā′-bel-shtarn′.
Neck, Nacken, nȧk′-ken; Hals, hȧls.
Necromancer, Geisterbeschwörer, gī′-ster-be-shvĭ′-rer.
Nectar, Nektar, nȧk′-tȧr.
Need, Mangel, mȧng′-el.
Negotiator, Unterhändler, un′ter-händl′-ler.

Negro, Neger, nā′-ger.
Neighbor, Nachbar, nȧch′-bȧir.
Nerve, Nerv, narv. [See Fem.]
Nestling, Nestling.
Nibbler, Tadler, tä′-dler.
Nick, rechter Augenblick, räh′-ter ou′-gen-blik′.
Nickel, Nickel.
Nickname, Spottname, shpot′-nā′-me.
Niggard, Knicker, knik′-ker.
Nightmare, Alp, ȧlp.
Nimbus, Nimbus.
Nitre, Salpeter, zȧl-pā′-ter.
Node, Knoten, knō′-ten.
Noise, Lärm, lȧrm.
Nonchalance, Gleichmuth, glīh′-moot.
None, keiner, kī′-ner.
Nonsense, Unsinn, un′-zin.
Nook, Winkel, ving′-kel.

N.

Naiad, Najade, nȧ-yä′-de.
Naivete, Naivetät, nȧ-ee′-ve-tait′.
Nakedness, Nacktheit, nȧkt′-hīt.
Nap, Schlaf, si-as′-tä. [See Neut.]
Narcissus, Narzisse, nȧr-tsis′-se.
Narration, Erzählung, er-tsai′-lung.
Nastiness, Schlüpfrigkeit, shlĭpf′-rig-kīt′.
Nation, Nation, nȧts-yōn′.
Naturalization, Einbürgerung, īn-bir′-ge-rung′.
Nature, Natur, nȧ-toor′.
Nausea, Uebelkeit, ü′-bel-kīt′.
Navigation, Schifffahrt, shif′-fȧrt.
Need, Noth, nōt.
Needle, [Näh-]Nadel, [nai′-]nā′-del.
Needlework, Nadelarbeit, nā′-del-ȧr′-bīt.
Negation, Verneinung, fer-nī′-nung.
Negligence, Nachlässigkeit, nȧch′-lȧs′-sig-kīt′.
Negotiation, Unterhandlung, un′-ter-händ′-lung.
Negress, Negerin, nā′-ge-rin′. [shȧft′.
Neighborhood, Nachbarschaft, nȧch′-bȧir-
Nephritis, Nierenentzündung, nee′-ren-ent-tsün′-dung.
Nerve, Kraft, krȧft.
Nicety, Nettigkeit, nȧt′-tig-kīt′.
Night, Nacht, nȧcht.
Nimbleness, Schnelligkeit, shnel′-lig-kīt′.
Nipple, Brustwarze, brust′-vȧr′-tse.
Nomination, Ernennung, er-nan′-nung.
Non-acceptance, Nichtannahme, niht′-ȧn′-nä′-me.
Nonage, Minderjährigkeit, min′-der-yai′-rig-kīt′.

N.

Nap, Schläfchen, shlaif′-ḥen.
Nape, Genick, ge-nik′.
Naphtha, Steinöl, shtīn′-ĭl.
Napkin, Tellertuch, tȧl′-ler-tooch′.
Narcotic, Betäubungsmittel, be-toi′-bungs-mit′-tel.
Nard, Nardenöl, nȧr′-den-ĭl′.
Naught, Nichts, nihts.
Nave, Schiff, shif.
Nebula, Gewölk, ge-vilk′.
Necklace, Halsband, hȧls′-bȧnt.
Needle gun, Zündnadelgewehr, tsint′-nā′-del-ge-vār′.
Negligee, Hauskleid, hous′-klīt.
Neigh, Wiehern, vee′-ern.
Nest, Nest, nȧst.
Nest-egg, Nestei, nȧst′-ī.
Net, Netz, nȧts.
Netting, Netzwerk, nȧts′-vȧrk.
Nettlerash, Nesselfieber, nȧs′-sel-fee′-ber.
Neuralgia, Nervenweh, nȧr′-ven-vā′.
Nicotine, Nikotin, nī′-ko-teen′.
Ninepins, Kegelspiel, kā′-gel-shpeel′.
Nitric acid, Scheidewasser, shī′-de-vȧs′-ser.
Noise, Geräusch, ge-roish′.
Nomenclature, Namensverzeichniß, nā′-mens-fer-tsīh′-nis.
Non-existence, Unding, un′-ding.
Non-suit, Fallenlassen, fȧl′-len-lȧs′-sen.
Nostril, Nasenloch, nā′-zen-loch′.
Note, Zeichen, tsī′-ḥen. [See Fem.]
Noun, Hauptwort, houpt′-vort.
Novitiate, Noviziat, no-vi-tsi-ät′.
Numeral, Zahlzeichen, tsäl′-tsī′-ḥen.

Noon, Mittag, mit'-tŭg.
North, Norden, nor'-den.
Notary, Notar, no-tār'.
Nucleus, Kern, karn.
Nugget, Klumpen, klum'-pen.
Nut-cracker, Nußknacker, nus'-knäk'-ker.
Nunchion, Besperbrod, vns'-per-brōt'.
Nunnery, Nonnenkloster, non'-nen-klō'-ster.
Nursemaid, Kindsmädchen, kints'-mait'-chen.
Nursling, Pflegekind, pflā'-ge-kint'.

Non-appearance, Nichterscheinung, niht'-er-shī'-nung.
Nonentity, Nichtexistenz, niht'-ak'-sistəns'.
Nonpayment, Nichtbezahlung, niht'-betsāl'-hung.
Nonsolvency, Insolvenz, in'-sol-vəns'.
Noose, Schlinge, shling'-e; Schleife, shlī'-fe.
Nose, Nase, nä'-ze.
Notation, Aufzeichnung, ouf'-tsīh'-nung.
Notch, Kerbe, kar'-be.
Note, Note, nō'-te. [See Neut.]
Notice, Notiz, no-tits'.
Notification, Meldung, məl'-dung.
Notion, Idee, i-dā'.
Novel, Novelle, no-vəl'-le.
Novelty, Neuigkeit, noi'-ig-kīt'.
Number, Zahl, tsāl.
Numbness, Erstarrung, er-shtär'-rung; Betäubung, be-toi'-bung.
Nun, Nonne, non'ne.
Nuptials, Hochzeit, hoch'-tsīt.
Nurse, Amme, äm'-me; Wärterin, vər'-te-rin'.
Nut, Nuß, nus.
Nutriment, Nahrung, nä'-rung.

Oath, Eid, īt; Schwur, shvoor.
Obedience, Gehorsam, ge-hōr'-zäm.
Obelisk, Obelisk.
Object, Gegenstand, gā'-gen-shtänt'.
Observator, Beobachter, be-ōb'-ächt'-ter.
Occident, Abend, ä'-bent; Westen, Westen, vŭs'-ten.
Occupant, Besitzer, be-zit'-ser.
Oak, Eiche, ī'-he.
Oasis, Dase, o-ä'-ze.
Objection, Einwendung, īn'-vən'-dung.
Obligation, Verpflichtung, fer-pflīh'-tung.
Obliquity, Schrägheit, shraig'-hīt.
Oblivion, Vergessenheit, fer-gəs'-sen-hīt'.
Obscenity, Unzüchtigkeit, un'-tsīh'-tigkīt'.
Oakum, Werg, vərg.
Oar, Ruder, roo'-der.
Oat meal, Hafermehl, hä'-fer-māl'.
Obstacle, Hinderniß, hin'-der-nis'.
Occurrence, Begegniß, be-gig'-nis.
Ocean, Weltmeer, valt'-mār.
Octagon, Achteck, ächt'-ak.
Octavo, Octavformat, ok-täv'-for-mät'.

176

M.

Ocean, Ocean, ō'-tse-ản'.
Oculist, Augenarzt, ou'-gen-ärtst'.
Odor, [Wohl-]Geruch, [vōl'-]ge-ruch'.
Offender, Uebertreter, ü'-ber-trāt'-ter.
Offense, Anstoß, ān'-shtōs. [See Neut.]
Officer, Beamter, be-äm'-ter; Offizier, of'-fi-tseer'.
Offset, Vorsprung, fōr'-shprung.
Offshoot, Auswuchs, ous'-vuks.
Offspring, Nachkomme, näch'-kom'-me.
Ogre, Wehrwolf, vār'-volf.
Olibanum, Weihrauch, vī'-rouch.
Omelette, Eierfuchen, ī'-er-koo'-chen.
Omnibus, Omnibus.
Onslaught, Angriff, än'-grif.
Onyx, Onyx.
Opal, Opal, o-päl'.
Operator, Operateur, ō'-pe-ra-tẏr'.
Opponent, Gegner, gāg'-ner.
Oppressor, Unterdrücker, un'-ter-drik'-ker.
Orator, Redner, rād'-ner.
Orchard, Obstgarten, ōpst'-gär'-ten.
Organist, Orgelspieler, or'-gel-shpee'-ler.
Orient, Osten, os'-ten; Orient, ō'-ri-aut'.
Orientalist, Morgenländer, mor'-gen-lān'-der.
Origin, Ursprung, oor'-shprung.
Ortolan, Gornfink, korn'-fink.
Outcast, Auswurf, ous'-vurf.
Outcry, Ausruf, ous'-roof; Aufschrei, ouf'-shrī.
Outline, Abriß, äp'-ris; Umriß, um'-ris.
Outpost, Vorposten, fōr'-pos'-ten.
Outset, Aufang, än'-fäng; Beginn, be-gin'.

F.

Observance, Beachtung, be-äch'-tung.
Observation, Beobachtung, be-ōb'-äch'-tung.
Obstinacy, Hartnäckigkeit, härt'-nak-kig-kīt'.
Obstruction, Verstopfung, fer-shtop'-fung; Versperrung, fer-shpar'-rung [of the road].
Obtrusion, Aufdrängung, ouf'-drang'-ung.
Occasion, Gelegenheit, ge-lā'-gen-hīt'.
Occupation, Beschäftigung, be-shaf'-ti-gung'.
Odds, Ungleichheit, un'-glīh'-hīt.
Offence, Beleidigung, be-lī'-di-gung'.
Ointment, Salbe, zäl'-be.
Olive, Olive, o-lee'-ve.
Omen, Vorbedeutung, fōr'-be-doi'-tung.
Omission, Auslassung, ous'-läs'-sung; Unterlassung, un'-ter-läs'-sung.
Onion, Zwiebel, tsvee'-bel.
Openness, Offenherzigkeit, of'-fen-har'-tsig-kīt'.
Operation, Operation, ō'-pe-rits-yōn'.
Opportunity, Gelegenheit, ge-lā'-gen-hīt'.
Opposition, Opposition, op'-po-zits-yōn'.
Optics, Optik, op'-tik.
Option, Wahl, väl.
Orange, Apfelsine, äp'-fel-zee'-ne.
Oration, Rede, rā'-de.
Order, Ordnung, ordt'-nung; Vorschrift, fōr'-shrift.
Ordinance, Ordenanz, or'-do-nans'.
Ordination, Einsegnung, īn'-zāg'-nung.
Organ, Orgel, or'-gel.

N.

Offense, Aergernis, ār'-ger-nis'. [See M.]
Offer, Anerbieten, än'-er-bee'-ten.
Oilcloth, Wachstuch, väks'-tooch.
Olive oil, Olivenöl, o-lee'-ven-īl'.
Omen, Vorzeichen, fōr'-tsī'-chen.
Opera glass, Opernglas, ō'-pern-glās'.
Opiate, Schlafmittel, shlāf'-mit'-tel.
Opium, Opium.
Opossum, Beutelthier, boi'-tel-teer'.
Orchestra, Orchester, or-shās'-ter.
Ordeal, Gottesgericht, got'-tes-ge-richt'.
Ore, Erz, arts.
Organ, Organ, or-gān'.
Oriel, Erkerfenster, ār'-ker-fen'-ster.
Orient, Morgenland, nor'-gen-länt'. [See Masc.]
Outlook, Aussicht, ous'-zāh'-en.
Outsider, Nichtmitglied, nīht'-mit'-gleet.
Outward, Aeußeres, oi'-sse-res'.
Oval, Oval, rund, ī'-runt.
Overmeasure, Uebermaß, ü'-ber-mās'.
Overpoise, Uebergewicht, ü'-ber-ge-viht'.
Oversight, Versehen, fer-zā'-en.
Ovule, kleines Ei, klī'-nes I.
Ownership, Eigenthumsrecht, ī'-gen-tums-raht'.
Oxide, Orid, ok-seet'.
Oxygen, Sauerstoffgas, zou'-er-shtoff'-gās.
Oyer, Anhören, än'-hī'-ren.
Ozone, Ozon, o-tsōn'.

Oven, Ofen, ŭ'-fen.
Overseer, Aufseher, ou'´-zā´-er.
Owner, Besitzer, bezit'-ser.
Ox, Ochs, oks.

Pack, Pack, păk; Ballen, băl'-len. [*See Neut.*]
Page, Page, păi'-je. [*See Fem.*]
Pagode, Heidentempel, hī'-den-tăm'-pel.
Pail, Eimer, ī'-mer.
Pain, Schmerz, shmarts.
Painter, Maler, mā'-ler.
Palace, Palast, pā'-lăst.
Palatine, Pfalzgraf, pfălts'-grăf.
Palfrey, Zelter, tsăl'-ter.
Palm, Palmbaum, pălm'-boum. [*See F.*]
Panther, Panther, păn'-ter.
Pantomine, Mimiker, mī'-mĭ-ker'.
Paper, Zettel, tsăt'-tel.
Papist, Papist, pā'-pist'.
Paragon, Ausbund, ous'-bunt.
Paragraph, Abschnitt, ăp'-shnit.
Paramour, Geliebter, ge-leep'-ter. [*See Fem.*]
Parasol, Sonnenschirm, zon'-nen-shirm'.
Parricide, Batermord, fă'-ter-mort'; — mörder, —mir'-der.
Parrot, Papagei, pā'-pā-gī'.
Parson, Pfarrer, pfăr'-rer.
Part, Theil, til; Anstheil, ăn'-til.
Participant, Theilnehmer, tīl'-nā'-mer.
Parting, Abschied, ăp'-sheet. [*See F. & N.*]

Orifice, Oeffnung, ĭf'-nung; Mündung, mĭn'-dung.
Ornament, Berzierung, fer-tsee'-rung.
Orphan, Waise, vī'-ze.
Orthography, Rechtschreibung, raht'-shrī'-bung.
Outrage, Gewaltthat, ge-vălt'-tăt.
Overture, Eröffnung, er-ĭf'-nung.

Page, Seite, zī'-te.
Pain, Mühe, mŭ'-e.
Paint, Farbe, făr'-be.
Palatinate, Pfalz, pfălts.
Palliation, Linderung, lĭn'-de-rung'.
Pallor, Blässe, bläs'-se.
Palm, flache Hand, flach'-e hănt. [*See M.*]
Palm, Palme, păl'-me.
Palpability, Handgreiflichkeit, hănt'-grīf'-lih-kīt'.
Pan, Pfanne, pfăn'-ne.
Panel. Geschworenliste, ge-shvōr'-nen-lĭs'-te. [*See Neut.*]
Pang, Angst, ăngst.
Pantry, Speisekammer, shpī'-ze-kăm'-mer.
Parabola, Parabel, pā-rā'-bel.
Paralysis, Lähmung, lai'-mung.
Parapet, Brüstung, brĭs'-tung.
Pardon, Berzeihung, fer-tsī'-ung.
Parentage, Herkunft, hăir'-kunft.
Parish, Pfarrei, pfăr'-rī.
Parity, Gleichheit, glīh'-hīt.
Particle, Partikel, păr'-tĭk'-el. [*See N.*]
Parting, Trennung, tran'-nung.
Partition, Scheidewand, shī'-de-vănt'.

Pack, Spiel, shpeel; Bolk, folk; Gesindel, ge-zin'-del. [*See Masc.*]
Package, Gepäck, ge-păk'.
Paddle, Ruder, roo'-der.
Paddle wheel, Schaufelrad, shou'-fel-rāt'.
Paganism, Heidenthum, hī'-den-tŭm'.
Pageant, Schaugepränge, shou'-ge-präng'-e.
Painting, Gemälde, ge-mail'-de.
Pair, Paar, pār.
Palmoil, Palmöl, pălm'-īl'.
Panel, Fach, fach; Feld, felt; Tafelwerk, tā'-fel-vark'. [*See Fem.*]
Paper, Papier, pā-peer'.
Papism, Papstthum, päpst'-tŭm.
Paradise, Paradies, pā'-rā-dees'.
Parcel, Stück, shtik.
Parish, Kirchspiel, kirh'-shpeel.
Parole, [Ehren-]Wort, [ā'-ren-]vort'.
Particle, Theilchen, tīl'-hen.
Parting, Scheiden, shī'-den.
Passion, Leiden, lī'-den.
Patch, Fleckchen, flăk'-hen.
Patent, Patent, pā-tănt'.
Patrimony, Erbgut, ărp'-goot. [dăl'.
Pattern, Muster, mus'-ter; Model, mo-

178

M.

Partner, Theilhaber, til'-häi'-ber.
Passage, Zug, tsug; Weg, väg.
Paste, Kleister, klī'-ster.
Path, Pfad, pfāt.
Pathos, Pathos, pā'-tos.
Pathway, Fußweg, foos'-väg.
Patrician, Patrizier, pät'-ree'-tsi-er'.
Patriot, Patriot, pat'-ri-ōt'.
Patron, Patron, pät-rōn'; Schutzheiliger, shuts'-hī'-li-ger'; Gönner, gin'-ner.
Pauper, Armer, ār'-mer.
Pavilion, Pavilion, pä'-vil-yōn'.
Pawn [chess], Bauer, bou'-er.
Peace, Frieden, free'-den.
Peacock, Pfau, pfou.
Peasant, Landmann, länt'-män.
Pebble, Kiesel, kee'-zel.
Peck [bird], Specht, shpaht.
Peddler, Hausirer, hou-zee'-rer.
Pedigree, Stammbaum, shtäm'-boum.
Pencil, Stift, shtift; Pinsel, pin'-zel.
Penitent, Büßer, bü'-sser.
Penny, Pfennig, pfän'-nig.
Pentecost, Pfingsten, pfing'-sten.
Pepper, Pfeffer, pfäf'-fer.
Period, Zeitraum, tsīt'-roum; Punkt.
Perjury, Meineid, mīn'-īt.
Pet, Liebling, leep'-ling.
Petitioner, Bittsteller, bit'-shtäl'-ler.
Petticoat, Unterrod, un'-ter-rok'.
Pettifogger, Winkelavokat, ving'-kel-ät'-vo-kät'.
Pew, Kirchstuhl, kirh'-shtool.
Pharos, Leuchtthurm, loiht'-turm.
Philologist, Philolog, fi'-lo-lōg'.

F.

Partnership, Handelsgesellschaft, hän'-dels ge-zäl'-shaft.
Party, Partei, pär-tī'.
Passion, Leidenschaft, lī'-den-shäft'. [See *Neut.*]
Past, Vergangenheit, fer-gäng'-en-hīt'.
Pastry, Pastete, päs-tā'-te.
Pasture, Weide, vī'-de.
Paternity, Vaterschaft, fā'-ter-shaft'.
Patrol, Patrolle, pät-rol'-le.
Paucity, Wenigkeit, vā'-nig-kīt'.
Pause, Pause, pou'-ze.
Paw, Pfote, pfō'-te; Klaue, klou'-e; Tatze, tät'-se.
Payment, [Be-]Zahlung, [be-]tsä'-lung.
Pea, Erbse, arp'-se.
Peach, Pfirsiche, pfir'-zih'-e.
Pear, Birne, bir'-ne.
Pearl, Perle, par'-le.
Peculation, Entwendung, ent-van'-dung.
Pen, Feder, fā'-der.
Penalty, Strafe, shträ'-fe; Buße, boo'-sse.
Peninsula, Halbinsel, hälp'-in'-zel.
Penitence, Buße, boo'-sse.
Pension, Pension, päng-syōn'.
Perdition, Verdammniß, fer-däm'-nis.
Perfection, Vollkommenheit, fol'-kom'-men-hīt'.
Performance, Aufführung, ouf'-fü'-rung.
Peril, Gefahr, ge-fär'.
Period, Periode, par-yō'-de.
Perishability, Vergänglichkeit, fer-gäng'-lih-kīt'.
Perpetuation, Verewigung, fer-ā'-vi-gung.
Perplexity, Verlegenheit, fer-lā'-gen-hīt'.

N.

Pawn, Pfand, pfänt.
Peasantry, Landvolk, länt'-folk.
Peck, Viertelbushel, fir'-tel-bush'-el.
Pectoral, Brustmittel, brust'-mit'-tel.
Pedal, Pedal, pe-däl'.
Pedestal, Fußgestell, foos'-ge-shtäl'.
Penknife, Federmesser, fā'-der-mäs'-ser.
People, Volk, folk; Leute, loi'-te [*pl.*].
Perdition, Verderben, fer-där'-ben. [See *Fem.*]
Petal, Blumenblatt, bloo'-men-blät'.
Petition, Bittschreiben, bit'-shrī'-ben; [i.] Gesuch, ge-zooh'.
Petroleum, Stein[Erd-]öl, shtīn'-[ärt'-] öl.
Pewter, Hartzinn, härt'-tsin.
Phantasm, Trugbild, troog'-bilt.
Phenomenon, Phänomen, fai-nō'-men.
Phlegm, Phlegma, flag'-ma.
Piano, Klavier, klä-veer'.
Pick, Spitzeisen, shpits'-ī'-zen.
Pickle, Eingemachtes, īn-ge-mach'-tes.
Picnic, Mahl im Freien, mäl im frī'-en.
Piece, Stück, shtük.
Pig, Schwein, shvīn; Ferkel, fär'-kel [young].
Pig iron, Roheisen, rō'-ī-zen.
Pillow, Kissen, kis'-sen.
Pinafore, Kinderschürzchen, kin'-der-shirts'-hen.
Pink, Resenroth, rō'-zen-rōt'.
Pint, halbes Quart, häl'-bes kvärt.
Pith, Mark, märk.
Pittance, Bißchen, bis'-hen [little bit].
Plagiarism, Plagiat, plä'-gi-ät'.
Plank, Brett, brät.

Philosopher, Philosoph, fi'-lo-zōf'.
Physician, Arzt, ärtst.
Pilgrim, Pilger, pil'-ger.
Pillar, Pfeiler, pfī'-ler.
Pillory, Pranger, prung'-er.
Pinnacle, Gipfel, gip'-fel.
Pique, Groll.
Pitcher, Krug, kroog.
Pivot, Zapfen, tsäp'-fen.
Place, Platz, pläts.
Plain, Plan, plän.
Plantain, Pfang, pee'-zäng.
Plate, Teller, tal'-ler. [See Fem.]
Plea, Einwand, In'-vänt.
Plenipotentiary, Bevollmächtigter, be-fol'-mäh'-tig-ter.
Plough, Pflug, pfloog.
Point, Punkt, punkt.
Pomegranate, Granatapfel, grä-nät'-äp'-fel.
Pond, Teich, tīh.
Poniard. Dolch, dolh.
Pontiff, Papst, päpst.
Pope, Papst, päpst.
Poppy, Mohn, mōn.
Port, Hafen, hä'-fen.
Porter, Träger, trai'-ger.
Portion, Theil, tīl.
Pot, Topf, topf.
Potter, Töpfer, tüp'-fer.
Powder, Puder, poo'-der. [See Neut.]
Praise, Preis, pris.
Precipice, Abgrund, äp'-grunt.
Priest, Priester, pree'-ster.
Principal, Vorsteher, fōr'-shtä'-er. [See Neut.]

Persecution, Verfolgung, fer-fol'-gung.
Perseverance, Ausdauer, ous'-dou'-er.
Persistence, Beharrlichkeit, be-här'-lih-kīt'.
Perturbance, Störung, shtī'-rung.
Perversion, Verkehrung, fer-kā'-rung.
Phrase, Redensart, rā'-dens-ärt'; Phrase, frä'-ze.
Piety, Frömmigkeit, frǐm'-mig-kīt'.
Pigeon, Taube, tou'-be.
Pin, Stecknadel, shtäk'-nä'-del.
Pincers, Zange, tsäng'-e.
Pine, Fichte, fih'-te; Tanne, tän'-ne.
Pipe, Pfeife, pfī'-fe; Röhre, rī'-re.
Pittance, kleine Gabe, klī'-ne gä'-be.
Plague, Plage, plä'-ge; Seuche, soi'-he [disease].
Plain, Ebene, ā'-be-ne'; Fläche, flah'-e.
Plant, Pflanze, pflän'-tse. [See Neut.]
Plate, Platte, plät'-te.
Plenitude, Fülle, fǐl'-le.
Plum, Pflaume, pflou'-me.
Plume, Feder[busch], fā'-der-[bush].
Pneumonia, Lungenentzündung, lung-ent-tsǐn'-dung.
Point, Spitze, shpit'-se.
Policy, Politik, po'-li-tik'.
Popalace, Menge, mäng'-e.
Pore, Pore, pō'-re.
Port, Pforte, pfōr'-te. [See Neut.]
Posterity, Nachkommenschaft, nähch'-kom'-men-shäft'.
Poststamp, Briefmarke, breef'-mär'-ke.
Power, Macht, mähcht; Gewalt, ge-vält'.
Precaution, Vorsicht, fōr'-ziht.
Precept, Vorschrift, fōr'-shrift.

Plant, Gewächs, ge-vaks'. [See Fem.]
Plaster, Pflaster, pfläs'-ter.
Pledge, Pfand, pfänt.
Plumb, Blei, blī.
Poem, Gedicht, ge-diht'.
Poise, Gewicht, ge-viht'.
Poison, Gift, gift.
Pomp, Gepränge, ge-präng'-e.
Pony, Pferdchen, pfärt'-hen.
Porcelain, Porzellan, por'-tsel-län'.
Pork, Schweinefleisch, shvī'-ne-flīsh'.
Port, Thor, tōr. [See Fem.]
Portal, Portal, por-täl'.
Portrait, Porträt, por-trät'; Bildniss, bilt'-nis.
Posse comitatus, Aufgebot, ouf'-ge-bōt'.
Possum, Beutelthier, boi'-tel-teer'.
Postern, Ausfallthor, ous'-fäl-tōr'.
Posy, Motto.
Poultry, Federvieh, fā'-der-fee'.
Pound, Pfund, pfunt.
Powder, Pulver, pul'-fer. [See Masc.]
Prayer, Gebet, ge-bāt'.
Preamble, Vorwort, fōr'-vort.
Prelude, Vorspiel, fōr'-shpeel.
Preponderance, Uebergewicht, ü'-ber-ge-viht'.
Prerogative, Vorrecht, fōr'-raht.
Presage, Vorzeichen, fōr'-tsī'-hen.
Prescription, Rezept, ra-tsäpt'. [See F.]
Present [gift], Geschenk, ge-shänk'.
Preserve, Eingemachtes, In'-ge-mäch'-tes.
Preterit, Präteritum, prai-tä'-ri-tum'.
Prime, Erstes, ǐr'-stes; Bestes, bäs'-tes. [See Fem.]
Principal, Kapital, kä'-pi-täl'. [See M.]

M.

Principle, Grundsaß, grunt'-zaits. [See Neut.]
Print, Druck, druk.
Prize, Preis, pris.
Proctor, Anwalt, an'-vält.
Profession, Stand, shtänt.
Progenitor, Vorfahr, för'-fär.
Promenade, Spaziergang, shpä-tseer'-gäng.
Proposal, Antrag, än'-träg.
Proprietor, Eigenthümer, i'-gen-tü'-mer.
Protection, Schutz, shuts.
Psalm, Psalm, psälm.
Puck, Kobold, kö'-bolt.
Pug, Mops, mops.
Pumice, Bimsstein, bims'-shtin.
Punster, Wortspieler, vort'-shpee'-ler.
Pupil, Schüler, shü'-ler. [See F. & Neut.]
Purse, Geldbeutel, gelt'-boi'-tel.
Pus, Eiter, i'-ter.
Putty, Kitt, kit.

F.

Predestination, Vorherbestimmung, för-här'-be-shtim'-mung.
Predilection, Vorliebe, för'-lee'-be.
Preliminary, Vorbesinnung, för'-be-shtim'-mung.
Preparation, Vorbereitung, för'-be-ri'-tung.
Prescription, Verschreibung, fer-shri'-bung.
Press, Presse, pras'-se.
Presumption, Muthmaßung, moot'-mä'-ssung.
Prevention, Verhinderung, fer-hin'-de-rung.
Prime, Blüte, blü'-te.
Primogeniture, Erstgeburt, ärst'-ge-burt'.
Probability, Wahrscheinlichkeit, vär'-shin'-lih-kit'.
Profanation, Entweihung, ent-vi'-ung.
Prominence, Hervorragung, här-för'-rä'-gung; Auszeichnung, ous'-tsih'-nung.
Prose, Prosa, prō'-zä.
Prospect, Aussicht, ous'-[än'-]zihṭ.
Prosperity, Wohlfahrt, völ'-färt.
Providence, Vorsehung, för'-zä'-ung.
Province, Provinz, pro-vints'. [See Neut.]
Pulpit, Kanzel, kän'-tsel.
Pupil, Pupille, pu-pil'-le—Iris—. [See M. & N.]
Pursuit, Verfolgung, fer-fol'-gung.
Puss, Katze, kät'-se.
Pyramid, Pyramide, pi'-rä-mee'-de.

N.

Principle, Element, a'-le-mant'. [See M.]
Printing, Drucken, druk'-ken.
Prism, Prisma, pris'-mä.
Prison, Gefängniß, ge-fäng'-nis.
Privateer, Kaperschiff, kä'-per-shif'.
Privilege, Privilegium, pri-vi-lä'-gi-um'.
Problem, Problem, prob-läm'.
Proceeding, Verfahren, fer-fä'-ren.
Prodigy, Wunder, vun'-der.
Profile, Profil, pro feel'.
Progress, Fortschreiten, fort'-shri'-ten.
Prominence, Ansehen, än'-zä'-en.
Promontory, Vorgebirge, för'-ge-bir'-ge.
Proverb, Sprichwort, shprih'-vort.
Province, Gebiet, ge-beet'; Amt, ämt. [See Fem.]
Public, Publikum, pub'-li-kum'.
Pullet, Hühnchen, hün'-hen.
Pun, Wortspiel, vort'-shpeel.
Pupil, Müntel, mün'-del. [See M. & F.]
Purgatory, Fegfeuer, fä'-ge-foi'-er.
Purpose, Vorhaben, för'-hä'-ben.
Pussy, Käßchen, käts'-hen.

Quack, Quacksalber, kväk'-zäl'-ber.
Quadrant, Quadrant, kväd-ränt'.
Quality, Rang, räng; Stamm, shtäm. [See Fem.]

Quab, Quapre, kväp'pe.
Quackery, Quacksalberei, kväk'-zäl'-be-ri'.
Quadrille, Quadrille, käd-ril'-ye.

Quadrat, kväd-rät'.
Quart, Quart, kvärt; Viertelmaß, fir'-tel-mäs'. [teer'.
Quarter, Viertel, fir'-tel; Quartier, kvär-

Qnantum, Betrag, be-trŭg'.
Quarrel, Streit, shtrĭt; Zank, tsănk.
Quay, Kai, kī; Damm, dăm.
Querist, Frager, frā'-ger; Forscher, for'-sher.
Quib, Sarkasmus, zär-käs'-mŭs.
Quill, Kiel, keel.
Quiver, Köcher, kĕh'-er.
Quotient, Quotient, kvō'-tsi-rănt'.

Quail, Wachtel, văch'-tel.
Qualification, Befähigung, be-fäi'-ĭ-gŭng'.
Quality, Eigenschaft, ī'-gen-shăft'. [See Masc.]
Quantity, Quantität, kvăn'-ti-tait'.
Quarantine, Quarantäne, kä'-rän-tai'-ne.
Queen, Königin, kī'-ni-gĭn'.
Query, Question, Frage, frăi'-ge.
Quilt, Decke, dăk'-ke.
Quinsy, Halsentzündung, hăls'-ent-tsĭn'-dung.
Quintessence, Quintessenz, kvint'-essăuts'.
Quire, Buch, booch [pl. the same].
Quotation, Anführung, ăn'-fŭi'-rŭng.

Quarto, Quartformat, kvärt'-for-măt'.
Quickening, Beleben, be-lä'-ben.
Quinine, Chinin, hi-neen'.
Quodlibet, Gemengsel, ge-măng'-sel; Quodlibet.
Quorum, Quorum.
Quotation, Citat, tsi-tät'. [See Fem.]

Rabbit, Hase, hä'-ze. [See Neut.]
Rabble, Pöbel, pī'-bel. [See Neut.]
Raccoon, Waschbär, väsh'-bair.
Racket, Lärm, lărm.
Radical, Radikaler, rä'-di-kä'-ler; Radikalbuchstabe, rä'-di-käl'-booch'-shtä'-be.
Radish, Rettig, rāt'-tĭg.
Rafter, Sparren, shpăr'-ren.
Rag, Lumpen, lŭm'-pen.
Ram, Widder, vĭd'-der.
Rancor, Groll, grol.
Rank, Rang, răng. [See Fem.]
Rapine, Raub, roup.
Rascal, Schuft, shŭft; Schurke, shŭr'-ke.
Rash, Hautausschlag, hout'-ous'-shläg.
Raven, Rabe, rŭt'-be.
Reason, Grund, grŭnt. [See Fem.]

Race, Rasse, răs'-se; Zucht, tsŭcht.
Rack, Reck, rek; Folter, fŏl'-ter.
Raiment, Kleidung, klī'-dŭng.
Raisin, Rosine, ro-zee'-ne.
Ramification, Verzweigung, fer-tsvī'-gŭng.
Range, Reihe, rī'-e; Tragweite, trăg'-vī'-te. [of a gun]; Linie, leen'-ye. [See Masc.]
Rank, Reihe, rī'-e; Linie, leen'-ye.
Rape, Nothzucht, nōt'-tsŭcht.
Rascality, Schurkerei, shŭr'-ke-rī'.
Rat, Ratte, răt'-te.
Ratification, Genehmigung, ge-nā'-mi-gŭng'.
Ravine, Schlucht, shlŭcht.
Reaction, Rückwirkung, rĭk'-vĭr'-kŭng.
Readiness, Bereitschaft, be-rīt'-shăft.

Rabbit, Kaninchen, kä-neen'-hen. [See Masc.]
Rabble, gemeines Volk, ge-mī'-nes folk. [See Masc.]
Race, Geschlecht, ge-shlăht'; Gezücht, ge-tsŭht'.
Racket, Getöse, ge-tī'-ze.
Railing, Geländer, ge-lăn'-der.
Ram's horn, Widderhorn, vĭd'-der-horn'.
Random, Ungefähr, ŭn'-ge-fair'.
Rank, Glied, gleet. [See Fem.]
Ransom, Lösegeld, lī'-ze-gĕlt'.
Ratio, Verhältniß, fer-hălt'-nĭs.
Real estate, Grundeigenthum, grŭnt'-ī'-gen-tŭm'.
Realm, [König-]Reich, [kī'-nĭg-]rĭh'.
Ream, Rieß, rees.
Reason, Recht, ruht. [See Masc.]

M.

Rebel, Rebell, re-bal'.
Rebuke, Verweis, fer-vīs'.
Receipt, Empfang, emp-fang'. [*See Fem.*]
Receiver, Empfänger, emp-fang'-er.
Receptacle, Behälter, be-hal'-ter.
Record, Bericht, be-riht'.
Recruit, Rekrut, rek-root'.
Reformer, Reformirer, re'-for-mee'-rer.
Refrigerator, Kühler, kü'-ler.
Regent, Regent, re-gant'.
Regulator, Regulator, re'-gu-lā'-tōr.
Relic, Reunant, Ueberrest, ü'-ber-rəst'.
Renard, Fuchs, fuks.
Renegade, Renegat, ra̤-ne-gät'; Abtrünniger, äp'-trǖn'-ni-ger'.
Rent, Zins, tsins. [*See Fem.*]
Repeal, Widerruf, vee'-der-roof'.
Report, Bericht, be-riht'.
Representative, Repräsentant, rep-rai'-zen-tänt'; Stellvertreter, shtəl'-fer-trā'-ter.
Reproach, Reproof, Vorwurf, för'-vurf.
Republican, Republikaner, re-puly-li-kä'-ner.
Repute, Ruf, roof; Name, nä'-me.
Reservoir, Reservoir, re-zar'-vo-är'.
Resonance, Wiederhall, vee'-der-häl'.
Resting place, Ruheplatz, roo'-e-pläts'.
Result, Erfolg, er-folg'; Ausfall, ous'-fäl.
Retail [business], Kleinhandel, klin'-hän'-del.
Retract, Widerruf, vee'-der-roof'.
Retrospect, Rückblick, rik-blik.
Return, Wahlbericht, väl'-be-riht'.

F.

Reason, Vernunft, fer-nunft'; Ursache, ur'-zäch'-e; Rechenschaft, rəh'-en-shaft'. [*See Masc.*]
Rebellion, Empörung, em-pö'-rung.
Receipt, Einnahme, īn'-nä'-me; Quittung, kvit'-tung. [*See Masc.*]
Recital, Hersagung, här'-zä'-gung; Recitation, rä-ssi-tāts-yōn'.
Reckoning, [Be-]Rechnung, [be-]rəh'-nung.
Recognition, An-[Wieder-]Erkennung, än'-[vee'-der-]er-kən'-nung.
Recompense, Belohnung, be-lō'-nung; Vergütung, fer-gü'-tung.
Record, Urkunde, oor'-kun'-de.
Rectification, Berichtigung, be-rih'-ti-gung'; Rettifizirung, rək-ti-fi-tsee'-rung.
Rectitude, Redlichkeit, rāt'-lih-kit'.
Redemption, Aus-[Er-]lösung, ous-[er-]lö'-zung.
Refuge, Zuflucht, tsoo'-fluht.
Regard, Aufmerksamkeit, ouf'-mərk'-zam-kit'. [byrt'.
Regeneration, Wiedergeburt, vee'-der-ge-
Rehearsal, Probe, prō'-be; Vorübung, för'-ü'-bung.
Reliance, Zuversicht, tsoo'-fer-ziht'.
Relief, Erleichterung, er-lih̥'-te-rung'; Unterstützung, un'-ter-shtüt'-sung.
Religion, Religion, re-lee'-gi-ōn'.
Remembrance, Erinnerung, er-in'-ne-rung'.
Remittance, Uebermachung, ü'-ber-mäch'-ung; Rimesse, ri-məs'-se.

N.

Receipt, Recept, re-tsəpt'. [*See Fem.*]
Receptacle, Behältniß, be-halt'-nis.
Receipt. Recept, re-tsəpt'.
Record, Protokoll, prō'-to-kol'. [*See Masc. & Fem.*]
Reed, Rohr, rōr; Schilf, shilf.
Roof, [Felsen-]Riff, [fəl'-zen-]rif'.
Refreshment, Erfrischungsmittel, er-frish'-ungs-mit'-tel.
Refrigerator, Kühlgefäß, kül'-ge-fais'. [*See Masc.*]
Regalia, Abzeichen, äp'-tsī'-hen.
Register, Register, re-gis'-ter.
Relievo, Relief, re-l-yaf'.
Remorse, Schuldbewußtsein, shult'-be-vust'-zīn.
Removal, Umziehen, um'-tsee'-en. [*See Fem.*]
Rent, Einkommen, In'-kom'-men. [*See Fem.*]
Reptile, Kriechendes, kree'-hen-des'.
Requiem, Seelenamt, zā'-len-ämt'.
Result, Resultat, re'-zul-tät'.
Revel, Schwärmen, shvär'-men.
Revenue, Einkommen, In'-kom'-men.
Reverse, Revers, re-värs'; Unglück, un'-glik. [*See Fem.*]
Revival, Wiederaufleben, vee'-der-ouf'-lā'-ben.
Ribbon, Band, bänt.
Right, Recht, rəht.
Rigmarole, Geschwätz, ge-shvats'.
Ring, Geläute, ge-loi'-te. [*See Masc.*]
Risk, Risiko, rēē'-zi-kō'.
Rivulet, Flüßchen, flis'-hen.

183

Revel, Schmauß, sĭhmous.
Reverend, Ehrwürden, är′-vĭr′-den.
Revolutioner, Revolutionär, re′-vo-luts′-yo-nair′.
Rhubarb, Rhabarber, rä-bär′-ber.
Rhyme, Reim, rim.
Rhythmus, Rhythmus, rit′-mŭs.
Rice, Reis, rĭs.
Ridge, Rücken, rĭk′-ken.
Rim, Rand, ränt.
Ring, Ring, ring; Kreis [circle], krĭs; Klang [sound], kläng.
Riot, Aufruhr, ouf′-roor; Aufstand, ouf′-shtänt.
Ripsaw. Fuchsschwanz, fŭks′-shvänts.
Rite. Ritus, ree′-tŭs; Gebrauch, ge-brouch′.
Rivulet, Bach, bäch.
Rock [spinning], Rocken, rok′-ken.
Rock, Fels, fäls; Stein, shtĭn.
Rogue, Schelm, shälm.
Romance, Roman, ro-män′.
Room [space], Raum, roum.
Row, lärmender Auflauf, lär′-men-der ouf′-louf.
Ruby, Rubin, ru̇-been′.
Rud, Röthel, rĭ′ tĕl.
Ruffian, roher Bursche, rō′-er bur′-she.
Ruin, Sturz, shtŭrts; Verfall, fer-fäl′. [See Fem.]
Rum, Rum, rŭm.
Rusk, Zwieback, tsvee′-bäk.
Rustic, Landmann, länt′-män.
Rye, Roggen, rog′-gen.

Remorse, Reue, roi′-e.
Removal, Wegschaffung, väg′-shäf′-fŭng.
Remuneration, Belohnung, be-lō′-nŭng; Vergütung, fer-gü̇′-tŭng.
Rent, Miethe, ran′-te; Miethe, mee′-te.
Repast, Mahlzeit, mäl′-tsit.
Repentance, Reue, roi′-e; Buße, boo′-sse.
Repetition, Wiederholung, vee′-der-hō′-lŭng.
Repose, Ruhe, roo′-e; Rast, räst.
Reprieve, Frist, frĭst.
Reprisal, Wiedervergeltung, vee′-der-fer-gäl′-tŭng.
Republic, Republik, ra′-pŭb-lik′.
Repugnance, Widerstrebung, vee′-der-shträ′-bŭng.
Reputation, Achtung, äch′-tŭng.
Resignation, Hin-[Er-]gebung, hĭn′-[er-]gā′-bŭng.
Resonance, Resonanz, rą-zo-nänts′. [See Masc.]
Resource, Ressource, re-soors′.
Respiration, Athmung, ät′-mŭng.
Result, Folge[rung], fol′-ge[rŭng]. [See Masc.]
Retribution, Vergeltung, fer-gäl′-tŭng.
Reunion, Wiedervereinigung, vee′-der-fer-ī′-ni-gŭng′.
Revenge, Rache, räch′-e.
Reverse, Rück-[Kehr-]seite, rĭk′-[kär′-]zī′-te.
Revolution, Revolution, re′-vo-lŭts-yōn′.
Reward, Belohnung, be-lō′-nŭng.
Rib, Rippe, rĭp′-pe.
Rifle, Büchse, bĭk′-se.
Risk, Gefahr, ge-fär′. [See Neut.]

Roast, Rostbeef, rost′-beef
Roof, Dach, däch.
Room, Zimmer, tsĭm′-mer. [See Masc.]
Rosin, Harz, härts.
Rudiment, Rudiment, ru̇′-di-mänt′.
Rule, Lineal, lee′-ne-äl′; Richtscheit, rĭht′-shĭt.
Rumor, Gerücht, ge-rĭht′.

M.

Sabre, Säbel, zai'-bel.
Sacrilege, Kirchenraub, kir'-hen-roup'.
Saddle, Sattel, zat'-tel.
Saffron, Saffran, zaf'-rän.
Saint, Heiliger, hī'-li-ger'. [See Fem.]
Salad, Salat, zä-lät'.
Saliva, Speichel, shpī'-hel.
Salmon Lachs, läks.
Saloon, Salon, zä-long'; großer Saal, grō'-sser zäl.
Sand, Sand, zänt.
Satan, Satan, sä'-tän.
Satchel, Schul- und Reisesack, shool- unt rī'-ze-zäk'.
Satin, Atlas, ät'-läs.
Saturday, Samstag, zäms'-täg.
Savage, Wilder, vil'-der.
Savor, Geschmack, ge-shmäk'; Duft, duft.
Scale, Maßstab, mäs'-shtäp. [See Fem.]
Scarlet, Scharlach, shär'-läch.
Scavenger, (Kotstenkehrer, gäs'-sen-kä'-rer.
Scent, (Geruch, ge-ruch'.
Scheme, Plan, plän; Entwurf, ent-vurf. [See Fem.]

F.

Rocket, Rakete, rä-kā'-te.
Rod, Ruthe, roo'-te; Stange, shtäng'-te.
Root, Wurzel, vur'-tsel.
Rose, Rose, rō'-ze.
Rostrum, Rednerbühne, rād'-ner-bü'-ne.
Rouge, Schminke, shming'-ke.
Row, Reihe, rī'-e.
Ruin, Ruine, ru-ee'-ne. [See Masc.]
Rule, Regel, rā'-gel.

Sack [woman's dress], Jacke, yäk'-ke.
Sadness, Traurigkeit, trou'-rig-kīt'.
Sage, Salbei, zäl'-bī.
Saint, Heilige, hī'-li-ge'.
Salutation, Begrüßung, be-grü'-ssung.
Salvation, Rettung, rĕt' tung; Seligkeit, zā'-lig-kīt'.
Sample, Probe, prō'-be. [See Neut.]
Sanity, Gesundheit, ge-zunt'-hīt.
Satiation, Sättigung, zät'-ti-gung'.
Satire, Satyre, zä-tee'-re.
Satisfaction, Befriedigung, be-free'-di-gung'. [See Neut.]
Saucer, Untertasse, un'-ter-täs'-se.
Sauciness, Unartigkeit, un'-är-tig-kīt'.
Sausage, Wurst, vurst.
Savoriness, Schmackhaftigkeit, shmäk'-häf'-tig-kīt'.
Saw, Säge, zai'-ge.
Scabbard, Scheide, shī'-de.
Scale [weighing], [Wag-] Schale, [vāg-]shā'-le.
Scala [in music], Scala, skä'-lä.
Scalp, Kopfhaut, kopf'-hout.
Scarf, Schärpe, shär'-pe. [See Neut.]

N.

Sacrament, Sakrament, zäk'-rä-mānt'.
Sacrifice, Opfer, op'-fer.
Safe-lock, Sicherheitsschloß, zih'-er-hīts'-shlos'.
Sail, Segel, zā'-gel; Schiff.
Salt, Salz, zälts.
Saltwork, Salzbergwerk, zälts'-barg'-vark.
Sample, Muster, mus'-ter; Beispiel, bī'-shpeel. [See Fem.]
Sanctuary, Heiligthum, hī'-lig-tum'.
Sandglass, Stundenglas, shtun'-den-gläs'.
Satisfaction, Vergnügen, fer-gnü'-gen.
Saving, Ersparnis, er-shpär'-nis.
Scaffold, Gerüst, ge-rist'; Schaffot, shäf-fot'.
Scalpel, Skalpirmesser, skäl-peer'-mas'-ser.
Scandal, Aergerniss, är'-ger-nis'.
Scarf, Halstuch, häls'-tooch. [See Fem.]
Scarifier, Schröpfeisen, shrüpf'-ī'-zen.
Schedule, Blatt, blät; Verzeichnis, fer-tsīh'-nis; Anhängsel [to inventory], än'-häng'-sel.

Scholar, Schüler, shü'-ler; Gelehrter, ge-lär'-ter.
Scoffer, Spötter, shpit'-ter.
Scorpion, Scorpion, skor-pyōn'.
Scoundrel, Schurke, shur'-ke.
Scream, Schrei, shrī.
Screech, Vogelschrei, fō'-gel-shrī'; Angstruf, ängst'-roof. [See F. & N.]
Screen, Schirm, shirm.
Scribe, Schreiber, shrī'-ber; Gelehrter, ge-lär'-ter; Schriftgelehrter, shrift'-ge-lär'-ter.
Sculptor, Bildhauer, bilt'-hou'-er.
Scurf, Schorf, shorf.
Seal, Seehund, zā'-hunt. [See Neut.]
Seaman, Matrose, mät-rō'-ze.
Sent, Sitz, zits; Schauplatz, shou'-pläts; Wohnsitz, vōn'-zits.
Secretary, Secretär, zak-re-tair'; Minister, mi-nis'-ter.
Seed, Samen, zä'-men.
Semblance, Anschein, än'-shīn. [See Neut.]
Senate, Senat, ze-nät'.
Senator, Senator, ze-nä'-tōr.
Sentence, Ausspruch, zin'-shpruch; Begriff, be-shīf'. [See Neut.]
Sergeant, Sergeant, särjänt'; Feldwebel, falt'-vä'-bel.
Servant, Diener, dee'-ner. [See Fem.]
Sexton, Küster, kis'-ter.
Shade, Schatten, shät'-ten.
Shark, Theil, til; Antheil, än'-tīl.
Shark, Haifisch], hī'-[fish].
Shawl, Shawl, shäl.
Shed, Schuppen, shup'-pen. [See Fem.]
Sheet, Papierbogen, pä-peer'-bō'-gen. [See Fem.]

Scene, Scene, ssā'-ne; Bühne [stage], bü'-ne.
Schene, Form, form. [See Masc.]
School, Schule, shoo'-le.
Scourge, Geißel, gī'-sel; Peitsche, prīt'-she.
Scrape, Klemme, klam'-me.
Screech-owl, Nachteule, nächt'-oi'-le.
Scrofula, Skrofel, skrō'-fel.
Scruple, Scrupel, skroo'-pel. [See Neut.]
Seuffle, Keilerei, kī'-le-rī'.
Sea, See, zā. [See Neut.]
Seam, Naht, nät.
Season, Jahreszeit, yä'-res-tsīt'.
Secession, Ausscheidung, ous'-shī'-dung.
Second, Secunde, ze-kun'-de.
Secrecy, Heimlichkeit, hīm'-lih-kīt'; Verschwiegenheit, fer-shvee'-gen-hīt'.
Sect, Sekte, zak'-te.
Section, Abtheilung, äp'-tī'-lung.
Selfishness, Selbstsucht, zalpst'-zucht.
Semblance, Aehnlichkeit, än'-lih-kīt'. [See Masc.]
Sensation, Empfindung, emp-fin'-dung.
Sensuality, Sinnlichkeit, zin'-lih-kīt'.
Sentiment, Gesinnung, ge-zin'-nung; Meinung, mī'-nung.
Sentinel, Sentry, Schildwache, shilt'-vach'-e.
Sermon, Predigt, prā'-dict.
Serpent, Schlange, shläng'-e.
Servant [maid, girl], Dienerin, dee'-ne-rin'; Magd, mägt.
Servitude, Dienstbarkeit, deenst'-bär-kīt'.
Session, Sitzung, zit'-sung.
Settee, Lehnbank, län'-hank.

Scope, Ziel, tseel.
Scrap, Stück, shtik; Stückchen, shtik'-hen; Bruchstück, bruch'-shtik.
Scrape, Gescharr, ge-shär'.
Screak, Gequiek, ge-kveek'.
Screech, Schreien, koits'-hen.
Scribble, Gekritzel, ge-krit'-sel.
Scrip, beschriebenes Stück Papier, be-shree'-be-nes' shtik pä-peer'; kleines Felleisen [wallet], klī'-nes fal'-ī'-zen.
Scruple, Bedenken, be-dang'-ken. [See F.]
Scrutoire, Schreibepult, shrī'-be-pult'.
Scull, Boot, bōt.
Sea, Meer, mär.
Seal, Siegel, zee'-gel; Petschaft, pat'-shaft. [See Masc.]
Sealing wax, Siegellack, zee'-gel-läk'.
Secret, Geheimniß, ge-hīm'-nis.
Secretaryship, Secretariat, zak-re-tä'-rī-ät'. [See M. & F.]
Semblance, Aeußeres, oi'-sse-res'.
Seminary, Seminar, zä'-mi-när'.
Semination, Säen, zä'-en.
Sensation, Aufsehen, onf'-zä'-en.
Sentence, Urtheil, ur'-tīl.
Sepal, Feldblatt, kalh'-blät.
Sepulcher, Grab, gräp; Begräbniß, be-graip'-nis.
Seraglio, Serail, se-rī'.
Serfdom, Serfthum, sarf'-tum.
Sex, Geschlecht, ge-shläht'.
Shake, Shaking, Schütteln, shit'-teln; Gestampf, ge-shtämpf'.
Shammy, Shamois, Gemsleder, gam'-zen-lä'-der.

186

M.

Shepherd, Schäfer, shai'-fer.
Shipwreck, Schiffbruch, shif'-bruch.
Shock, Stoß, shtōs; Anstoß, án'-shtōs.
Shop, Laden, lä'-den.
Shot, Schuß, shus; Schütze, shit'-se. [See Neut.]
Shrub, Strauch, shtrouch; Busch, bush. [See Neut.]
Shutter, Fensterladen, fan'-ster-lä'-den.
Sight, Anblick, án'-blik. [See F. & N.]
Singer, Sänger, zäng'-er.
Skate, Schlittschuh, shlit'-shoo.
Skater, Schlittschuhläufer, shlit'-shoo-loi'-fer.
Sky, Himmel, him'-mel.
Slime, Schleim, shlīm; Schlamm, shläm.
Slipper, Pantoffel, pán-tof'-fel.
Smell, Geruch, ge-ruch'.
Smelter, Schmelzer, shmel'-tser.
Snob, Großthuer, grōs'-too'-er.
Snow, Schnee, shnā.
Snuff, Schnupftabak, shnupf'-tä-bák'.
Somersault, Luftsprung, luft'-shprung; Purzelbaum, pur'-tsel-boum'.
Song, Gesang, ge-záng'.
Sorrow, Kummer, kum'-mer.
Sortie, Ausfall, ous'-fál.
Sound, Ton, tōn; Laut, lout; Schall, shál; Klang, kláng; Ausdruck, ous'-druk'.
South, Süden, zü'-den; Mittag, mit'-täg.
Sovereign, Souverän, sṳ'-ve-rain'.
Spade, Spaten, shpä'-ten.
Spasm, Krampf, krämpf.
Spawn, Laich, līh. [See Fem.]

F.

Sewer, Wasserableitung, vás'-ser-áp'-lī'-tung.
Shame, Scham, shäm; Schande, shán'-de.
Sheaf, Garbe, gár'-be.
Sheath, Scheide, shī'-de.
Shed, Hütte, hit'-te; Werkstätte, vȧrk'-shtät'-te. [See M. & N.]
Sheet [land or sea], Fläche, fläh'-e. [See M. & N.]
Shell, Schale, shä'-le; Muschel, mushʹ-el.
Sherd, Scherbe, shȧrʹ-be.
Shoulder, Schulter, shulʹ-ter.
Shovel, Schaufel, shouʹ-fel; Schippe, shipʹ-pe.
Shrub, Staude, shtonʹ-de. [See M. & N.]
Shyness, Schüchternheit, shüh'-tern-hīt'.
Sickness, Krankheit, kránk'-hīt.
Side, Seite, zī'-te.
Siege, Belagerung, be-lä'-ge-rung'.
Sight, Ansicht, án'-ziht. [See M. & N.]
Signature, Unterschrift, un'-ter-shrift'.
Silence, Verschwiegenheit, fer-shvee'-gen-hīt'. [See Neut.]
Silk, Seide, zī'-de.
Silk mill, Seidenfabrik, zī'-den-fäh-rikʹ.
Sill [of door], Schwelle, shvál'-le.
Sin, Sünde, zin'-de.
Sincerity, Aufrichtigkeit, ouf'-rih'-tig-kīt'.
Sinfulness, Sündhaftigkeit, zint'-häf'-tig-kīt'.
Skin, Haut, hout.
Slander, Verleumdung, fer-loim'-dung.
Slavery, Sklaverei, shklä-fe-rīʹ..

N.

Shamrock, Kleeblatt, klā'-blát.
Shearing, Scheren, shä'-ren.
Sheet [in bed], Leintuch, līn'-tooch. [See M. & F.]
Sheet copper, Kupferblech, kup'-fer-bláh'.
Sheet glass, geblasenes Tafelglas, ge-blä'-ze-nes'tä'-fel-glás'.
Sheet iron, Eisenblech, ī'-zen-bláh'.
Sheet lead, Walzblei, válts'-blī.
Shelf, Sims, zims; Gesims, ge-zims'.
Shin, Schienbein, sheen'-bīn.
Ship, Schiff.
Shirt, [Manns-]Hemd, [mánsʹ-]hamt.
Shirt of mail, Panzerhemd, pán'-tser-hamt'.
Shooting, Schießen, shee'-ssen; Feuern, foi'-ern.
Shooting in [weaving], Einschießen, In'-shee'-ssen.
Shot, Schrot, shrōt. [See Masc.]
Show, Schauspiel, shou'-shpeel'; äußeres Gepränge, oi'-sse-res' ge-präng'-e.
Shrinkage, Schrumpfen, shrump'-fen; Krimpen, krim'-pen.
Shroud, Grabtuch, gräp'-tooch; Leichentuch, lī'-hen-tooch'.
Shrub, Gebüsch, ge-bish'.
Shrug, Achselzucken, äk'-sel-tsụk'-ken.
Shuffle, Kartenmischen, kär'-ten-mish'-en.
Sieve, Sieb, zeep.
Sight, Gesicht, ge-ziht'; Sehvermögen, zā'-fer-mȫ'-gen.
Sign, Zeichen, tsī'-hen.
Signal, Zeichen, Signal, sig-nä'l.
Signet, Siegel, zee'-gel.

Spear, Spieß, shpees. [See Fem.]
Speck, Sped, flak.
Spectacle, Anblick, än´-blik. [See F. & N.]
Spell, Zauberspruch, tson´-ber-shpruch´.
Spelt, Spelz, shpalts; Dinkel, ding´-kel.
Spern, Samen, zä´-men; Rogen, rō´-gen.
Spigot, Zapfen, tsäp´-fen; Hahn, hän.
Spine, Rückgrat, rik´-grät; Dorn [thorn], dorn.
Spirit, Geist, gīst.
Spite, Groll, grol; Haß, häs.
Spittle, Speichel, shpī´-chel.
Splint, Splitter, shplit´-ter; Spahn, shpän.
Sponsor. Pathe, pä´-te.
Spoon, Löffel, lif´-fel.
Sport, Zeitvertreib, tsīt´-fer-trīp´; Scherz, shgrts.
Sportsman, Waidmann, vīt´-män.
Spot, Fleck, flak; Flecken, flak´-ken.
Spring, Lenz, lnuts; Frühling, frü´-ling.
Sprout, Sproß, shpros.
Spy, Spion, shpī-on´.
Stable, Stall, shtäl.
Staff, Stab, shtäp; Stock, shtok; Schaft, shaft.
Stain, Flecken, flak´-ken.
Stake, Pfahl, pfäl; Satz [in playing], zäts.
Stalk, Stengel, shtng´-el; Stiel, shteel.
Stall, Stall, shtäl; Stand, shtänt.
Stand, Stand, shtänt.
Standstill, Stillstand, shtil´-shtänt.
Staple, Stapel, shtä´-pel.
Stare, starrer Blick, shtär´-rer blik.

Slide, [Eis-], [Gleit-], [Schleif-]bahn, [īs-], [glīt-], [shlīf-]bän.
Sloe, Schlehe, shlā´e.
Sloth, Faulheit, foul´-hīt.
Slovenliness, Nachlässigkeit or Unreinlichkeit im Aeußern, näch´-läs´-sig-kīt´ or un´-rīn´-lih-kīt´ im oi´-ssern.
Smallpox, Blattern[n], blät´-ter[n], used only in pl.
Snout, Schnauze, shnou´-tse.
Soap, Seife, zī´-fe.
Solder, Lethe, lī´-te.
Solidity, Gediegenheit, ge-dee´-gen-hīt´.
Solstice, Sonnenwende, zon´-nen-vn´-de.
Somnolence, Schläfrigkeit, shläf´-rig-kīt´; Schlafsucht, shläf´-zucht.
Sonata, Sonate, zo-nä´-te.
Sorrow [rare], Sorge, zor´-ge.
Source, Quelle, kvl´-le.
Sow, Sau, zou. [See Neut.]
Sow machine, Sämaschine, zai´-e-mäshee´-ne.
Span, Spanne, shpän´-ne.
Spawn, Brut, broot.
Spear, Lange, län´-tse.
Species, Art, ärt; Gattung, gät´-tung.
Specimen, Probe, prō´-he.
Spectacle, Brille, bril´-le. [See M. & N.]
Speculation, Spekulation, shpa´-ku-läts-yōn´.
Speed, Eile, ī´-le.
Sphere, Sphäre, sfai´-re; Kugel, koo´-gel.
Spider, Spinne, shpin´-ne.
Spindle, Spindel, shpin´-del; Achse, äk´-se.
Spontaneity, Selbstbestimmung, zlpst´-be-shtim´-nung.

Silence, Schweigen, shvī´-gen. [See F.]
Sill, Gesims, ge-zims´.
Silver, Silber, zil´-ber.
Skeleton, Skelett, ske-lat´; Gerippe, ge-rip´-pe.
Skimmings, Abgeschäumtes, äp´-ge-shoim´-tes.
Skin, Fell, fäl.
Skirmish, Scharmützel, shär-mit´-sel.
Skunk, Stinkthier, shtink´-teer.
Slam, Zuschlagen, tsoo´-shlä´-gen.
Slaughter, Gemetzel, ge-mats´-el; Blutbad, bloot´-bät.
Slop, [schlechtes] Getränk, shlah´-tes getrank´; Spülwasser, shpül´-väs´-ser.
Sloth, Faulthier, foul´-teer.
Smartmoney, Schmerzengelb, shmar´-tsen-galt´.
Snore, Schnarchen, shnär´-hen.
Sob[bing], Geschluchz, ge-shluchts´; Schluhz, ge-shtjn´.
Solder, Loth, lōt.
Sonnet, Sonett, zo-nat´.
Soreness, Weh, vä.
Sound, Eutschel, zank´-bll.
Sourkrout, Sauerkraut, zon´-er-krout´.
Sow, Mutterschwein, mut´-ter-shvīn´.
Specimen, Exemplar, äk´-sem-plär´.
Spectacle, Schauspiel, shou´-shpeel. [See M. & F.]
Specter, Gespenst, ge-shpanst´.
Spectrum, Spektrum.
Spelling, Buchstabierren, booch´-shtä-bee´-ren.
Spice, Gewürz, ge-vīrts´.
Spinning wheel, Spinnrad, shpin´-rät.

M.

Start, Anlauf, ān'-louf; Anfang, ān'-fäng; Antrieb, ān'-treep. [*See Neut.*]
State, Stand, shtänt; Zustand, tsoo'-shtänt; Staat, shtāt.
Statement, Bericht, be-riht'; Entwurf, ent-vurf'. [*See Fem.*]
Steam, Dampf, dämpf'.
Steer, Stier, shteer.
Stem, Stamm, shtām; Stiel, shteel; Stengel, shtäng'-el.
Stench, Gestank, ge-shtānk'.
Step, Schritt, shrit; Tritt, trit.
Steward, Verwalter, fer-väl'-ter; Aufseher, out'-zā'-er; Proviantmeister, prō'-vi-änt'-mī'-ster.
Stirrup, Steigbügel, shtīg'-bü'-gel.
Stock, Stamm, shtām; Vorrath, fōr'-rāt.
Stocking, Strumpf, shtrumpf.
Stomach, Magen, mä'-gen.
Store, Laden, lä'-den; Vorrath, fōr'-rāt.
Stork, Storch, shtorh.
Storm, Sturm, shturm.
Stove, Ofen, ō'-fen.
Strain, Ton, tōn; Stil, shteel.
Strand, Strand, shtränt.
Strap, Riemen, reec'-men.
Stream, Strom, shtrōm.
Stress, Nachdruck, näch'-druk.
Strip, Streifen, shtrī'-fen.
Stroke, Streich, shtrih; Schlag, shlāg; Hieb, heep; Strich, shtrih.
Strop, Streichriemen, shtrīh'-reec'-men.
Stud, Stumpf, shtumpf; Baumstock, boum'-shtok.
Stud, Hemdeknopf, hām'-de-knopf'.

F.

Spontaneousness, Spontaneität, shpon'-tā-nā'-i-tait'.
Squaw, Indianerin, in'-di-ä'-ne-rin'.
Stair, Treppe, trāp'-pe.
Starch, Stärke, shtār'-ke. [*See Neut.*]
Starvation, Aushungerung, ous'-hŭng'-e-rŭng'.
Statement, Specifizirung, shpā'-tsi-fi-tsee'-rŭng. [*See Masc.*]
Station, Stelle, shtāl'-le; Station, shtāts-yōn'.
Stature, Statur, shtä-toor'.
Stay, Schnürbrust, shnür'-brust.
Stiffneckedness, Hartnäckigkeit, härt'-nāk'-kig-kīt'.
Storage, Lagerung, lä'-ge-rŭng'. [ge-shih'-te; Sage, zä'-Story, Geschichte, Sage, zä'-
Stratagem, Kriegslist, kree'-ges-list'.
Street, Straße, shtrā'-sse.
Strength, Stärke, shtär'-ke.
Strike, Arbeitseinstellung, är'-bīts-īn'-shtāl'-lung.
Stuff, Materie, mä-tā'-ri-ye'; Masse, mäs'-se.
Stupefaction, Betäubung, be-toi'-bŭng.
Stupor, Erstarrung, er-shtär'-rŭng, and the preceding.
Subjection, Submission, Unterwerfung, un'-ter-vär'-fŭng.
Subscription, Unterschrift, un'-ter-shrift'; Subscription, zup'-skrips-yōn'.
Substance, Substanz, zup-stants'.
Subterfuge, Ausflucht, ous'-fluht.
Subtility, Feinheit, fīn'-hīt; Spitzfindigkeit, shpits'-fin'-dig-kīt'.

N.

Splitrod, Spalirohr, shpält'-l'-zen.
Splutter, Gepolter, ge-pol'-ter.
Sportsmanship, Waidwerk, vīt'-vārk.
Spray, Reis, rīs.
Spree, andauerndes Trinken, än'-dou'-eru-des'tring'-ken; Saufgelage, souf'-ge-lit'-ge.
Sprig, Reis, rīs.
Sprit, Spriet, spreet.
Spy glass, Fernglas, fārn'-gläs.
Squadron, Geschwader, ge-shvä'-der.
Square, Viereck, feer'-āk; Winkelmaß, ving'-kel-mäs'.
Square roof, Sattelbach, zāt'-tel-däch'.
Square root, Quadratwurzel, kväd-rät'-vur'-tsel.
Stampmill, Pochwerk, poch'-vārk.
Standard, Richtmaß, ih'-mäs; Normalmaß, nor-mäl'-mäs; Verhältniß, fer-hält'-niss.
Starboard, Steuerbord, shtoi'-er-bort'.
Starch, Stärkemehl, shtär'-ke-mäl'.
Starlight, Sternenlicht, shtār'-nen-liht'.
Start, Auffahren, ouf'-fä'-ren; Erschrecken, er-shrāk'-ken. [*See Masc.*]
Startle, Stutzen, shtüt'-sen; Zurückfahren, tsu-rik'-fä'-ren.
Steak, Steak.
Steam bath, Dampfbad, dämpf'-bāt.
Steam vessel, Dampfboot, dämpf'-bōt.
Steel, Roß, ros.
Stigma, Brandmal, bränt'-mäl.
Still life, Stillleben, shtil'-lā'-ben.
Stipend, Stipendium, sti-pän'-di-ŭm'.
Stoneware, Steingut, shtīn'-goot.

Student, Student, shtu-dent'; Schüler, shü'-ler.
Stuff, Stoff, shtof.
Stump, Stumpf, shtumpf; Stummel, shtŭm'-mel.
Sturgeon, Stör, shtör.
Sty [stable], Schweinestall, shvī'-ne-shtäl.
Style, Stil, shteel; Griffel, grif'-fel.
Subject, Gegenstand, gā'-gen-shtänt'; Unterthan, un'-ter-tän'.
Subpœna, Gerichtsbefehl, ge-rihts'-be-fāl'.
Substitute, Stellvertreter, shtal'-fer-trāi'-ter.
Sugar, Zucker, tsuk'-ker.
Suit, Anzug, än'-tsug. [See Fem.]
Summary, Inbegriff, in'-be-grif'; Auszug, ous'-tsug.
Summit, Gipfel, gip'-fel.
Superstition, Aberglaube, ä'-ber-glou'-be.
Supply, Vorrath, fōr'-rāt; Zufluß, tsoo'-shus.
Surname, Zuname, tsoo'-nāi'-me.
Surplus, Ueberschuß, ü'-ber-shus'.
Surtout, Ueberrock, ü'-ber-rok'.
Suspender, Hosenträger, hō'-zen-trāi'-ger.
Suspicion, Verdacht, fer-dächt'; Argwohn, ärg'-vōn.
Sutler, Marketender, mär'-ke-ten'-der.
Sweat, Schweiß, shvīs.
Syrup, Syrup, sī'-rup.

Table, Tisch, tish.
Table spoon, Eßlöffel, as'-lŏf'-fel.
Taboo, Bann, bän.
Tack, Stift, shtift. [See Fem.]

Suburb, Vorstadt, fōr'-shtät.
Sufferance, Duldung, dul'-dung.
Suffrage, Wahlstimme, väl'-shtim'-me.
Suit, Folge, fol'-ge; Reihe, rī'-e; Gefolge, ge-fol'-ge. [See Masc.]
Sum, Summe, zum'-me.
Summit, Anhöhe, än'-hö'-e.
Sun, Sonne, zon'-ne.
Supplement, Ergänzung, er-gän'-tsung.
Support, Unterstützung, un'-ter-shtit'-sung; Versorgung, fer-zor'-gung.
Surrender, Uebergabe, ü'-ber-gā'-be.
Suspense, Verzögerung, fer-shee'-bung; Ungewißheit, un'-ge-vis'-hīt.
Sycamore, Sycamore, sī'-kā-mō'-re.
Synagogue, Synagoge, zī'-nä-gō'-ge.
Syntax, Syntax, zin'-täks.

Tack, Zweck, tsvęk'-ke.
Taint, Ansteckung, än'-shtak'-kung.
Tale, Erzählung, er-tsāi'-lung.
Talent, Anlage, än'-lā'-ge.

Story [tale], Mährchen, mair'-ḥen.
Story [of a house], Stockwerk, shtok'-vęrk; Geschoß, ge-shos'.
Strap, Band, bänt.
Straw, Stroh, shtrō.
Stray, Herumirrendes, her-ŭn'-ir'-ren-des'.
Stroking, Streicheln, shtrī'-ḥeln.
Structure, Gebäude, ge-boi'-de; Bauwerk, bou'-vęrk.
Stucco, Stuck, shtuk.
Sty, Gerstenkorn, gär'-sten-korn'.
Subject, Subject, sub-yękt'.
Sublimate, Sublimat, sub'-li-mät'.
Suds, Seifenwasser, zī'-fen-väs'-ser.
Suet, Nierenfett, nee'-ren-fät'.
Sulphate, schwefelsaures Salz, shvā'-fel-zou'-res zälts.
Supper, Abendmahl, ä'-bent-mäl'.
Surplice, Chorhemd, kōr'-hämt.
Symbol, Symbol, sin-bōl'.
System, System, zis-täm'.

Tabernacle, Stifshütte, shtifts'-tsält.
Tableau, Tableau, tä-blō'.
Table cloth, Tischtuch, tish'-tooch.
Table linen, Tafelzeug, tāi'-fel-tsoig'.

M.

Tact, Takt.
Tadpole, Kaulfrosch, koul'-frosh.
Tail, Schwanz, shvants; Schweif, shvīf.
Tailor, Flicken, flak'-ken.
Talbot, Windhund, vint'-hunt.
Tallow, Talg, talg.
Tally, Kerbholz, karp'-shtok. [ter.
Tank, Wasserbehälter, vas'-ser-be-hal'-
Tape worm, Bandwurm, bänt'-vurm.
Taper, Wachsstock, väks'-shtok.
Tar, Theer, tär; Matrose, mät-rō'-ze.
Tare, Abgang, äp'-gang; Abzug, äp'-tsug.
Tart, Kuchen, koo'-chen.
Tartar, Weinstein, vīn'-shtīn.
Taste, Geschmad, ge-shmak'.
Taunt, Hohn, hōn.
Tax, Zoll, tsol.
Tea, Thee, tā.
Teacher, Lehrer[in], lā'-rer-[in'].
Team, Zug, tsoog; Flug [birds], floog.
Teetotaler, Temperenzler, tam'-pe-rants'-ler.
Telegraph, Telegraph, te'-le-gräf.
Tempest, Sturm, shturm; Tumult, tu-mult'.
Tenant, Pächter, päh'-ter; Miethsmann, meets'-män.
Tender, Vorweis, fōr'-vīs; Truber. [See Neut.]
Tenor, Tenor, te-nōr'; Tenorist, te'-no-rist'; Inhalt, in'-hält. [See F. & N.]
Term, Ausdruck, ous'-druk; Termin, ter-meen'. [See F. & N.]
Terrier, Dachshund, daks'-hunt.

F.

Tallness, Höhe, hüh'-e; Länge, läng'-e; Größe, grē'-se.
Talon, Klaue, klou'-e; Kralle, kral'-le.
Tamarind, Tamarinde, tä'-mä-rin'-de.
Tan, [Gerber-]Lohe, [gar'-ber-]lōh'-e.
Tank, Zisterne, tsi-star'-ne.
Tan yard, Gerberei, gar'-be-rī'.
Tap, Schenkstube, shank'-shtoo'-be.
Tardiness, Langsamkeit, läng'-säm-kīt'.
Tare, Widke, vik'-ke.
Tare [in goods], Tara, tä'-rä.
Target, Schießscheibe, shees'-shī'-be.
Tarpaulin, Theerdede, tär'-dak'-ke.
Tartness, Schärfe, shar'-fe; Säure, zoi'-re.
Task, Aufgabe, ouf'-gä'-be.
Tassel, Quaste, kväs'-te.
Taunt, Schmähung, shmā'-ung.
Tavern, Schenke, shäng'-ke.
Tawery, Weißgerberei, vīs'-gar'-be-rī'.
Tax, Steuer, shtoi'-er.
Teacup, Thee-[Kaffee-]tasse, tā'-[käf'-fe-]täs'-se.
Team, Reihe, rī'-e. [See M. & N.]
Tear, Thräne, trai'-ne; Zähre, tsai'-re.
Tedium, Langweile, läng'-vī'-le.
Tegument, Bedechung, be-dak'-kung; Hülle, hül'-le.
Temper [of metals], Temperirung, täm'-pe-reer'-rung.
Temperance, Mäßigkeit, mai'-ssig-kīt'.
Temptation, Versuchung, fer-zoo'-chung.
Tenderness, Zärtlichkeit, tsairt'-lih-kīt'; Zartheit, tsärt'-hīt; Weichheit, vīh'-hīt.

N.

Table plate, Tafelservice, tä'-fel-ser-vees'.
Tablet, Täfelchen, tai'-fel-hen'.
Talent, Talent, tä-lant'.
Talk, Gespräch, ge-shpraih'; Geplauder [of no weight], ge-plou'-der.
Tallow, Unschlitt, un'-shlit.
Tally, Kerbholz, karp'-holts.
Tambourine, Tamborin, täm'-bu-reen'.
Tare, Unkraut, un'-krout.
Task, Geschäft, ge-shäft'; Tagewerf, tä'-ge-vark'.
Tattle, Geschwätz, ge-shvats'.
Team, Gespann, ge-shpan'.
Telegram, Telegram, te'-le-grim'.
Telescope, Fernrohr, farn'-rōr.
Temper, Temperament, tam'-pe-rä-mant'.
Tender, Anerbieten, än'-er-bee'-ten. [See Masc.]
Tennis, Ballspiel, bäl'-shpeel.
Tenor, Wesen, vā'-zen. [See M. & F.]
Tent, Zelt, tsält.
Tenth, Zehntel, tsān'-tel.
Term, Ziel, tseel. [See M. & F.]
Terror, Entsetzen, ent-zats'-en.
Territory, Gebiet, ge-beet'.
Testament, Testament, tas'-tä-mant'. [See Masc.]
Texture, Gewebe, ge-vā'-be.
Thanksgivings day, Danksagungsfest, dänk'-zä'-gungs-fast'.
Thatch, Dachstroh, dach'-shtrō.
Theme, Thema, tā'-mä.
Thicket, Dichicht, dik'-kiht.
Third, Drittheil, drit'-tīl.

Terror, Schrecken, shrak'-ken.
Testament, letzter Wille, lăts'-ter vil'-le. [See Neut.]
Text, Irrt; Leitfaden, līt'-fā'-den.
Thanks, Dank, dănk.
Theft, Diebstahl, deep'-shtāl.
Theologian, Theolog, tā'-o-lōg'.
Theorem, Theorem, tā'-o-rĕm'; Lehrsatz, lā'-zăts.
Theorist, Theoretiker, tā'-o-rā'-ti-ker.'
Thief, Dieb, deep.
Thimble, Fingerhut, fing'-er-hoot'.
Thinker, Denker, dăng'-ker.
Thirst, Durst, durst.
Thorn, Dorn, dorn.
Thought, Gedanke, ge-dăng'-ke.
Thread, Faden, fā'-den; Zwirn, tsvirn.
Throat, Hals, hăls; Schlund, shlunt.
Throne, Thron, trōn.
Thrust, Stoß, shtōs.
Thumb, Daumen, dou'-men.
Thump, Stoß, shtōs; Puff, puf; Schlag, shlāg.
Thunder, Donner, don'-ner.
Thyme, Thymian, tee'-mi-ān.
Tie, Knoten, knō'-ten. [See Fem.]
Tile, Ziegel, tsee'-gel.
Tinder, Zunder, tsųn'-der.
Tin-glass, Wismuth, vis'-moot.
Tinker, Kesselflicker, kas'-sel-flik'-ker.
Title, Titel, tsip'-fel.
Tittle, Tüpfel, tip'-fel; Punkt.
Toast, Trinkspruch, trink'-shpruch. [See Fem.]

Tenor, Beschaffenheit, be-shăf'-fen-hīt'. [See Mase.]
Tension, Spannung, shpăn'-nung.
Tepidity, Lauheit, lou'-hīt.
Term, Frist; Grenze, grān'-tse. [See M. & N.]
Terrace, Terrasse, ter-răs'-se.
Tetter, Flechte, flăh'-te.
Thankfulness, Dankbarkeit, dănk'-bār-kīt'.
Thanksgiving, Danksagung, dănk'-zā'-gung.
Theology, Theologie, te-ō-lo-gee'.
Therapeutic, Heilkunst, hīl'-kunst.
Thickness, Dicke, dĭk'-ke.
Thistle, Distel, dis'-tel.
Thoughtlessness, Gedankenlosigkeit, ge-dăng'-ken-lō'-zig-kīt'.
Thrashing floor, Dreschtenne, drĕsh'-ten-ne.
Threat, Drohung, drō'-ung.
Threshold, Thürschwelle, tür'-shvĕl'-le.
Throat, Kehle, kā'-le; Gurgel, gur'-gel.
Throttle, Kehle, Luftröhre, luft'-rī'-re.
Thrush [bird], Drossel, dros'-sel.
Tide, Zeit, tsīt; Fluth, floot; Strömung, shtrī'-mung.
Tidiness, Nettigkeit, năt'-tig-kīt'; Sauberkeit, zou'-ber-kīt'.
Tidings, Nachricht, năch'-riht.
Tie, gleiche Stimmenzahl, glī'-he shtĭm'-men-tsāl'. [See Mase.]
Tillage, Bebauung, be-bou'-ung.
Timbre] Handpauke, hănt'-pou'-ke.
Time, Zeit, tsīt.

Throng, Gedränge, ge-drăng'-e.
Thunderstorm, Ungewitter, uņ'-ge-vĭt'-ter.
Ticket, Billet, bĭl-yāt'.
Tie, Band, bănt. [See M. & F.]
Tiffany, Flortuch, flōr'-tooch.
Tiller, Schubläden, shŭp'-lait'-hen.
Timber, Bauholz, bou'-holts.
Time, Mal, māl [2 × 2].
Tin, Weißblech, vīs'-blăh.
Tinsolder, Zinn [Weiß-] loth, tsĭn'-[vīs'-] lōt.
Tip [end], Ende, ăn'-de.
Tissue, Gewebe, ge-vā'-be; Gewirk, ge-virk'.
Tissue paper, Seidenpapier, zī'-den-pā-peer'.
Titter, Gekicher, ge-kih'-er.
Toll, Geläute, ge-loi'-te.
Tomb, Grab, grāp; Grabmal, grāp'-māl.
Tonic, Stärkungsmittel, shtŏr'-kungs-mit'-tel.
Tool, Werkzeug, věrk'-tsoig; Geräth, ge-rāt'.
Tooth-ache, Zahnweh, tsān'-vā.
Topic, Thema, tā'-mā.
Torchlight, Fackellicht, făk'-kel-liht'.
Torsel, Gewundenes, ge-vun'-de-nes'.
Tort, Unrecht, uņ'-raht.
Totality, Ganzes, gān'-tses.
Touch, Gefühl, ge-fül'. [See M. & F.]
Toupee, Toupet, tu-pā'.
Tourney, Turnier, tųr-neer'.
Tow, Werg, vŭrg.
Tower, Kastell, kăs-tĕl'. [See M. & F.]

M.

Tobacco. Tabaf, tă-băk'.
Tokay, Tofayer, to-kī'-er.
Tonne, Tonne, Bant, bănt.
Tonnage, Tonnengehalt, ton'-nen-ge-hălt'; —zoll, —tsol'.
Tooth, Zahn, tsain.
Top, Gipfel, gip'-fel.
Topaz, Topas, tō'-pas.
Tornado, Orfan, or-kān'.
Torrent, Strom, shtrom; Guß, gus.
Touch [stroke], Schlag, shlăg; Strich, shtrih. [See Fem. & Neut.]
Tourist, Reisender, rī'-zen-der'.
Tower, Thurm, turm.
Trade, Traffic, Handel, hăn'-del.
Tragedian, Trauerspieldichter, trou'-er-shpeel'-dih'-ter; Tragöde, tră-gī'-de. [See Neut.]
Train, Zug, tsoog.
Transit, Durchgang, durh'-găng.
Trash, Andwurf, ous'-vurf.
Traveler, Reisender, rī'-zen-der'.
Treason, Verrath, fer-rāt'.
Treasure, Schatz, shăts.
Treasurer, Schatzmeister, shăts'-mīs'-ter.
Trial, Versuch, fer-zooch'; Prozeß, pro-tsĕs'.
Tribe, Stamm, shtăm.
Tribunal, Richterstuhl, rih'-ter-shtool'.
Tributary, Tribut, tri-boot'; Nebenfluß, nā'-ben-flus'.
Trick, Trick; Kniff, knif; Pfiff, Strich, shtrih. [See Neut.]
Trident, Dreizack, drī'-tsăk.
Trimming, Besatz, be-zăts'.

F.

Timidity, Zaghaftigkeit, tsŭg'-hăf'-tig-kīt'.
Tincture, Tinctur, tink-toor'.
Tip, Spitze, shpit'-se.
Tiptoe, Zehenspitze, tsăh'-en-slpit'-se.
Toast, geröstete Brotschnitte, ge-rüs'-te-te' brōt'-shnit'-te.. [See Masc.]
Tocsin, Sturmglocke, shturm'-glok'-ke.
Toe, Zehe, tsäh'-e.
Toil, Mühseligkeit, mü-zā'-lig-kīt'.
Ton, Tonne, ton'-ne.
Tone, Spannung, shpăn'-nung; Elastizität, e-lăs'-tī-si-tait'; Stimme, shtim'-me.
Tong, Zange, tsăng'-e.
Tongs, Zange, tsăng'-o; Schere, shā'-re.
Tongue, Zunge, tsung-e; Sprache, shprā'-che.
Tonsil, Halsdrüse, hăls'-drü'-ze.
Tonsure, Tonsur, ton'-zoor'; Schur, shoor.
Top, Spitze, shpit'-se.
Torch, Fackel, făk'-kel.
Tornado, Windsbraut, vints'-bront.
Tortoise, Schildkröte, shilt'-krī'-te.
Torture, Folter, fol'-ter; Marter, mar'-ter; Pein, pīn.
Totality, Totalität, to-tā'-li-tait'.
Touch, Berührung, be-rü'-rung. [See Masc. & Neut.]
Tour, Reise, rī'-ze.
Tower, Burg, burg. [See Masc.]
Track, Spur, shpoor; Fährte, fair'-te.
Tradition, Ueberlieferung, ü'-ber-lee'-fe-rung'.

N.

Toy. Spielzeug, shpeel'-tsoig.
Tracing paper, Kalfirpapir, kăl-keer'-pā-peer'.
Track, Geleise, ge-lī'-ze.
Trade, Gewerbe, ge-var'-be; Geschäft, ge-shäft'.
Train [suite], Gefolge, ge-fol'-ge.
Transom, Querholz, kvar'-holts.
Tray, Theebrett, tā'-brăt.
Treadboard, Trittbrett, trit'-brăt.
Treadwheel, Tretrad, trāt'-rīt.
Treat, Traktament, trăk'-tā-mant'.
Trellis, Gitter[-werf], git'-ter[-vark'].
Tremor, Beben, bā'-ben; Zittern, tsit'-tern.
Trencher, Tranchirbrett, trän-sheer'-brăt.
Trespass, Vergehen, fer-găh'-en.
Trestle, Gestell, ge-shtăl'.
Trial, Experiment, ăks'-pe'-ri-mant'. [See M. & F.]
Tribe, Geschlecht, ge-shlăht'.
Tribunal, Tribunal, trī'-bŭ-nāl'.
Trick, Kunststück, kunst'-shtĭk. [See M.]
Trill, Triller, ge-tril'-ler.
Trink, Büchernß, tĭsh'-er-năts'.
Trio, Trio, tree'-ō.
Tripping, Getrippel, ge-trip'-pel; Straucheln, shtrou'-cheln.
Trophy, Siegeszeichen, zee'-ges-tsī'-hen.
Truss, Bruchband, bruch'-bănt.
Trust, Vertrauen, fer-trou'-en.
Tumbler, Trinkglas, trink'-glăs.
Tumult, Getümmel, ge-tüm'-mel.
Tune, Tonstück, tōn'-shtĭk.
Twang, Näseln, nai'-zeln.

Tripod, Dreifuß, drī'-foos.
Triumph, Triumph, tri-ŭmf'.
Truant, Tagedieb, tā'-ge-deep'; Schwänzer, shvạn'-tser.
Truck, Tausch-[handel], toush-[hän'-del].
Truck [ear], Karren, kär'-ren.
Trunk, Stamm, shtäm; Rumpf, rụmpf; Koffer, kof'-fer.
Tumult, Tumult, tụ-mụlt'.
Tune, Ton, tōn; Laut, lout.
Tunner, Stimmer, shtim'-mer.
Tunnel, Trichter, trih'-ter; Tunnel, tụn-nal'.
Turf [fuel], Torf, torf; Rasen, rä'-zen.
Turkey, Puter, poo'-ter.
Tutor, [Unter-]Lehrer, [ụn'-ter-]lā'-rer; Hofmeister, hof'-mīs'-ter.
Twig, Zweig, tsvīg.
Twin, Zwilling, tsvil'-ling.
Twine, Zwirn, tsvirn.
Type, Druckbuchstabe, drụk'-booch-shtā'-be. [See F. & N.]
Type founder, Schriftgießer, shrift'-gee'-sser.
Typhus, Typhus, tee'-fus.
Typographer, [Buch-]Drucker, [booch'-]drụk'-ker.

Traduction, Uebertragung, ü'-ber-trä'-gụng.
Train [dress], Schleppe, shlạp'-pe; Reihe, rī'-e; Folge, fol'-ge.
Trance, Verzückung, fer-tsük'-kụng.
Transcription, Abschreibung, ạp'-shrī'-bụng.
Transmigration, Durchwanderung, dụrh'-vän'-de-rụng'.
Transportation, Versendung, fer-zạn'-dụng; Verbannung, fer-bän'-nụng.
Travel, Reise, rī'-ze.
Treachery, Treasonableness, Verrätherei, fer-rä'-te-rī'.
Treatise, Abhandlung, äp'-händ'-lụng.
Tress, Locke, lok'-ke; Flechte, fleh'-te.
Trial, Untersuchung, ụn'-ter-zoo'-chụng. [See Masc. & Neut.]
Tribe, Gattung, gät'-tụng; Familie, fä-mee'-li-ye'.
Trifle, Kleinigkeit, klī'-nig-kīt'.
Trinity, Dreieinigkeit, drī'-nig-kīt'.
Triviality, Trivialität, trī'-vi-ä'-li-tait'.
Trouble, Mühe, mü'-e; Unruhe, ụn'-roo'-e.
Trout, Forelle, fo-rạl'-le.
Trowel, Kelle, kạl'-le.
Trumpet, Trompete, trom-pā'-te.
Truth, Wahrheit, vär'-hīt.
Tune, Melodie, mạ'-lo-dee'.
Twine, Schnur, shnoor.
Type, Type, tee'-pe; Schrift, shrift. [See Masc. & Neut.]
Tyranny, Tyrannei, tī'-rän-nī.

Twine, Nähgarn, naī'-gärn.
Twist, Geflecht, ge-flạht'.
Twitch, Zupfen, tsụp'-fen; Zucken, tsụk'-ken.
Twitter [of birds], Gezwitscher, ge-tsvit'-sher.
Twittle-twattle, Gewäsch, ge-vạsh'.
Type, Vorbild, fōr'-bilt; Gepräge, ge-prai'-ge. [See M. & F.]

13

M.

Ultimatum, Endbeschrieb, ant'-be-shit'. [See Neut.]
Umpire, Schiedsrichter, sheets'-rih'-ter.
Unbelief, Unglaube, un'-glou'-be.
Underdrain, unterirdischer Abzugskanal, un'-ter-ir'-di-sher' äp'-tsugs-kä-näl'.
Underofficer, Unterbeamter, un'-ter-be-äm'-ter.
Underplot, heimlicher Anschlag, hīm'-li-her'-än'-shlig.
Understanding, Verstand, fer-shtänt'.
Undertaker, Unternehmer, un'-ter-nā'-mer; Leichenbesorger, lī'-hen-be-zor'-ger. [ter.
Undertenant, Unterpächter, un'-ter-päh'-
Underwriter, Assekurant, äs'-se-ku-ränt'.
Unitarian, Unitarier, u'-ni-tä'-ri-er.
Uproar, Aufruhr, ouf'-roor.
Upstart, Emporkömmling, em-pör'-kim'-ling; Glückspilz, gliks'-pilts; Parvenü, pär'-ve-nü'.
Urchin, Bube, boo'-be; Knirps, knirps.
Usage, Gebrauch, ge-brouch'.
Usufruct, Nießbrauch, nees'-brouch.

Vagabond, Vagrant, Bagabund, vä'-gä-bunt'; Landstreicher, länt'-shtrī'-her.
Valet, Bedienter, be-deen'-ter; Lakei, lä-kī'.
Valetudinary, Siechling, zeeh'-ling.
Valiant, tapfere Helb, täp'-fe-re' halt.
Value, Mantelfack, män'-tel-zäk'.
Value, Werth, wärt; Betrag, be-träg'.
Valve, Flügel, flü'-gel. [See Fem.]
Vanguard, Vortrab, för-träp.

F.

Ugliness, Häßlichkeit, hās'-lih-kīt'.
Uncouthness, Ungeschlachtheit, un'-ge-shlächt'-hīt.
Unction, Salbung, zäl'-bung.
Undercurrent, Unterströmung, un'-ter-shtrī'-mung.
Underlip, Unterlippe, un'-ter-lip'-pe.
Underplot, Nebenhandlung, nā'-ben-händ'-lung.
Understanding, Einsicht, īn'-ziht.
Unfaithfulness, Treulosigkeit, troi'-lō'-zig-kīt'.
Ungodliness, Gottlosigkeit, got'-lō'-zig-kīt'.
Union, Vereinigung, fer-ī'-ni-kung; Union, oo'-ni-ön, for U. S., Vereinigte Staaten, fer-ī'-nig-te' shtä'-ten.
Unit, Einheit, īn'-hīt.
University, Universität, oo'-ni-vạr'-zi-tait'.
Urbanity, Höflichkeit, hīf'-lih-kīt'.
Usage, Sitte, zit'-te.
Usufruct, Nußnießung, nuts'-nee'-ssung. [See Masc.]

Vacancy, Leere, lā'-re; Bafanz, vä-känts'; erledigte Stelle, er-lā'-dig-te' shtäl'-le.
Vacation, Mußzeit, moo'-sse-tsīt'; Baslaus.
Vaccination, Kuhpockenimpfung, koo'-pok'-ken-impf'-ung.
Vacuity, Leere, lā'-re.
Vagary, Grille, gril'-le.
Vagrancy, Landstreicherei, länt'-shtrī-he-rī'.

N.

Udder, Euter, oi'-ter.
Ulcer, Geschwür, ge-shvür'.
Ultimatum, Ultimatum, ul'-ti-mä'-tum. [See Masc.]
Umpirage, Schiedsrichteramt, sheets'-rih'-ter-ämt'.
Understanding, Verständniß, fer-shtänt'-nis.
Universe, Universum, oo'-ni-vạr'-zụm; Metall, vạlt'-äl.
Upland, Hochland, hoch'-länt.
Upper leather, Oberleder, ō'-ber-lā'-der.
Upside down, Oberste unterst, ō'-ber-ste' un'-terst.
Utensil, Gefäß, ge-fais'; Geschirr, ge-shir'; Werkzeug, vạrk'-tsoig.

Vat, Faß. [See Fem.]
Vault, Gewölbe, ge-vīl'-be. [See M. & F.]
Vaunt, Geprahl, ge-präl'.
Veal, Kalbfleisch, kälp'-flīsh.
Vegetable, Gemüse, ge-mü'-ze.
Vehicle, Fuhrwerk, foor'-vạrk; Gefährt, ge-fairt'; Vehikel, vā'-hī'-kel.
Venom, Gift.
Venture, Wagniß, väg'-nis.
Verb. Zeitwort, tsīt'-vort.

195

Vapor, Dampf, dümpf; Dunst, dunst; Qualm, kvälm. [shtrih.
Varnish, Firniß, fir'-nis; Anstrich, än'-
Vassal, Lehnsmann, läns'-män.
Vault, Keller, kel'-ler. [See F. & N.]
Vaunt, Stolz, shtolts.
Veil, Schleier, shlī'-er.
Velvet, Sammet, zäm'-met.
Ventilator, Windfang, vint'-fäng.
Verdict, Wahrspruch, vär'-shpruch.
Verdigris, Grünspan, grün'-shpän.
Vermilion, Scharlach, shär'-lach. [See F.]
Verse, Vers, fars.
Vertex, Scheitel, shī'-tel.
Veteran, alter Soldat, äl'-ter zol-dät'.
Veterinarian, Thierarzt, teer'-ärtst.
Vice [tool], Schraubstock, shroup'-shtok.
Victor, Sieger, zee'-ger.
Victual, Mundvorrath, munt'-fōr'-rät.
Vine, Weinstock, vīn'-shtok.
Virtuoso, Kunstkenner, kunst'-kän'-ner.
Visit, Besuch, be-zooch'.
Visitor, Besucher, be-zoo'-cher.
Vitriol, Vitriol, vit'-ri-ōl'.
Vocation, Ruf, roof; Beruf, be-roof'.
Vogue, Gang, gäng.
Voice, Schall, shäl. [See Fem.]
Volume, Band, bänt. [See F. & N.]
Volunteer, Freiwilliger, frī'-vil'-li-ger'.
Vortex, Wirbel, vir'-bel.
Voucher, Gewährsmann, ge-vairs'-män';
Schein, shīn.
Vow, Schwur, shvoor. [See Neut.]
Vowel, Vokal, vo-käl'; Selbstlaut, zälpst'-lout.
Vulture, Geier, gī'-er.

Valedictory, Abschiedsrede, äp'-sheets'-rā'-de.
Valve, Klappe, kläp'-pe. [See Masc.]
Vanilla, Vanilla, vä-nil'-lä.
Variety, Mannigfaltigkeit, män'-nig-fäl'-tig-kīt.'
Vat, Bütte, büt'-te; Kufe, koo'-fe. [See N.]
Vault, Gruft, gruft; Höhle, hū'-le. [See Masc. & Neut.]
Vegetation, Pflanzenleben, pflän'-tsen-lā'-ben.
Veil, Hülle, hül'-le. [See Masc.]
Velocity, Geschwindigkeit, ge-shvin'-dig-kīt'.
Vengeance, Rache, räch'-e.
Vent, Oeffnung, öff'-nung; Luft, luft.
Ventilation, Ventilirung, vän'-ti-lee'-rung.
Verberation, [Luft-]Erschütterung,[luft'-]er-shüt'-te-rung.
Vermilion, Scharnille, kosh'-e-nil'-ye.
Vernacular, Muttersprache, mut'-ter-shprā'-che.
Vest, Weste, vus'-te. [See Neut.]
Vestry, Sakristei, zäk'-ris-tī.
Vicarage, Pfarrstelle, pfär'-shtäl-le.
View, Aus-, An-, Absicht, ous', än', äp'-ziht.
Viol, Violine, vee'-o-lee'-ne.
Violin, Violine; Geige, gī'-ge.
Viper, Viper, vee'-per; Natter, nät'-ter.
Virgin, Jungfrau, yung'-frou.
Virtue, Tugend, too'-gent; Kraft, kräft.
Virulence, Giftigkeit, gif'-tig-kīt'; Bösartigkeit, bös'-är'-tig-kīt'.
Vision, Erscheinung, er-shī'-nung.

Verdure, Grün, grün.
Vermicule, Würmchen, vīrm'-hen.
Vermifuge, Wurmmittel, vurm'-mit'-tel.
Vermilion, Carmesin, kär'-me-zeen'. [See M. & F.]
Vertebra, Wirbelbein, vīr'-bel-bīn'.
Vesicatory, Blasenpflaster, blä'-zen-pfläs'-ter.
Vessel, Schiff; Gefäß, ge-fäis'.
Vest [garment], Gewand, ge-vänt'. [See Masc.]
Vicariate, Vikariat, vi-kä'-ri-ät'.
Victim, Opfer, op'-fer.
Villa, Landhaus, länt'-hous.
Violet, Veilchen, fīl'-hen.
Vision, Gesicht, ge-ziht.
Vocabulary, Wörterbuch, vīr'-ter-booch'.
Volume, Volumen, vo-loo'-men. [See M. & F.]
Vote, Votum, vō'-tum.
Vow, Gelübde, ge-lüp'-de.

M.

Wag, Schalf, shaĺk; Schelm, shalm.
Wages, Lohn, lōn; Solb, zolt.
Wagon, Wagen, vä'-gen.
Wagoner, Fuhrmann, foor'-main.
Waiter, Kellner, kal'-ner.
Walk, [Spazier-]Gang, [shpa-tseer'-] gäng.
Walker, Fußgänger, foos'-gäng'-er.
Wallet, Quersack, kvär'-zäk.
Wanderer, Wanderer, vän'-de-rer'.
Want, Mangel, mäng'-el
Wanton, Muthwille, moot'-fil'-le.
War, Krieg, kreeg.
Warbler, Sänger, zang'-er.
Ward, Stadtbezirk, shtät'-be-tsirk'. [fäl.
Warrant, Verhaftsbefehl, fer-häfts'-be-
Way, Weg, vāg
Weakling, Schwächling, shväh'-ling.

F.

Visitation, Heimsuchung, hīn'-zoo'- chung; Besichigung, be-zih'-ti-gŭng.
Vitality, Lebenskraft, lā'-bens-kräft';
Vivacity, Lebhaftigkeit, läp'-häf'-tig-kīt'; Munterkeit, mun'-ter-kīt'.
Vixen, Kaiferin, kī'-fe-rin'.
Vogue, Mode, mō'-de.
Voice, Stimme, shtim'-me.
Volley, Salve, zäl'-ve; Ladung, lä'- dung.
Volume, Rolle, rol'-le. [See M. & N.]
Vote, Stimme, shtim'-me; Abstimmung, äp'-shtim'-mung.
Voyage, [See-]Reise, [zā-]rī'-ze.
Vulgarity, Gemeinheit, ge-mīn'-hīt'.
Vulgate, Vulgata, vŭl-gä'-tä.

Wadding, Watte, vät'-te.
Wafer [to eat], Waffel, väf'-fel; Oblate [sticking], ob-lä'-te; Hostie [in the Eucharist], hos'-ti-e'.
Wager, Wette, vät'-te.
Wagtail, Bachsteiß, bäch'-shtaI'-tse.
Wail, [Web-]Klage, [vī'-]klā'-ge.
Wainscot, Wandbekleidung, vänt'-be-klī'- dŭng.
Waist, Taille, tal'-ye.
Wake, [Todten-]Wache,[tō'-ten-]vach'-e.
Wall, Wand, vant; Mauer, mou'-er.
Wall paper, Tapete, tä-pā'-te.
Ward, Vormundschaft, fōr'-munt-shäft. [See M. & N.]
Watch, Wache, väch'-e; Wacht, vächt; Taschenuhr, täsh'-en-oor'.

N.

Want, Bedürfniß, be-dirf'-nis.
Warble, Gewirbel, ge-vir'-bel.
Ward, Mündel, mĭn'-del
War-office, Kriegsministerium, kreegs'- mi-nis-tā'-ri-um'.
Water, Wasser, väs'-ser. [hen.
Watermark, Wasserzeichen, väs'-ser-tsī'-
Waterwork, Wasserwerk, väs'-ser-vąrk'.
Wax, Wachs, väks.
Weal, Wohl, vōl.
Weaving, Entwöhnen, ent-vī'-nen.
Weasel, Wiesel, vee'-zel.
Weather, Wetter, vąt'-ter.
Weaving, Gewebe, ge-vā'-be.
Weed, Unkraut, un'-krout. [wänt'.
Weed, [Trauer-]Gewand, [trou'-er-]ge-

Wealth, Wohlstand, vōl'-shtant; Reichthum, rīh'-tum.
Wedge, Keil, kīl.
Weigher, Wagmeister, vāg'-mīs'-ter.
Welcome, Willkommen, vil'-kom'-men.
West, Westen, vṳst'-en; Abend, ä'-bent.
Whale, Wallfisch, väl'-fish.
Whiff, Zug, tsoog; Puff, puff. [del.
Whirl, Wirbel, vir'-bel; Strudel, shtroo'-
Whisk, kleiner Besen, klī'-ner bā'-zen; Kehrwisch, kār'-vish.
Whisker, Backenbart, bak'-ken-bārt'.
Whiskey, Branntwein, bränt'-vīn.
Whistle, Pfiff. [See Fem.]
Whitewasher, Weissbinder, vīs'-bin'-der;
  Tüncher, tīn'-ḥer.
Widower, Wittwer, vit'-ver.
Will, [letzter] Wille, [lṳts'-ter] vil'-le.
Wind, Wind, vint.
Wine, Wein, vīn.
Wing, Flügel, flü'-gel. [blik'.
Wink, Wink, vink; Augenblick, ou'-gen-
Wire, Draht, drāt.
Wit, Witz, vits; Verstand, fer-shtänt'.
Witness, Zeuge, tsoi'-ge.
Wizard, Zauberer, tsou'-be-rer'.
Wolf, Wolf, volf.
Woodpecker, Specht, shpuht.
Workman, Arbeiter, är'-bī'-ter.
Worm, Wurm, vųrm.
Wrapper, Einwickler, īn'-vik'-ler; Umschlag, um'-shlāg; kleiner Mantel, klī'-ner män'-tel.
Wreath, Kranz, kränts. [er.
Wrestler, [Preis-]Ringer, [prīs-]ring'-
Wretch, Elender, ā'-lan'-der.

Way, Strasse, shträ'-sse; Strack, shtrak'-ke.
Weight, Last, läst.
While, Weile, vī'-le.
Whim, Whimsey, Grille, gril'-le; Laune, lou'-ne.
Whip, Peitsche, pīt'-she.
Whistle, Pfeife, pfī'-fe.
Wicker, Weide, vī'-de.
Widow, Wittwe, vit'-vū.
Width, Breite, brī'-te; Weite, vī'-te.
Willow, Weide, vī'-de.
Wisdom, Weisheit, vīs'-hīt.
Witch, Here, haks'-e; Zauberin, tsou'-be-rin'.
Woman, Frau, frou.
Wool, Wolle, vol'-le.
Work, Arbeit, är'-bīt. [See Neut.]
Workshop, Werkstatt, vųrk'-shtät.
Worship, Anbetung, an'-bā'-tųng; Verehrung, fer-ā'-rųng.
Worthiness, Würdigkeit, vir'-dig-kīt'
Wound, Wunde, vųn'-de.
Wrinkle, Runzel, rųn'-tsel; Falte, fäl'-te.
Writ, Schrift, shrift.

Weight, Gewicht, ge-viht'
Welcome, Willkomm, vil'-kom.
Wharf, Werft, vųrft.
Wheel, Rad, rät.
Whisper, Geflüster, ge-flüs'-ter.
Whist, Whist, vist.
Wish, Sehnen, zā'-nen; Wünschen, vin'-shen.
Witness, Zeugniss, tsoig'-nis. [See Masc.]
Woe, Wehe, vā'-e.
Wood, Holz, holts.
Word, Wort, vort.
Work, Werk, vųrk. [See Fem.]
Workhouse, Arbeitshaus, är'-bīts-hous'.
Wraith, Geispenst, ge-shpaust'.
Wrapper, [cigars], Deckblatt, dṳk'-blät.
Wreath, Gewinde, ge-vin'-de.
Wreck, Wrack, vräk.
Wrist, Handgelenk, hänt'-ge-lęnk'.
Writing, Schreiben, shrī'-ben; Werk, vųrk; Buch, booḥ.
Wrong, Unrecht, ųn'-ruht.

198

M.	F.	N.
Yankee, Neuengländer, noi'-ang-län'-der.	Yacht, Jacht, yácht.	Yarn, Garn, gärn.
Yard, [Bau-]Hof, [bou'-]hōf; Hofraum, hōf'-roum.	Yard, Elle, al'-le.	Year, Jahr, yär.
Yeoman, Freisasse, frī'-zas'-se.	Yeast, Hefe, hā'-fe.	Yearning, Sehnen, zā'-nen.
Yolk, Dotter, dot'-ter.	Youth, Jugend, yoo'-gent. [See Masc.]	Yoke, Joch, yoch.
Youth, Jüngling, yīng'-ling; junger Mensch, yung'-er maŭsh. [See Fem.]	Youthfulness, Jugendlichkeit, yoo'-gent-lih-kīt'.	Yolk, Eigelb, ī'-galp.
Zeal, Eifer, ī'-fer.	Zone, Zone, tsō'-ne.	Zebra, Zebra, tsā'-brä.
Zealot, Zelot, tse-lōt'; Eiferer, ī'-fe-rer'.	Zoology, Thierkunde, teer'-kun'-de; Zoologie, tsō'-o-lo-gee'.	Zinc, Zink, tsink.
Zest, Zusatz, tsoo'-zats; Beigeschmack, bī'-ge-shmäk'.	Zoophyte, Thierpflanze, teer'-pflän'-tse.	Zoophyte, Pflanzenthier, pflän'-tsen-teer'.
Zodiac, Thierkreis, teer'-krīs.		

NOTE.—The student, in glancing over the columns of this vocabulary, cannot fail to notice that English nouns admitting of divers German renderings are subject to a corresponding change of gender. For instance: *table* means Tisch, *m.*, and Tafel, *f.*; *apparatus*, Apparat, *m.*, and Zurüstung, *f.*; *bidding*, Befehl, *m.*, Einladung, *f.*, Gebot, *n.*, etc. Making allowance for this characteristic peculiarity of the language, the following observations may prove an excellent help in determining the gender of a substantive, viz.:

(*a*) Nouns (English) beginning with *sp* and *st*, others carrying *ck*, and others again ending in —*ary*, —*er*, —*ism*, —*tor*, are mostly *masculine*, unless the nature of the subject designated by the respective word point to a different gender.

(*b*) Nouns ending in —*acy*, —*age*, —*ance*, —*ancy*, —*ation*, —*cy*, —*dom*, —*ence*, —*ency*, —*ery*, —*ity*, —*ment*, —*ness*, —*ship* and —*tude* are mostly of the *feminine* gender.

(*c*) Where a verb in its participle (—*ing*) is used as a noun, corresponding to the German infinitive (Ex.: *walking*, Gehen), or where the suffix —*let* is added, the word may be safely taken as being of the *neuter* gender.

More particulars will be found in the "Rules to determine the gender of the nouns," page 216.

GERMAN AND ENGLISH PROVERBS,

ALPHABETICALLY ARRANGED.

I. GERMAN.

The number following any proverb indicates the current number of the corresponding version in the English list.

1. Aller Anfang ist schwer, 48.
2. Aller guten Dinge sind drei, 164.
3. Alte Liebe rostet nicht, 167.
4. Am Lachen erkennt man die Narren, 6.
5. Andere nach sich selbst beurtheilen, 294.
6. Anderer Stand, andere Sitte, 37.
7. An Gottes Segen ist Alles gelegen, 68.
8. Arbeit macht das Leben süß, 228.
9. Armuth schändet nicht, aber thut weh, 182.
10. Art läßt nicht von Art, 132.
11. Auf dem Sprunge stehen kann auch im Sitzen geschehen, 305.
12. Auf den Bergen ist Freiheit, 145 a.
13. Auf den Busch schlagen und den Schall behorchen, 301.
14. Auf den Sack schlägt er, den Esel meint er, 301.
15. Auf einen groben Klotz gehört ein grober Keil, 188.
16. Aufgeschoben ist nicht aufgehoben, 59.
17. Auf Regen folgt Sonnenschein, 7 a.
18. Auf Regiment's Unkosten leben ist bequem, aber faul, 288.
19. Auf Schuster's Rappen reiten ist billig und gesund, 280 a.
20. Aus anderer Leute Leder ist gut Riemen schneiden, 115.
21. Aus dem Regen in die Traufe kommen, 276.
22. Aus den Augen, aus dem Sinn, 177.
23. Aus der Noth eine Tugend machen, 290.
24. Aus einer Mücke einen Elephanten machen, 289.
25. Aus Kindern werden Leute, 211.
26. Aus Nichts wird Nichts, 66.
27. Außer dem Süßen auch Bitteres genießen, 281.
28. Baar Geld lacht, 36.
29. Bei Nacht sind alle Katzen grau, 14.
30. Berg und Thal kommen nicht zusammen, aber Menschen wohl, 65.

(199)

31. Besser hab' ich, denn hätt' ich, 168.
32. Besser Neider als Mitleider, 119.
33. Besser Unrecht leiden, als Unrecht thun, 186 a.
34. Borgen macht Sorgen, 95.
35. Böse Gesellschaften verderben gute Sitten, 54.
36. Bringst Du mir die Wurst, so lösch' ich Dir den Durst, 170.
37. Da liegt der Has' im Pfeffer, 206.
38. Da liegt der Hund begraben, 206.
39. Das Blatt hat sich gewendet, 225.
40. Das Ei will klüger sein, als die Henne, 125.
41. Das Eisen schmieden, weil (or so lange) es warm ist, 310.
42. Das Futter sticht ihn, 76, 88.
43. Das hat sich gewaschen, 204.
44. Das heißt, beim Teufel zur Beichte gehen, 215.
45. Das Hemd ist mir näher, als der Rock, 151.
46. Das ist die Braut, um welche man tanzt, 207.
47. Das ist für die Katze, 208.
48. Das ist Knochen für Fleisch, 60 a.
49. Das ist mein Acker und Pflug, 205.
50. Das ist nicht auf seinem Mist gewachsen, 203.
51. Das ist Wasser auf seiner Mühle, 238.
52. Das Kennen der Gefahr schwächt sie wunderbar, 60.
53. Das Kind beim rechten Namen nennen, 263.
54. Das sind ihm böhmische Dörfer, 114.
55. Das soll ihm theuer zu stehen kommen, 122.
56. Das Spiel hat sich gewendet, 225.
57. Da stehen die Ochsen am Berge, 222.
58. Das Werk lobt den Meister, 220.
59. Dem lieben Gott die Tage abstehlen, 198.
60. Dem Tage die Augen ausbrennen, 261.
61. Den Baum erkennt man an den Früchten, 226.
62. Den Vogel in der Hand haben, 282.
63. Den Wald vor lauter Bäumen nicht sehen, 163.
64. Der Apfel fällt nicht weit vom Stamm, 131.
65. Der Bauer stößt ihn immer in den Nacken, 221.
66. Der gerade Weg ist der beste, 103.
67. Der Hafer sticht ihn, 76, 88.
68. Der Hehler ist so gut wie der Stehler, 223.
69. Der Hunger treibt's herein, 13.
70. Der Klügste giebt nach, 227.
71. Der Krug geht so lange zu Wasser, bis er bricht, 166.
72. Der Kuckuck ruft seinen eigenen Namen aus, 72.
73. Der Kuckuck spricht nur von sich selbst, 93.
74. Der Mensch denkt und Gott lenkt, 140.
75. Der Mißbrauch hat keine Stimme gegen den guten Gebrauch, 2.
76. Der Teufel ist los, 92.

77. Der Weg zur Hölle ist mit guten Vorsätzen gepflastert, 92 a.
78. Der Wolf frißt auch die gezählten Schafe, 16.
79. Die Bolzen verschießen, die ein Anderer gedreht hat, 248.
80. Die Katze im Sack kaufen, 262.
81. Die Katze läßt das Mausen nicht, 209.
82. Die Kinderschuhe noch nicht ausgetreten haben, 259.
83. Die Kutte macht keinen Mönch, 213.
84. Die Ochsen halten am Berge, 222.
85. Die Pferde hinter den Wagen spannen, 303.
86. Die Rechnung ohne den Wirth machen, 304 a.
87. Die Saiten zu hoch spannen, 309.
88. Die Sprache dient dazu, die Gedanken zu verbergen, 217.
89. Die Suppe ausessen müssen, 254.
90. Die Welt will betrogen sein, 150.
91. Die Wurst nach dem Gaste braten, 268.
92. Die Wurst nach der Speckseite werfen, 312.
93. Durch die Finger sehen, 267.
94. Durch Mark und Bein gehen, 298 a.
95. Durch Schaden wird man klug, 33.
96. Durch zu große Vertraulichkeit geht die Achtung verloren, 296.
97. Ehrlich währt am längsten, 103.
98. Eigenlob stinkt, 93, 191.
99. Eigner Herd ist Goldes werth, 102 a, 233.
100. Eile mit Weile, 138.
101. Eine blinde Henne findet auch ein Korn, 117.
102. Eine böse Sieben, 23.
103. Eine gute Partie thun, 293.
104. Eine Hand wäscht die andere, 170.
105. Ein Ei in der Hand ist besser, als ein Sperling auf dem Dache, 168.
106. Eine Krähe hackt der andern die Augen nicht aus, 71.
107. Eine kurze Kette für einen bösen Hund, 58.
108. Einem das Wamms ausklopfen, 279.
108a. Einem den Pelz waschen, 253.
109. Einem den Staar stechen, 311.
110. Einem die Kastanien aus dem Feuer holen, 248.
111. Einem einen blauen Dunst vormachen, 283.
112. Einem einen Strich durch die Rechnung machen, 313.
113. Einem geschenkten Gaul guckt man nicht in's Maul, 9.
114. Einem Lügner glaubt man nicht, und wenn er auch die Wahrheit spricht, 46.
115. Einen Korb bekommen, 295.
116. Einen Rath giebt Jeder gern, 48 a.
117. Einen Scheffel Salz mit Jemandem essen, 287.
118. Einen Wurm im Kopfe haben, 247.
119. Einen zum Besten haben, 292.
120. Eine Schlange im Busen nähren, 333.
121. Eine Schwalbe macht keinen Sommer, 174.

122. Eine Tracht Prügel, 24.
122a. Eine zu stark gespannte Saite bricht, 1.
123. Ein gelindes Feuer macht süßes Malz, 194.
124. Ein gutes Wort findet eine gute Statt, 11.
125. Ein Handwerk hat einen goldenen Boden, 143.
126. Ein Jeder kehr' vor der eignen Thür, 201.
127. Ein Keil treibt den andern, 171.
128. Ein magerer Vergleich ist besser, als ein fetter Prozeß, 12.
129. Ein Mann von altem Schrot und Korn, 18.
130. Ein Narr macht mehrere, 169.
131. Ein räudiges Schaf steckt die ganze Herde an, 172.
132. Ein Schelm, der es böse meint, 104.
133. Ein Tausch ist kein Raub, 55.
134. Ein treuer Freund ist Goldes werth, 8.
135. Ein Wort, ein Mann, 20.
136. Ende gut, Alles gut, 17.
137. Er geht wie der Bauer in den Thurm, 75.
138. Er hat den Namen mit der That, 100 a.
139. Er hat's hinter den Ohren, 75.
140. Er hat sein Schäfchen geschoren, 77.
141. Er hat sich selbst eine Ruthe gebunden, 78.
142. Er hat weder Kind noch Kegel, 80.
143. Er ist nicht weit her, 86.
144. Er ist noch nicht trocken hinter den Ohren, 82.
145. Er ist weder kalt noch warm, 85.
146. Er kann mehr als Brod essen, 84.
147. Er kann nicht Fünf zählen, 74.
148. Er läßt die Ohren hängen, 83.
149. Er läuft vor seinem eigenen Schatten, 81.
150. Er lügt, daß sich die Balken biegen, 91.
151. Er lügt wie gedruckt, 90.
152. Er reicht ihm das Wasser nicht, 73, 87.
153. Er sieht es an, wie die Kuh das neue Thor, 94.
154. Er spinnt keine Seide dabei, 80 a.
155. Er stiehlt wie ein Rabe, 102.
156. Es geht nichts über Gesundheit, 232.
157. Es giebt nichts Neues unter der Sonne, 234.
158. Es ist ihm kein Sitzfleisch gewachsen, 192.
159. Es ist kein Messer, das schärfer schiert, als wenn der Bauer zum Edelmann wird, 159.
160. Es ist nichts so fein gesponnen, es kommt endlich an die Sonnen, 235.
161. Es ist noch nicht aller Tage Abend, 216.
162. Es ist, um des Teufels zu werden, 120.
163. Es ist weder gehauen, noch gestochen, 231.
164. Es paßt wie die Faust auf's Auge.
165. Es sei Kunz oder Klaus, 31.
166. Es steht Keinem an der Stirn geschrieben, was er im Herzen hat, 334.

167. Es wird ihm zu Hause und zu Hofe kommen, 122.
168. Es wird noch viel Wasser verrinnen, bevor dieses Werk kann beginnen, 224.
169. Freunde in der Noth gehen zehn auf ein Loth, 64.
170. Frisch gewagt ist halb gewonnen, 61. [Haus, 43.
171. Frühzeitig zu Bett und zeitig heraus, bringt Kräfte dem Körper und Segen in's
172. Für den Tod ist kein Kraut gewachsen, 157.
173. Geben ist besser als nehmen, 187.
174. Geduldige Schafe gehen viele in einen Stall, 332.
175. Geduld ist ein heilsames Kraut, 180.
176. Geld ist die Losung, 145.
177. Geld reicht weit, 144.
178. Gelindere Saiten aufziehen, 266.
179. Geschehene Dinge sind nicht zu ändern, 320.
180. Gestrenge Herren regieren nicht lange, 39.
181. Gewalt geht vor Recht, 148.
182. Gleiche Brüder, gleiche Kappen, 44, 132.
183. Gleich und Gleich gesellt sich gern, 32.
184. Goldene Berge versprechen, 302.
185. Gott schickt die Kleider nach der Kälte, 219.
186. Gut angefangen ist halb vollbracht, 10.
187. Gut das Pferd, das nimmer fällt, gut die Frau, die keine Predigt hält, 118.
188. Gut Ding will Weile haben, 138.
189. Guter Dinge sein, 255.
190. Guter Rath ist theuer, 69.
191. Gute Waare lobt sich selbst, 70.
192. Hab' mich ein bischen lieb, hab' mich lang lieb, 137.
193. Hahn im Korbe sein, 250.
194. Haus in allen Gassen, 124.
195. Hast Du mich lieb, lieb' auch meinen Hund, 136.
196. Heu machen so lang die Sonne scheint, 291.
197. Heute mir, morgen Dir, 271.
198. Heute roth, morgen todt, 270.
199. Hinter dem Berge halten, 257.
200. Hinter den Ohren noch nicht trocken sein, 251.
201. Hinter Eines (or Einem auf die) Sprünge kommen, 272.
202. Hochmuth kommt vor dem Fall, 184.
203. Hunger ist der beste Koch, 105.
204. Ich wasche meine Hände in Unschuld, 123.
205. Im Rohr ist gut Pfeifen schneiden, 116.
206. Im Trüben ist gut fischen, 113, 230.
206a. In der Tinte sitzen, 252.
207. Irren ist menschlich, 45.
208. Ist der Tag auch noch so lang, dennoch kommt der Abend, 218.
209. Jedem Narren gefällt seine Kappe, 50.
210. Jeder Arbeiter ist seines Lohnes werth, 53.
211. Jeder ist seines Glückes Schmied, 49.

212. Jeder Krämer lobt seine Waare, 52.
213. Jedes Ding hat seine Zeit, 51.
214. Je gieriger, desto schmieriger, 62.
215. Jemandem die Hölle heiß machen, 302 a.
216. Je mehr man trinkt, desto durstiger wird man, 47.
217. Jung gewohnt, alt gethan, 26.
218. Kalte Hände, warme Liebe, 3.
219. Kein Baum fällt auf den ersten Hieb, 173.
220. Keine Antwort ist auch eine Antwort, 156.
221. Keine Regel ohne Ausnahme, 229.
222. Keine Rose ohne Dornen, 161.
223. Kein Meister fällt vom Himmel, 160.
224. Kein Pulver riechen können, 246.
225. Kinder und Betrunkene haben ihre Schutzengel, 42.
226. Kinder und Narren sagen die Wahrheit, 212.
227. Kleider machen Leute, 56.
228. Kommt Zeit, kommt Rath, 242.
229. Ländlich, sittlich, 195.
230. Lange geborgt ist nicht geschenkt, 22.
231. Lange Gewohnheit wird endlich zur (zweiten) Natur, 133.
232. Leben und leben lassen, 286.
233. Leeres Stroh dreschen, 274 a.
234. Liebe ist blind, 135.
235. Lunten riechen, 306.
236. Lust und Lieb' zu einem Ding macht alle Müh' und Arbeit g'ring, 274.
237. Mai kühl und naß füllt Scheuer und Faß, 4.
238. Man muß sich strecken nach der Decken, 335.
239. Man sieht es dem Säugling nicht an, was er einstens noch werden kann, 63.
240. Man sorgt sich eher alt als reich, 35.
241. Mit dem Interesse hört auch die Freundschaft auf, 158.
242. Mit doppelter Kreide schreiben, 298.
243. Mit einem blauen Auge davon kommen, 266 a.
244. Mit fremdem Kalbe pflügen, 300.
245. Mit Jemandem unter einer Decke spielen, 283.
246. Mit Speck fängt man Mäuse, 121.
247. Mit Vielem hält man Haus, mit Wenig kommt man aus, 190.
248. Morgenstunde hat Gold im Munde, 43.
249. Mücken seihen und Kameele verschlucken, 308.
250. Müßiggang ist aller Laster Anfang, 106.
251. Nach gethaner Arbeit ist gut ruh'n, 228.
252. Nach Jemandes Pfeife tanzen, 269.
253. Noch einen Fußtritt dem Gefallenen, 107.
254. Noth bricht Eisen, selbst die Ketten der Trägheit, 152.
255. Noth ist der Liebe Tod, 325.
256. Noth kennt kein Gebot, 153.
257. Noth lehrt beten, 154.

258. Oel in's Feuer gießen, 245.
259. Pack schlägt sich, Pack verträgt sich, 165.
260. Perlen vor die Säue werfen, 265.
261. Saure Trauben, 197.
262. Scheiden thut weh, 179.
263. Schönheit ohne Tugend, sagt der Spruch, gleicht der Blume ohne Wohlgeruch, 28.
264. Schuster bleib' bei deinem Leisten, 127.
265. Schlösser in die Luft bauen, 260.
266. Seine Augen sind größer als sein Magen, 101.
267. Sein Schäfchen in's Trockne bringen, 277.
268. Selbst der Teufel ist gut, wenn man seinen Willen thut, 214.
269. Selbst Hunger leiden, damit Andere nicht essen sollen, 299.
270. Sich auf's hohe Pferd setzen, 280.
271. Sich etwas hinter die Ohren schreiben, 314.
272. Sich in's Fäustchen lachen, 285.
273. Sich kein Blatt vor den Mund nehmen, 256.
274. Sich (halb) krank lachen, 307.
275. Sich vom Pferd auf den Esel setzen, 276.
276. Sich weiß brennen, 315.
277. Sich zum Narren machen, 288 a.
278. Sieht doch die Katze den Kaiser an, 210.
279. Spare in der Zeit, dann hast Du in der Noth, 30.
280. Sprechen, wie einem der Schnabel gewachsen ist, 256.
281. Sprich wie Du sollst und denke wie Du wollest, 217.
282. Stille Wasser sind tief, 199.
283. Träume sind Schäume, 41.
284. Trunken Mund spricht aus Herzens Grund, 112.
285. Tugend geht über Alles, 318.
286. Ueber die Klinge springen lassen, 304.
287. Ueber die Schnur hauen, 275.
288. Uebung macht den Meister, 183.
289. Um des Kaisers Bart streiten, 273.
290. Undank ist der Welt Lohn, 111.
291. Unrecht Gut gedeihet nicht, 109.
292. Unter dem Pantoffel stehen, 258.
293. Unter uns gesagt, 200, 317.
294. Verkehrte Welt, 236.
295. Verstand kommt nicht vor Jahren, 176.
296. Viele Hunde sind des Hasen Tod, 189.
297. Viele Köche verderben den Brei, 141.
298. Viele Köpfe, viel Sinn, 186.
299. Viel Geschrei und wenig Wolle, 146.
300. Viel Geschwätzigkeit, wenig Herzlichkeit, 147.
301. Viel Lärm um nichts, 146.
302. Volksstimme ist Gottes Stimme, 319.
303. Vor die unrechte Schmiede kommen, 278.

304. Vorsicht ist die Mutter der Weisheit, 185.
305. Wasch' mir den Pelz und mach mich nicht naß, 316.
306. Was Hänschen nicht lernt, lernt Hans nimmermehr, 21, 321.
307. Was ich nicht weiß, macht mich nicht heiß, 237.
308. Was man nicht im Kopfe hat, muß man in den Beinen haben, 19.
309. Wasser in den Brunnen tragen, 264.
310. Was sich liebt, das neckt sich, 239.
311. Wem nicht zu rathen ist, dem ist nicht zu helfen.
312. Wenn alle Stränge reißen, 327.
313. Wenn das Kind in den Brunnen gefallen ist, macht man den Brunnen zu, 7.
314. Wenn die Katze nicht zu Hause ist, tanzen die Mäuse auf den Tischen, 326.
315. Wenn man ihm einen Finger reicht, will er gleich die ganze Hand, 67.
316. Wenn man unter den Wölfen ist, muß man mitheulen, 328.
317. Wenn man vom Wolf spricht, ist er nicht weit, 202.
318. Wenn Schelme sich zanken, kommen ehrliche Leute zu ihrem Gelde, 324.
319. Wer Alles will, bekommt Nichts, 15.
320. Wer Andern eine Grube gräbt, fällt selbst hinein, 330.
321. Wer das Glück hat, führt die Braut heim, 98.
322. Wer den Schaden hat, darf für den Spott nicht sorgen, 100.
323. Wer einmal lügt, dem glaubt man nicht, und wenn er auch die Wahrheit spricht, 46.
324. Wer erst kommt, mahlt erst, 57.
325. Wer gern tanzt, dem ist leicht gepfiffen, 97.
326. Wer gewinnt, hat gut lachen, 126.
327. Wer lügt, der stiehlt auch, 193.
328. Wer nicht hören will, muß fühlen.
329. Wer nichts wagt, gewinnt nichts, 162.
330. Wer Pech angreift, besudelt sich, 181.
331. Wer sich getroffen fühlt, der zupfe sich bei der Nase, 331.
332. Wer sich mit Hunden niederlegt, der steht mit Flöhen auf, 99.
333. Wer sich zum Schafe macht, den frißt der Wolf, 38.
334. Wer zuerst so leicht gewann, ward zuletzt ein armer Mann, 96.
335. Wer zuletzt lacht, lacht am besten, 89.
336. Weß' das Herz voll ist, davon läuft der Mund über, 323.
337. Wie der Herr, so der Knecht, 129.
338. Wie der Vater, so der Sohn, 128.
339. Wie die Alten sungen, so zwitschern die Jungen, 128.
340. Wie die Arbeit, so der Lohn, 27.
341. Wie die Frage, so die Antwort, 25.
342. Wie die Katze um den heißen Brei herumgehen, 249 a.
343. Wie die Mutter, so die Tochter, 130.
344. Wie? Einen Hund halten und selbst bellen? 322.
345. Wie gewonnen, so zerronnen, 110.
346. Wie man in den Wald hineinruft, so schallt es wieder heraus, 175.
347. Wie man's treibt, so geht's, 5.
348. Wo nichts ist, da hat der Kaiser sein Recht verloren.
349. Wo Tauben sind, da fliegen Tauben zu, 329.

350. Wo viel Licht ist, da ist viel Schatten, 149.
351. Wurst wider Wurst, 142.
352. Zeit bringt Rosen, 240.
353. Zeit ist Geld, 241.
354. Zupfe Dich bei Deiner Nase, 134.
355. Zur Besserung ist es nie zu spät, 155.
356. Zu viel ist ungesund, 297.
357. Zwischen Thür und Angel stecken, 249.
358. [Nachträglich]: Biegen oder brechen, 29.

II. ENGLISH.

The number following any proverb indicates the current number of the corresponding version in the German list.

1. A bow long bent at last grows weak, 122 a.
2. Abuse is not an argument against proper use, 75.
3. A cold hand, a warm heart, 218.
4. A cold May and windy, makes the barn fat and findy, 237.
5. Act well, and you will fare well, 347.
6. A fool is known by his laughing, 4.
7. After death comes the physician, 313.
7a. After rain comes sunshine, 17.
8. A friend in need is a friend indeed, 134.
9. A gift-horse I'm not so bold to ask if it's young or old, 113.
10. A good beginning is half the work, 185.
11. A good word always tells, 124.
12. Agree, for the law is costly, 128.
13. A hungry dog will eat dirty pudding, 69.
14. All cats are grey in the dark, 29.
15. All grasp, all lose, 319.
16. All is one to him who wants to have his will, 78.
17. All is well that ends well, 136.
18. A man of the old stamp, 129.
19. A miss of the brain makes a run of the feet, 308.
20. An honest man is as good as his word, 135.
21. An old dog will learn no tricks, 306.
22. A prolonged credit does not cancel a debt, 230.
23. A shrew, 102.
24. A sound thrashing, 122.
25. As the question, so the answer, 341.
26. As the twig is bent, so is the tree inclined, 217.
27. As the work, so the pay, 340.

28. Beauty without virtue is like a flower without fragrance, 263.
29. Bend or break, 358.
30. Better spare at the brim than at the bottom, 279.
31. Be who it will, 165.
32. Birds of one feather flock together, 183.
33. Bought wit is best, 95.
34. By foul means never try to gain that which in a fair way thou canst attain.
35. Cares will make us sooner old than rich, 240.
36. Cash is the thing, 28.
37 Change of station produces change of manners, 6.
38. Daub yourself with honey, and you will never want flies, 333.
39. Despots seldom rule long, 180.
40. Do a kindness, receive a kindness, 104.
41. Dreams are empty, 283.
42. Drunken folks seldom come to any harm, 225.   [171, 248.
43. Early to bed and early to rise makes a man healthy and wealthy and wise,
44. Equal mind, equal rank, 182.
45. Error is natural to man, 207.
46. Even truth in a liar's mouth is taken for an untruth, 114, 323.
47. Ever drunk, ever dry, 216.
48. Every beginning is difficult, 1.
48a. Everybody is ready to give advice, 116.
49. Every man is the creator of his own fortune, 211.
50. Every man has his hobby, 209.
51. Everything has its time, 213.
52 Every tradesman praises his goods, 212.
53. Every worker is worth his deserts, 210.
54. Evil communications corrupt good manners, 35.
55. Exchange is no robbery, 133.
56. Fine feathers make fine birds, 227.
57. First come, first served, 324.
58. For a vicious dog a short chain, 107.
59. Forbearance is no acquittance, 16.
60. Forewarned, forearmed, 52.
60a. For meat they had striven, and bones they were given, 48.
61. Fortune favors the brave, 170.
62. Fox in stealth, wolf in greediness, 214.
63. Foul in the cradle and fair in the saddle, 239.
64. Friends in need, a wondrous breed, 169.
65. Friends may meet, but mountains never greet, 30.
66. From nothing nothing comes, 26.
67. Give him an inch, and he'll take an ell, 315.
68. God's blessing gained, everything obtained, 7.
69. Good advice is precious, 190.
70. Good wine needs no bush, 191.
71. Hawks don't pick out hawk's een, 106.

72. He betrays himself, 72.
73. He cannot hold a candle to him, 152.
74. He cannot say boo to a goose, 147.
75. He goes like a bear to the stake, 137, 139.
76. He grows insolent from being too well fed, 42, 67.
77. He has feathered his nest, 140.
78. He has made a halter to hang himself, 141.
79. He has more cunning than virtue, 139.
80. He has neither legitimate nor illegitimate issue, 142.
80*a*. He hopes to gain, but 'tis in vain, 154.
81. He is afraid of his own shadow, 149.
82. He is a stripling, 144.
83. He is dispirited, 148.
84. He is half a sorcerer, 146.
85. He is neither fish nor flesh, 145.
86. He is no great shakes, 143.
87. He is not worthy to hold a candle to him, 152.
88. He is too well fed, 42, 67.
89. He laughs best who laughs last, 335.
90. He lies like truth, 151.
91. He lies prodigiously, 150.
92. Hell is broke loose, 76.
92*a*. Hell is paved with good intentions, 77.
93. He recognizes nobody but himself, 73, 98.
94. He stares at it like a fool, 153.
95. He that goes borrowing, goes sorrowing, 34.
96. He that once in gain began, died a poor and wretched man, 334.
97. He who likes to dance, will easily find a chance, 325.
98. He wins whom luck favors, 321.
99. He who lies down with dogs, rises with fleas, 332.
100. He who loses is sure to be laughed at, 322.
100*a*. His doing answers his name, 138.
101. His eyes want more than his stomach can bear, 266.
102. His fingers are lime twigs, 155.
102*a*. Home is home, let it never be so homely, 99.
103. Honesty is the best policy, 66, 97.
104. *Hony soit qui mal y pense*, 132.
105. Hunger is the best sauce, 203.
106. Idleness is the mother of vice, 250.
107. If a man once fall, he will be kicked by all, 253.
108. If thieves fall out, honest men will recover their money, 318.
109. Ill-gotten goods don't prosper, 291.
110. Ill gotten, ill spent, 345.
111. Ingratitude is the currency of this world, 290.
112. *In vino veritas*, 284.
113. It is good fishing in troubled waters, 206.

114. It is all Greek to him, 54.
115. It is an easy thing to gain at other people's expense and experience, 20.
116. It is easy to buy if you have the money, 205.
117. It is not always folly what a fool does, 101. [187.
118. It's a good horse that never stumbles, and a good wife that never grumbles,
119. It's better to be envied than to be pitied, 32.
120. It's enough to drive one mad, 162.
121. It's not hard to catch a mouse with lard, 246.
122. It will come home to him, 55, 167.
123. I wash my hands of it, 204.
124. Jack of all trades, 194.
125. Jack Sprat will teach his grandam, 40.
126. Let him laugh that wins, 326.
127. Let the shoemaker not go beyond his last, 264.
128. Like father, like son, 338, 339.
129. Like master, like man, 337.
130. Like mother, like daughter, 343.
131. Like sire, like son, 64.
132. Like sticks to like, 10, 182.
133. Long custom grows into second nature, 231.
134. Look to home first, 354.
135. Love makes blind, 234.
136. Love me, and love my dog, 195.
137. Love me a little, love me long, 192.
138. Make haste slowly, 100, 188.
139. Make hay while the sun shines, 196.
140. Man proposes, God disposes, 74.
141. Many cooks spoil the broth, 297.
142. Measure for measure, 351.
143. Mechanics are gold mines, 125.
144. Money goes a great way, 177.
145. Money is the watchword, 176.
145a. Mountains rise above the law of man, 12.
146. Much ado about nothing, 299, 301.
147. Much talk, little sympathy, 300.
148. Might is above right, 181.
149. Much light, much shadow, 350.
150. *Mundus vult decipi*, 90.
151. Near is my shirt, but nearer is my skin, 45.
152. Necessity breaks iron bars, even the fetters of laziness, 254.
153. Necessity has no law, 256.
154. Necessity teaches many things, 257.
155. Never too late to mend, 355.
156. No answer is an answer anyhow, 220.
157. No escape from death, 172.
158. No longer foster, no longer son, 241.

159. No man looks to be accounted more than a beggar mounted, 159.
160. No one is born a master, 223.
161. No rose without a thorn, 222.
162. Nothing venture, nothing have, 329.
163. Not to be able to see wood for trees, 63.
164. Number three is always fortunate, 2.
165. Offending to-day, commending to-morrow, 259.
166. Oft goes the pitcher to the well, and comes home broken at last, 71.
167. Old love is never forgotten, 3.
168. One bird in the hand is better than two in the bush, 31, 105.
169. One fool makes many, 130.
170. One good turn deserves another, 36, 104.
171. One nail drives out another, 127.
172. One scabby sheep will mar a whole flock, 131.
173. One stroke fells no tree, 219.
174. One swallow makes no summer, 121.
175. One Yate for another, good fellow, 346.
176. Our mind expands with our years, 295.
177. Out of sight, out of mind, 22.
178. Out of the abundance of the heart the mouth speaketh its part, 336.
179. Parting is smarting, 262.
180. Patience overcomes tribulations, 175.
181. Pitch defileth, 330.
182. Poverty does not stain, but it produces pain, 9.
183. Practice makes perfect, 288.
184. Pride will have a fall, 202.
185. Providence and prudence are healthy twins, 304.
186. *Quot homines, tot sententiae*, 298.
186a. Rather be wronged than do wrong, 33.
187. Rather give than take, 173.
188. Rudeness is to be met with rudeness, 15.
189. Safety there is none where many are against one, 296.
190. Saving is the art of good housekeeping, 247.
191. Self-praise is no recommendation, 98.
192. Sitting long in any place tires him more than the hottest race, 158.
193. Show me a liar and I'll show you a thief, 327.
194. Soft fire makes sweet malt, 123.
195. So many countries, so many customs, 229.
196. So many men, so many minds, 298.
197. Sour grapes, 261.
198. Spending the days on the bed of sloth, 59.
199. Still waters are deep, 282.
200. *Sub rosa*, 293.
201. Sweep before your own door, 126.
202. Talk of the devil and he is sure to appear, 317.
203. That has not grown on his soil, 50.

204. That is *comme il faut*, 43.
205. That is my bread and butter, 49.
206. That's the rub, 37, 38.
207. That's the cream of the business, 46.
208. That's worth nothing, 47.
209. That which is bred in the bone will never out of the flesh, 81.
210. The cat may look upon a king, 278.
211. The child is the father of the man, 25.
212. The children and the simple-minded are unsophisticated, 226.
213. The cowl makes no monk, 83.
214. The devil himself is kind, if his will you mind, 268.
215. The devil rebukes sin, 44.
216. The end of it is still to be seen, 161.
217. The language of man hides his thoughts, 88, 281.
218. The longest day must have an end, 208.
219. The Lord will provide, 185.
220. The master is known by his work, 58.
221. The peasant smells after the soil, 65.
222. The progress sticks fast, 57, 84.
223. The receiver is as bad as the thief, 68.
224. The stream will quietly run on a long while yet ere this is done, 168.
225. The tables are turned, 39, 56.
226. The tree is known by its fruit, 61.
227. The wisest will give way, 70.
228. The work done, repose is sweet, 8, 251.
229. There is an exception to every rule, 221.
230. There is good fishing in troubled waters, 206.
231. There is neither rhyme nor reason in it, 163.
232. There is nothing like good health, 156.
233. There is nothing like home, 99.
234. There is nothing new under the sun, 157.
235. The sun will bring to light what's hidden in the dark of night, 160.
236. The world upside down, 294.
236a. Things done belong to times gone, 179.
237. Things unknown to me never bother me, 307.
238. This is grist to his mill, 51.
239. Those who love each other like to tease each other, 310.
240. Time brings everything to pass, 352.
241. Time is money, 353.
242. Time will show a plan, 228.
243. 'Tis all Greek to him, 54.
244. 'Tis enough to drive one mad, 162.
245. To add fuel to the fire, 258.
246. To be a coward, 224.
247. To be a little cracked, 118.
248. To be another's cat's paw, 79, 110.

249. To be at a pinch, 357.
249a. To beat carefully about the bush, 342.
250. To be cock of the walk, 193.
251. To be green, 200.
252. To be in a sad pickle, 206 a.
253. To belabor one, 108 a.
254. To be obliged to suffer for ...., 89.
255. To be of good cheer, 189.
256. To be plain spoken, 273, 280.
257. To be reserved, 199.
258. To be under petticoats government; henpecked, 292.
259. To be yet in leading strings, 82.
260. To build castles in the air, 265.
261. To burn daylight, 60.
262. To buy a pig in a poke, 80.
263. To call a spade a spade, 53.
264. To carry coals to Newcastle, 309.
265. To cast pearls before swine, 260.
266. To come a peg or two lower, 178.
266a. To come off with a scratch, 243.
267. To connive at, 93.
268. To cut the cloth according to the man, 91.
269. To dance after one's pipe, 252.
270. To-day blooming, to-morrow drooping, 198.
271. To-day my turn, to-morrow yours, 197.
272. To discover one's tricks (pranks), 201.
273. To dispute about trifles, 289.   [ure, 236.
274. To do a thing with love and pleasure reduces the trouble to a slight meas-
274a. To do a useless thing, 233.
275. To exorbitate; overdo a thing, 287.
276. To fall out of the frying pan into the fire, 21, 275.
277. To feather one's nest, 267.
278. To get into the wrong box, 303.
279. To give one a sound thrashing, 108.
280. To give one's self high airs, 270.
280a. To go on foot is a cheap and healthy exercise, 19.
281. To have sweet meat and sour sauce, 27.
282. To have the bird in the hand, 62.
283. To have underhand dealings with one, 111, 245.
284. To humbug one, 111.
285. To laugh in one's sleeve, 272.
286. To live and let live, 232.
287. To live seven years with a person, 117.
288. To live upon the common, 18.
288a. To make a fool of one's self, 277.
289. To make a mountain of a molehill, 24.

290. To make a virtue of necessity, 23.
291. To make hay while the sun shines, 196.
292. To make sport of one, 119.
293. To marry a fortune, 103.
294. To measure other men's corn by one's own bushel, 5.
295. To meet with a refusal, 115.
296. Too much familiarity breeds contempt, 96.
297. Too much of one thing is good for nothing, 356.
298. To overcharge, 242.
298a. To pierce to the quick, 94.
299. To play the dog in the manger, 269.
300. To plough with another man's ox, 244.
301. To point to the house and meaning the tenant, 13, 14.
302. To promise gold mines, 184.
302a. To put one in great fear, 215.
303. To put the cart before the horse, 85.
304. To put to the sword, 286.
304a. To reckon without one's host, 86.
305. To remain ready at any moment, 11.
306. To smell a rat, 235.
307. To split one's sides with laughing, 274.
308. To strain at a gnat and swallow a camel, 249.
309. To strain the strings too high, 87.
310. To strike the iron while it is hot, 41.
311. To tell one the plain and bitter truth, 109.
312. To throw a sprat to catch a salmon, 92.
313. To thwart one's designs, 112.
314. To treasure up a thing, 271.
315. To whitewash one's self, 276.
316. Treat me with great nicety, 305.
317. Under the rose, 293.
318. Virtue is above all things, 285.
319. *Vox populi vox Dei*, 302.
320. What has happened cannot be altered, 179.
321. What is not learned in youth, will not be learned in old age, 306.
322. What? keep a dog and do the barking myself? 344.
323. What the heart thinketh, the mouth speaketh, 336.
324. When knaves fall out, honest men will recover their money, 318.
325. When poverty comes in at the door, love leaps out of the window, 255.
326. When the cats are away, the mice will play, 314.
327. When the worst comes to the worst, 312.
328. When you are in Rome, you must do as the Romans do, 316.
329. Where there is much, still more will come, 349.
330. Who lays a snare for others, falls therein himself, 320.
331. Whom the slipper fits, let him put it on, 331.
332. With patience as his daily fare, man finds a shelter everywhere, 174.

333. You bring up a bird to pick out your eyes, 120.
334. You cannot read a man's heart upon his face, 166.
335. You must cut your coat according to your cloth, 238.

ADDENDA.

Alter schützt vor Thorheit nicht.
Old age is no safeguard against folly.

Aug' um Auge, Zahn um Zahn.
An eye for an eye, and a tooth for a tooth.

Darüber läßt man sich keine grauen Haare wachsen.
There is no use crying over spilled milk.

Der Schein trügt.
Appearances are deceitful.

Ein Wort giebt das andere.
One word provokes the other.

Es ist dafür gesorgt, daß die Bäume nicht in den Himmel wachsen.
Trees may grow ever so high, their top will never reach into heaven.

Es paßt wie Schiller's „Handschuh" auf Göthe's „Faust".
It fits like Shakespeare's "Merchant of Venice" in Dickens' "Old Curiosity Shop."

Heute reich und morgen arm,
Heute Lust und morgen Harm,
Was heute steigt, das morgen fällt,
Das ist der alte Gang der Welt.
Rich to-day and poor to-morrow,
Happiness followed by woe and sorrow,
To-morrow will fall, what rises to-day,
Such is the world's unchangeable way.

***

Sage mir, mit wem Du umgehst, und ich sage Dir, wer Du bist.
Show me thy company, and I show thee thyself.

Unter fleißigen Händen wächs't kein Unkraut.
A rolling stone gathers no moss.

Was Du nicht willst, das man Dir thu', das füg' auch keinem Andern zu.
As ye would have men do unto thee, so do ye also unto them likewise.

Wer sich gut bei der Mutter steht, dem die Tochter nicht entgeht.
The mother's favor gained, the daughter's hand obtained.

Wo man singt, da laß' Dich nieder, böse Menschen haben keine Lieder.
Among the singers tarry long, wicked people have no song.

Zwei Fliegen auf einen Schlag tödten.
To kill two birds with one stone.

Occupation is life's panacea, 8.

RULES
TO DETERMINE THE GENDER OF NOUNS.

I. GENERAL RULE.

Nouns designating persons, male or female, with or without reference to their position, occupation and quality, require the article according to the sex they belong to, except: (das) Weib, *woman* and *wife*; (das) Kind, child, *boy* and *girl*; (das) Gemahl (1) spouse *or* consort, for both *husband* and *wife*; (der) Mündel (2) *ward, minor, pupil*, male and female; (der) Mensch, *man*, comprising both sexes; (die) Waise, *orphan*, male and female.

(1) It is customary to say: (der) Gemahl, *husband*, and (die) Gemahlin, *wife*.
(2) It is also correct to say: (die) and (das) Mündel.

In accordance with this rule, masculine naturally are: Vater, *father*; Mann, *man*; Gärtner, *gardener*; Professor; König, *king*; Arzt, *physician*; Apotheker, *apothecary*; Schuldner, *debtor*, etc. Feminine are: Mutter, *mother*; Frau, *woman*; Amme, *nurse*; Nonne, *nun*; Königin, *queen*; Hebamme, *midwife*; Wäscherin, *laundress*, etc. And neuter are those which either represent both sexes, as „das Kind," or which, by virtue of the terminable syllables —chen and —lein [see C, 8], are characterized as neuter, for instance: (das) Mädchen, *girl*; (das) Knäblein, *little boy*, etc.

Be it furthermore understood that Latin words retained in the German language with the terminable syllables of —*us* (*ius*), —*a* (*ia*), —*um* (*ium*), designating the respective gender, generally have the corresponding article in German, as: der Focus, der Jesuitismus, der Radius; die Fama, die Aula, die Concordia; das Factum, das Factotum, das Gymnasium. (Das) Dogma is neuter also in Latin.

NOTE.—It is of the highest importance to know that, with very few exceptions, the suffixes and the final letters of the words, in so far as both serve to indicate the gender [see A, 9,—B, 3,—C, 8 and 9], are conclusive in determining the same, irrespective of the bearing of the prefixes or other marks of distinction on the respective words. Example: (der) Beruf, *calling*, but (die) Berufung, *appeal*; (der) Einwand, *objection*, but (die) Einwendung, *objection*; (der) Bedarf, *need*, but (das) Bedürfniß, *need*; (die) Verlobung, *affiance*, (das) Verlöbniß, *affiance*, etc., etc.

II. SPECIFIC RULES.

(A) MASCULINE ARE—WITH FEW EXCEPTIONS:—

(1) The names of most of the larger domestic and wild animals, birds and fish, as: Hund, *dog*; Esel, *ass*; Hirsch, *stag*; Wolf, *wolf*; Löwe, *lion*; Adler, *eagle*; Fasan, *pheasant*; Hai(fisch), *shark*, etc. Exceptions: (die) Katze, *cat*; (das) Pferd, *horse*; (die) Hyäne, *hyena*; (die) Gemse, *chamois*; (die) Forelle, *trout*, etc., which exceptions, das Pferd excluded, are accounted for in B, 3;

(2) The names of mountains, except (die) Alpen, *Alps*, pl.; (die) Karpathen, pl., etc.;

(3) The names of minerals, and of metals the following: (der) Stahl, *steel*; (der) Nickel, *nickel*; (der) Glimmer, *mica*;

(4) The names of the various kinds of grain, (die) Gerste, *barley*, excepted, [see B, 3];

(5) The names of the days, months and seasons;

(6) The designation of atmospheric phenomena, as: Wind, *wind*; Blitz, *lightning*; Donner, *thunder*; Regen, *rain*, etc. Exceptions: (das) Wetter, *weather*; (das) Gewitter, *thunderstorm*; (das) Wetterleuchten, *lightning without thunder*;

(7) Nouns with the following initials:—

    (a) Fl—, except (das) Fleisch, *flesh*; (das) Floß, *raft*; (die) Flur, *field, plain* (Flur, *floor*, is masculine); (die) Fluth, *flood*;

    (b) Gl—, except (das) Glück, *luck*; (die) Gluth, *glowing fire*;

    (c) Gr—, Kl—, Kr—, except (das) Kraut, *herb*; Krokodill, *crocodile* (also used masculine);

    (d) Pf—, except (das) Pferd, *horse*; (das) Pfund, *pound*; (das) Pflaster, *plaster*;

    (e) Pr—, Sch—, except (die) Schachtel, *box*; (das) Schaf, *sheep*; (die) Schaufel, *shovel*; (die) Scham, *shame*; (die) Schande, *shame*; (das) Scheit, *log*; (die) Schicht, *layer*; (das) Schiff, *ship*; (das) Schilf, *reed*;

    (f) Sp—, except (das) Spiel, *play*;

    (g) St—, except (die) Stadt, *town*; (das) Stück, *piece*;

    [With regard to all other nouns from *a* to *g*, which are exceptions to this rule, see B, 3 and 5.]

(8) Nouns with the prefixes Auf—, Aus—, Be—, Bei—, Ein—, (Ent—), Er—, Um—, Ver—, Vor—, Zu—. Exceptions, besides those that come under B, 3 and 5, are: (die) Aufsicht, *control*; Aussicht, *prospect*; Umsicht, *circumspection*; Vorsicht, *precaution*.

(9) Most of the nouns ending in —en, —f (pf and mpf), —ig, —ich, —ing, —l, —ling, —m, —ch, —ck and —z (nz and tz). Exceptions: (das) Buch, *book*; (das) Tuch, *cloth*; (das) Fach, *shelf*; (das) Reich, *empire*; (das) Netz, *net*, etc.;

[Verbs used as nouns, of which see C, 1, do not belong to this class.]

(10) The greater part of monosyllabic nouns derived from verbs, as: (der) Gang, *walk*, from gehen, *to walk*; (der) Sitz, *seat*, from sitzen, *to sit*, etc. Likewise: (der) Entschluß, *resolve*, from entschließen, *to resolve* [see 8 above];

(11) Masculine are finally a large number of English nouns beginning with *sp*— or *st*—, or carrying —*ck*—, or ending in —*ck*, or in —*er*, —*ian*, —*or*, —*tor*, —*ary*, and —*ory*, especially when the nouns with such terminations represent persons. This includes also the German terminal syllable —er, designating a person according to position or occupation. [See "General Rules."]

[The English —*ism* is in German —ismus, with reference to which see "General Rules" on "Latin words retained in the German language."]

NOTE.—In compound nouns the last word determines the gender, as: (die) Haustaube, *tame pigeon*—(das) Taubenhaus, *pigeon house*; (das) Lastpferd, *sumpter horse*—(die) Pferdelast, *horse load*; (der) Oelbaum, *olive tree*—(das) Baumöl, *olive oil*, etc.

In connection with this rule we deem it necessary to call attention to the fact that of fourteen (apparently all) compound nouns (the last—*i. e.* the second—word of each being —mut(h), six are of the masculine, and eight of the feminine gender. These nouns are: (die) Armut, *poverty;* (die) Demut, *humility;* (die) Großmut, *generosity;* (die) Langmut, *forbearance;* (die) Sanftmut, *mildness;* (die) Schwermut, *dejection;* (die) Wehmut, *wofulness,* and (die) Anmut, *gracefulness;*—(der) Freimut, *frankness;* (der) Gleichmut, *equanimity;* (der) Hochmut, *haughtiness;* (der) Kleinmut, *faint-heartedness;* (der) Unmut, *dejection,* and (der) Uebermut, *presumptuousness.* This difference of gender in spite of the same terminal word is to be ascribed to the fact that this termination of —mut has only in the last six (masculine) words the meaning of (der) Mut(h), *courage* or *spirit,* while in the immediately preceding six instances it is tantamount to the English "*mood,*" (die) Stimmung, (die) Gesinnung, and in Armut and Demut the ending is not —mut at all, but —ut, viz.: Arm—ut, Dem [in the sense of the Greek "demos," *common people,* dependent on the higher classes]—ut.

(B) FEMININE ARE—WITH FEW EXCEPTIONS:—

(1) All nouns as described in A; those designating position or occupation require the ending —in = English —*ess*, which is retained in Prinzessin, *princess;*

(2) The names of most of the large rivers in Germany, England and France, except (der) Rhein, (der) Main, (der) Neckar, (der) Rhone;

(3) All nouns ending in —e, except (der) Knabe, *boy;* (der) Bote, *messenger;* (der) and (das) Erbe, *heir* and *inheritance;* (der) Gedanke, *thought;* (der) Glaube, *thought;* (das) Gelübde, *vow,* and three or four more;

(4) The names of vegetables and fruit, except (der) Spargel, *asparagus*; (der) Apfel, *apple;* (der) Kohl, *cabbage* [see A, 9]; (das) Kraut, *herb* [see C, 4];

(5) The nouns ending in —acht and —ucht, except (der) Schacht, *pit* or *shaft* (of a mine);

(6) Nouns ending in —unft, whence (die) Vernunft, *reason,* as exception to A, 8;

(7) All nouns ending in —ei, —erei, —heit, —in [see B, 1], —keit, —schaft, —thum, —ung, and —ur (the latter in words of foreign origin). But Reichthum, *riches,* and Irrthum, *error,* are masculine, and Petschaft, *seal, signet,* is neuter, for properly and originally it means Petsch-haft, *i. e.* a Haft, O. G. for *haft* or *handle,* here used in closing a letter with some sticking matter, say *pitch,* hence Petsch, Lat. *pix,* and the O. G. petschieren for *sealing.*

These terminations or suffixes correspond to the English terminations —*age,* —*ance* (*cy*), —*ation,* —*cy,* —*dom,* —*ence* (*cy*), —*ess,* —*ety,* —*ice* (short), —*ity,* —*ment* [see C, 10], —*ness,* —*ship,* —*tude,* —*ture* and —*y,* forming with any preceding consonant an accentuated syllable, each of which endings indicates the feminine gender of the noun in German, though the nature of the language admits in many a translated word the use of a different gender.

The termination —*y* (*v. s.*) is rendered in German —ie, when the same word is used without translation, as: *dynasty,* Dynastie; *epilepsy,* Epilepsie, with the exception, however, of *tyranny,* which is in German Tyrannei. Thus also the terminations —*ety* and —*ity* are rendered in German etät and ität, as: *society,* Societät; *humanity,* Humanität.

The short —*ice* is in German —iz: *justice,* Justiz; —*ance* is —anz: *arrogance,* Arroganz; —*ence* is —enz: *excellence,* Excellenz; —*tion* is —tion or zion (o long): *subscription,* Subscription or —zion; *nation,* Nation or —zion; *combination,* Combination or —zion; and —(*t*)*ure* is —(t)ur: *nature,* Natur; *mixture,* Mixtur, etc.

(C) NEUTER ARE—WITH FEW EXCEPTIONS:—

(1) All verbs in the infinitive mood, used as nouns, as: (das) Essen, *eating;* (das) Denken, *thinking,* etc. Consequently the English verbal substantive in —*ing* is exactly equivalent to the German verbal substantive in —en, and thus indicates the neuter gender, with the exception of the *understanding,* (der) Verstand [see A, 8], which, however, is nothing but another (stronger) form for (das) Verständniß, *i. e.* fundamentally the same as, though in its application more concrete than (das) Verstehen;

(2) The names of metals, [but see exceptions in A, 3];

(3) The names of the young ones in the animal kingdom, as: (das) Lamm, *lamb;* (das) Rind, *heifer;* (das) Füllen, *colt;* (das) Kalb, *calf;* (das) Kind, *child,* etc.;

(4) The slender productions of the soil covering large areas, as: (das) Gras, *grass;* (das) Kraut, *herb;* (das) Korn, *grain,* etc. ;

(5) The names of countries, cities, and villages, the two terms Land, *country,* and Dorf, *village,* included. Even the compound name [see note at close of A] of a city ending in —stadt is neuter, though Stadt, *city,* is of the feminine gender. Thus we say: das schöne Halberstadt, das feste Kronstadt, etc. But feminine are: (die) Schweiz, *Helvetia;* (die) Krimm, *Crimea,* and those ending in —ei [see B, 7] as: (die) Türkei, *Turkey;* (die) Wallachei, Wallachia, etc. ;

(6) The following kinds of terms when used substantively:—

   (*a*) Adjectives, as: (das) Mehr und Minder;

   (*b*) Pronouns, as: (das) Mein und Dein;

   (*c*) Prepositions, as: (das) Für und Wider, *pro* and *con;*

   (*d*) Conjunctions, as: (das) Wenn und Aber;

   (*e*) Interjections, as: (das) Ach und Weh;

(7) The terms for quantities, measures and weight, *unless they be subject to the various rules derived from the terminal syllables of words,* as: (das) Dutzend, *dozen,* etc.; (das) Quart; (das) Pfund, *pound;* but (der) Zentner, *hundredweight;* (die) Million;

(8) All nouns ending in —chen and —lein, being thus diminutives, as the English nouns are ending in —*let,* —*ling* and —*kin,* as: *leaflet,* Blättchen; *gosling,* Gänslein; *mannikin,* Männchen;

(9) Nouns ending in —sal and —sel, as: (das) Labsal, *restorative;* (das) Räthsel, *riddle,* etc., and those with the suffix —niß, with the exception of (die) Erlaubniß, *permission*; (die) Kümmerniß, anxiety ;

(10) English nouns ending in —*ment,* when (like the French with the French pronunciation) they are used in German, as: (das) Argument, (das) Firmament, (das) Amusement (French), (das) Reglement (French), etc.;

(11) The great majority of nouns with the prefix Ge—, numbering about seven hundred, closes this list of nouns of the neuter gender.

    [*It will prove advantageous to the student to look for the application of these rules in the Vocabulary, p. 148, and to read the note at the close thereof, p. 198*].

PUBLICATIONS OF I. KOHLER,
No. 911 ARCH STREET, PHILADELPHIA.

Schiller's sämmtliche Werke.
Imperial-Ausgabe in zwei Bänden,
auf schönem Papier.
Mit 58 großen Illustrationen
von den besten Künstlern Deutschland's.

Nr. 1. In 1 Band gebunden, feine Leinwand, Gold- und Schwarzdruck $4 00
Nr. 2. In 2 Bänden, feine Leinwand, Gold- und Schwarzdruck 5 00
Nr. 3. In 2 Bänden, halb Marocco, einfach 5 50

In zwölf Bänden, klein Octav.

Nr. 1. In 12 Bänden, in Leinwand mit Goldtitel und Schwarzdruck $8 00
Nr. 3. In 6 Bänden, Lwd., Rücken u. Seiten in Gold- u. Schwarzdruck, fein... 7 00
Nr. 4. In 12 Bänden, halb Marocco, extra 15 00

Inhalt:

1r Bd. Gedichte, mit Illustrationen.
2r Bd. Die Räuber, Schauspiel.—Die Räuber, Trauerspiel.—Die Verschwörung des Fiesco in Genua.
3r Bd. Kabale und Liebe.—Don Carlos.—Der Menschenfeind.
4r Bd. Wallenstein, ein dramatisches Gedicht. 1r Theil: Wallenstein's Lager; die Piccolomini. 2r Theil: Wallenstein's Tod.
5r Bd. Maria Stuart.—Die Jungfrau von Orleans.—Die Braut von Messina.
6r Bd. Wilhelm Tell.—Die Huldigung der Künste.—Iphigenie in Aulis.—Scenen aus den Phönizierinnen. Macbeth, ein Trauerspiel.
7r Bd. Turandot, Prinzessin von China.—Der Parasit.—Der Neffe als Onkel.—Phädra.—Nachlaß: I. Warbeck; II. Die Maltheser; III. Die Kinder des Hauses; IV. Demetrius.
8r Bd. Geschichte des Abfalls der Vereinigten Niederlande von der spanischen Regierung.
9r Bd. Geschichte des dreißigjährigen Krieges.
10r Bd. Prosaische Schriften, erste und zweite Periode.
11r Bd. Kleine Schriften vermischten Inhalts.
12r Bd. Schriften vermischten Inhalts.

☞ Of the German Edition in 12 vols. each volume will be delivered separately at 75 cts., of which all Educational Institutions should take special notice.

❧ Schiller's Gedichte. ❧
Klein Octav. Auf feinem Tonpapier mit Illustrationen.

Schön in Leinwand gebunden $0 75

Schiller und seine Zeit.
Von Johannes Scherr.—Mit zahlreichen Illustrationen.

In Leinwand gebunden $1 50

SCHILLER'S COMPLETE WORKS

IN ENGLISH.

The only COMPLETE Edition ever published!

Selected from the best translations by S. T. COLERIDGE, E. L. BULWER, MELISH, A. J. W. MORRISON, T. MARTIN, J. CHURCHILL, CHAS. J. HEMPEL and others.

Edited by Dr. CHAS. J. HEMPEL.

In two Volumes, Imperial Octavo. Large, clear and legible type.
1282 Pages.
WITH 56 FULL-PAGE ILLUSTRATIONS
FROM THE BEST GERMAN ARTISTS.

STYLE OF BINDING AND PRICES.—EDITION ON GOOD WHITE PAPER.

No. 1. In 1 vol., cloth, extra, gilt back and gold centre	$4 00
No. 2. In 2 vols., " " " " "	5 00
No. 3. In 1 vol., half morocco	5 00

FINE EDITION ON TONED PAPER.

No. 5. In 2 vols., cloth, extra, gilt back and gold centre	$6 50
No. 7. In 2 vols., half morocco, plain	7 00
No. 8. In 2 vols., half mor., super extra, gilt back, gold centre, marble edges	8 50

SCHILLER'S POEMS.

Published both in German and English (the two languages on opposite pages).

Small 8vo. 750 pp. Illustrated.

No. 1. Bound in cloth	$2 00
No. 2. On tinted paper, bound in fine cloth	2 50
Bound in fine cloth, gilt edge	2 75
In half morocco, extra, red edge	3 00
In full Turkey Morocco, superfine, extra	5 00

IN ENGLISH ONLY. ON TINTED PAPER. ILLUSTRATED.

No. 1. Bound in cloth	$0 75
No. 2. Bound in fine cloth, gilt edge	1 50
In half morocco, extra	1 75
In full Turkey morocco, superfine	3 00

SCHILLER AND HIS TIMES.

BY JOHANNES SCHERR.

Translated from the German by ELISABETH McCLELLAN.

Nearly 500 pages. With Illustrations.

On fine toned paper, bound in cloth, extra, black and gold, and gold centre	$1 50
" " " " " " " " gilt edge	2 00
Half morocco, extra	3 00

In SCHILLER'S WORKS we find mirrored a pure and unstained life and a noble mind attuned to all that is good and great, but only a careful picture of his life and character can teach us fully to appreciate him as an author. And such a picture we find in DR. SCHERR'S book, which far excels all others of the kind.

JUST PUBLISHED:

ENGLISH-GERMAN
MODEL LETTER WRITER AND BOOK-KEEPER.

A FAITHFUL COMPANION

IN THE VARIOUS SOCIAL AND BUSINESS RELATIONS AND USEFUL ADVISER AT HOME AND IN SCHOOLS.

WITH AN APPENDIX,

Containing: Poems for Special Occasions; Postal Matters; Etiquette on Invitations; Money and Interest Tables; Abbreviations and Contractions and Technical Law Terms.

By Dr. JACOB MAYER.

12mo. Second Edition.

German and English on opposite pages (502 pp.), bound in cloth............	..$1 50
German part, 258 pages, bound in cloth..	0 75
English part, 258 pages, bound in cloth..	0 75

Ein werthvolles Buch für jeden Deutschen!

„Germania."

Zwei Jahrtausende deutschen Lebens

kulturgeschichtlich geschildert von **Johannes Scherr.**

Mit einem prachtvollen Titelbilde der „Germania", einer Vorrede von Prof. J. B. Herzog, 40 Vollbildern und circa 250 Text-Illustrationen von den besten Künstlern Deutschland's.

Groß-Royal-Octav. 528 Seiten.

Schön in Leinwand gebunden, Schwarzdruck und Goldtitel...............	$3 50
Extra fein geb. in Leinwand, roth, Rücken und Seiten voll vergoldet, Schwarzdruck mit Goldschnitt..	5 00
Halb Marocco, mit Goldschnitt...	6 00

Mein Bruder.

Ein Bild aus der Wirklichkeit. Von **Auguste Bender.**

12mo.

In Umschlag brochirt..	25 Cts.
Schön in Leinwand gebunden..	50 Cts.

Tafel, Dr. J. E. Leonh., & L. H., *A. B.*

New and complete English-German and German-English Pocket Dictionary, with the Pronunciation of both languages, enriched with the Technical Terms of the Arts and Sciences for the use of Business Men and Schools. 874 pages. 13th Edition. Bound $1 00

Kunst, L. J.

American Dictionary of the English and German Languages, containing all the words in general use; designating the various parts of speech in both languages, with the Orthography, Accentuation, Division and Plan of Pronunciation according to Webster. With two sketches of Grammar, English and German. Newly enlarged. 12mo. 830 pages. Bound in Half Morocco $1 50

Grieb, Chr. Fr.

Dictionary of the English and German Languages.
In Half Morocco, complete in 2 vols $12 00

Rupp, Prof. J. Daniel.

Author of several Historical Works. A collection of upwards of 30,000 names of German, Swiss, Dutch, French and other Immigrants in Pennsylvania, from 1727 to 1776, with a statement of the names of ships, whence they sailed and the date of their arrival at Philadelphia, chronologically arranged. Together with the necessary historical and other notes; also, an Appendix containing lists of more than 1000 German and French names in New York prior to 1712 ....$5 00

Horn, W. O. von.

Erzählungen. Vollständig in 14 Bänden, wovon 2 Bde. Schmied-Jakob's Geschichten. Mit vielen Illustrationen von Prof. L. Richter. Jeder Band von 300–400 Seiten stark, schön gebunden.

Nr. 1.	In Leinwand gebunden, 14 Bände			$9 00
Nr. 2.	In	„	„ 7 „	8 00
Nr. 1.	In	„	„ @ Band	0 75
Nr. 2.	In	„	„ 2 Bände zusammen	1 25

Franklin, Benjamin.

Sein Leben, von ihm selbst beschrieben. Ein Buch für Jung und alt. Mit Illustr'n. Schön in Muslin gebunden, mit Gold- und Schwarzdruck ....75 Cts.

Erlernung des Deutschen nach der natürlichen Methode.

Mit besonderer Rücksicht auf den Kinder-Unterricht.

Von Otto Heller, Professor der deutschen Sprache am *Sauveur College of Languages.*

(Erste Stufe.)

Schön in Leinwand gebunden ....40 Cts.

www.ingramcontent.com/pod-product-compliance
Lightning Source LLC
Chambersburg PA
CBHW021833230426
43669CB00008B/957